Flights of Fancy : The Great Fantasy Films

This book is for
Ray Harryhausen
and for
all the dedicated special effects artists
who make the imaginary real

Flights of Fancy

The Great Fantasy Films

by

Kenneth Von Gunden

McFarland & Company, Inc., Publishers
Jefferson, North Carolina, and London

Also by Kenneth Von Gunden

Twenty All-Time Great Science Fiction Films
(with Stuart H. Stock, 1982)

Alec Guinness: The Films (McFarland, 1987)

British Library Cataloguing-in-Publication data available

Library of Congress Cataloguing-in-Publication Data

Von Gunden, Kenneth.
  Flights of fancy : the great fantasy films / by Kenneth Von
Gunden.
     p.   cm.
  Bibliography: p. 275.
  Includes index.
  ISBN 0-89950-397-7 (lib. bdg.; 50# acid-free natural paper) ∞
  1. Fantastic films—Plots, themes, etc. 2. Fantastic films—
History and criticism. I. Title.
PN1995.9.F36V57   1989
016.79143′09′0915—dc19   88-38028
                                                                CIP

Printed in the United States of America.

McFarland & Company, Inc., Publishers
  Box 611, Jefferson, North Carolina 28640

Contents

Acknowledgments

I would like to extend my appreciation to the following people, who helped make this book possible by providing me with films, stills, books, opinions, criticism, and support: Allen Street Video, Lane Carpenter, Steve and Nancy Gould, Ray Harryhausen, Jeffrey Lang, Carolyn Meredith, Kathy Smith, Stuart H. Stock, Patrick Trimble, and Video Center.

And, as always, special thanks to my wife, Donna, whose affectionate support is no fantasy.

Introduction

fan-ta-sy, noun. Fancy: *esp*: the free play of creative imagination . . . imaginative fiction featuring especially strange settings and grotesque characters. . . .

— *Webster's New Collegiate Dictionary*

The first fantasies were stories told around prehistoric campfires late at night. As listeners sat with their mouths agape, storytellers spun wonderous tales of creatures half human and half animal, or of giant beings whose horrid visages would cause an onlooker to instantly harden into stone. Monstrous beings from within the earth or from out of the night populated these tales — told to entertain, to frighten, and to teach obedience to the tribe's rules.

With the invention of writing, these oral fantasies were recorded for posterity. With the invention of the printing press, they were made available to a wider audience than ever before possible. *Frankenstein,* Mary Shelley's 1818 gothic tale of science gone mad, was one of the first fantasies to thrill and horrify readers around the world.

And then came motion pictures.

Fantasy films have existed since the movies' beginnings. People of all ages have responded to the magic of fantasy films since such pioneering efforts as Georges Melies' *Cinderella* (1899) and *A Trip to the Moon* (1902).

Film's ability to trick the eye, as well as encompass a multitude of sets and locations, was put to good use in the filming of such early fantasies as *The Golem* (1914), *The Avenging Conscience* (1914), *The Cabinet of Dr. Caligari* (1919), *Sigfried* (1924), and Douglas Fairbanks' effects-laden *Thief of Bagdad* (1924).

Even though the stage version of *Ben-Hur* included the climactic chariot race, the 1925 filming of the biblical epic contained wondrous effects and shots the theater could not hope to duplicate. Perhaps more than any other type of motion picture, the fantasy film makes full use of the tools available to the filmmaker: stop-motion animation, miniatures, hanging miniatures, optical effects, tricks of perspective, blue screens, matte paintings, glass shots, reverse projection, slow motion, rear and front projection, makeup, and so on.

This book differs from most other fantasy film books in that it is *not,* per se, an overview of the entire fantasy film genre. Such surveys, treating each film at greater or lesser length, usually depend solely upon the whims of the author, though this is not usually made clear. Since surveys try to cover every fantasy film ever made, their information concerning any one film is often confined to a paragraph or two. This book, however, is intended to remedy that situation by treating in depth each of the fifteen films chosen. By limiting myself to fifteen films, I hope to provide information on each film that is as complete and accurate as I can make it.

Each film in this book is a superior fantasy film — although I anticipate disagreements with some of my choices. Such disagreements are only natural since no two people would independently come up with the same fifteen fantasy films. However, I hope my treatment of each film justifies its inclusion in the book.

Each film I've selected to examine in detail stands for a subgenre of fantasy films, and I will briefly mention some of the other films in that category (more often than not in the Appendix). For instance, *Beauty and the Beast* represents the Classic Fairy Tale, *Jason and the Argonauts* represents Ancient Mythology, *King Kong* the Giant Monster film, and so on.

Sharp-eyed readers will quickly note that the list of films contains no animated or "cartoon" features. This is not an oversight; neither does it mean that I think there are no classic animated fantasies (how could this be the case when masterpieces such as *Snow White and the Seven Dwarfs* and *Pinocchio* exist?). Simply put, my task of selection was difficult enough without considering the many fine animated fantasy films, so I precluded them from consideration; all the films I examine, then, are principally live-action features.

Fantasy films are a passport to a world of wonder. They reach and activate the child that still resides in all of us. They take us away from the humdrum world of everyday life and, for one glorious moment in time, hold us spellbound in darkness.

1. Beauty and the Beast: The Classic Fairy Tale

> Children believe what we tell them, they have complete faith in
> us.
> They believe that a rose plucked from a garden can bring drama to
> a family. They believe that the hands of a human beast will smoke when
> he slays a victim, and that this beast will be ashamed when confronted by
> a young girl.
> They believe a thousand other simple things.
> I ask of you a little of this childlike simplicity, and to bring us luck,
> let me speak four truly magic words, childhood's "Open Sesame."
> "Once upon a time...."

With those words, in white on a black background, begins Jean
Cocteau's wonderful fairy tale for all ages, *Beauty and the Beast* (*La Belle
et la Bête* in its original French). This now-classic motion picture, produced
just months after the end of World War II, is a visual masterpiece, and the
purest rendering of Mme. Leprince de Beaumont's popular story ever
filmed.

Most attempts to film fairy tales have been either lackluster live-action
productions marred by a paucity of imagination, juvenile scripts, bad acting, hamfisted direction, and cheesy sets; or animated cartoons with limited
appeal to adults (excepting most of the Disney canon). Because *Beauty* was
made by a true artist, the poet and filmmaker Jean Cocteau, it transcends
all other filmed fairy tales and most other motion pictures.

Unfortunately for English-speaking audiences, Cocteau's poetic
dialogue is essentially rendered limp and lifeless by the English subtitles.
This, and the fact that Cocteau was forced to shoot his film in black and
white instead of in color are *Beauty*'s two major shortcomings. The
characters' speeches are obviously longer and more complex when spoken
in French by the actors. Long passages are compressed or simplified to the
point of ridiculousness. For instance, near the end of the film, when Avenant begins a climb to the top of Diana's Lodge, the subtitles have him say,
"You're scared of course." Ludovic replies, "No," and then looks startled and
a bit ruffled—and we haven't a clue why if we don't speak French. If we do,

1

---

we know that Avenant actually says, "Let's go. A little courage. You're afraid naturally." Ludovic replies, "I'm not afraid. I'm thinking." Avenant then says, "That's the same thing." And *that* is why Ludovic does a small doubletake!

In the diary Cocteau kept during the shooting of the film (*La Belle et la Bête: Journal d'un film*, 1946), he bemoans having to film his story in black and white: "What a pity France cannot afford the luxury of films in color. . . ." While photographer Henri Alekan's sharp-edged black-and-white photography is impeccable and exquisitely shaded, Escoffier and Castillo's costumes and the opulent settings by Christian Berard are denied the impact they would have in color. (I'm arguing for the original film to have been shot in color, *not* for the film to now be "colorized"—an abominable process which distorts a picture's original photographic values.)

Variety's "Bron." wrote, "This Jean Cocteau French film is a fairytale—for grownups. It is slow-moving and quite obvious, but on the other hand it has the charm of simplicity, and a good deal of imagination. In the delicate hands of Cocteau and an excellent cast, this yarn becomes palatable. Early scenes in the forest castle are gruesome . . . with the beast wearing makeup that would scare the Hunchback of Notre Dame."

In *The New York Times*, Bosley Crowther raved, "The oft-tried but seldom-known accomplishment of telling a familiar fairy-tale with pure imagery and enchantment through the sensuous devices of the screen has been almost perfectly realized by the French poet-playwright, Jean Cocteau, in his beautifully measured French production of the old fable, *Beauty and the Beast*. Except that it isn't in color, this film . . . is an eminent model of cinema achievement in the realm of poetic fantasy. Although [Jean Marais'] grossly feline make-up is reminiscent of some of the monsters of Hollywood (and could drive the little kiddies to hysterics), he wears it exceedingly well."

Stephen Belcher's review in the *National Board of Review Magazine* was typical but for his reaction to Marais' beast makeup: "And the Beast! He is magnificent with his long legs and princely shoulders. He would be almost too beautiful to be true. *Beauty and the Beast* requires complete submissiveness from its audience which is no easy demand to make. Yet it will be worth it, whether one's eye is drawn to the implications within the text or to the visual delights of its make-believe."

Because Cocteau's film is so rich, texturally and visually, my synopsis of it is necessarily long:

Two young men, Avenant (Jean Marais) and Ludovic (Michel Auclair), are shooting at a target near the window of a house. Inside are Ludovic's three sisters, Adelaide (Mila Parely), Felicie (Nane Germon), and Beauty

(Josette Day) — the youngest child. Beauty is helping her two sisters prepare for a concert at a Duchess' chateau. When Avenant is distracted, his arrow flies in the open window and almost strikes Cabriole, the dog.

As Beauty removes the arrow from the floor, Avenant embraces her and tells her she wasn't meant to be a servant. She says since her father's ships have been lost in a storm she must work. When Avenant tells her she's the fairest of the fair and asks her to marry him, she refuses, saying she must stay with her father. Avenant tries to kiss her as her brother comes in. When Beauty tells Ludovic that she refused Avenant's proposal, he's glad because he doesn't want her to marry a good-for-nothing like himself. Furious, Avenant knocks him down with a punch.

Downstairs, Beauty's father, the Merchant (Marcel Andre), enters with good news — one of his ships has made port, and they'll all be rich. Ludovic now thinks Avenant must have known this before asking for Beauty's hand. When her father asks Beauty if she wishes to leave him, she says no.

As the Merchant goes to reap his profits, the two sisters ask for dresses, jewelry, ostrich feathers, a monkey and a parrot. Beauty simply asks for a rose, causing the sisters to laugh and mock her.

When a moneylender presses Ludovic for payment, the youth signs a note which requires his father to pay or give up the family furniture if Ludovic defaults. Meanwhile, at his lawyer's office, the Merchant discovers that his creditors have seized his cargo, leaving him penniless once again. Unable to stay the night, the Merchant must return through the forest in the dark.

During a storm, the branches part, revealing a chateau to the Merchant. He enters after the chateau's front door swings open by itself. Down an entryway lit by candelabra held by human arms, he finds a large and luxurious room with a table set for one. Human heads decorating the fireplace move and silently watch him as the clock strikes 11. Human hands pour out a cup of wine for him.

Fast asleep in the chair, the Merchant is awakened by an animal's death cry and a ferocious roaring. Rushing outside, he cannot find his horse. He pauses to pick a lovely rose for Beauty . . . and sees a dead deer at his feet. A Beast appears, dressed in finery and furious at the theft of the flower. The Beast tells him, "You're stealing my roses which I love more than anything in the world. You are unlucky, for you could take anything here except my roses. It happens that this simple theft merits death."

The Merchant will die unless one of his three daughters agrees to take his place. If none will, the Merchant must swear to return in three days. When the Merchant says he'll lose his way in the forest, the Beast replies, "You will find in my stable a white horse. His name is Magnifique [Magnificent]. All you have to do is say in his ear: 'Go where I'm going Magnifique, go, go, go.'"

The Merchant recounts his story to his family and her sisters berate Beauty for her request. When Beauty says she'll go in his place, the Merchant says no. Amid anger and recriminations, Avenant slaps Felicie twice. Nothing more happens because they discover that the Merchant has become ill.

Beauty secretly rides Magnifique to the Beast's chateau. Inside, she strides through the house, goes upstairs, and finds a door, which whispers "Beauty, I am the door of your room." Inside, she finds a mirror which says, "I am your mirror, Beauty. Reflect for me and I will reflect for you." In the mirror, she sees her sickly father, with a trace of blood at his mouth.

Beauty runs from the chateau and confronts the Beast. Swooning, she collapses. The Beast picks her up and carries her in his arms to her room. As she passes through the doorway, her rough garments are magically transformed to a beautiful dress and tiara. As the Beast places her on her bed, she awakens and peers up at him. He draws back, telling her she must never look straight into his eyes and that she will see him each night at seven when she is to dine.

At seven, the Beast enters. At his prodding, she admits that she finds him ugly. He says, "My heart is good, but I am a monster." Beauty replies, "There are many men who are more monsters than you and who hide it." The Beast tells her each night he will ask the same question: "Beauty, will you be my wife?" When she gets up and says, "No, Beast," he withdraws.

Later, Beauty hears the same shrieks and roaring that her father heard. After she runs off, the Beast enters her room, looking for her. He sees in her mirror that she is outside the door. When she enters and asks what he is doing there, the Beast gives her a beautiful pearl necklace then leaves at her bidding.

Hearing a strange sound one day, Beauty observes the Beast lapping up water from a pond. Another time, when the Beast thirsts, Beauty allows him to drink from her cupped hands. Beauty and the Beast walk in his gardens — she's growing accustomed to him and his voice is growing less animal-like. Suddenly the Beast freezes, distracted by a nearby deer — his ears pricking at the sound.

Later, Beauty opens her door to find the Beast outside. His shirt is opened, and he is disheveled and blood-smeared. Smoke rises from his hands. Softly, he says, "Excuse me . . . for being an animal . . . forgive me." After she tells him to clean himself up, he says, "Close your door. Quickly . . . your eyes are burning me. I can't bear your eyes."

At the Merchant's, the moneylender is taking all of the furniture — including the table on which Ludovic and Avenant are playing chess. Ludovic confesses to his father that it's all his fault.

Beauty begs to see her father. The Beast says he'll die of grief if he sends her home and she fails to return. When Beauty strokes his head,

A portrait of Jean Marais as the tortured Beast.

he says, "You stroke me the way you stroke an animal." Beauty naively replies, "But you are an animal." Beauty then admits that someone has asked to marry her, someone young and handsome, but that she has refused because of her father. Later, Beauty lies despondently upon her bed. She tells the Beast her father is dying and agrees to the Beast's demand to return in exactly one week.

The Beast then takes her to the window and points. "You see this lodge," he says. "It is Diana's Lodge. It is the only place on the estate that no one may enter, not even I. All I possess, I possess by magic, but my true wealth is in this lodge. It is entered by means of a golden key."

The Beast gives her the golden key to the lodge and tells her that if she doesn't return, he will die. He also tells her, "Beauty, a rose which has played its role, my mirror, my golden key, my horse, and my glove are the five secrets of my power. I deliver them up to you." The Beast's glove, when placed on her right hand, takes her instantly to where she wishes to go.

Beauty appears in her father's bedroom and he first thinks he's dreaming. When she says the Beast allowed her to see him, he says, "You mean this monster has a *soul?*" Beauty says she must return to him and adds, "Father, this monster is good." When she weeps for him, her tears turn to diamonds.

The sisters are hanging up washing with Avenant and Ludovic when Beauty appears with the Merchant. He tells them she has cured him. Beauty gives her pearl necklace to Felicie, but it turns into an old burned rope — clearly the Beast's gifts are meant for Beauty alone.

Ludovic and Avenant plot to kill the Beast and take his treasures. The sisters rub onions in their eyes to make them cry so they can pretend that don't want Beauty to leave again. As Beauty comforts them, Felicie secretly takes the golden key.

After the Beast sends Magnifique , with the mirror in a saddlebag, Avenant and Ludovic decide to use him to find the Beast's estate. When Adelaide looks into the mirror, she sees herself reflected with an old hag's face; Felicie sees a monkey. Angry, they take the mirror to Beauty and leave it with her. In it, Beauty sees the Beast silently weeping.

Putting on the glove, Beauty is transported. But she remembers the key and returns home to find it; when she cannot locate it, she returns to the Beast's chateau. Searching for the Beast, she finds him lying on the ground by the pond, near death. She says that *she* is the monster.

Avenant and Ludovic find Diana's Lodge, but fear the key could trigger a trap. They climb on the roof.

When Beauty implores to Beast to fight death, he says that "poor animals who want to prove their love know only how to lie down and die." Beauty cries out, "My Beast! My Beast!" as swans hiss and peck at the dying Beast.

Peering into the lodge, Ludovic and Avenant see a gleaming treasure . . . and a statue of Diana with bow and arrow. Avenant prepares to lower himself inside.

Beauty sobs, "My Beast! My Beast! Pardon me. I'll be your wife. I *am* your wife, I love you."

As Avenant hangs from Ludovic's hands, Diana shoots him in the back with her arrow. Avenant's face becomes the face of the Beast, Ludovic releases him, and he falls to the floor.

The Beast is transformed into a prince — with the face of Avenant — and magically rises to his feet. "The Beast is no more. Avenant is no more. I am called Ardent. I am a Prince to adore you and serve you," he tells the startled Beauty. "My parents didn't believe in fairies, so the fairies punished them through me as a result. Only a look of love could change me into a man and give me the form of your dream."

When Beauty says that he looks like a friend of her brother's, the Prince asks, "Does it displease you that I look like this friend of your brother's?" Beauty replies, "Yes," then coyly, "No."

By means of a fairy cloak, the two are carried off to the Prince's kingdom, where Beauty will be a queen. Her father will be there, and her sisters will serve her. Leaping into the air, they fly off . . . to live happily ever after.

Fairy tales are the means by which young children begin to understand life's hidden dimensions and society's norms. They help the child to identify and confront basic fears — of death, dismemberment, abandonment — and inexplicable longings and desires: the male child for his mother and the female child for her father. (For more filmed fairy tales, see Appendix.)

Madame Leprince de Beaumont's 1757 version of the story, an elaboration of an even earlier telling of the tale by Madame de Villeneuve, begins with, "Once upon a time there was a merchant who was extremely wealthy. He had six children, three boys and three girls, and, as this merchant was a man of sense, he spared nothing for his children's education and gave them all manner of teachers."

De Beaumont's is a very middle-class telling, emphasizing money, family, and education in the very first paragraph. Thus, the author passes on basic bourgeois values. The tale is also the clearest example of a subgenre of the fairy tale known as "the Animal Groom."

In most such stories, the absent mother is represented by a wicked sorceress who causes the child to view sex as animal-like. In Cocteau's filming, however, that role is assumed by the coarse Avenant. Bruno Bettelheim, in *The Uses of Enchantment*, writes, "Thrown into a conflict between her love for her father and the Beast's needs, Beauty deserts the Beast to attend her father. But then she realizes how much she loves the Beast — a symbol of the loosening of ties to her father and transference of her love to the beast." Only then "does sex, which before was repugnant, become beautiful."

Bettelheim notes that the Beast's chateau — where Beauty, once all but a slave to her sisters, is waited upon by invisible hands — represents each child's wish for a place where nothing is asked of him and his wants are immediately met. Beauty soon learns that such an existence is empty and boring, and begins to appreciate her time with the Beast and look forward to his visits.

Beauty, then, is a story of a daughter's transference of affection from her father to her husband and lover. What she feared might be a "beastly" experience turns out to be nothing of the sort. Beauty discovers that sex need not be feared, that it can be accompanied by love and understanding, and lead to a "happily ever after" life of fulfillment.

The need for such middle-class tales of reassurance comes from the fact that children, especially young girls are taught little or nothing about sex. Parents believe that just before marriage (as a virgin) is the proper time for such information. At that juncture, what was taboo and unmentionable is suddenly not only proper but expected of the young woman.

Cocteau's film version adds and subtracts elements from the classic tale. Mirrors were a favorite device of Cocteau, appearing in all his films, and Beauty uses them to great effect: Beauty seeing her father "dying" and the Beast weeping, the two sisters seeing themselves reflected as an old hag and a monkey. Perhaps Cocteau's most subtle yet important contribution was to use Jean Marais in three roles, refining the psychological underpinnings of the tale.

As Avenant, Marais is handsome and virile—he appears in one scene with his shirt off, revealing broad shoulders and a granite-hard chest. But his Avenant is coarse and brutal: He is a rounder and a gambler. Brutal and impetuous, he twice slaps Felicie hard across the face. Further, he is lustful and all too macho, not romantic. "Marry me," he says to Beauty at the film's beginning, and it is more a demand than a request.

Marais' Beast, on the other hand, asks tenderly, "Beauty, will you be my wife?" The Beast, aware of his "animal" tendencies, is embarrassed by them and fights to overcome them. But no matter how much the tale is meant to show that "ugly" is okay, that it may hide a loving heart, the Beast is considered imperfect marriage material.

Marais' prince (Charming) is the fusion of the two imperfect halves: Avenant, handsome and virile, but corrupt and lustful; the Beast, loving and pure, but dull and "homely." When Diana's arrow enters Avenant's back, his face becomes the face of the Beast and the two halves come together to produce the Prince: "The Beast is no more. Avenant is no more. I am called Ardent. I am a Prince to adore you and serve you."

"Where is the Beast?" Beauty asks of this too-perfect stranger. Although she soon accepts the handsome Prince with Avenant's face, we do not. As Pauline Kael wrote in Kiss Kiss Bang Bang, "The transformation of the Beast into Prince Charming is ambiguous—what we have gained cannot take the place of what we have lost. (When shown the film, Greta Garbo is reported to have said at the end, 'Give me back my beast.')"

Jean Cocteau was born in the Paris suburb of Maisons-Laffitte on July 5, 1889. The young poet-to-be's father committed suicide when Cocteau was nine years old. Fathers were often portrayed ingloriously in Cocteau's works, reflecting the fear and anger his father's death induced in him.

Cocteau's poetry was often "visual," so it was no surprise that he eventually made a number of motion pictures, beginning with *Le Sang d'un Poete (The Blood of a Poet)* in 1930, which he wrote and directed. By the time he made *Beauty*, between 1945 and 1946, he had written (but not directed) four other films: *La Comedie du Bonheur* (1940), *Le Baron Fantome* (1943), *L'Eternel Retour* (1943), and *Les Dames du Bois de Boulogne* (1944).

Jean Marais, whom Cocteau had met in 1937, suggested to Cocteau that he film the fairy tale. For the classically handsome Marais, it would be an opportunity, underneath the fur and fangs of the Beast, to stress acting over his physique.

Producing such a complex film would be no easy task in war-damaged France. The easiest part of the enterprise was finding the proper locations. Cocteau discovered the Rochecorbon manor house in Ille-et-Vilaine in Touraine and deemed it perfect for Beauty's home. Well, almost perfect — the film company had to reach an understanding with the commanding officer of a nearby military airfield. Even with his cooperation, many scenes were ruined by training flights roaring overhead during filming.

For the Beast's chateau, Cocteau utilized the Chateau de Raray near Senlis. It was there, in "the most bizarre park in Paris," that Cocteau found the strange animal statuary — hunting dogs and stags — that give the Beast's estate such an otherworldly look.

The equipment the production had to work with was, for the most part, old and in disrepair. Many shots were ruined by jamming cameras, flawed lenses, damaged film stock, or careless processing. Cocteau confided to his diary: "Seven breakdowns in the electricity during the day. Work almost at a standstill. Nothing is more demoralizing than the Saint-Maurice studio when everything goes dead, the cold takes possession and only a few scene-shifters work furiously on the set by candlelight. . . . Haven't seen the work of the last few days. The laboratory does not dare develop it for fear of a breakdown. I tremble before the possibility of a catastrophe that would oblige me to do over again what can never be done again."

Cocteau and his actors persevered under the draining conditions. Things were still so bad in France when production started in the summer of 1945, that Cocteau was receiving food packages from actor Jean-Pierre Aumont in Hollywood.

Josette Day refused to ride Aramis (the white horse known as Magnifique in the film), so Cocteau was forced to ask a local girl, a neighbor of the owner of Rochecorbon, to double for her. And, when a deer carcass was needed for the scene between the Merchant and the Beast, the markets selling game were on strike. When the carcass was finally obtained, Cocteau himself opened its throat "and poured the haemoglobin down."

At one point, when Jean Marais emerged from the bushes wearing the Beast's makeup, he terrified the local children who'd come to watch the filming.

Beauty (Josette Day) and the Beast (Jean Marais) talk in his garden.

Marais' mask, gloriously feline and expressive, was constructed by an elderly gentleman who first made a cast of the actor's face. As Marais recalled in his autobiography, "M. Pontet made my mask like a wig, hair on a webbing base, but in three parts—one down to the eyes, a second as far as the upper lip, and the third to the base of the neck. . . . It took me five hours to make up—that meant thirteen hours a day in the studio. Because of the fangs attached to my teeth, all I could eat was mush, and that by the spoonful. Between takes I scarcely dared open my mouth lest the makeup become unglued: No one understood what I said, and that exasperated me."

Cocteau was overwhelmed by Marais' dedication as the Beast. He wrote in his diary, "Marais gave a striking performance last night of the Beast drinking. He drank and then spat it out. He actually *drank* this disgusting water. No other artist I know would have done that."

Art director Christian Berard is, after Cocteau, the man most responsible for the film's look. It was when Cocteau wrote about Berard's "immense role in this enterprise"—his costumes, sets, and interiors which fully realize the director-writer's vivid ideas and amazing conceits—that he bemoaned France's inability to afford color films.

Photographer Henri Alekan's crisp black-and-white images are stunning, but he did not initially agree with Cocteau's idea of the film's look. "Alekan is timid," Cocteau wrote. "He hesitates. He does not dare to work for harsh effects in his photography. The result is a certain softness that I have to correct. Everything is still too pretty. I want it rougher, with more contrasts."

Slowly, Cocteau forced his director of photography to see it his way: "Yesterday's pictures were a thousand times more robust. . . . By degrees Alekan is finding his equilibrium and getting into his camera work what corresponds to the particular way I tell a story, gesticulate, write. Alekan has heard people say in the studio that everything I find admirable is spoiled, badly lit, 'cheesy.' Strange he should not yet know what I have taken for granted for years, that whenever one attempts something new people become blind, seeing only the parts that are like the things they already know. It has been decided that anything soft and fuzzy is poetic. Now since, in my opinion, poetry is precision itself, is mathematics, I drive Alekan toward the opposite of what appears poetic to fools. . . ."

Cocteau's special effects, magical and enchanting, were almost all what are called "mechanical" effects, requiring little more than reverse projection. Among the most prominent of these "backwards" shots is the Merchant's entry into the hallway of candelabras held by human arms. It appears that, as he enters, the candles are lit by an unseen hand. In reality, Cocteau filmed numerous tedious retakes of the candles being blown out by what he calls a "gadget," as Marcel Andre moves and gestures backwards. Another reverse action shot created the illusion that Beauty was emerging from the wall in her father's room. Josette Day simply pushed herself up the "wall" (really the floor) and slowly was lowered through a trap door.

The most obvious shots involved Marais as the Prince. In one, he simply fell backwards onto the ground. When projected in reverse, it appeared that the Prince was springing up in place of the dead Beast. Later, Marais and a stunt double jumped from a 12-foot-high stage to the ground. Projected backwards and in slow motion, this gave the illusion that the Prince and Beauty were leaping into the air to fly away to his kingdom.

One of *Beauty's* most psychologically disturbing effects is Cocteau's conceit of having statues and stone heads in the Beast's chateau played by young men and women whose eyes silently follow the principals as they move about the rooms. The two heads on either side of the fireplace which open their eyes and stare intently at the Merchant are especially unnerving. The heads were portrayed by "kids" who were forced to kneel behind the set with their shoulders immobilized by plastic casings. Their faces were blackened and their hair "gummed and bepowdered" while powerful arc lamps shone in their faces.

"These heads are alive; they look, they breathe smoke from their nostrils, they turn following the artists who are unaware they are being watched," Cocteau wrote in his diary. Then he added a chilling thought: Perhaps they behaved "as objects which surround *us* behave, taking advantage of the fact that we believe them to be immobile."

Beauty constantly proves Cocteau's thesis that it is possible to achieve magical effects by simple, almost mundane, means. When the Beast, walking with Beauty in his gardens, scents a stag, his ears prick. Cocteau merely had a technician, hidden behind Jean Marais, animate his ears by moving them with a forked twig.

Another visually striking effect was achieved by equally uncomplicated means. Beauty's passage down the corridor to her room without moving her feet was filmed by having her stand on a wheeled platform which was pulled by a string. This scene's rushes convinced producer Paulve to finance the film.

For the scenes in which the sisters see themselves reflected in the Beast's mirror as, respectively, an old hag and a monkey, Cocteau used magician's tricks. An old woman stood beside actress Nane Germon (Felicie) and her face was reflected into the camera lens. A monkey dressed in a ruff and bonnet was placed behind ordinary glass in the mirror frame to represent actress Mila Parely (Adelaide). Cocteau found the little creature "charming."

When Beauty offers to give her necklace to Felicie, it turns into an old burned rope. Felicie then drops it, and it magically transforms itself back into the necklace. Another simple sleight of hand trick accomplished the change in mid-fall: The rope is seemingly dropped, but it is really just whisked out of sight behind the actors as the pearl necklace is dropped. The camera, tilting down, catches the pearl necklace as it hits the ground.

The effects, whether complex or simple, whether startling or merely interesting, are compelling but not really what give *Beauty* its power. That comes from the two major performers and from Cocteau's inspired direction.

Jean Marais gives a tortured, romantic performance of uncommon intensity. His Beast is regal yet humble, powerful yet weak. Cocteau was impressed by Marais' willingness to do anything to give his performance verisimilitude—from drinking the vile pond water, to allowing the tethered swans to attack the dying Beast: "With their wings spread, they come on hissing with fury. And Marais, with his usual courage, doesn't flinch but lets them come on; the sight of these swans attacking their sick master lying helpless and deprived of his power, added a terrible pathos to the scene."

Josette Day's Beauty is almost a tour de force of acting—for the beautiful actress must project innocence, naivety, simplicity, dignity, and patrician superiority. Beauty loves her father, but she does not weep for him. Mme. de Beaumont wrote that Beauty "never weeps in public," disdaining crocodile tears—unlike her sisters, who even resort to rubbing onions on their eyes to bring tears.

At 32, Josette Day was a bit old for the part (Marais was a mature 33 as well), yet the wisdom of her years, her radiant charm, and aristocratic good looks give her Beauty an authority not likely to be found in a younger actress. (Sadly, Miss Day died in 1978, at the age of 64, having appeared in only a handful of films.)

Jean Cocteau's direction, under daunting technical and personal conditions (he was afflicted by both eczema and jaundice during the shooting), is nothing short of marvelous. There are countless memorably staged and photographed shots: Beauty's slow-motion passage through the hall of candelabras; Beauty seeming to float, her legs immobile, down the hallway to her room; Beauty's first encounter with the Beast; the unforgettable shot of the shadow of the Beast's glove on Beauty's face; and the fireplace heads following the Merchant's every move.

Beauty was only the second film Cocteau had directed, and he was not above making novice mistakes . . . and then charmingly dismissing them out of hand: "I shot the father's bedroom with the furniture still there — and this, of course, had all be taken away previously by the money-lender. But I've got around it and made my mistake into a discovery. For of course, when Beauty comes back, so must the furniture return too in its place, as if by magic."

For the music, Cocteau used composer Georges Auric, whom he had worked with before on *The Blood of a Poet*. Cocteau asked Auric to compose the score without letting him hear it until the picture was completed. Auric, at Cocteau's request, deliberately avoided wedding the music to the images. Yet the result was what Cocteau called "this miracle of synchronization" which "could only happen by the grace of God." As Cocteau wrote, "His music marries my picture, impregnates it, exalts it, completes it." Cocteau is correct — Auric's superb score adds yet another dimension of meaning and power to the images on the screen.

Cocteau showed the completed film to the assembled technicians in the Joinville studio. The reception from the workers was warmly appreciative, and Cocteau said, "Whatever happens, nothing will ever equal the grace of that ceremony organized very simply by a little village of workmen whose trade is the packaging of dreams."

2. Conan the Barbarian: Sword and Sorcery

> Between the time when the oceans drank Atlantis and the rise of the sons of Aryes, there was an age undreamed of. And onto this Conan, destined to bear the jeweled crown of Aquilonia upon a troubled brow. It is I, his chronicler, who alone can tell you of his saga. Let me tell you of the days of high adventure.
> — *The Wizard of the Mounds.*

These words are spoken by actor Mako (following an earlier printed quote by Friedrich Nietzsche, "That which does not kill us makes us stronger"), to open the saga of Robert E. Howard's Cimmerian barbarian as brought to the screen by self-proclaimed "Zen fascist" John Milius.

Conan the Barbarian is a controversial choice to represent the "Sword and Sorcery" subgenre — decried for its comic book violence, its "brainless" plot, and its lusty endorsement of killing and revenge. Yet *Conan* is a remarkably well-made film which takes its hero and its subject matter seriously — no tongue-in-cheekiness or condescending camping it up here.

Conan, released in 1982, was an immediate hit with audiences (admittedly heavily populated by adolescent boys), earning North American rentals of $22.5 million against a production cost of approximately $17.5 million (it was the thirteenth-highest rental film of 1982). The yardstick is that a film must earn at least its production cost in North American rentals to be considered profitable (it makes the rest of its money from overseas rentals and ancillary income sources like videocassette, pay cable, and network rights).

Oddly enough, the diehard Conan fans were less than enthusiastic about Milius' *Conan*. As Robert Garcia, in an otherwise appreciative review in *American Fantasy* #2 notes, "This Conan is less powerful, less talkative, and less educated than Howard's, and therein lies the betrayal to the fans." Critic Bill Warren quotes production designer Ron Cobb, in *Fantasy Newsletter*, on the fans: "They would have made a lukewarm, predictable, orthodox film. They'd faithfully recreate the stories over and over. Fan mentality . . . has a great love of orthodoxy . . . Milius emulates Howard while infusing him with a whole new direction."

14

SF and fantasy fans forget that film is a mass medium, if less so than television. They also tend to believe they number in the millions. At one World Science Fiction Convention, a producer told startled purists that if *all* the diehard fans turned out to support a film based on a certain popular comic book series, they'd sustain the box office for just one day—if even to that extent.

So Milius' Conan is as metaphysical as he is physical. He does more than cut horses in half or face a grinning, unspeakable "evil." Conan is, in a very real sense, made and shaped by the sophisticated cult leader Thulsa Doom; while Doom lives, Conan cannot be a free man, an unfettered "barbarian" reveling in the pleasures of the sword.

To say *Conan's* reviews were mixed would be truthful, if misleading. For every positive review the film garnered, it received two negative ones. Predictably, a film starring a former bodybuilder and titled *Conan the Barbarian* had to face the wrath of the critics. (Just as predictably, those who wanted to see such a film ignored those same critics.)

David Sterritt, writing in the *Christian Science Monitor*, complained, "This isn't fantasy, it's just a rehash of the latest obsessions; all Milius has done is transplant them to a stock Hollywood setting, updating the explicitness but not the sophistication. There's more Neanderthal than Nietzsche in it—which is appropriate, but hardly appealing."

Writing for the *Los Angeles Times'* "Calendar," Kevin Thomas produced one of the film's few enthusiastic reviews. "*Conan the Barbarian* does for the heroic epic what *Star Wars* did for space fantasy and *Raiders of the Lost Ark* for Saturday serials: It revives a beloved genre in all its innocent pleasures on a spectacular scale and with sophisticated style."

In *New Leader*, Robert Asahina wrote, "Preferring action to words and thought, the writers manifest virtually no regard for such matters as characterization or motivation. A series of battle sequences reveal Milius at his best, borrowing liberally and unabashedly from Akira Kurosawa's *Seven Samurai*, Sergi Eisenstein's *Alexander Nevsky*, and Leni Riefenstahl's *Triumph of the Will*. It has been some time since the large screen was so filled with the clatter of swords, the thunder of hooves, and the mayhem of primitive hand-to-hand combat. Missing is any sense of fun. *Conan the Barbarian* plods along with the lead grace of its tongue-tied, muscular hero."

Accusing the filmmakers of racism, John Preston wrote in the *New Statesman*, ". . . The guilty party is religious nut Thulsa Doom, played by the only black actor in the cast, James Earl Jones. Just in case anyone misses the point, Doom has a habit of changing into a snake thus making him not only black but slimy too. Fortunately, the chances of anyone taking this at all seriously, much less granting it any kind of political credibility, are negligible since the film is abominably bad."

David Denby's *New York* review was predictably negative: "Milius

never finds a consistent tone or style. The dreary, uninvolving narrative
lurches from brutal 'realism' to cruddy oracular pomp to zippy fantasy to
Christian and phallic symbolism. In brief, Milius worships force, but he
doesn't have the consistency or the visual skills to be a good fascist filmmaker."

Archer Winsten's review in the *New York Post* was generally upbeat.
"There is no need for *Conan the Barbarian* to be acted by Sir Laurence
Olivier. Arnold Schwarzenegger is quite enough. All he has to do is flex a
muscle, set a jaw, and that's that. Barbarous. Writers John Milius and Oliver
Stone have given director Milius great stuff to work with. If Schwarzeneg-
ger were more of an actor he might have ruined it. As it is, he's the Barbarian
Incarnate. This is a hero who looks the part."

Less enthralled with Arnold's pecs was Joseph Gelmis, writing in *Newsday*. "*Conan the Barbarian* opens and closes with decapitations. In between,
there's nonstop mayhem, mutilation, phallic worship, orgy, and cannibal-
ism. Based on the character created in 1932 by Robert E. Howard, the
movie's style is tongue-in-cheek, soft-core pornography. *Conan* is a $17.5-
million, kinky kid culture flick."

Newsweek's Jack Kroll wrote that "the film has a heavy, murky, pig-iron
quality; it's oppressive rather than heart-stirring."

Similarly, in *Time*, Richard Schickel argued, "Instead of the giddy lift
one sometimes obtains from improbably heroic adventures, one gets a grim
endorsement of the uses of primitive mysticism and brutality. *Conan* is a
sort of psychopathic *Star Wars*, stupid and stupefying."

Finally, *Variety*'s "Berg." wrote, ". . . With the exception of a handful
of scenes, the uninitiated will once again marvel at how a picture as
monumentally boring and uncentered as this ever captures the fancy of
anyone. With real life heroes scarcer all the time, it's probably not at all surprising that audiences are even less choosey on the big screen."

Conan's father, the Master (William Smith), is seen forging a mighty
sword. He takes the young Conan to the mountains and tells his son of their
god, Crom, and of the "riddle of steel."

A raiding party attacks Conan's tribe's village, killing and burning.
Conan's father fights back but is torn to pieces by vicious dogs. Conan and
his mother (Nadiuska), the only survivors, wait fearfully as the raiders'
leader (James Earl Jones), whose standard is a pair of snakes facing each
other, approaches them. He decapitates Conan's mother, and Conan is
taken in chains to a grinding mill called the Wheel of Pain.

Pushing the great wheel, day and night, season after season, Conan
grows to a powerful man (Arnold Schwarzenegger). Purchased by "Red
Hair" (Luis Barboo), Conan is led away in chains to become a pit fighter.
Awkward and unsure in his first fight, Conan quickly catches on and uses

his great natural strength to defeat his first opponent. Soon, Conan is a mighty battler and realizes a harsh truth: His skill at death makes him special; he has value. Red Hair furthers Conan's fighting skills, employing a Sword Master (Kiyoshi Yamasaki) to teach him how best to handle a blade.

One night, Red Hair frees Conan, striking off his chains. Later, running from wild dogs, Conan falls into an underground crypt where he finds the rotted body of a warrior king . . . and a magnificent Atlantean sword.

Conan comes upon the hut of a beautiful woman (Cassandra Gaviola), who asks him in to share her fire. She says he'll one day be king by his own hand . . . and crush the snakes of the earth. As they make love, her eyes become cat-like and she grows fangs and claws, attacking Conan. He throws her into the fire, and she bursts from the hut as a fireball. Conan then frees a Mongol chained to a rock, who calls himself Subotai the Thief (Gerry Lopez).

Traveling together, they come upon several towns, where Conan asks about the snake design; he learns of the Snakes of Set, Thulsa Doom's cult. Conan and Subotai plan to enter the Tower of Set and steal the cult's "Eye of the Serpent"—a fabulous gem. Outside the Tower, they meet another thief, Valeria (Sandahl Bergman). These three climb and enter the Tower.

A willing victim is prepared for sacrifice to the cult's great snake—which awakens when Conan's sweat falls on it as he steals the Eye. Conan sees the two-snake emblem of his mother's killers as the giant snake slithers up behind him. Subotai pins the serpent to the wall with arrows and Conan hacks off its head with his sword. The maiden victim leaps into the pit only to find the snake dead; her screams alert the guards, but Conan, Subotai, and Valeria escape.

Conan demonstrates his feelings to Valeria, and they make love. Afterwards, the trio drink and carouse until they are seized and taken before King Osric (Max Von Sydow), who offers them a fortune to bring back his daughter, Princess Yasimina (Valerie Quennessen), a follower of Thulsa Doom.

Valeria says she's been alone all her life; she wants Conan to decline the offer of the fortune and forget about Thulsa Doom. In the morning, she awakes to find Conan gone. Conan rides to the east, toward Thulsa Doom. After meeting the Wizard of the Mounds (Mako) and leaving his sword behind, Conan rides off to seek Thulsa Doom.

Joining Doom's followers, Conan kills a priest and takes his robes. At the Temple of Set, however, Conan is discovered and taken prisoner by Rexor (Ben Davidson) and Thorgrim (Sven Ole Thorsen), who beat him. Doom tells him that flesh is stronger than steel, proving it by gesturing to a follower, who gladly leaps to her death.

Conan is crucified upon the Tree of Woe and left to die. Vultures circle and, when one comes too close, Conan tears its neck out. Conan is near

Crucified upon the Tree of Woe and left to die, Conan is rescued by his friend Subotai (Gerry Lopez).

death when Subotai appears and rescues him. The Wizard paints Conan's face and hands with runes to protect him from the spirits. Ghostly apparitions come in the night seeking Conan, but Valeria wards them off and Conan lives.

Restored, Conan and the others enter Doom's mountain through a gorge to kidnap the Princess. Inside, their bodies painted for battle, they find a hellish scene of gutted human bodies and flesh cooking in cauldrons. In Thulsa Doom's orgy chamber, they see the Princess and Doom—who turns into a large snake. Repelled, they initiate an orgy of killing. Valeria snatches the Princess as Rexor and Thorgrim arrive to battle Conan. Conan overturns the cauldron, and they escape.

As they ride off, Doom turns a serpent into an arrow and fires it, striking Valeria. Dying, she asks Conan to hold her close and to "keep me warm." Heeding her plea, Conan burns her body on a funeral pyre as Subotai cries for Conan—who, being a Cimmerian, will not cry for himself.

Conan, Subotai, and the Wizard prepare for Thulsa Doom's attack by placing stakes in the ground, setting up spears, and rigging booby traps. Armed men ride to the attack, but the defensive measures prove effective as Conan faces Thorgrim, who is impaled by a booby-trapped stake. Subotai is wounded but saved when the Wizard comes to his aid.

Finally, Conan faces Rexor, aided by the spirit of Valeria, who momentarily blinds his opponent. Conan kills Rexor, shattering the giant's sword, which he stole from Conan's father. Thulsa Doom attempts to shoot the Princess, but Subotai deflects the snake arrow with his shield.

As Thulsa Doom addresses his followers at the Temple of Set, Conan confronts and beheads him and burns the Temple to the ground.

Created by Robert E. Howard in 1932 and appearing first in the December issue of the pulp magazine *Weird Tales* ("The Phoenix and the Sword"), Conan the Barbarian was an immediate hit with the readers, and 16 more stories and serials featuring the mighty Cimmerian appeared in *WT*. (See the Appendix for a listing of *Conan* stories, books, collections, and re-issues.)

Robert E. Howard (1906–1936) was born in Peaster, Texas, and lived most of his short life in Cross Plains, Texas. After attending Brownwood High School and Howard Payne Academy in Brownwood, he took several courses at Brownwood College. He then dropped out of school to pursue free-lance writing. His first published story, "Spear and Fang," appeared in *Weird Tales* in 1925, when he was only nineteen.

At first bullied for his puny physique, his obvious intelligence, and for being a "momma's boy," Howard, in a classic case of compensation, took up exercise and sports to build his body. The adult Howard weighed over 200 pounds and was six feet tall, but he never forgot the taunts and humiliations of his childhood. One needn't be Sigmund Freud to see that in creating Conan, Howard was creating a romantically powerful alter ego, one free to crush his enemies and mete out punishment to his tormentors.

Howard corresponded with fantasy writers Clark Ashton Smith and H.P. Lovecraft, whose works he read and admired, and became a prolific writer of pulp fiction. The "pulps" were 6½″ × 9½″ magazines printed on cheap wood pulp paper—the kind guaranteed to turn to cellulose dust on your shelves in a few years. Howard wrote for *Spicy, Adventure Stories, Top-Notch, Action Stories, Thrilling Mystery, Oriental Stories, Sports Story Magazine*, and *Weird Tales*, the major market for his Conan and other fantasy sword-and-sorcery adventures.

He produced many heroic fantasy figures—among them King Kull, Solomon Kane, and Bran Mak Morn—but none was as popular as Conan. Conan the barbarian was a Cimmerian, from a land in Howard's imaginary Hyborian Age, set in the period after the sinking of Atlantis and before the recording of history, about twelve thousand years ago.

While noting that L. Sprague de Camp's later Conan stories and novels have a verisimilitude that Howard's stories lacked, critic Damon Knight nonetheless believed the original Conan tales have something missing in de Camp's work: "a vividness, a color, a dream-dust sparkle, even when they're most insulting to the rational mind," adding, "Howard had the maniac's advantage of believing whatever he wrote; de Camp is too wise to believe wholeheartedly in anything."

Despite the outward changes wrought by his athletic pursuits, Howard was reclusive and emotionally dependent upon his mother. Upon learning she was dying, he committed suicide by shooting himself in the head with a pistol. He was only thirty.

Producer Edward R. Pressman, whose credits include *The Revolutionary* (1970), *Badlands* (1973), cult favorite *Phantom of the Paradise* (1974), and *The Hand* (1981), felt that Howard's creation could be realized on the screen . . . *if* the rights to the books could be attained and *if* someone could be found to play the giant Cimmerian. After two years of complex legal maneuvering, Pressman secured the rights to Conan. When Pressman saw Arnold Schwarzenegger in the 1977 documentary *Pumping Iron,* he was convinced he'd found his Conan.

Pressman and Schwarzenegger met at a restaurant on the Sunset Strip in 1977, and Schwarzenegger finally agreed to play Conan. Setting the initial budget at approximately two and a half million dollars, Pressman hired Oliver Stone, who would later write *The Hand* for him, to write the screenplay.

Stone's screenplay was loosely based on two of Howard's Conan tales, "Black Colossus" and "A Witch Shall Be Born." Stone's script had its oddities and production stumbling blocks, however. Stone intimated that Conan's savage world was a dark age that lay in our future, after a nuclear apocalypse. Even worse, Stone's script would have cost a daunting $40 million to produce.

Meanwhile, after deciding Stone was not the right person to helm the production, Pressman was looking for a director for his Conan film. John Milius read Stone's screenplay and was intrigued by the project but wary. Milius' friend, and the production designer of the film, Ron Cobb kept after him to accept. Finally, when it was clear that Stone wouldn't be the director, Milius made up his mind to direct the film on the condition he rewrite Stone's screenplay to reflect his interests.

John Milius was born in St. Louis, Missouri, in 1944. When Milius was seven years old his father, a shoe manufacturer, moved the family to Los Angeles. In L.A., Milius discovered two things which were to have a profound effect upon his life and personality. As a teenager, he became an avid surfer, reveling in the sport's danger and the fact that he needed to rely on no one but himself. Secondly, Milius discovered Japanese culture. He read Japanese books, studied the martial arts, and became enamored of the films of Akira Kurosawa and Masaki Kobayashi, especially *Seven Samurai* and *Kwaidan* (the influence of each is visible in *Conan*).

Since the surfer's credo in the early '60s was to live life to the fullest and then die young—on the crest of a giant wave, so to speak—Milius planned to attend USC in Los Angeles for a few semesters before going into the armed forces to "die." But Milius, the soon-to-be director of bad-guy, hard-ass films like *Dillinger* and glory-and-guts militaristic movies like *Red Dawn*, was labeled 4-F because of chronic asthma. So instead of becoming a soldier and dying in Viet Nam, Milius took English and history courses before drifting into art classes. Without really planning it, he found himself in the film school. (See the *Dragonslayer* chapter for more on Milius' USC film school buddies.)

Intending to be a writer, not a director, Milius' first script to be produced was a bikers-in-'Nam slam-bang action picture called *The Devil's 8* (1969). Produced by American-International Pictures, with Willard Huyck and James Gordon White, the film was a reworking of *The Dirty Dozen*. Also in 1969, Milius began writing the screenplay that would eventually become *Apocalypse Now*, Francis Ford Coppola's highly regarded attempt to "explain" the futility of the Viet Nam war.

Milius did a fast rewrite on *Evel Knievel*, the film about the motorcycle daredevil, and worked extensively on the script for 1971's *Dirty Harry* without receiving screen credit. He did, however, receive screen credit for the 1973 sequel, *Magnum Force*. Milius saw his script for 1972's *The Life and Times of Judge Roy Bean* subverted by the inappropriate (in Milius' view) casting of the too-good-looking Paul Newman in the title role.

Milius got a chance to direct his own script with 1973's slam-bang gangster epic, *Dillinger*, starring Warren Oates and Richard Dreyfuss. Milius found the transition to director difficult but turned in a credible performance. By the time he directed his second film, 1975's *The Wind and the Lion*, Milius was more confident, and it showed on screen. A box-office and critical disaster, Milius' paen to surfing, 1978's *Big Wednesday*, taught the young filmmaker that self-indulgence can be boring and off-putting. It was a mistake he vowed never to repeat.

Milius began rewriting Stone's original screenplay for *Conan*, picking up Stone's story and running with it. He introduced the Wheel of Pain, to which the young Conan is sentenced, to convincingly explain Conan's/Schwarzenegger's impressive musculature.

Stone had gone back to two of Howard's stories for elements of his script which remained in Milius' rewrite. From "Black Colossus" (*WT*, June 1933) Stone took Howard's use of a 20-foot snake and a fabulous jewel, and from "A Witch Shall Be Born" (*WT*, December 1934) he took Howard's quintessential Conan scene: the mighty Cimmerian, hanging on a cross, nails driven through his hands and feet, tearing out the throat of a vulture which comes to peck out his eyes.

From Howard's "The Tower of the Elephant" (*WT* March 1933), Milius derived the scene of Conan and his companions climbing the Tower of Set. In "Elephant," however, the Tower is guarded by lions on the outside, and, instead of a giant serpent inside, by a giant venomous spider. In Howard's original, the goal is also a fabulous gem.

A non–Howard Conan story, "The Thing in the Crypt," by L. Sprague de Camp and Lin Carter, was the inspiration for the scene in which Conan finds the dead Atlantean warrior-king and takes his sword.

While he was whipping the screenplay into its final form, Milius had one group of researchers unearthing mounds of material on ancient snake and assassination cults. Another group researched early weapons and their use in warfare and hand-to-hand combat. Production designer Rob Cobb and Milius wanted a consistent, believable world, so they studied Celtic and Nordic designs and then imagined what had influenced them—what things had looked like one or two thousand years *earlier*.

Artist William Stout was hired to contribute storyboards to the earliest phases of the production, but left after providing sketches for only a few sequences, including the attack on Conan's tribe that opens the film.

Cast as Conan, Arnold Schwarzenegger, born in Austria in 1947 and the son of a police chief, had suffered through an early childhood blighted by sickness. Like Robert E. Howard before him, and to fulfill a desire to excel in at least one thing, the fifteen-year-old Schwarzenegger began working out with weights. When his father insisted he could not go to the local gym more than three nights a week, the young bodybuilder simply constructed his own facilities in the family's basement and continued his training every night.

By the time Arnold came to the United States in 1968 to compete in bodybuilding contests, he was a legend in the sport. Eventually, he owned five "Mr. Universe" titles and was crowned "Mr. Olympia" seven times. Always ambitious, Schwarzenegger looked around for new conquests. Director Bob Rafelson cast him in a role patterned on his real-life achievements in the 1976 film *Stay Hungry*, and the Hollywood Foreign Press Association awarded Schwarzenegger a Golden Globe for Best Acting Debut, for his appearance. Critics were charmed by this hunk who revealed a complex and intelligent inner self, a judgment confirmed by Arnold's backstage bantering in the 1977 documentary *Pumping Iron* (which fea-

Arnold Schwarzenegger as Conan, the mighty Cimmerian.

tured outclassed muscleman Lou Ferrigno in his pre–*Incredible Hulk* days).

At the pinnacle of his bodybuilding career, Schwarzenegger retired to become an actor. He told one interviewer that continuing his bodybuilding would have prevented him from putting his full effort into acting.

Although it was *because* of his bodybuilding achievements that Pressman signed Schwarzenegger, Milius and his star agreed that Conan should look less like a bodybuilder and more like a man who'd gotten his physique from the Wheel of Pain. Consequently, Arnold pared 30 pounds from his frame, dropping from his competitive weight of 240 to a more athletic-looking 210. Since the start of filming was twice postponed, Schwarzenegger spent 18 months in rigorous training. Besides his routine running and lifting, Schwarzenegger added stretching exercises, horseback riding, rope climbing, and took long swims in the ocean near his Venice, California, home.

In addition to his other training, Schwarzenegger and his three co-stars—Sandahl Bergman, Gerry Lopez, and Ben Davidson—spent two hours a day, three days a week beginning in summer 1980 learning how to wield their swords under the stern eye of martial arts master Kiyoshi Yamasaki (who portrays the Sword Master in the film).

Sandahl Bergman was hired after John Milius decided to cast a dancer as Valeria. He looked at Bergman after Bob Fosse (who'd used her in the steamy "Air Rotica" number in *All That Jazz*, a grim, modern-day fantasy) recommended her. Milius cast his old surfing buddy Gerry Lopez as Subotai the Mongol. Lopez played his role adequately, but his voice had to be dubbed after production by Japanese actor Sab Shimomo. Max Von Sydow, a De Laurentiis fixture, was signed to play King Osric, another take-the-money-and-run part for the great Swedish actor.

Ben Davidson, 6'8" and 280 pounds of quarterback-crushing power (just ask Joe Namath), who played defensive end for the Oakland Raiders in the '60s and '70s, was cast as Rexor, Thulsa Doom's massive high priest. Joining him as the hammer-wielding Thorgrim was Sven Ole Thorsen, a champion bodybuilder and karate expert from Denmark. William Smith, a veteran of numerous biker films and typecast as a bad guy, played Conan's father.

After Ron Cobb had scouted locations in Yugoslavia, political uncertainty following the death of Marshal Tito made filming there impossible. The second choice, Spain, proved more amenable to the production, and Spanish construction crews began building a number of the required sets in a massive warehouse outside of Madrid. Other interiors were filmed in an aircraft hangar on a Spanish military base.

Cobb and Milius, reluctant to rely on matte paintings—which both of them considered too "artificial looking"—instead opted to build a number of sets full size, disguise and extend others with hanging miniatures, and construct the rest as models.

Approximately $350,000 of the production's $3,000,000 budget for sets was spent on constructing Thulsa Doom's "Temple of Set" on a Spanish mountainside. The immense Temple, built of wood in anticipation of its fiery destruction by Conan at the film's conclusion, measured 150 feet long and was over 65 feet high. The steps and the foundation were concrete, not wood, to bear the weight of the thousands of Spanish extras used in the two sequences shot at the Temple.

After several weeks of filming in Spain, Milius grew dissatisfied with the work of director of photography Gil Taylor (who'd clashed with George Lucas during the filming of *Star Wars* and was replaced for the two

Conan (Arnold Schwarzenegger) and Valeria (Sandahl Bergman) strike a fierce pose.

sequels). As Milius told an interviewer, "He was terminated with extreme prejudice [because] his methods were unsound." Duke Callaghan took Taylor's place.

Bothered by his asthma, Milius found the five-month shoot in Spain a terrible experience; the production was beset by cold and rain and voracious mosquitoes. Then there were the inevitable accidents. During one sword fight, an extra's fiberglass safety sword slid down the blade of Sandahl Bergman's sword and sliced her right index finger to the bone. In another incident, powerful Ben Davidson, during the shooting of the fight scene in Doom's orgy chamber, swung a wood-handled axe at Schwarzenegger's head. When Arnold fell to one knee and caught the swing with his sword, Davidson's steel axehead snapped off and grazed Schwarzenegger's neck, drawing blood. The incident further reminded people that these were large persons swinging potentially dangerous "weapons."

Besides her cut finger, Bergman's breast was burned during the sequence in the tavern and the constant physical action bruised and marred her long legs. But she and the rest of the cast bore up stoically under the many injuries. Milius' morale-booster, Schwarzenegger later recalled, was to remind his cast that the pain would be temporary, the film permanent.

Apart from Schwarzenegger's first spoken line of dialogue in the film, which is memorably bad (asked what is best in life, Conan replies, "To crush your enemies — see dem driven before you, and to hear the lamentations of dair vimen"), his acting is serviceable, if not great.

As the "lamentations" quote indicates, Schwarzenegger's difficulties centered on his accent and his delivery of lines. The first was shrugged off, but Schwarzenegger and Milius did what they could to improve the second. Every day before lunch, the director and his star would retreat to Milius' trailer, where Arnold would practice his longer monologues. By the time he had to deliver his long speeches in the film, Schwarzenegger had rehearsed them perhaps forty or fifty times.

Aware of fine stage actor James Earl Jones' desire to keep in shape with physical training, Schwarzenegger worked out an equitable arrangement with him. Arnold helped him with his workouts, and Jones helped the bodybuilder with his acting, showing him different ways to read different lines.

The acting in *Conan* ranges from very good to indifferent. Good are Mako as the Wizard, and Sandahl Bergman as Valeria. Mako injects needed doses of humor and humanity into the film, and Bergman's statuesque Valeria is an appealing mixture of bravado and femininity. Her love for Conan, shining from her eyes, somehow makes him more human and worthy of our respect and affection — as does his sense of loss when she dies.

Schwarzenegger's sessions with Milius and Jones paid off, and he brings to the part a certain style of "physical acting" rarely seen in films anymore. Belying the term "muscle-bound," his Conan is lithe and light-footed — and no one else, save Bergman, can handle a sword as well as he can.

The other actors, having little to do — like Davidson and Thorsen — are passable. Oddly enough, the film's most experienced actor (in a major role, which you can't call Von Sydow's King Osric), James Earl Jones, gives the least satisfactory performance. Leaden and hammy by turns, Jones seems to have wandered in from another film. With his flowing locks and long robes, he might be better suited for the part of the High Priest in a mummy movie.

Basil Poledouris' music is thunderous and continuous and more than a little pompous. Yet where James Earl Jones' pomposity as Thulsa Doom is overdone, Poledouris' overly dramatic music matches the air of solemnity that hangs over much of the film.

In accordance with Milius' desire to eschew stop-motion models, special effects sculptor Peter Voysey sculpted a one-piece, 36-foot-long snake that special effects supervisor Nick Allder (*Dragonslayer*) used to make a number of molds to construct a duraluminium skeleton. The giant snake took ten weeks to build and cost $20,000. Unlike De Laurentiis and Rimbaldi's mechanical Kong (used in only one scene) in *King Kong*, the snake is, for the most part, convincingly menacing. Milius realized his goal of having Conan fighting what is clearly a full-size giant serpent.

The film's most impressive effect—Thulsa Doom turning into a giant snake—was accomplished in several stages. First, James Earl Jones' head was immobilized and yellow contacts placed in his eyes to suggest the onset of the metamorphosis. After this "establishing shot" was achieved, a foam-rubber mask of Jones' face was placed over a hollow head and a snakelike puppet pushed through the head and against the mask, suggesting Doom's face beginning to stretch into the shape of a serpent.

The film's most gruesome effect—the close-ups of Conan's mother being beheaded and her head lying on the ground, spouting blood as its eyes roll about and its lips move—was cut by Milius before the film's release, probably to avoid receiving an "X" rating. Other cuts, to remove "excessive" violence and get the film down to a reasonable running time, included a scene with the "Beast with Three Eyes," a creature Conan and his companions encountered at the top of the Tower, and a scene where Conan cuts off the arm of a pickpocket who unwisely chooses the wrong victim. While Ron Cobb remained in the film in a cameo as the "Haga vendor," director Milius' bit as the "lizard on a stick" vendor was excised.

Conan the Barbarian is an example of what can be done with a moribund subgenre—Sword and Sorcery—when the people making the film *believe* in what they're doing. John Milius, production designer Ron Cobb, and star Arnold Schwarzenegger faithfully transposed Robert E. Howard's fantastic Hyborian Age from the page to the screen.

Admittedly, not everything in *Conan* works. Cobb's marvelous designs—the Wheel of Pain is a good example—are outstanding, but Duke Callaghan's moody photography hides too many details in shadow. Perhaps it's because we've seen too many cheapie "B" epics shot in Spain's landscapes, but the location shooting fails to convey the necessary sense of "differentness" a fantasy like *Conan* requires.

The action and other set pieces work well, and Milius' references to

Conan struggles to free himself from the giant serpent in the Tower of Set.

other films are as inspired as they are obvious: *Alexander Nevsky*, with its bizarrely helmeted knights; *Seven Samurai*, with its climactic confrontation between a small band of warriors who make good use of booby-traps and reserves of arrows to blunt the attack of mounted men; and *Kwaidan*, for the scene where the Wizard of the Mounds paints Conan's body with mystic runes to protect him from the spirits of the dead.

Conan represents one of the strongest, most satisfying fantasies around: to be a powerful giant who lives by no rules but his own. Howard, in virtually every Conan story, stresses his hero's distance from the niceties of civilized life; freed of the constraints that limit and contain modern men and women, Conan takes what he wants. He *is*, after all, a barbarian.

The appeal of Conan to Robert E. Howard, his creator, and to Milius and Schwarzenegger, is obvious. Milius, Schwarzenegger, and Howard are men who overcame sickness and infirmity in childhood to reshape their bodies to match the strength of their minds (although Milius, because of his chronic asthma, remains in fragile health).

Much of the appeal of moviemaking is the opportunity for everyone, but especially the actor, to indulge his fantasies; this is even more gratifying if those fantasies are impossible to realize in everyday life. As Schwarzenegger told Stephen Farber in the May 1982 *Moviegoer*, "It was fun to swing a sword, see the blood, [and] still know that . . . the director would yell 'cut,' and . . . the little ladies [would] come in and clean up the fake blood." Most filmgoers shared Schwarzenegger's sense of fun and took *Conan* for what it was—a romp, a chance to live in an age of violence and excitement, to experience wielding a sword against your enemies. Too many pointy-headed critics, however, saw the blood-and-gore as a reflection of our basest instincts instead of the escape valve it was meant to be. Indeed, for a picture called *Conan the Barbarian* and not *Conan the Librarian*, there is really not all that much blood (another sticky point with Conan purists!).

Next time the boss is hassling you, go down to your local video store, rent a copy of *Conan*, kick off your shoes, and relive the "days of high adventure."

3. The Dark Crystal: Other Worlds, Other Times

"Another world . . . another time . . . in the age of wonder."
— *From the opening narration.*

The Dark Crystal is a difficult film to categorize, evaluate, and appreciate. For every positive thing one can say about it, a corresponding negative can be cited: It is a brilliantly conceived world . . . inhabited by less than compelling central characters; it is a marvel of technological achievement . . . all but undone by the limitations of technology; it is a very adult fantasy . . . that works best for undemanding adolescents; and, finally, it is a triumph of the puppeteer's art . . . which cannot escape its Muppet origins.

Crystal is a frustrating film, a 'yes, but. . .' film. Because of its many virtues, however, and despite its many faults, *Crystal* deserves a place among the great fantasy films.

David Sterritt's review in the *Christian Science Monitor* was one of many lauding Henson's achievement: "*The Dark Crystal* takes a fresh approach to fantasy filmmaking. Using sophisticated puppets and high-tech production devices—there's not one human character in the whole movie—directors Jim Henson and Frank Oz . . . have opened up new territory between traditional cartooning and 'live action' drama.

"My 11-year-olds enjoyed the film, but noted how standard the story line was. . . . At its most effective, *The Dark Crystal* has the sneaky verisimilitude of a very vivid dream. It's an engaging fantasy."

Kevin Thomas' review in the *Los Angeles Times* also noted the film's similarity to a dream: "Unlike many screen fantasies, *The Dark Crystal* casts its spell from its very first frames and proceeds so briskly that it's over before you realize it. You're left with the feeling that you have just awakened from a dream."

Less enthralled was John Pym, writing in the *Monthly Film Bulletin*. As Pym notes, ". . . *The Dark Crystal* requires a voice-over explanation: the Great Conjunction, the Crystal itself. Life-giving forces in this context turn out to be rather fey notions. The Skeksis have an appetite for evil in the same way—deep down—that the Cookie Monster has an appetite for cookies. This said, however, *The Dark Crystal* carries a greater fantastical jolt than *Star Wars*.... Chewbacca was a prop in a fantasy: the Chamberlain is a creature, alive to his creators, who has wandered into a rather awkwardly contrived story."

In the *New Statesman*, John Coleman gave the film a similarly mixed review. "*The Dark Crystal*, directed by Jim Henson and Frank Oz, suffers from plot trouble, giving us a fabulous world a millennium ago doomed to everlasting evil unless a boy Gelfling can find a shard from the eponymous Crystal and replace it when the Three Suns coincide. The saving magic is to be performed at the time of the 'Great Conjunction.' In the last resort, the small and crabby conjunction has to be 'but....'"

Alex Keneas, of *Newsday*, had his quibbles with the film, but ended his review by saying, "In all, though, *The Dark Crystal* is joyous fun."

Time magazine's Richard Corliss was less forgiving: "The invention is impressive, but there is little indication of the Henson-Oz trademark: a sense of giddy fun."

Finally, in a free-wheeling review in the *Village Voice*, J. Hoberman gleefully leaps into the fray: "The trend presaged by the mutant baby in David Lynch's *Eraserhead* and epitomized by Steven Spielberg's lovable E.T.—movies constructed around high-tech ventriloquist acts with glum actors playing second fiddle to uncannily expressive animated whatzits—reaches its logical conclusion in *The Dark Crystal*, a sci-fi fantasy dispensing with human performers altogether."

An opening narration tells the viewer that, after 1,000 years, there are ten Skeksis and ten Mystics still living. A Gelfling named Jen, according to a prophesy, is the chosen one. Jen's Mystic teacher, the wisest of them, is dying; he tells Jen to go to Aughra, who has the secret of the lost shard.

The evil Skeksis emperor dies, dissolving away to nothingness; simultaneously, Jen's master dies and also disappears. Jen now sets off on his quest for Aughra and the lost shard.

Both wishing to become the new emperor, the Skeksis chamberlain and the general undergo a "trial by stone"—each seeking to strike the strongest blow. A mighty swing from the general's sword shatters the stone, and he is proclaimed the new emperor. The defeated chamberlain is stripped and banished. The Crystal now "calls" the Skeksis and reveals to them the existence of Jen—a hated Gelfling. The Skeksis send their armored, beetle-like Garthim warriors after him.

Jen meets Aughra and asks for her help in finding the shard. Inside her Orrery—which shows the motions of the heavenly bodies—Aughra tells Jen a time is coming, the Great Conjunction, when the planet's three

The Gelfling Jen (center front) beholds the wonder of Aughra's Orrery.

suns will line up. Jen must use the shard to "heal" the Crystal at exactly that moment. Suddenly, the monstrous Garthim break in and destroy Aughra's Orrery, capturing her. Meanwhile, the Mystics begin a long, slow journey back to the Skeksis castle, back to the Crystal.

Jen cautiously proceeds through an eerie swamp when suddenly he's frightened by Fizzgig, a hairball with teeth. Fizzgig is the pet of Kira, a female Gelfling raised by the gentle Pod People. Jen and Kira touch, sharing their memories.

The captured Aughra reveals Jen's quest to the Skeksis—who immediately send out flying crystal bats to determine the Gelfling's whereabouts. Kira and Jen join a joyous Pod People party that is disrupted by a Garthim attack. As the Garthim carry off Pod People to become Skeksis slaves, the chamberlain sees Jen and Kira escape and prevents a Garthim from capturing them.

Amidst ancient Gelfling ruins, Jen and Kira find an engraved prophecy on a wall: "When single shines the triple sun, what was sundered and undone shall be whole, the two made one, by Gelfling hand or else by none." Jen and Kira now realize the shard is from the dark Crystal and must be returned to it to make it whole once again.

The chamberlain shows up and tries to talk them into going to the castle with him, telling them he wants to arrange peace between their races. But Jen and Kira run away and Kira calls Landstriders to carry them to the castle. Mounted on the spindly-legged Landstriders, Kira, Jen, and Fizzgig all but fly toward the castle. Outside the castle, Jen and Kira's Landstriders battle the same Garthim who kidnapped Kira's Pod People but are defeated and killed. Driven to the edge of the cliff, Kira and Jen jump. As they fall, Kira opens her wings and they gently settle to the ground.

Once in the lower depths of the castle, Jen and Kira are captured by the ever-present chamberlain. With Jen seemingly dead under a rock fall, the chamberlain takes Kira before the emperor—who wishes to drink her essence. For his service, the chamberlain's banishment is lifted and his robes returned.

As Kira's essence is being drained, the imprisoned Aughra shouts to her to call the animals. When Kira does, a multitude of small furry beasts attack the Skeksis scientist, and he falls into the fiery pit and vanishes—as does another Mystic on the plains outside.

Jen finds his way inside the Crystal Chamber pit as the Mystics approach and enter the castle. Jen makes his way above the Crystal and spots Kira across the chamber. As Jen beholds the dark Crystal, the Skeksis approach for their moment of triumph. Jen leaps onto the Crystal . . . but drops the shard. Kira grabs the fallen shard and throws it to Jen before being fatally struck down by a Skeksis. As the moment of the Great Conjunction arrives, Jen fulfills the prophecy by replacing the shard in the Crystal.

There is a dazzling eruption of energy and light, and the Mystics arrive just as the castle begins to fall apart. The Mystics and the Skeksis merge into each other to be replaced by ethereal beings—Urskeks. It was the Urskeks, in their folly, who shattered the Crystal a thousand years earlier.

Jen has made their world whole again—and Kira is given back her life. The world is restored.

Jim Henson's career as a puppeteer began in his hometown of Hyattsville, Maryland. In 1953, at the age of 16, Henson got his start in television with *The Junior Morning Show*, a Washington, D.C., children's program which lasted all of three weeks. Later, calling his weird combination of puppets lip-synching to records The Muppets, Henson landed a five-minute late-night show called *Sam and Friends* on an NBC affiliate in 1955.

Henson and his Muppets debuted on network television in 1956 when they appeared on Steve Allen's NBC show. Kermit the Frog, wearing a blonde wig, sang "I've Grown Accustomed to Your Face" to Yorick, one of Henson's "monster" puppets. It was on ABC's *The Jimmy Dean Show* (1963–1966) that Henson's Muppet dog, Rowlf, achieved enormous popularity. Rowlf (a forerunner to Fozzy Bear, although with Henson's voice) bantered with—and often bested—host Dean.

Henson's creations continued to appear on television with mixed results until 1969 and *Sesame Street*. "With *Sesame Street*, the Muppets suddenly took off under their own power," Henson told Judith P. Harris in *Cinefantastique*. "We just went with it."

Further ventures included *The Frog Prince,* on ABC in 1971, starring the ever-popular Kermit. Henson's Muppets were then hired to produce a weekly segment for NBC's *Saturday Night* (which, after the demise of a similarly titled Howard Cosell live prime-time variety show, was called *Saturday Night Live).*

Henson and company's contribution to the show, "The Land of Gorch," never clicked with the writers and cast or the youthful audiences and, after a few appearances, their segments were cancelled by mutual agreement. The more realistic-looking creatures had glass eyes and included The Mighty Favog, King Ploobis, Scred, Peuta, Wazh, and Wisss.

Henson later noted that these creatures were a sort of step on the path toward *The Dark Crystal.* He believed that if he made the puppets more realistic and less cartoonish than the Muppets he'd be able to do more dramatic things.

Henson saw an illustration in *The Pig Tale,* based on a poem by Lewis Carroll, that further directed his thinking. As he told Alan Jones in *Cinefantastique,* ". . . I saw this drawing of some crocodiles in very ritzy surroundings and it became the key image that kicked off the whole [*Crystal*] project." So enamored of this image was Henson that it eventually showed up as the SkTeksis banquet in *Crystal.*

Henson had a title for the film he wanted to make — *The Crystal* — but little else. In 1977, in the midst of producing *The Muppet Show,* Henson's New York Muppet workshop staff began preproduction work for a film which didn't even have a story line much less a script.

It was about this time that Henson saw a copy of *The World of Froud,* a book of illustrations of trolls, fairies, and other mythical creatures. The book's creator was a young English artist named Brian Froud. "I loved the style and richness of Froud's illustrations," Jim Henson said in *Cinefantastique.* "I knew intuitively that his work could be turned into three dimensional characters for our film — it was that translatable."

Froud met Henson at the ATV Studios outside London where *The Mupper Show* was taped. When Henson showed Froud photos of Scred and the other *Saturday Night Live* Muppets, the young artist began to see the possibilities inherent in a collaboration. "Their eyes were the key," Froud recalled in *The Making of the Dark Crystal.* "It was almost as if we designed everything around the eyes."

Won over, Froud flew to Henson's New York workshop to join the film's brain trust. Also joining the team that same day was Wendy Midener, a young dollmaker from Detroit. Later, she and Froud were married.

Froud immediately began to produce hundreds of illustrations and sketches for the puppetmakers to discuss and consider. In *American Cinematographer,* Froud recalled those days: "We started off with a small group of people in New York, just talking about what the world might be and what the creatures might be in this world. Jim had a fairly strong idea about what the Skeksis might be. They are evil creatures, and he felt that they were reptiles dressed up in very extravagant and opulent clothes, living in a castle."

Froud and the others in New York were generating lots of creature designs—but for a so-far nonexistent story. Excited by their efforts, which were producing marvelously alien and unique life forms, Henson and his people made a decision (probably more by default than by conscious action) that would have a strong negative impact on the project later: They went forward without any real idea where they were going, trusting that somehow a story would miraculously emerge from all their brainstorming sessions.

Henson's teenage daughter Lisa wanted her dad to create a world derived from the eternal elements of the classic fairy tale, something with totally heroic and totally villainous characters. So when a blizzard stranded Jim Henson at a motel at Kennedy Airport in New York City, he finally began to put some ideas on paper. He wrote a detailed story treatment which he titled *The Crystal.*

As preproduction on *Crystal* began to accelerate in 1978, Henson was contacted by Gary Kurtz, then producing the second installment of the *Star Wars* trilogy, *The Empire Strikes Back.* Kurtz sold an initially reluctant Henson on the idea of the two organizations exchanging information on the creation of lifelike puppets for film; Kurtz and George Lucas were having difficulties achieving a workable Yoda. Henson agreed to provide expertise—and Frank Oz—for Yoda's creation for *Empire,* and Kurtz would offer his services as advisor for Henson's *Crystal.*

Recalling her work with the 800-year-old Jedi Master, Wendy Midener told Alan Jones in *Cinefantastique:* "Yoda was the forerunner of everything we were trying to achieve on *The Dark Crystal.* It gave us a taste of what it was like using that kind of sophisticated puppet on a set where you had a limited amount of time and very elaborate scenes that you had to get done. That sort of training was vital to *The Dark Crystal.*"

Later, after departing Lucasfilm, Gary Kurtz agreed to sign on as co-producer and second-unit director of *Crystal,* bringing with him invaluable experience in working, not only with big-budget fantasy films, but also with British crews. Kurtz, in fact, was already operating out of an office at the once-shuttered EMI Studios, which he had reopened when he produced *Star Wars.*

The production team moved to England in 1979, and Henson's "animatronic fabrication group" expanded from a mere seven people to more than 60. Henson's creative supervisor for this crew was Sherry Amott, a young woman with a background in theatrical costuming.

Sherry Amott had the herculean task of assembling the artisans needed

Jen, Kira, and Fizzgig find a revealing prophecy amid ancient Gelfling ruins.

for this unusual production. "My job was to get the ideas from Jim Henson, Frank Oz, and Brian Froud . . . and then find someone to do it," she recalled in *American Cinematographer*. It was necessary for Amott to learn completely how the puppets were made before she knew what sort of people to look for. Amott searched out puppeteers in the unlikeliest professions: jewelry designers and watch repairers became mechanical designers, and pottery and ceramic majors still in art school were hired to make the company's molds.

Trying to find workable eyes for the characters ("They just don't exist," she said), Amott went from Madame Tussaud's ("very fragile") to an artificial-eye maker, to a company that finally was able to produce what the production was looking for.

The job of turning Froud's sketches into actual physical settings went to Harry Lange. Lange, who'd been an artist for NASA when he was discovered by Stanley Kubrick and brought to London to conceptualize the future of *2001: A Space Odyssey*, was hired as *Crystal's* production designer. Lange had worked on both of Kurtz' *Star Wars* productions.

Stage armorer Fred Nihda and his crew had been mass-producing the Garthim shells since mid–1980. Assembled from 59 fiberglass pieces, each Garthim weighed 70 pounds. A special harness distributed much of that weight over the performer's back and shoulders and gave him the mobility and speed he needed to be sufficiently scary.

The heroes of the story, the Gelflings, were traditional Muppet hand puppets fitted over the hands of performers Jim Henson and Kathryn Mullen. While Henson and Mullen operated the mouths, radio control devices were responsible for giving Jen and Kira lifelike facial and eye movements.

The urRu Mystics were operated by performers inside who squatted on their haunches, heads bowed, with their right arms thrust forward into the creatures' heads. More complicated than the Mystics, the Skeksis were cable-operated puppets in closeups and costumed midgets in long or walking shots. Since each Skeksis puppet took five performers to operate, the council chamber scenes with all nine of them in attendance required 45 performers trying to stay out of each other's way and out of sight of the camera.

The Landstriders began as Froud-inspired spiderlike creatures which moved by leaping. When Henson remembered that performer Robby Barnett could stiltwalk, he asked the young man to attempt to gallop on four stilts. When Barnett easily ran, Froud refined his original design, and the Landstriders were born.

The script for *Crystal* was an afterthought. Henson knew he had to have one, but considered words almost superfluous. "From my first experience with film," Henson told Christopher Finch in *The Making of the Dark Crystal*, "I just loved what could be done with the montaging of visual images. I was fascinated with a kind of flow-of-consciousness form of editing, where one image took you to another image, and there was no logic to it but your mind put it together. I've always felt that music and image work on one level, and the spoken word and dialogue work on another, much shallower one. That's one of the reasons why in *The Dark Crystal* I started off trying to do a film with as little dialogue as possible."

David Odell, who'd written *Between Time and Timbuktu*, a fantasy based on the works of Kurt Vonnegut, for PBS, was hired to turn Henson's slender quest outline into a screenplay. Odell had written many episodes of *The Muppet Show* for Henson, as well as scripting *The Muppet Movie*.

Mystic Valley was the first set built and, like all the others, had to be constructed 4½ feet off the floor to allow the puppet operators to manipulate their charges off camera. One huge set, when dressed with different props, served as both the Crystal and council chambers.

While most of the sets were constructed full size, the ruins of the ancient Gelfling civilization and the Pod People's village were built to the scale of the three-foot-tall puppets. Although it is not made clear in the film, the Pod People's civilization is dependent upon giant gourds that the Pod People use for both food and shelter.

John Coppinger, a technical advisor on loan from London's Natural History Museum, offered advice concerning the plant and animal life that might be found in a swamp like the one in which Jen and Kira meet, and his expertise found its way into the finished swamp set.

John Harman, an electrical supervisor, recalled in *American Cinematographer* the difficulties the huge swamp set on Stage 4 presented: "Because of the vastness of the complicated lighting on this picture we spent several weeks beforehand planning with Ossie [Morris], rigging the lights and working out the colors."

Because the huge lamps burning down from overhead sent the temperature soaring between 100 and 130 degrees, the lighting electricians took salt tablets to prevent dehydration and spent no more than an hour at a time in the rigging above the set.

Oswald Morris was hired as the film's director of photography. Morris' credits are impressive; the many films he has shot include *Moulin Rouge, Moby Dick, Lolita, The Pumpkin Eater* (British Film Academy Award for Best B/W Cinematography), *Oliver!, Fiddler on the Roof* (Academy Award for Best Cinematography), and *The Man Who Would Be King*. He was also the director of photography on Henson's *The Great Muppet Caper*.

Morris found *Crystal* a difficult film to photograph. As he wrote in *American Cinematographer*, "It is difficult because there is no visual yardstick whereby each . . . member of the unit can talk with the same basic understanding. By that I mean, visual realism. A fairy tale is not real, it is an interpretation . . . which is . . . different in every person's mind."

Morris decided to use the Lightflex, a "device whereby color overlays can be laid onto images while they are being photographed and is at the total command . . . of the cinematographer. I could increase or decrease the color effects as I so wished. I could change the colors scene by scene or indeed during the course of a scene. . . ."

Shooting the battle between the Garthim and the Landstriders took days to film on a manmade plateau on EMI's backlot. This single outdoor set—utilized not only for the Garthim/Landstrider battle, but also for the entry of the Mystics into the castle—was a full-scale facsimile of a Yorkshire rock formation. Unfortunately, the artificial plateau reflected the rays of the sun upwards. The performers were affected by the heat and could act only for brief periods. When the heat got to be too much for the Landstrider actors (Hugh Spight, Swee Lim, and Robbie Barnett), they doffed their characters' heads and were cooled off by portable electric fans.

Because the Landstrider performers were on stilts, piano wires tethered them to a huge crane arm overhead. When, in the course of the "battle," as often happened, Robbie Barnett or one of the others was knocked off balance, the wires prevented him from crashing to the floor of the plateau.

Henson and Oz found directing such a logistically complicated movie a near-nightmare. Henson noted that in shooting a normal film, the director first shoots a "master" shot, which takes in the whole scene and all the characters. On *Crystal,* however, Henson and Oz discovered that they couldn't shoot a continuous master because of concerns unique to working with puppets and cable crews: keeping character performers and crew members out of the shot. What the two directors found themselves doing was breaking the master into several shots, then shooting any closeups and inserts.

The special mechanical effects and special photographic effects were supervised by Brian Smithies and Roy Field, respectively. "We started with special effects very early on," said co-producer Kurtz in *American Cinematographer.* "We knew we would have to have some miniatures, some matte paintings, a lot of optical composite work. We [built] the dark Crystal in two miniature sizes, one about 10th scale and one about 25th scale so that we could build a a fairly large landscape over Stage 7 with mountains and terrain and put the castle in the middle."

At the film's end, the Crystal Chamber was to be revealed in its original glory when the stone slabs with which the Skeksis had covered the crystal walls fell away. Three cameras were positioned to catch the peeling away of the slabs in a single take. Smithies built a glass miniature, lining its walls with plaster blocks.

As Kurtz recalled, "The only way we could get the stonework to fall away effectively was to shoot at a very high speed, so we brought in a 360 frames-per-second camera to shoot the falling away and set many explosive charges all around the plaster stonework so that it would fall apart in small enough pieces for this scale to work." The first take was ruined when there was a malfunction; it took five days to set up a second attempt which, fortunately, went perfectly.

Other effects included creating roiling clouds for a storm sequence at the film's beginning. The clouds were colored liquids suspended in a glass-walled water tank. The film's matte paintings were executed by Michael Pangrazio and Chris Evans of Kurtz and Lucas' effects company, Industrial Light & Magic.

While the puppets were being fabricated, Henson and Kurtz were casting the actors who would perform inside the finished characters. Henson took it upon himself to act Jen, the dying Skeksis emperor, and the ritual-master. Co-director Frank Oz, after initially vowing he wanted nothing to do with the acting side, accepted the roles of Aughra and the chamberlain. Longtime Muppet puppeteer Dave Goetz assumed the roles of the Garthim-master and Kira's pet pest, Fizzgig.

Henson was uncomfortable with his decision to play Jen. "Jen was murder," Henson later complained to Alan Jones. "For the first third of the filming I was terribly unhappy with my performance. I was constantly frustrated by what I felt were the character's shortcomings." Specifically, Henson discovered that while Jen was the central character around which everything else was constructed, he was "white-bread" pure—a boring goody-goody.

Sherry Amott had spotted Swiss mime Jean-Pierre Amiel at the London Mime Festival and immediately hired him to recruit and train other performers. Amiel auditioned hundreds of mimes, clowns, and dancers to find the small group of performers who would augment Henson and Oz's normal contingent of Muppet regulars. Among the recruits was Brian Muehl, who had been a performer with Mummenschanz, a dance/performance group famous for sketches in which they contort themselves into unusual positions, usually inside fabric, tubes, or other flexible materials.

After three months of rehearsal, Crystal finally went before the cameras on May 4, 1981. Amiel was assigned the role of the Mystic weaver and also one of the Garthim. Brian Muehl played Jen's dying master.

The Mystics were the first of the character groups (Skeksis, Landstriders, etc.) to be shot. After the first week of production, Kurtz selected several scenes from the rushes and had them screened at the Leicester Square Cinema, a huge London movie theater. As Henson, Oz, and members of the workshop and character group looked on, Brian Froud's Mystic illustrations came to convincing life.

Frank Oz, like Henson, found his acting and directing chores demanding and often in conflict. When he was directing, he wished he could be free of all responsibilities except acting; and when he was acting he wanted to be lining up shots and talking to the other actors. Oz found it difficult to keep his mind on directorial concerns, like the lighting, when he wanted to be focusing his energy and his acting skills into performing his characters.

Both Frank Oz and Dave Goetz, who played the Garthim-master, stressed the close coordination they needed to establish with their cable crews. "At first we had to give rather precise instructions—'Pop his eyeballs on the count of three,'" said Dave Goetz, "but then it became much easier. Most of the time I would just tell my crew what emotion I wanted the Garthim-master to register."

All along, Henson and Oz had determined that a female puppeteer would perform Kira. In Kathryn Mullen, they found an actress who'd also done a little puppeteering. In *The Making of the Dark Crystal*, Henson recalls that he always thought that "her puppeteering skills could be developed. What was more important was that we sensed she had the acting ability to take on Kira." Mullen got much-needed experience and seasoning by acting as a backup performer on *The Muppet Show* while *Crystal* was in preproduction. She also served as Oz's "performing assistant" for Yoda on *The Empire Strikes Back*.

Mullen soon found herself frustrated by Kira's cable-controlled limitations—she hated being trailed by technicians and wires. With Henson's approval, Faz Fazakas, a Muppets technician, then built two robot heads containing radio-controlled ears, eyelids, lips, and eyes.

Mullen was astonished and relieved at the degree of freedom the remote-controlled Kira gave her, calling the difference between cable and remote control "like night and day." Without having to worry about her movements quite so much, Mullen was able to focus on performing instead of on whether or not cables or crew were in the shot.

Jen and Kira were played in long shots by children Abbie Jones and Natasha Knight. If Jen or Kira had to climb or do physical actions, they were played by midget Kiran Shah. Likewise, Aughra and the scenes of the Skeksis walking were filmed with midgets inside the costumes: Jack Purvis, Deep Roy, Peter Burroughs, Mike Cottrell, Lisa Esson, Malcolm Dixon, Gerald Stradden, and others. Not credited for the characters they played, all the little people were listed in the final credits only as "Additional Performers."

One of the funniest and most memorable scenes in *Crystal* is the Skeksis banquet sequence. Henson and Oz were behind schedule and had to shoot the scene as quickly as possible, giving the actors little time to consider their performances.

"In the beginning," puppetmaker Lyle Conway states in *Cinefantastique*, "we were ever so careful with the Skeksis: white gloves, special bags, careful grooming. By the end of shooting we couldn't care. They had become too much like *real* Skeksis—rotting rubber, permeated with cold KY jelly and putrifying noodles. Fortunately the banquet scene turned out to be the last Skeksis shot."

Without time to over-prepare their actions and no longer overprotective of the puppets since it was the last shot (one Skeksis even plunges his head into a bucket of water), the performers were free to wallow in the Skeksis' lack of table manners and disgusting eating habits.

Aiming for a May 28 release (the golden *Star Wars, Alien* and *Raiders of the Lost Ark* pre-summer launch time), Henson and Oz proudly previewed a rough cut of their nearly finished film in Washington, D.C.

Henson and distributor Universal Pictures' high hopes were dashed when the demographically chosen sample audience found the film too long and plodding, Aughra's dialogue all but unintelligible, and the unsubtitled foreign speech of some characters baffling. Henson had hired linguist Alan Garner to devise the alien tongues, but according to Gary Kurtz, the mystified Washington audience couldn't avoid believing that something was going on they weren't privy to.

Now painfully aware that his efforts to be linguistically innovative were resented rather than appreciated, Henson was forced to scramble to save the film. So, it was back to the cutting room for a disappointed Henson and Oz. Word of the reception of the film had received in Washington got out, and the film's original May release date was scrubbed until the picture could be salvaged.

Henson began the restructuring process—with help from unexpected sources: George Lucas, who knew both Frank Oz and Gary Kurtz, dropped by an early screening of the film and offered several suggestions that Henson gladly incorporated into the new version.

Henson also sent writer David Odell a videotape of the film so new English dialogue could be written and matched to the lip movements of the various characters—a necessary evil since none of the footage could be reshot. Relying on what worked for *The Muppet Show*, Odell added a number of zingers and one-liners for the Skeksis. The voice of Aughra was recast, with actress Billie Whitlaw delivering a performance that cleverly mixed grouchiness and humor to produce a more appealing—and audibly intelligible—character.

Since the preview audience had found the film's beginning slow and ponderous, Henson trimmed a number of scenes which duplicated action or which ran on far too long. In so doing, Henson slimmed the film down from its original 101 minutes to a more svelte 94.

After adding a voice-over narration by Joseph O'Connor, Henson nervously previewed *Crystal* before a Detroit audience on July 11. This time, the audience evaluation cards were more appreciative of the film's wonders. Despite this improved reception, however, industry wags were predicting disaster.

Aware of the industry rumors that Henson had produced a turkey, Associated Communications Corporation, which had financed the picture and was deeply in debt, wanted to release *Crystal* immediately—before the end of the lucrative summer play period. Henson, believing his film would not have time to find its way, dug into his own pockets and came up with $2 million to pay for the increased interest charges until the film could be released at Christmas.

Still nervous about *Crystal*'s money-making potential, ACC agreed to sell the $26 million picture to Henson for approximately $18 million—a figure which included the $2 million Henson had already paid to under-write the interest charges.

Henson's faith in the picture and his investment were rewarded when the film went on to earn $23,552,592 in domestic rentals (source: *Variety*). With foreign rentals and subsidiary rights like videocassette and laserdisc sales and merchandising spinoffs (*The Making of the Dark Crystal*), the film has surely proved to be profitable, if not overwhelmingly so.

Analyzing *The Dark Crystal* forces one to conclude that while it is a great fantasy film, it is not a great film. *Crystal* has wonderous flights of imagination; its world is a marvelous creation whose inhabitants are as diverse and convincing as one could ask for; its technical aspects are flawless. However, the film suffers from several weaknesses common to many fantasy and science fiction films.

As the set designers, puppet fabricators, illustrators, creature designers, and mimes and other performers toiled to produce incredibly realistic results, Henson proceeded without a finished script in hand. "The story would evolve later," Henson said as his Muppet artisans built Garthim and searched for perfect glass eyes. What Henson, Oz, and Kurtz failed to realize — or chose not to acknowledge — is that special effects and wondrous worlds are not enough. The story, the plot, must come first.

Crystal is saddled with a flabby plot, poor logic, and weak central characters whose motivation is muddled or unclear. Gary Kurtz, of all peo-ple, should have been aware of this problem. The myriad of trashy *Star Wars* imitators learned the wrong lessons from its tremendous success, assuming it was the film's special effects, space ships, and weird creatures that tickled audiences' fancies. The truth is, *Star Wars* and its sequels were based on myths fundamental to western civilization — separation, initiation, return.

The world of *Crystal* is populated by creatures great and small, good and evil, but its central characters, the two Gelflings Jen and Kira, are lackluster heroes. Henson admitted the choice was his. Wanting the Gelflings to be "very attractive" and humanoid, but not actually human, Henson believes he made the correct choice for an epic. Arguing that mak-ing them more "elfin-like" would have made them and the film more appeal-ing, Henson nonetheless stuck to his guns and produced two one-dimensional and not-very-involving characters.

Henson's comment about his performance as Jen ("I was constantly frustrated by what I felt were the character's shortcomings") reveals the puppet master's growing awareness that the Gelflings were too bland and unheroic to hold the film together. But, in the midst of a major production, when the costs are running at a rate of $3.40 *per second*, it's too late to iron out script or character problems which should have been considered before the cameras started rolling.

While in all fantasies we are aware that good will ultimately triumph, the outcome of *Crystal* seems almost too preordained to sustain suspense. We know (there's a prophecy, after all) that a Gelfling will heal the Dark Crystal at the time of the Great Conjunction, and Jen never seems to be in much real danger.

Crystal also is burdened by its Muppet origins, especially when it mixes convincing puppets like the Skeksis and the Mystics with the usual assortment of Muppet fuzzies and cutesies like Fizzgig and the Gelflings. Henson ought to consider finding more voices from outside his Muppet regulars since many of their voices are recognizable to us from *Sesame Street* or *The Muppet Show* (this problem plagued Oz's portrayal of Yoda in *The Empire Strikes Back* as well).

Oswald Morris' photography is often too dark and depressing, contributing to the film's lack of exuberance. I must admit, though, that the Pod People's party, filled with dancing and music, is great fun (it owes a lot to Henson's perennial cable special, *Emmet Otter's Jug-Band Christmas*).

The film's strength is in its ability to cast us into a world unlike any we have ever seen before—and to make us believe in that world. Aughra, the Skeksis, the Mystics, and the Garthim are creatures from our dreams—and nightmares.

Froud's design of the film is flawless. Froud's success at creating a totally new world is matched by the success attained by Tim Miller and John Coppinger in creating the film's "environmental creatures"—those walking plants and flying flowers seen in the swamp scenes.

Two months before the start of principal photography, Henson hired young composer Trevor Jones to write the musical score. Jones was scoring John Boorman's *Excalibur* (then called *The Knights*). Jones' score is one of the best things about *Crystal*; it's powerful, heroic, and even majestic. The film would be much less successful without Jones' music.

Henson, Oz, and Froud dared to try to put an original and compelling fantasy adventure on film. That they failed to completely realize their goal is less remarkable than the fact that they so often succeeded in translating Brian Froud's visions to the screen.

4. Dragonslayer:
Mythic Beasts/Genrebuster

> And the great dragon was cast out, that old serpent, called the Devil,
> and Satan, which deceiveth the whole world: he was cast out into the
> earth, and his angels were cast out with him.
> — *Revelation 12, the King James Version of the Bible.*

When *Dragonslayer* was released in the summer of 1981 — the summer
of *Raiders of the Lost Art, Clash of the Titans, Superman II, For Your Eyes
Only,* and *Time Bandits* — fans and critics alike praised its ground-breaking
special effects, including a "go-motion" dragon that was as realistic and
magnificent as any movie monster put on celluloid. It also got some of the
best reviews of any film to debut in this hottest of movie-going seasons.

In *Films in Review,* Tom Rogers wrote, "Paramount and the Disney
studios have teamed up again to produce a fine fantasy fare. The film is often
captivating due to Matthew Robbins' fine direction. Everything builds to an
utterly phenomenal climax of action and destruction, and this is what fantasy films are all about."

In his review in the *Christian Science Monitor,* David Sterritt observed
that "there's not an original bone in the entire picture: The hero is straight
from *Star Wars,* and the plot is a steal from King Arthur, complete with a
twinkly Merlin character played by Ralph Richardson. Otherwise, though,
it's a fast-moving and uncommonly good-looking movie, with powerful settings in a brooding Welsh countryside."

Writing in the *Los Angeles Times,* Kevin Thomas enthused, "Forget
Godzilla. Forget all the other dinosaurs and firebreathers and make way for
the greatest dragon yet, the wondrously scary Vermithrax Pejorative, the
terror of the 6th-Century British kingdom of Urland . . . *Dragonslayer* itself
is a meticulous work, a thoroughly convincing evocation of the Dark
Ages. . . ."

Less enthralled, the *Monthly Film Bulletin*'s Tim Pulleine wrote that
"the movie never really acquires sufficient narrative drive and clarity to support its sundry effects: the early stages of the plot are confusing and slow-
moving, and the visual treatment sometimes oddly sombre and heavy."

John Coleman's review in *New Statesman* was equally blunt, calling the film a "turgid sword-and-sorcery fable, with Ralph Richardson in a backdated kind of *Star Wars* or Alec Guinness role . . . ."

However, the often-demanding David Denby, writing in *New York*, began his review this way: "In *Dragonslayer*, the splendid new spectacle about magic and terror in the Dark Ages, the dragon is called Vermithrax Pejorative, and the beast fully lives up to its wonderful name. This is a much better movie than the incoherent *Excalibur*, and also much better, I think, than a machine-tooled, soulless winner like *Raiders of the Lost Ark*."

Archer Winston's *New York Post* review ended with this: "This picture is another in the endless stream of fabulous creations that are aimed to delight the child's mind, and all those others who have never lost their childish belief in magic, adventure, and a whole world beyond reality."

Not so, says Alex Keneas' *Newsday* review. "*Dragonslayer* is so closed off from everything but its own ethers — the magic of cauldron and amulet, Latin hocus-pocus, sulphurous smoke — that it drew laughs from the audience when one of its dragon-menaced villagers remarked, 'What kind of a life can you have here?' In fact, *Dragonslayer* is so bereft of any real sense of medieval time, place, and society that after a while we begin wishing for the humanized lethargy of *Excalibur*."

Finally, writing in *Variety*, "Berg." notes, "A well-intentioned fantasy with some wonderful special effects, *Dragonslayer* falls somewhat short on continuously intriguing adventure . . . there is a smokey atmosphere to *Dragonslayer* that will initially absorb audiences at the expectation of a journey taking them far away from the problems of contemporary life. Yet what is lacking here is the proper combination of action, humor, and character necessary to keep people interested. Several individual scenes work quite well but, on the whole, the film just doesn't have enough bite."

Despite its impressive reviews, *Dragonslayer* bombed at the box office. It cost an estimated $18 million to produce and returned less than $7 million in domestic rentals (source: *Variety*). The film thus did not place among the top 45 films of the year.

Why did *Dragonslayer* fail to find an audience in a summer when film attendance was breaking records? There are many reasons, and I'll attempt to present several explanations for the film's poor showing in this chapter. (A number of the films in this book were box-office failures; I'm *not* equating financial success with artistic success, simply seeking explanations for audience rejection.)

Let us begin with the most successful cinematic trilogy in the history of motion pictures, one which grossed over a billion dollars worldwide: George Lucas' *Star Wars* trilogy. Lucas had studied and relied upon Joseph Campbell's *The Hero with a Thousand Faces*, the seminal 1949 work detailing the universality of the myths that permeate our society and our lives. Other filmmakers and studios, unaware of Lucas' reliance on Campbell's work, thought the success of *Star Wars* and its sequels was due to the marvelous special effects. The wave of derivative films which followed brimmed with special effects, but what their makers failed to realize was the mythic depth of Lucas' seemingly simple saga.

I am placing *Dragonslayer* not only in the subgenre I call "Mythic Beasts," but also in a special category I've chosen to call "genrebuster." By genrebuster, I mean that *Dragonslayer* willfully goes against long-established elements of popular myth and storytelling. The reason most of the other films in this book work, and have become classics in many cases, is that they are original and well-made films *within* the requirements of the fantasy and heroic genres.

Beauty and the Beast, for instance, reaffirms our belief that beauty is only skin deep and that love can transform what is feared and "ugly" into something beautiful and wonderful. In *Jason and the Argonauts,* Jason is heroic, persevering, and ultimately successful. *King Kong* represents our submerged primal desires—to smash and destroy normal societal constraints, to be an unfettered Id seeking self-satisfaction and the rest of the world be damned; but the film's message is that we are all part of the larger society around us and cannot live out our basest animal desires. Some conformity is not only desirable, says *Kong*—it is necessary for civilized life as we know it.

Dragonslayer is a compelling and often brilliant fantasy film; it is also, however, a movie which is at odds with the normal internal structure of the typical "hero myth." It first tries hard to evoke a certain time and place—and then tries just as hard to reject the necessary, and expected, limitations its particular setting and historical era impose. To put it bluntly, *Dragonslayer* is not content to conform to the strictures of the genre and to tell a rousing good story; it seeks, as well, to impose modern sensibilities on its medieval characters and plot—twentieth-century political, sociological, and religious sensibilities which only serve to dilute its particular strengths.

Dragonslayer confounds our normal genre expectations in many ways. Rather than being about an age of sorcerers and dragons, it is, at times, all too modern. When the king's counselor draws the Princess' name in the lottery, Casiodorus Rex intones, "That is *not* the name; the good Horsrik misspoke himself." "Misspoke" is a twentieth-century term born during the Watergate hearings. The filmmakers are making an obvious—and forced—connection between the kingdom's rigged lotteries and modern political chicanery.

While Princess Elspeth is beautiful and brave—as any fantasy princess should be—the film fumbles her fate. If myths and heroic tales have one

absolute, one unbreakable rule, it is this: the hero *must* rescue the fair
princess (whether she is his love or not). What happens in *Dragonslayer?*
Not only does the callow Galen fail to save Princess Elspeth (perhaps the
purest character in the film), but we see her dead and mangled body feasted
upon by the dragon's dreadful spawn. In a grotesque scene, unworthy of a
Disney film, we see one of the infant dragons actually *tear off* the Princess'
leg!

Brother Jacopus—the monk who vainly invokes the name of Christ in
an attempt to stop the dragon, only to be burned alive by its fiery breath—
represents the new faith that is displacing the ancient arts of magic and
sorcery. The monk's evocation of Christ's name is as futile against the fiery
breath of the dragon as is Pastor Collins' recital of the twenty-third Psalm
against the heat rays of the Martian war machines in *War of the Worlds.*
(What are Barwood and Robbins trying to say here?)

At the film's conclusion, the religious and political elements are
cynically linked when Greil and the other Christians thank God for destroying the dragon, and when the king plunges a sword into the already-dead
dragon's body and Horsrik proclaims, "All hail Casiodorus Rex—
dragonslayer!" This slap at the mythic tale's normally satisfying ending left
audiences discomforted and muttering to themselves: After proving himself
a conniving villain, the king (with the villagers) takes the glory rightfully
belonging to Galen (or, at least, Ulrich).

Given all these genrebusting elements, then, it is not hard to see why
the film, despite its state-of-the-art special effects got lost in the flood of
emotionally satisfying fantasies released that spring and summer.

In Castle Cragganmore, ancient sorcerer Ulrich is casting spells, looking to a future full of fire and death. Seeking his aid, a party of travelers led
by a youth named Valerian arrives. Ulrich sees the visitors, after first predicting his own death to his young apprentice, Galen.

The visitors are from far-off Urland and beset by a dragon. Ulrich, one
of the last sorcerers alive, is their only hope. Twice a year, they tell him,
the king selects a virgin in a lottery to appease the dragon. Ulrich tells them
that without sorcerers there'd be no dragons and that this dragon is old and
in pain . . . and spiteful.

Before Ulrich can set off, Tyrian, the king's centurion, shows up to
"test" the wizard and seemingly kills the old man with his own dagger.
Galen inherits Ulrich's magic amulet and burns the old man's body. Setting
off with Ulrich's servant, old Hodge, Galen pulls off a series of cheap parlor
tricks, including making Hodge's pack float and his clothes disappear.
Galen then offers his "sorcerer's" skills to the travelers.

Meanwhile, a virgin is taken to the mouth of the dragon's lair for
sacrifice. As she struggles to free herself, the dragon comes—a horned head

rising from the pit. She is incinerated by the dragon's breath before she can escape.

While swimming, Galen discovers Valerian's secret — "he's" a girl. Her father, Simon the blacksmith, has protected her from the lottery — just as the nobles' daughters have been protected by paying bribes to the king.

Old Hodge is mortally wounded by the evil Tyrian. Dying, he gives Galen a sack with Ulrich's ashes which Ulrich ordered him to throw into "burning water."

In Urland, the travelers pass near the lair. Galen, wishing to see it, insists they visit the single entrance and then casts a spell, causing an earthquake which buries the entrance. The Urlanders celebrate and fete Galen in the village of Swanscombe. Valerian shocks everyone by appearing in a dress. Easing the moment, Galen dances with her, but the partying is interrupted by soldiers who arrive to take Galen to the king.

Casiodorus Rex is unimpressed by Galen's second-rate conjuring tricks and unsure the dragon is really dead. The king tells Galen that the dragon is capable of terrible reprisals and, guessing that it holds the youth's power, tears the amulet from Galen's neck and has him imprisoned.

At the lair, the ground trembles and shakes. Galen, without Ulrich's amulet, is powerless. From his cell, he sees the Princess Elspeth. Galen speaks to her and she naively insists she's always participated in the lotteries. She confronts her father and learns the truth.

Elspeth frees Galen as the earth trembles with the dragon's fury. A monk, Brother Jacopus, ventures to the lair, invoking Christ's name; his followers flee, and the dragon burns the flesh from his bones.

The village and fields burn as the dragon swoops vengefully overhead; dawn reveals ruin and death. The king's soldiers search unsuccessfully through the smithy for Galen, and Tyrian tells Simon there's to be a new lottery. The soldiers leave and Galen emerges from beneath the anvil. Simon then produces a weapon for Galen — a "dragonslayer." Even so armed, Galen knows he must have the power of the amulet.

Princess Elspeth rigs the new lottery so that only her name is chosen. Meanwhile, Galen searches the castle for the amulet. Eager to save his daughter, Casiodorus Rex returns the amulet to Galen. Braving the lair and the dragon's young, Valerian gathers dragon scales to make a shield which will protect Galen from the beast's fiery breath. Valerian presents the shield to Galen, warning him of the dragon's young. Galen professes his love for Valerian and kisses her.

The Princess is chained to a stake when Galen appears, ready to save her. But first he must fight Tyrian, who says the kingdom needs the sacrifice. The Princess flees into the lair as Galen kills Tyrian. Hastening into the lair, Galen finds Elspeth's body being feasted upon by the dragon's young and angrily kills all three of them.

Galen (Peter MacNichol) holds the lance—a "dragonslayer"—Simon the blacksmith (Emrys James) has made for him while Valerian (Caitlin Clarke) looks on uneasily.

From burning pools of liquid, the dragon rises and is finally revealed, unleashing fiery breath as Galen hides behind his shield. Galen then runs, with the dragon scuttling and crabbing in pursuit. The dragon finds the bodies of her offspring and mourns for them, nudging one with her snout. Hatred in her eyes, she rages after Galen.

Hiding above her, Galen leaps onto the back of her neck, stabbing at her. He is thrown off and stabs the dragon in the throat, hanging on as she tosses her head from side to side. His lance shatters, and she pulls the tip from her throat.

Valerian finds the shield, the lance . . . and then the wounded Galen. At the smithy, Valerian says they must leave. Simon, saying magic and magicians are fading from the world, gives Valerian a crucifix.

Galen has a vision of the "burning water"—he knows all was a plan of Ulrich's—and returns to the lair to throw in Hodge's sack of ashes and restore Ulrich. The amulet glows and a green flame from the water produces Ulrich.

Simon and others are being baptized as the dragon soars overhead during an eclipse. The dragon senses her enemy, Ulrich, as the sorcerer sees Valerian's cross. Ulrich tells Galen to destroy the amulet and him with it, while life is still in him. The dragon engages Ulrich in battle, after which the dragon seizes Ulrich in her talons and flies off with him. Galen smashes the amulet and it explodes, killing the dragon; the eclipse passes.

The next morning, as Galen and Valerian inspect the body of the dragon, the king appears and pierces the corpse with his sword as his counselor Horsrik intones, "All hail Casiodorus Rex—dragonslayer!" Galen and Valerian ride off on a white horse that magically appears.

Early man, ignorant of the causes of day and night, watched uneasily as nightly the sun disappeared into the yawning blackness of night—perhaps never to reappear. It seemed to such fearful onlookers that the god of the sun each night fought a great battle against an awesome night monster that tried to prevent him from returning to the earth with life-giving light and warmth. The sun god, and his heroic descendants, came to represent good; the night beast, the dragon, likewise came to represent darkness and evil. (The Chinese, however, believed in dragons that were both evil *and* good—some protected the heavenly mansions of the gods; others governed the wind, the clouds, and the rain that fell.)

The ancient Greeks told tales of battles between men and dragons. The warrior Cadmus fought and killed a mighty dragon, sowing its teeth and watching in wonder as a crop of fully grown warriors emerged from the soil. These strange warriors engaged each other in battle until only five remained; these then made peace. With Cadmus' help, they threw the dragon's body high into the air. The dragon soared higher and higher until, according to legend, coiling among the stars, the dragon became the constellation Draco.

One of Hercules' twelve labors was to steal the golden apples of the Hesperides. As he did so, he killed the many-headed dragon which guarded the tree. Jason fought the many-coiled dragon that guarded the grove of the Golden Fleece, luring it to sleep with the magic potion given him by Medea (see the *Jason and the Argonauts* chapter).

The Roman Empire collapsed—and with it the civilization it had imposed on the barbaric tribes. Thus, Europe in the Middle Ages, its gods and heroes slowly being replaced by saints and knights of the Church, found itself in a period of terrifying violence and societal decay. The dragon came to represent the dark forces seeking to tear the established order apart and replace it with barbarism and death.

With fear and ignorance rampant, dragons represented palpable, direct causes for the otherwise unexplainable natural disasters that befell medieval towns and villages. A devastating flood was seen as coming not from rain falling from the sky, but from a dragon, deep in the swollen river, roiling the water with massive strokes of his mighty tail. Droughts and famines were assumed to be the result of a rapacious dragon laying waste to farmers' fields with his poisonous or fiery breath, and of his devouring of the "beeves ahoof" in the fields. Dragons dwelt in wells and poisoned the water, causing contagion and death.

During these dark times, the dragon assumed an even more awful mantle, representing the shape taken by Satan. St. John's vision of Lucifer as the red dragon of the Apocalypse promised a cataclysmic battle between mankind and horrendous monsters and dragons almost beyond imagining. This Armageddon, preached by the bringers of the new religion, Christianity, was a vivid warning of the fate awaiting those unwashed in the blood of the lamb. Medieval artists, as powerful in their depictions of this final collision between the armies of good and evil as the special effects artists of the most gut-wrenching horror film, struck fear into the hearts of poor, everyday sinners.

With visions of the Apocalypse dancing in their heads, people saw dragons everywhere, and their sightings and legends grew exponentially. (This is comparable to the rash of flying saucer sightings of the early 1950s, produced by the fear of the bomb and the possible end of the world. Just as medieval paintings of dragons induced stories of dragons, so did reports of flying saucers induce more U.F.O. sightings.)

It is appropriate that *Dragonslayer* was filmed partly in Wales. The national emblem of Wales is a dragon, known variously as the *afanc*, the *ceffyl dwr* (water horse), or *Y ddraig Coch* (red dragon). There are many dragon legends attached to England and Wales, with tales of fierce beasts lurking in lakes to seize and devour the unwary. Many of these monsters were known as worms or *wyvern*. The wyvern, a two-legged dragon, derives its name from the Saxon word *wivere*, or serpent. Thus, we have legends of the Wyvern of *Cynwch* Lake, the Worm of Spirdleston Heugh, the Serpent of Handale, the Bromfield Dragon, and many others.

To commemorate the slaying of a dragon upon that site, many English towns have names like Worms Head, Great Ormes Head, Ormesleigh, Ormskirk, Wormelow, and Wormeslea. All these monstrous creatures — all Wyvern, Serpents, Peistes, Worms, and Dragons — come from lakes or the sea; they come from water, as does Vermithrax Pejorative, the flying dragon of *Dragonslayer*.

The great English dragons that fly are pictured as primarily land or sea beasts with hilariously inadequte wings. If medieval artists did show the creature in the air, they presented it as entirely aerodynamic, but lacking any clear means of propulsion when on the ground. In any event, the dragon prefers to avoid flying unless it is to wreak destruction upon the countryside, as Vermithrax Pejorative is seen doing after Galen fails to seal the lair.

Unlike Galen and Ulrich, the medieval dragonslayers of legend rarely achieved their victories by sorcery. The defeat of the beast usually came only after a titantic struggle, in doubt until the hero finally succeeded in his noble task. St. George, the best-known dragonslayer, was a mighty warrior and pure of heart. He slew the great dragon of Silene to rescue a princess of Libya.

In the Gottfried of Strassburg's medieval poem *Tristan and Iseult*, Tristan battles a ferocious dragon: "Then Tristan drew forth his sword, thinking to slay the monster easily, but 'twas a hard strife . . . and in truth he thought it would be his death. For the dragon had as aids smoke and flame, teeth and claws sharper than a shearing knife. The fight was so fierce that the shield he held in his hand was burnt well nigh to a coal."

Sigfried was a great Nordic warrior whose slaying of the dragon Fafnir is celebrated in Wagner's opera cycle, *The Ring*. He bathed in the slain Fafnir's blood and gained the ability to speak the language of the birds. *Beowulf*, the famous seventh- or eighth-century epic, recounts the slaying of several dragons, including one by Beowulf himself, who is fatally poisoned in the effort.

Hal Barwood and Matthew Robbins were film students at USC in the mid-1960s. The period between 1965 and 1970 saw many leaders of the new Hollywood graduate from the Southern California school: George Lucas, director Randal Kleiser (*Grease, The Blue Lagoon*), editor-turned-director Walter Murch (*Apocalypse Now, Return to Oz*), writer-producer Bob Gale (*Used Cars*), writer-director Robert Zemeckis (*Back to the Future, Who Framed Roger Rabbit?*), writer-director John Milius (*Conan the Barbarian, Red Dawn*), producer Howard Kazanjian (*Return of the Jedi*), writer-turned-director Dan O'Bannon (*Alien, Return of the Living Dead*), writer-director John Carpenter (*Halloween, Big Trouble in Little China*), and other lesser-known lights.

The members of the USC "mafia" referred to themselves as the Dirty Dozen, in deference to Robert Aldrich's 1967 film. They worked together and in competition with each other and each other's student crews. Robbins and Barwood became friends with all of the Dirty Dozen, especially George Lucas.

Barwood and Robbins were given their first Hollywood screenwriting assignment not by one of the Dirty Dozen, however, but by a young television and film director who'd attended Long Beach State: Steven Spielberg. Together, the two young writers cobbled out the script for the boy wonder's first feature film, 1974's critically acclaimed *Sugarland Express*.

The Hal Barwood–Matthew Robbins team then wrote the script for 1976's *The Bingo Long Travelling All-Stars and Motor Kings*, director John Badham's film about star Billy Dee Williams' attempt to start his own team in the Negro National League.

Barwood and Robbins then appeared, respectively, as "Returnee #2, Flight 19" and "Returnee #3, Flight 19" for Spielberg's 1977 SF hit, *Close Encounters of the Third Kind*. That same year saw the release of *MacArthur*, another of their joint screenwriting efforts.

Their first teaming as writer-producer and writer-director occurred with 1978's *Corvette Summer*, a disappointing film starring *Star Wars'* Mark Hamill and the sports car of the title.

In 1979, after shopping around a romantic comedy which no studio could be induced to support, the duo turned their attentions to making a fantasy film. Once they decided upon *Dragonslayer* as the appropriate vehicle, Matthew Robbins recalled, the most important thing was to deliver a dragon.

A fateful — and perhaps fatal — decision was to feature the dragon itself as little as possible while not cheating the audience of what they'd come to see. The dragon does not make its appearance until the eighty-third minute of the 108-minute movie. Given that much of the rest of the film — the political, religious, and sociological elements — weakened the film's appeal, the relatively few appearances of the awesome dragon could not offset this imbalance. (The giant ants in *Them!* are not seen until near the end of that film, but they then play a major role; this is also true of "Bruce" the shark in *Jaws*. The hideous monster in *Alien* is only glimpsed throughout, but that film is marvelously paced and directed, and has interesting characters.)

When Paramount (which later signed a co-production agreement with Walt Disney Productions similar to that of their earlier joint venture, 1980's *Popeye*) gave the team the go signal, they began hiring some of the best special effects people in the business: Dennis Muren, Brian Johnson, Phil Tippett, Ken Ralston, Chris Walas, and others. Robbins and Barwood wanted miniature and model work convincingly mixed with full-size effects like the dragon's head and neck.

While artist David Bunnell was creating a dragon which would look magnificent and convincing both in the air and on the ground, production designer Elliot Scott began designing the many sets, including the four-acre medieval village of Swanscombe. The largest set was constructed on Pinewood's so-called "007" set; this was the external entrance to the dragon's lair. The most impressive set was the underground lake of fire, made to look larger by carefully placed mirrors, and its "flaming water" provided by jets of flammable gas.

Because it took more than a dozen people several days just to get the shot of the dragon's full-scale head rising from the lake to tower over Galen, Barwood and Robbins realized they needed a second, less complex, head. Dubbed the "B" head, this styrofoam head was used in a number of shots, notably in the scene where Brother Jacopus is incinerated. To further speed production, a hand puppet — just the dragon's neck and head — was devised by Chris Walas for closeups. Much easier to operate than the full-size head, the puppet was used in a number of scenes, including the one where the dragon stops to nuzzle one of the babies killed by Galen.

Aware that standard stop-motion photography would be too limiting for the production's needs, Stuart Ziff designed and constructed a special rod-actuated motion control mechanism. This complicated piece of machinery consisted of six "legs," each a separate unit to control various parts of the articulated dragon model positioned above.

Galen (Peter MacNichol) battles the great dragon Vermithrax (here, a full-size head and neck).

A nightmare of wires and motors, this amazing contraption makes two things possible which had previously been impossible. First, it allows the puppet being animated to move slightly while a single frame is being exposed. This slight blurring is more natural than the "strobing" associated with standard stop-motion animation, where each movement of the creature being animated is seen with crystal clarity. Second, this "go-motion" unit permitted multiple takes. Although programming the go-motion dragon mover took a great deal of time—longer than conventional stop-motion animation—the sequence of movements shot could be refined and changed. Effects supervisor Dennis Muren believes that go-motion can replace stop-motion if several units, all operating at the same time, are used. Otherwise, conventional stop-motion is still faster. (For an in-depth look at *Dragonslayer's* superior special effects, see Steven S. Wilson's comprehensive article in *Cinefex #6*, October 1981.)

Alex North's music is richly textured, yet powerfully discordant at times. North received an Academy Award nomination for his first score, 1951's powerful *A Streetcar Named Desire*. Born in Philadelphia of Russian parents in 1910, North attended the Juilliard School of Music in New York on a scholarship. To support his studies, North worked nights as a telegraph operator for the four years of his schooling. Unable to keep up with this routine, North was allowed to study music in the Soviet Union for two years.

Back in the States, North scored films for government agencies—the State Department, the Health Department, etc. After director Elia Kazan campaigned on his behalf, North was assigned to score *Streetcar.* His jazz-oriented score was widely hailed, and its impact upon film music was enormous.

North went on to score *Viva Zapata!* for Kazan, and among his other film scores are *Desiree* (1954), *The Rose Tattoo* (1955), *The Rainmaker* (1956), *Spartacus* (1960), *The Misfits* (1961), *Who's Afraid of Virginia Woolf* (1966), *Willard* (1971), *Wise Blood* (1970), and *Carny* (1980). One that "got away" was *2001: A Space Odyssey.* After North had scored the entire picture, director Stanley Kubrick decided against discarding the "temporary" tracks he'd been using and eliminated the other music in favor of sound effects, like breathing sounds.

Before he succumbed to digestive ailments in October, 1983, Ralph Richardson had solidified his position as the "Grand Old Man" of British acting. During his 63-year career on stage and in films, he had come to represent the elite group of British thespians known as the "actor-knights": Sir John Gielgud, Sir (now Lord) Laurence Olivier, and Sir Alec Guinness.

In *Dragonslayer,* Richardson appears onscreen only at the film's beginning and confrontational conclusion, but he steals the show—as he did in his last film, *Greystoke: The Legend of Tarzan,* and as he nearly did in *Time Bandits* (as the Supreme Being).

As Galen, Peter MacNichol, forced into playing the part as a Luke Skywalker/Mark Hamill clone, seems too twentieth-century for the role. He was better cast in *Sophie's Choice,* playing "Stingo." The Dallas-born Mac-Nichol is likeable but, ultimately, too callow in the role to make for a convincing hero.

More suited to her role of brave-lad-turned-brave-lassie is Caitlin Clarke, a Pittsburgh native. Clarke's Valerian seems masculine enough when we first meet "him"—a believable medieval youth. Then, revealed as a young woman—and wearing a dress—Clarke effortlessly becomes a beautiful heroine.

A strong, appealing character, Clarke's Valerian is betrayed by Barwood and Robbins' script. She is capable, brave, and self-realized as a boy, but, as a girl, Valerian is suddenly incapable of the bold acts she exhibited as a "male," becoming timid and typically film-feminine—cautious, fearing, and in need of a protector.

The other actors in *Dragonslayer* are competent professionals who deliver the goods. Included among their numbers was one whose small role would give way to a more central part in one of the most successful and eagerly anticipated SF/fantasy films of all time: *Return of the Jedi.* Ian McDiarmid, who plays the ill-fated Brother Jacopus, was later to portray the evil, goading emperor in *Jedi*. (For more about the actors and their other films, see the Appendix.)

Although *Dragonslayer* is flawed because of its genre-deficient aspects and miscasting, it is a well-done, superior fantasy film. For the most part, Robbins' direction is self-assured and his set-ups carefully considered. The photography by Derek Vanlint stunningly captures the grimy realism of production designer Elliot Scott's sets and the moody bleakness of the Welsh and Scottish terrain. Unfortunately, however, the somber photography and the necessity of keeping the dragon in the dark (one of the reasons the final confrontation takes place during an eclipse), give the film a depressing air and lessen the fun.

The film did not do well at the box office during a time of intense competition, but its magnificent dragon—a smashing debut for the new animation process known as "go-motion"—lingers in the mind and in the imagination.

Dragonslayer's Vermithrax Pejorative is the finest, scariest, most affecting cinematic monster since King Kong and Moby Dick and deserves a special place among the mythic beasts of the silver screen.

5. The 5,000 Fingers of Dr. T: A Child's Fantasy

In the 1950s in the United States, the only films I'm aware of to have largely succeeded at being films not only made for children, but which are plotted as if they were made *by* children are *Invaders from Mars, The 5,000 Fingers of Dr. T* (both 1953), and *The Invisible Boy* (1957).
— *Bill Warren, in* Keep Watching the Skies! Volume I.

The 5,000 Fingers of Dr. T was one of the strangest films released in 1953 . . . or any year, for that matter.

As Bill Warren noted above, perhaps the key element in this well-produced and crafted fantasy film was its adherence to a child's point of view. The film is a child's dream — or, rather, nightmare. Although the film's Terwilliker is portrayed as being the absolute dictator of his own peculiar preserve, the freedom being denied is not something adult or abstract, it's the freedom to play baseball instead of the piano! There are no large moral issues involved about having to do something against your will, albeit something "good for you." Instead, the issues are kids' normal, everyday longings: going fishing, or collecting baseball cards, or trapping frogs, or just goofing off.

The film's key message, if it has one, is contained in the song Bart, the film's young hero, sings after being let down — again — by the picture's "father figure," Mr. Zabladowski: "You have no right . . . to push us little kids around."

The film's plot is simple (as befits a dream or nightmare). Everything is filtered through the eyes and sensibilities of a young boy (Bart's mother, Mrs. Collins, is the only female in the film). Bart is forced to practice the piano for Dr. Terwilliker's grand recital, which will utilize the 5,000 fingers of 500 little boys. After this triumph, Dr. T plans to wed Bart's mother (a classic fairytale element — the evil or unworthy stepparent), and Bart will be condemned to an eternity of getting up at dawn to practice at Dr. T's enormous piano. Bart, then, with some help from the plumber–father figure, Mr. Zabladowski, must thwart Dr. T's evil scheme and save his mother and himself.

58

Produced by Stanley Kramer and directed by Roy Rowland, the film owes its special feel and look to one man—Dr. Seuss (Theodor Geisel), whose script, lyrics, and visual conception are so different from those to be found in any other movie of the time as to be beyond easy absorption by moviegoers and critics.

Dr. Seuss' script, written with Allan Scott, can quickly escalate from the ordinary to the ridiculous. For instance, when we first see Mrs. Collins in Bart's nightmarish Terwilliker Institute, she's talking on the phone: "Dr. Terwilliker does not believe in baseballs, golf balls, basketballs, or tennis balls; ping pong balls, snowballs, croquet balls, or hockey pucks. Dr. Terwilliker believes only in the piano." Similarly, a solicitous Dr. T asks Mr. Zabladowski, "Hot cakes, layer cakes, fish cakes, peanut brittle, the blue-plate special, or chicken potpie?" Clearly, Dr. Seuss is a man with a well-developed sense of the ridiculous and one who likes to play with words and how they work in juxtaposition.

Geisel revealed to *Time*'s anonymous interviewer that, as a child, he took piano lessons "from a man who rapped my knuckles with a pencil whenever I made a mistake . . . I made up my mind I would finally get even with that man. It took me 43 years to catch up with him. He became the Terwilliker of the movie."

The reviews were not nearly as appreciative as one might assume they would be. Much as they did with *The Wizard of Oz*, the adult reviewers apparently missed those very elements that make the film so compelling for kids. (The reviewers *did* know that the strange dreamscape setting that opens the film was called the "Mound Country." How? Reviewers get advance press kits which reveal such esoterica.)

Variety's "Brog." began his review by stating, "The mad humor of Dr. Seuss (Ted Geisel) has been captured on film in this odd flight into chimerical fiction," and called the film's dungeon ballet "a mad creation that is well worth the admission price."

In his *New York Times* review, Bosley Crowther began by observing that "The trickiest sort of entertainment—symbolic fantasy—is attempted in Stanley Kramer's *The 5,000 Fingers of Dr. T.*" Crowther opined that, apart from one musical number, "there is little or no inspiration or real imagination in the thing."

Similarly, Parker Tyler's *Theatre Arts* review said that in the film "love appears strange enough, to be sure, on the surface of a fantasy that is nothing if not deliberately and daringly quaint." Further, Tyler commented, "Songs and dances . . . appear in fairly recognizable forms in this film, but here they conceal a newfangled way of entertaining the public: a way that might be dubbed 'Dr. Seuss's Freudian Fantasy Method.'"

In *America*, Moira Walsh said *Dr. T* "certainly qualifies as one of the oddest movies of the year." Although noting that it was staged "in

Technicolor with taste and imagination," Ms. Walsh ended her review by calling the film "too subtle for the juvenile audience and too single-mindedly committed to a juvenile problem to command the full attention of adults."

However, Philip T. Hartung, writing in *Commonweal*, described *Dr. T* as "a delightful fantasy," and ended his review by observing that "the film as a whole has enough surprises to win both young and old in the audience."

Newsweek's anonymous reviewer had this to say: "On a personal level the story is sometimes a little too corny for comfort. But as fantasy it is highly successful, from the H.G. Wellsian gadgets, gangsters, and twin snoopers with the Siamese Smith Brothers' beard to a brilliantly conceived ballet . . . staged in the madhouse where Terwilliker has confined all those musicians who dare to play any instrument but the piano."

Less enthralled with the film was John McCarten, the *New Yorker*'s reviewer. "A boy's mind . . . is explored at some length, and to no particular purpose, in the movie called *The 5,000 Fingers of Dr. T.*" While McCarten enjoyed the dungeon scene, he believed that "Dr. Seuss has been handicapped by Hollywood's insistence on plot."

Finally, *Time*'s uncredited reviewer called the film "a freshly told, more than slightly screwball little film fantasy. . . . Fantasy without coyness is rare, and fantasy about childhood without overdoses of syrup is even rarer. *The 5,000 Fingers*, even at its most fantastic, contrives to keep its brisk sense of humor and its matter-of-fact, child's eye view."

In the eerie "Mound Country," a fog-shrouded place of enormous ball-bearing-like cylinders, a young boy (Tommy Rettig) is pursued by strange green-clad men who attempt to capture him with their colored "butterfly" nets.

The boy, named Bart, awakens from what was a literal nightmare to a figurative nightmare: he's seated at a piano and being lectured at about his playing by his haughty piano teacher, Dr. Terwilliker (Hans Conried). Speaking directly to the audience, Bart complains about Dr. T and introduces his widowed mother (Mary Healy). As Bart, who'd rather be playing baseball, fusses about his lessons, his mother sings "Ten Happy Fingers," a piece written by Dr. Terwilliker extolling piano practice.

Bart thinks Dr. Terwilliker must have his mother hypnotized and tells us that their plumber, Mr. Zabladowski (Peter Lind Hayes), also dislikes Dr. T. Bart's mother and Mr. Zabladowski speak about Bart's piano lessons. Saying, "practice makes perfect," Bart falls asleep at the piano.

Dreaming, Bart finds himself playing an immense, two-tier piano with hundreds of stools. He's in the Terwilliker Institute, directed by his old nemesis, Dr. Terwilliker. Dr. T reveals that he has a dream, which is to come true the following day: to conduct 500 boys—5,000 fingers—as they play his compositions. When they're not performing, the boys will be practicing 24 hours a day, 365 days a year.

Dr. T tells Bart to return to his cell and put on his official Terwilliker beanie (it bears the words "Happy Fingers," and is topped by five outstretched fingers). As Bart marches off, we learn that the Institute is a strange and eerie place of steps and stairways, trap doors, tunnels, and hallways — surrounded by barbed wire and watched over by stone gargoyles.

Bart speaks to Mr. Zabladowski, installing sinks in the cells for the 500 boys, and learns that his own mom ("Mrs. C") is "Number Two" at the Institute and is scheduled to marry Dr. T after the next day's concert.

Learning that Bart is not in his cell, Dr. T vows to toss him into the dungeon and sends out the roller-skating twins Uncle Judson (Robert Heasley) and Uncle Whitney (John Heasley) — who are joined by one long white beard — to look for him. The goons capture Bart, but he escapes and climbs a tremendously high ladder to nowhere. At the top, he leaps off and uses his shirt as a parachute.

Seeking out Mr. Zabladowski, Bart learns the plumber won't help him. "I'd hate to have you as a father," Bart tells him. Bart and Mr. Zabladowski then pretend they're fishing, and Mr. Zabladowski sings "Dream Stuff," joined later by Bart.

Suddenly, Mr. Zabladowski jumps up and again refuses to help. Bart asks him to accompany him to the living quarters and Mr. Z reluctantly agrees. Once there, Mr. Zabladowski is almost hypnotized by Dr. Terwilliker, and the two of them have a gesturing battle which leaves them exhausted. After Dr. T sings "Get Together Weather," Mr. Zabladowski is won over and leaves. After he departs, Dr. T calls the "Physics Department" and orders them to disintegrate Mr. Zabladowski after he's installed the last sink.

Telling Bart that Dr. Terwilliker is okay, Mr. Zabladowski will have none of Bart's attempts to warn him of his fate, saying, "Listen to a kid, it gives you nothing but trouble." Dismayed and alone, Bart sings "The Kid's Song." Flip-flopping again, Mr. Zabladowski says he's sorry, and Bart insists he'll get some money to pay the plumber for his help. Sneaking into the sleeping Dr. Terwilliker's room, Bart steals a key and opens Dr. T's safe. Bart takes $30 and leaves an I.O.U. behind. He finds the signed order for Zabladowski's execution and steals it as well.

Running away, Bart slides down a *long* fireman's pole, only to find himself in the dungeon confronting Stoogo (Henry Kulky), one of Dr. T's minions. A sign says, "Dungeon for Scratchy Violins, Screechy Piccolos, Nauseating Trumpets, etc., etc." This is the place where Dr. T keeps prisoner the musicians who play those instruments.

Bart flees the dungeon and shows Mr. Zabladowski his execution

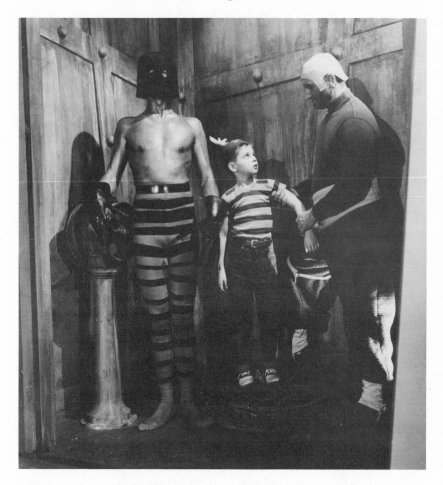

Restrained by one of Dr. Terwilliker's goons, Bart (Tommy Rettig) is taken to the dungeon while the masked operator sings "Dungeon Elevator," one of the film's many songs.

order, finally convincing the plumber. Wanting no more changes of heart, Bart insists their partnership be sealed in blood, and they cut their thumbs and press them together. Saying that this makes Mr. Zabladowski his "old man," Bart and the plumber free Mrs. C—who reveals that her first name is Heloise. Mr. Zabladowski's first name is August.

Drinking the powerful pickle juice, Mr. Zabladowski puts on skates and ventures forth to combat the bearded skaters, using pruning shears to separate them at their mutual beard. But all appears lost as Dr. T and his goons appear and capture them, singing "Victorious." Again, the inconstant Mr. Zabladowski rejects Bart.

To the dungeon with them ("Dungeon Elevator"), where Bart and Mr. Zabladowski can look forward to endless torture: Every day, at dawn, Bart will have to begin practice. In their cage, Mr. Zabladowski reveals he's brought along a bottle of "AirFix" with him, noting that it pulls smells from the air. Bart begins to think of a way to create a "MusicFix" — to pull the music from the air.

While Bart and Mr. Z attempt to produce their MusicFix, the 499 other boys arrive, and their suitcases are opened so that Dr. Terwilliker's goons can remove any baseball bats and gloves and other "useless" toys and items. Bart finally steals Stroogo's hearing aid to bring noises into the bottle, and the MusicFix works!

Bart is taken to join the other boys as Dr. Terwilliker dresses for his big day, singing "The Dressing Song (My Do-Me-Do-Duds)." At the giant piano, Dr. Terwilliker gets ready for his moment of triumph — the boys will play his own "Ten Happy Fingers." But Bart unleashes the MusicFix, capturing the sound. Confusion erupts. When Dr. Terwilliker sees what Bart is doing, Bart holds up the bottle, says "It's atomic," and forces his tormentor to free everyone. Bart then has the boys play a ragged version of "Chopsticks."

After Bart's MusicFix blows up, destroying the Institute, he awakens, saying, "No, no, no." Bart and Mr. Z still have their bandaged thumbs, and Mrs. Collins and Mr. Zabladowski strike some tentative romantic sparks. Abandoning his lessons, Bart goes outside to play baseball.

Theodor Seuss Geisel was born on March 2, 1904, in Springfield, Massachusetts. Geisel attended Dartmouth College in Hanover, New Hampshire, earning his A.B. in 1925. While in school, Geisel was the editor of the college's humor magazine, and it was there that he published his first cartoons, filled with strange animals.

After his graduation from Dartmouth, Geisel enrolled in Lincoln College at Oxford as a graduate student. While at Oxford, the young Geisel met Helen Marion Palmer, and the two were married in 1927. The new Mrs. Geisel encouraged her husband to pursue his artistic interests, and he dropped out of school to see if he could make a living from his "funny animals."

Keeping his real name for the "serious" work he was certain he would be producing, Geisel began to sign his cartoons as "Dr. Seuss." Before long, the moniker Dr. Seuss was appearing on many cartoons in publications like the *Saturday Evening Post*. A Dr. Seuss cartoon in the humor magazine *Judge* showed a dragon with a knight and was captioned, "What! Another Dragon! And just after I sprayed the joint with Flit!" An advertising executive at Standard Oil Company of New Jersey saw the cartoon and quickly hired Dr. Seuss to draw a number of "Quick Henry, the Flit!" ads.

The expression entered the national consciousness as one of the catch phrases of the time, and Geisel stayed with Standard Oil from 1928 to 1941.

After nearly ten years of success with his cartoons and his advertising work, Geisel grew restless and began to write and illustrate a children's book. The result, *And to Think That I Saw It on Mulberry Street*, was rejected by several publishing houses before Vanguard Press published the book in 1937. A "tall tale" told by a young boy, *Mulberry Street*'s success encouraged Geisel to produce *The 500 Hats of Bartholomew Cubbins*. When it too was successful, many other books for children followed: from *The King's Stilts* and *Horton Hatches the Egg* in 1939 and 1940, to *How the Grinch Stole Christmas* in 1957, to *Hunches in Bunches* in 1982.

After brief stints as an advertising cartoonist for the Ford Motor Company and as an editorial cartoonist for *PM* Magazine (no, not THAT *PM Magazine!*), Geisel became a lieutenant colonel in the Army Signal Corps (Information and Education Division) and did publicity work for various governmental agencies to promote wartime efficiency and solidarity. Geisel oversaw the production of educational and training films, and performed his duties so meritoriously that he was awarded the Legion of Merit.

After his wartime introduction to the possibilities of film, Geisel wrote a number of screenplays for the medium. One script, written with his wife, concerned the rise of the generals and militarism in pre-war Japan. Titled *Design for Death*, it won the Academy Award in 1947 for Best Feature Documentary. His animated cartoon, *Gerald McBoing-Boing*, won the Oscar for Best Cartoon of 1950.

In 1955, Geisel's alma mater, Dartmouth College, awarded the writer-illustrator-filmmaker an honorary Doctorate in Humane Letters. "Dr. Seuss" was now officially Dr. Geisel.

After reading an article in *Life* magazine by John Hersey, which denigrated the "learn to read" books used in elementary schools, Geisel wrote and published the first of his "Beginner Books" series, *The Cat in the Hat*. This 1957 picture book combined fanciful Dr. Seuss illustrations with a limited vocabulary, and started a trend toward such easy-to-read picture books. (For more on Theodor Seuss Geisel's works, see the Appendix.)

With the exception of Hans Conried, *Dr. T*'s cast was made up of relative unknowns. The show-business couple of Peter Lind Hayes and Mary Healy are best known for their radio and television appearances. Indeed, a search through the usual film credit sources failed to uncover any other films either of the two may have appeared in. *The Complete Directory to Prime Time Network TV Shows: 1946–Present*, an immensely helpful reference work by Tim Brooks and Earle Marsh, lists a number of Peter Lind Hayes and Mary Healy series.

In 1950, both Hayes and Healy appeared on a CBS talk show called *The*

Stork Club. Joining owner Sherman Billingsley on a set located in the celebrated nightclub itself, Hayes and Healy interviewed celebrities at "Table 50."

The Peter Lind Hayes Show, a live 1950 NBC situation comedy, was telecast from the home of its stars and featured Mary Wickes. When that week's guest stars arrived at the Hayes home, they somehow always found a way of showing off their singing, dancing, or comedy abilities. Originally called *The Peter and Mary Show*, the series underwent a title change in December 1950.

Star of the Family, a CBS comedy-variety show which debuted in September 1950, featured original host Morton Downey interviewing people related to celebrities. Downey, a singer, was replaced as host by Peter Lind Hayes and Mary Healy in the summer of 1951, and they remained until the last telecast on June 26, 1952.

Hayes and Healy starred in the 1960 NBC situation comedy, *Peter Loves Mary*, playing—appropriately enough—a show business couple who'd moved from Manhattan to the suburbs. This one-season comedy featured Bea Benaderet as their housekeeper, Wilma.

Perhaps the most intriguing television appearance the dynamic duo of Hayes and Healy have to their credit was guest hosting *The Tonight Show* on NBC for a week during the period after Jack Paar left in March 1962 and before Johnny Carson took over in October 1962. Other substitute hosts during this time included Art Linkletter, Joey Bishop, Bob Cummings, Jerry Lewis, Groucho Marx, and Soupy Sales.

Tommy Rettig, of course, will forever be known for playing Jeff Miller on the long-running children's television series *Lassie*. Rettig was there for the show's beginning, in September 1954, on CBS on Sunday evenings. The master of heroic and intelligent Lassie, the loyal collie, Rettig co-starred with Jan Clayton, who played Ellen Miller, his mother, and with George Cleveland, who played "Gramps" Miller. After Rettig's three seasons, a new cast, including Jon Provost as "Timmy," took over. (Provost was on *Lassie* for more years than Rettig: seven seasons to three. The show ran for seven more seasons after Provost left in 1964, and Robert Bray, as forest ranger Corey Stuart, became Lassie's last master.)

Tommy Rettig's film career was entirely in the 1950s. Born in 1941, Rettig's first film was *Panic in the Streets* (1950). That same year, he was in *The Jackpot, Two Weeks with Love*, and *For Heaven's Sake*. His other films are: *Elopement* (1951), *Weekend with Father* (1951), *Paula* (1952), *The Lady Wants Mink, Dr. T, So Big* (all 1953), *River of No Return, The Raid, The Egyptian* (all 1954), *The Cobweb* (1955), *At Gunpoint* (1955), and *The Last Wagon* (1956).

After Rettig's film career faltered as he pursued adult roles, "he retired with his wife to a California farm, where he was arrested in 1972 for growing marijuana," according to Ephraim Katz in *The Film Encyclopedia*. After serving two years on probation, Rettig was again arrested in 1975—this time for allegedly smuggling cocaine—and was sentenced to a five-year term in a federal prison. The charge was later dismissed on appeal. Today, Tom Rettig owns a computer software company in Marina del Rey.

Hans Conried (1917–1982) is probably the best-known actor in *Dr. T* and best remembered for playing "Uncle Tonoose" for 13 years on *The Danny Thomas Show* (*Make Room for Daddy* for its first three seasons). According to Tim Brooks and Earle Marsh, Conried had been seen in several guest roles—Cousin Carl, Uncle Oscar, and Derik Campbell—before landing his continuing role as Uncle Tonoose in the fall of 1958. A later generation of kids remembers Conried (his voice, if not his name) as Dudley Do-Rights' nemesis, the dastardly Snidley Whiplash, on the 1961 cult cartoon show *The Bullwinkle Show* (later *Rocky and Bullwinkle*).

Conried's film career began with *Dramatic School* in 1937, but he landed only a smattering of roles until World War II began. With the war, Conried then specialized in playing Nazis in such films as *Saboteur* (1942), *Journey Into Fear* (1942), *Hitler's Children* (1943), and *Passage to Marseille* (1944). (See the Appendix for Conried's frequent genre appearances, as listed in *Science Fiction, Horror & Fantasy Film and Television Credits* by Harris M. Lentz, III.)

Dr. T's producer was Stanley Kramer, a filmmaker who later began directing his own productions. Kramer, serious about the art of motion pictures, has been responsible for a steady flow of well-intentioned films which often tackle troublesome or difficult topics. He's probably best known for producing *Death of a Salesman* (1951), *High Noon* (1952), *The Wild One* (1954), and *The Caine Mutiny* (1954). He was both producer and director for *On the Beach* (1959), *Inherit the Wind* (1960), *Judgment at Nuremberg* (1961), *Ship of Fools* (1965), and *Guess Who's Coming to Dinner* (1967).

Kramer chose an old veteran, Roy Rowland, to direct *Dr. T*. According to Katz' *Encyclopedia*, Rowland studied law at USC before getting a job as a script clerk and then advancing to assistant director. After directing numerous shorts in the mid-'30s, including the *Pete Smith Specialties* series, Rowland directed his first feature, *Lost Angels*, in 1944. Apart from *Dr. T*, few of Rowland's films are well remembered today. (For more on Rowland's films, see the Appendix.)

Although color film had been around since the mid-to-late '30s (and even earlier in certain productions), it still presented a number of lighting problems by the early '50s. Color film required much more intense and brilliant lighting (see the *Wizard of Oz* chapter) and most films had their own "Technicolor Color Consultant"—*Dr. T*'s was Francis Cugat.

Before the production actually began shooting, director of photography Frank Planer, A.S.C., realized that the immense piano courtyard in the Terwilliker Institute — where the 500 boys were to fulfill Dr. T's mad fantasy and where much of the film's action took place — would require special lighting. The set, which was built on Columbia's stages 8 and 9, was one of the largest indoor sets the studio had ever constructed.

Instead of wallboard, which would have been too costly to use to provide the backing for such an immense set, Planer and art director Cary Odell covered the supporting framework with 3500 square yards of white muslin. Fortunately for Planer, Columbia's lighting engineers were experimenting with a new lighting system: cone lights. Planer observed that the cone lights provided a soft, almost shadowless illumination capable of filling even a large set with bright, yet diffuse, light.

"The use of cone lights," Planer told *American Cinematographer*'s Arthur Rowan, "made it easier to light those sets which called for the addition of matte shots at the top. The piano courtyard set especially, while it extended clear to the ceiling of the soundstage, was heightened further pictorially in the finished result through effect matte shot photography."

Wanting something visually striking for the dungeon scenes, Planer asked makeup man Clay Campbell to apply a luminous green makeup to the extras. Abandoning traditional lighting setups, Planer lowered the "key light" (the primary lighting instrument) and utilized ultraviolet and fluorescent light sources as well. This unusual approach to altering the mood and look of a scene was only partially successful, working as intended only in the closeups. The problem, Planer discovered, was that ultraviolet light is an inherently low-volume source of illumination. (In 1986, for the film *Legend*, director of photography Alex Thompson, B.S.C., attempted to use ultraviolet light to make Tim Curry's eyes and fingernails glow green for the "Darkness" scene. Thompson found the same problems and limitations with ultraviolet light that Planer had experienced over 30 years earlier.)

Time reported that director Rowland had a peculiar difficulty shooting the scene where all 500 boys (actually no more than 400) play chopsticks on the giant piano at Bart's direction. While the scene was being set up, the impatient boys filtered outside into the rain, discovered a nearby hot dog stand, and proceeded to gorge themselves silly. Recalling the situation, Geisel winced and said, "Have you ever tried to get 400 sick, wet boys to play a piano?"

For some reason, whether the film is *The Wizard of Oz, Popeye, Dr. T,* or *Willie Wonka and the Chocolate Factory,* many fantasies aimed at children contain songs and musical numbers. Maybe these are directed at the adult who accompany the kids to the showings, or maybe adding music and dance numbers to such films is an attempt to make them more palatable to kids. I'm not sure about that last — perhaps I'm a special case, but I mostly (*Oz* is the exception) disliked music and dancing in the movies I went to as a child.

In any event, with a few exceptions, like "The Kid's Song," "Victorious," and the wacky ballet in the dungeon, the musical numbers work against the movie's flow, stopping the action cold while the adults (as in "Get Together Weather") take center stage. Bart and Zabladowski's duet, "Dream Stuff," is "mushy" and uninspired—as are "Ten Happy Fingers" and "The Dressing Song."

The five-minute, thirty-second dungeon ballet, featuring musician prisoners in torn pants and suspenders playing a succession of enormous or otherwise distorted instruments, is the film's musical and imaginative highlight—worth the price of admission, as one critic noted.

Dr. T is not well remembered today, except by those who saw it as children. The film is unequivocally a kid's film, filled with the discomforting and unavoidable terrors of childhood—abandonment, the loss of a parent's affections, the fickleness of adults, and the inscrutability of their world. *Dr. T* gives us a child's perception of the child-parent relationship eerily similar to *Invaders from Mars*—an exaggerated view in which parents are loving and kind one moment and in the next, for no apparent reason, cruel and hateful.

As Stuart H. Stock notes in *Twenty All-Time Great Science Fiction Films*, "*Invaders* offers the child a convenient explanation for such changes. It's not that the child has misbehaved, or that parents might have problems of their own, but that some outside force—in this case, Martians—has interfered to cause the change. To a child this is the most reasonable way of explaining why Mommy and Daddy no longer seem to love him."

Stock's analysis applies to Bart's situation in *Dr. T* as well. Instead of "Martians," Bart rationalizes at the film's beginning that Dr. Terwilliker must have "hypnotized" his mother; how else to explain her callous declaration to keep him practicing at the piano "forever" if necessary? In Bart's nightmare, this is indeed the case.

Just as *Invaders*' David MacLean knows the "truth" about the Martian invasion, Bart also knows the truth about Dr. T and his nefarious plans, including disintegrating Mr. Zabladowski. And, just like the adults in *Invaders*, the plumber remains skeptical about Bart's insistent warnings until he's shown proof—in this case, his own excecution order.

The similarities between *Invaders* and *Dr. T* continue. Both films' sets are spare and stark—emphasizing distortions of size and space—just as they would appear to a child trapped in a nightmarish adult world. (Perhaps coincidentally, the men with the butterfly nets in the opening dream sequence look eerily similar to the green-clad Martians in *Invaders*.) The logic employed in both films is a childish logic, emphasizing things only a child would think important while ignoring things an adult would focus on. And, ultimately, in both films it is the child protagonist who is the clearest thinker, the able one, and the hero.

Needing to get $30 from the sleeping Dr. T's safe, Bart ingeniously matches the ticking of the metronome that regulates Dr. T's sleep by tapping on its side with a stone to mimic its sound while he stops its incessant motion to steal the key inside it. Later, when Mr. Zabladowski is grousing about once again getting into trouble because of Bart, it's Bart who comes up with the idea of transforming the AirFix into a MusicFix—utilizing Stroogo's hearing aid—foiling Dr. T's scheme and freeing his mom, the 500 boys, and the musicians in the dungeon.

After they cut their thumbs to seal their new "father-and-son" relationship, it's Mr. Zabladowski who exclaims, "Ouch!" Bart just says it doesn't really hurt. This scene throws doubt on who the "kid" and the "adult" really are.

Rarely shown today, even on TV, *The 5,000 Fingers of Dr. T* remains both an imaginative delight and an admonition to adults to take kids seriously.

6. It's a Wonderful Life:
The Guardian Angel

"Every time you hear a bell ring, it means that some angel's just got his wings."
— *Clarence, in* It's a Wonderful Life.

It's a Wonderful Life is a warm-hearted fantasy in the "guardian angel" subgenre. Although affectionately greeted upon its original release at Christmas 1946, only later did the film take its place as one of the best-loved and most fondly emembered films of all time.

Wonderful Life has become an eagerly anticipated Christmas tradition on many television stations across the country—so much so that when it was "colorized" (color added to the black-and-white print by computer), there were cries of outrage from many people, including Frank Capra and James Stewart.

A bitter and angry Capra compared the colorization of his classic film to someone painting over marble statues. James Stewart told an interviewer that colorizing was completely "unfair"—to the film and to the people who worked hard to create its "look," achieved by careful attention to details of lighting, design, costuming, and the like. Coloring a black-and-white film, Stewart explained, destroys the details created by light and shadow. "I think it's terrible," he said.

Like many others, I've viewed *Wonderful Life* many times. I've laughed and cried. Unlike most others, however, the film brings me to tears for totally different reasons than it does other viewers; rather than accepting *Wonderful Life* as a triumph for the "little people," I'm frustrated and annoyed that poor George Bailey never sees any of *his* wishes come true, that he never escapes the clutches of his miserable little home town and its selfish and onerous inhabitants who can't seem to exist without George to protect them from not only Mr. Potter but also themselves.

Despite my reservations about *Wonderful Life*'s central message, I admire it as gloriously photographed, impeccably scripted, and ingeniously detailed fantasy film that has grown in stature with each viewing.

70

Wonderful Life's reviews were generally positive, but hardly glowing. As usual, many critics liked the film *despite* its fantasy elements; apparently, the reviewers of the time believed fantasy (as well as science fiction and horror) was somehow inferior to more conventional fare.

Variety's "Bert." turned in one of the more supportive and appreciative notices: Capra "again proves he can fashion what ordinarily would be homilizing hokum into gleaming, engaging entertainment for all brows — high, low, or beetle. Capra may not have taken here the stride forward in film-making technique he achieved in *It Happened One Night*, but no past Capra celluloid possessed any great or more genuine qualities of effectiveness."

Richard Griffith's review in the *National Board of Review Magazine* was less enthusiastic. Griffith wrote, "Years ago I called the Capra films 'fantasies of good will' because their plots pivoted upon the fanciful premise that kindness of heart is in itself enough to banish injustice and cruelty from the world. However pleasant it may have been for Capra and his audiences to toy with that idea, it is out of place in the new picture."

After berating Capra for sugar-coating reality with fantasy, Griffith admits that Capra's "way with incident and situation has never been more brilliant, his understanding and mastery of the film medium is more complete than ever." Griffith ends his piece by calling for Capra to "trust us a little bit more next time."

Newsweek's reviewer wrote, "Like any number of Capra films that you can name at random . . . his new film reiterates his identification with the kindly, possibly oversentimentalized, 'little' people of these United States. Capra's trick is that he can make it stick without being sticky. *Wonderful Life* is sentimental, but so expertly written, directed, and acted that you want to believe it. Some of it is unashamed fantasy, but it is fantasy that beguiles rather than bewilders. And, by luck and good timing, it is a movie in the Christmas spirit released in the holiday season."

Bosley Crowther was another critic who found too much "Capra-corn" in the film. In the *New York Times* he wrote, "Indeed, the weakness of this picture, from this reviewer's point of view, is the sentimentality of it — its illusory concept of life. Mr. Capra's nice people are charming, his small town is a quite beguiling place, and his pattern for solving problems is most optimistic and facile. But somehow they all resemble theatrical attitudes rather than average realities."

Writing in *The Nation*, James Agee said, "*It's a Wonderful Life*, Frank Capra's first film since those he made for the army, is one of the most efficient sentimental pieces since *A Christmas Carol*. Often, in its pile-driving emotional exuberance, it outrages, insults, or at least accosts without introduction, the cooler and more responsible parts of the mind; it is nevertheless recommended. . . ."

It is Christmas Eve in the little town of Bedford Falls, and a number of people are praying for George Bailey. In response, God sends for an "angel second-class" named Clarence. Clarence is to help save George, which will win him his wings, but first he must be shown George's life up to this moment.

In 1919, twelve-year-old George (Bobby Anderson) saves his brother Harry from drowning, catching an infection which destroys the hearing in his left ear.

George works part-time at Gower's Drugstore and comes to work to find Mr. Gower (H.B. Warner) drinking heavily. Two little girls, Mary and Violet, vie for George's attention, and Mary whispers into George's bad ear, "I'll love you 'til the day I die." George sees a telegram to Gower notifying the druggist that his son has died of influenza, and then he notices that Gower has put the wrong pills into a prescription. Mr. Gower then tells George to deliver the pills.

George decides to ask his father if he should deliver the pills and goes to the building and loan institution his father owns. After seeing his father confronting Mr. Potter, the richest and meanest man in town, George returns to the drugstore and Gower cuffs his bad ear for not delivering the drugs. George tearfully explains that the pills were poisoned; Gower embraces him, and George never tells a soul.

Next Clarence (and the audience) sees an adult George (James Stewart) picking up a suitcase for his planned travels, telling his father (Samuel S. Hinds) that after college he's leaving Bedford Falls for good.

At Harry's high school graduation dance, George enters a Charleston contest with the now-grown-up Mary (Donna Reed). A jealous rival presses a button which opens the dance floor to reveal a pool underneath. Dancing closer and closer to the edge, George and Mary finally tumble in—and are joined by all the seniors.

Dressed in a football uniform which he scrounged up in the locker room, George escorts Mary—who's wearing a robe—home. They pass the old Granville house, and George throws a rock at a window to make a wish; he tells her he's "shaking the dust of this crummy little town off." Mary breaks a window and makes an unspoken wish. After a neighbor startles them, Mary loses her robe and has to hide in a bush. George's appreciation of the situation is ended when Uncle Billy (Thomas Mitchell) shows up to tell him his father has had a stroke.

After Mr. Bailey's death, Mr. Potter (Lionel Barrymore) wants to dissolve Bailey Brothers Building and Loan. George counters Potter's cynical arguments and calls him a "warped and frustrated old man." All set to leave for college, George is trapped into taking over his father's position to save the business. Clarence next learns that George's brother Harry (Todd Karns) got George's college money and became a football star.

When Harry returns from college four years later, he's newly married and has been offered a good job. Instead of handing over the business and its responsibilities to Harry, George is again left holding the bag.

George's mother (Beulah Bondi) suggests he visit Mary, back from college. Outside Mary's home, George is reluctant to enter. He converses tersely with Mary and learns she *likes* Bedford Falls. After a few uncomfortable moments, George leaves. Mary gets a call from Sam Wainwright (Frank Albertson) as George returns for his hat. Talking to Sam, George realizes—against his better judgment—that he loves Mary, and they are soon married.

Leaving on their honeymoon, George and Mary see a run on the bank and on the building and loan. Potter takes over the bank and threatens to do the same for the B&L. George's customers demand their money instantly. Mary offers up their honeymoon savings—$2,000—and George halts the panic.

Ernie the cabbie (Frank Faylen) takes George to his new home: the dilapidated old Granville house, where Mary waits for him. She confesses that *her* wish, to live there some day, came true.

A number of brief scenes show us the success of George's enlightened business policies—poor families moving into decent houses in "Bailey Park"—and underscore the fact that George is barely keeping his head above water financially.

Potter, his "Potter's Field" hurt by competition from George's housing park, offers George a $20,000-a-year job with his company. Potter shrewdly sums up George's feelings and his obvious predicament—George is trapped. Although tempted, George angrily rejects Potter's offer. Mary becomes pregnant, and George is bound even tighter to his town and his job.

When World War II comes, George is 4-F (because of his ear) and serves the home front. Harry becomes a pilot who saves a transport full of soldiers, winning the Congressional Medal of Honor.

The story now moves to today, December 24. Making an $8000 deposit at the bank, Uncle Billy (Thomas Mitchell) accidently wraps the money in a newspaper, which he gives to Potter. Learning that Uncle Billy has lost the money, a distraught George returns home to find Mary and the kids decorating for Christmas. Little "Zuzu" (Susan) has come home from school with a fever, and George berates her teacher, Mrs. Welch, on the telephone. Angry and frustrated, more trapped than ever and facing prison, George kicks and throws things before rushing out.

George asks Mr. Potter for help, but the old man chides him and laughs in his face, calling George a "warped and frustrated young man," worth more dead than alive because of an insurance policy.

Nursing a drink at Martini's, George prays for help. Instead, he is

To satisfy George's depositors during a run on the building and loan, Mary (Donna Reed) gives George (James Stewart) the $2000 they had saved for their honeymoon. Uncle Billy (Thomas Mitchell, on the right) looks on.

immediately punched in the mouth by an angry Mr. Welch (Stanley Andrews). After driving his car into a tree, George runs onto a bridge and prepares to leap into the icy water. Before he can act, Clarence (Henry Travers) leaps into the water, and George jumps in to save him.

Clarence tells him he's from heaven and that he saved George from suicide; Clarence is George's guardian angel. When George wishes he'd never been born, Clarence grants his wish. Immediately, George can hear in his left ear.

Accompanied by Clarence, George walks back to town to find that his car is gone, and Bedford Falls is now a ghastly little place called Pottersville. Martini's has become Nick's place, where Nick (Sheldon Leonard) ejects a pathetic old rummy. Horrified, George sees that it's Mr. Gower—since George wasn't there to stop him, he poisoned the the child in 1919 and spent 20 years in prison.

Violet (Gloria Grahame) is a prostitute, and neither Ernie nor Bert the cop (Ward Bond) knows George. After George finds his house an empty shell, Bert attempts to arrest him. Clarence helps George escape . . . but only into a deepening nightmare. Pottersville is full of gin joints, girlie shows, pawnshops and gambling dens. George's widowed mother takes in boarders and tells him that Uncle Billy is in an insane asylum. Bailey Park is a cemetery—where Harry Bailey, who drowned in 1919, is buried.

As Clarence (Henry Travers, left) tells George (James Stewart, right) that he's George's guardian angel, the tollhouse keeper (Tom Fadden) looks on in obvious disbelief.

Mary, an old maid librarian, is accosted by George. She screams in terror and the police arrive, shooting at the fleeing George. Returning to the bridge, George begs to live again. Bert arrives and knows him; his car is back where he abandoned it; he is once again deaf in his left ear.

George returns to his home, where the bank examiner stands waiting. But the townspeople arrive with enough money to bail George out. Sam Wainwright also cables money, and Harry flies in to be at George's side, calling him "the richest man in town."

Among the Christmas presents is a copy of *Tom Sawyer*—a present from Clarence. A bell rings to signify that the angel has won his wings. George realizes that his is, indeed, a wonderful life.

Wonderful Life was a triumphant return to the big screen for producer-director-writer Frank Capra and for the film's star, James Stewart. Returning to Hollywood from the War Department, where he'd made the hugely successful "Why We Fight" series, Capra was afraid the reaction to him would be a blank "Frank who?" Since his first film after the war would also be the first film for his independent film company, Liberty Pictures, Capra was doubly cautious about choosing the right property for his initial production. Aware that his first film after returning to directing features would draw close inspection, Capra reportedly said that he wished he could "sneak out somewhere and make a couple of quickie Westerns first—just to get the feel of things again." (For more on Capra's background, see Chapter 9.)

Capra was casting about fruitlessly for a story, growing more and more despondent. He was being offered a lot of war pictures but, having come out of the war a confirmed pacifist, Capra wanted to do something that didn't involve violence.

Liberty Films was quartered at RKO Studios, and it was there that RKO's studio chief, Charles Koerner, stuck his head into Capra's office and described an original story he'd bought, a little tale called "The Greatest Gift," written by Philip Van Doren Stern as a three-page Christmas card to be mailed to his friends. RKO had spent a lot of money attempting to turn Stern's modest parable into a workable script. Three complete scripts, each by a fine writer—Dalton Trumbo, Clifford Odets, and Marc Connelly—had been commissioned, written, and rejected by Koerner and RKO.

Koerner's wife then suggested to him that only one man could turn the story into a film: Frank Capra. Hoping to be well rid of Stern's story, Koerner asked Capra to read it and judge its value for himself. If Capra liked the story, Koerner told him, he could have it AND the three scripts for what RKO originally paid for the rights to the Christmas card—$50,000. Capra agreed.

After reading the story, Capra barged into Koerner's office and offered to buy the story then and there.

Capra threw out the first three scripts except for a couple of scenes from Clifford Odets' version of the story—those between the young George Bailey and Mr. Gower, the drugstore proprietor. Capra then hired a husband-and-wife writing team, Albert Hackett and Frances Goodrich, to write a fourth script. While Capra found most of their scenes "bright and sensitive," he was unmoved. So, sitting down, Capra wrote a number of key scenes of his own, melded them with the Hacketts' effort, and came up with the script he wanted.

Meanwhile, James Stewart, who'd won an Academy Award for best actor in 1940's *The Philadelphia Story*, also returned from the war. Stewart had enlisted in the army air corps in March 1941 and was initially treated as a movie star rather than just another enlistee—understandably so. After achieving the rank of captain, Stewart joined the 445th Bombardment Group and was shipped overseas. By the time of his discharge in September 1945, Stewart was a colonel and wing commander. Highly decorated, he was awarded the DFC and cluster, the Croix de Guerre with palm, and seven battle stars.

Stewart had been out of the army air corps for months without having had an offer to do a film. Feeling forgotten, he was delighted when Capra, the director of several of his biggest hits, called with an idea for a picture and invited Stewart to his house.

Stewart later recalled Capra rambling on about guardian angels and a man who wished he had never been born, to the point that Stewart became a little confused; but, trusting Capra's instincts, he asked few questions and simply said that he'd gladly play the part of George Bailey.

As soon as the sets were constructed on the RKO Ranch, the four-month-long shooting commenced on April 8, 1946. Capra had begun the production with a capable director of photography, but was not pleased with the results. Without hesitating, Capra called Columbia Pictures and asked his longtime cameraman on his Columbia productions, Joseph Walker, if he would take over the film. Harry Cohn, Columbia's head, grudgingly gave Walker permission to join Capra's production, contingent upon his return to Columbia if Cohn and the studio needed him. (When Walker was indeed recalled by Cohn before filming was wrapped, his place was taken by Joseph Biroc, after the latter's new status as director of photography was approved by the union.)

On Walker's first day on the set he faced an immediate production difficulty. Walker was to light an entire Bedford Falls street, which was to be seen at night as snow gently fell. The film's assistant director, Art Black, told Walker that the RKO Special Effects department had come up with a special chemical snow to use in place of the untoasted cornflakes films had relied upon in the past.

After Walker had lit the block-long street, Capra shouted "Action!" and the new snow began to fall—beautifully and realistically. However, after Capra called "cut," Black was besieged by extras. The new "snow" had caused the colors in their clothing to run. After the extras were mollified, the snow again fell—but this time it was the traditional cornflakes.

Walker later recalled one fortuitous accident during shooting. In the long shot where Bert the cop fires at an escaping George Bailey, a light in one of the electric signs at the end of the street immediately goes out, as if hit by the bullet. It was not until many years later, when a fan asked Capra if this piece of business had been planned or was an ad lib on the set, that the director first noticed this "great touch." Capra chuckled and replied that he had never noticed it; he guessed it was a coincidence.

A piece of business which *was* planned but which was also the result of a happy coincidence was the famous high school dance sequence which culminates with James Stewart and Donna Reed falling into a swimming pool under the dance floor. Capra, shooting at Beverly Hills High, had no idea there was a pool under the floor. The Charleston contest had been choreographed well in advance, and Stewart and Reed had diligently been rehearsing their moves. On the first day of shooting someone asked Capra if he knew there was a pool under the dance floor. "A swimming pool?" Capra said. "Let's see it." After the hidden pool was revealed, Capra just knew they had to use, and it was worked into the story.

Capra, although always well prepared, was open to changes or suggestions that would improve the film. For the "run on the bank" scene in the
building and loan, when George Bailey was asking his depositors how much
money they would settle for to tide them over, Ellen Corby (later the grand-
mother on TV's *The Waltons*) had only one line: She was to ask James
Stewart for $20. Capra took her aside and, without saying a word to Stewart,
told her to ask for $17.50. When Corby looked at Stewart and delivered her
line, Stewart — surprised, but totally in character — grabbed her and kissed
her.

Donna Reed remembered that Capra was open to suggestions and
ideas from anyone, and that he even would close down the shooting for a
day or so to rethink scenes that he believed needed more work, whether
technically or dramatically.

Wonderful Life is James Stewart's favorite film, and for good reason: He
gives what is perhaps his finest performance as George Bailey. He ages from
a fresh-faced 21-year-old man with a bright future before him to an angry
and frustrated 39-year-old who knows that his dreams are never going to
come true. The role of George Bailey gave Stewart a chance to show off his
considerable range — from cheerful optimism and boundless enthusiasm, to
the devouring despair that can visit a man's soul when he faces the cruel
realities of his unfulfilled life.

Capra even allows Stewart to first manhandle Uncle Billy, telling him
that "one of us is going to jail, and it's not going to be me," and then break
down and snap at his wife and children, smashing furniture and ruining
their Christmas Eve with his uncharacteristic anger.

One of Stewart's many memorable moments in *Wonderful Life* occurs
in the long sequence which follows the high school prom. Stewart's George
Bailey breaks a window in the old Granville house and makes a wish:

> Oh, it's not just one wish, it's a whole hatful, Mary. I'm shakin' the dust
> of this crummy little town off my feet and I'm going to see the world. Italy,
> Greece, the Parthenon, the Colosseum — then I'm coming back and I'm go-
> ing to college and see what they know — and then I'm going to build
> things — I'm gonna build skyscrapers a hundred stories high, I'm gonna
> build bridges a mile long, I'm gonna build. . . . Hey, what? What? You got
> a rock. You gonna throw it, too, Mary? What do you want? You want the
> moon? If you want the moon, say the word and I'll throw a lasso around
> it and bring it right down to you. And then, you know — you could swallow
> it — and it'd all dissolve, see, and moonbeams'd shoot out of your fingers
> and your toes and the ends of your hair, and . . . say, am I talkin' too much?

James Stewart was born on May 20, 1908, in Indiana, Pennsylvania,
where his father owned a hardware store. Because the elder Stewart often
accepted odd items in trade in place of cash at his store, he one day ended
up with an accordion. Mrs. Stewart played the organ in church and was able

Surrounded by Mary and their children, George realizes that his has truly been "a wonderful life."

to teach young Jimmy how to play the family's new musical instrument. While not an outstanding accordion player, Jimmy played well enough to be accepted into Princeton's Triangle Club, and he performed in the Club's 1929 show.

After graduating from Princeton in 1932 with a degree in architecture, Stewart was asked by a classmate, Joshua Logan, to join the University Players at Falmouth, Massachusetts. Stewart initially rebuffed Logan's entreaties to become an actor, insisting he'd promised his father he'd help him run his hardware store that summer, but finally relented and agreed to join the troupe. (Thus, unlike poor George Bailey, Stewart escaped having to take over his father's small-town business.)

Stewart met Henry Fonda at Falmouth and, after agreeing with his new friend and fellow actor that he might have a better future in acting than in architecture since few buildings were being erected, the lanky Pennsylvanian moved to New York with Fonda to try to make it on Broadway. Stewart, Fonda, Josh Logan, and Myron McCormick moved into a two-room apartment on West 64th Street.

His first play, *Carry Nation,* quickly closed, but Stewart landed a number of small parts before finally seeing his name in lights in 1934's *Yellow Jack.*

In 1935, Stewart moved to Hollywood. Fonda's ex-wife, Maureen Sullivan, saw to it that he was cast in small roles in several of her films, and he was on his way.

Donna Reed, a beautiful leading lady of 25, was chosen to play Mary Hatch, the woman George Bailey marries almost against his will. Reed's casting as Mary was consistent with her lifelong typecasting as a wholesome girl-next-door type. While Reed's part and her acting ability are no match for co-star Stewart's, she brought a genuine sense of warmth and humanity to the film.

Born Donna Belle Mullenger, in 1921, in Denison, Iowa, and raised on a farm, Reed won a beauty queen contest at her high school and attended Los Angeles City College. After being chosen campus queen in 1940, she was courted by several studios before signing with MGM following a successful screen test with Van Heflin.

After acting under the name Donna Adams, Reed became a leading lady in the mid-40s. Years of being typecast in roles like Mary in *Wonderful Life* led Reed to attempt to shatter her image by playing Alma, the prostitute, in 1953's *From Here to Eternity*. Although she received an Oscar for best supporting actress for the part, it did not lead to further challenging roles, and she essentially retired from the screen.

Reed is perhaps best known for her long-running television series, *The Donna Reed Show*, which aired from 1958 to 1966. In 1978, Reed starred in a made-for-TV film, *The Best Place to Be*, and acted in a two-part *Love Boat* special before being approached by the popular TV series *Dallas* to play "Miss Ellie."

Replacing an ailing Barbara Bel Geddes, Reed played the part in 1984–1985. Reed herself was replaced—by a recovered Bel Geddes—and sued the producers, settling out of court for a reported $1 million.

Donna Reed died on January 14, 1986, from complications from pancreatic cancer; she was 64 years old.

Lionel Barrymore, who played the venal Mr. Potter, was born Lionel Bythe, in Philadelphia, Pennsylvania in 1878, the son of Maurice Barrymore (Herbert Bythe) and Georgiana Drew. He was just one of the three famous Barrymore acting siblings: His younger brother and sister were John and Ethel.

Barrymore, who often appeared on stage with his uncle, John Drew, became a leading Broadway actor. He briefly abandoned the stage and moved to Paris to attempt to become an artist. After several years he returned to the New York stage. Barrymore later acted in many of D.W. Griffith's early films, and even wrote several scripts for Griffith.

Barrymore won a Best Actor Oscar for his performance in 1931's *A Free Soul*. A fine character actor, he became best known for his portrayal of crusty old Dr. Gillespie in MGM's 15-film *Doctor Kildare* series. After a combination of of illness and injury confined him to a wheelchair in 1938, Barrymore carried on as before and appeared in many more films before his death at age 75 in 1954.

Capra cast Henry Travers, who he felt was truly heaven-sent for the part, as Clarence, the bumbling, if goodhearted, angel second-class. Danny Peary, in *Cult Movies*, called it "fitting that Travers be the one to help Stewart see clearly, for in the previous year's *Bells of St. Mary's* (1945), the film which is on the marquee of the one movie house in Bedford Falls, Travers plays the skinflint who becomes exceedingly generous under the prodding of nun Ingrid Bergman and *her* heavenly contacts."

Travers' Clarence, looking like an overgrown leprechaun, provides a much-needed dose of whimsy and charm to the otherwise dark and jarring *film noir* sequences in which George Bailey has never been born.

George Bailey's guardian angel was born Travers Heagerty in Ireland in 1874. After beginning on the British stage in 1894, he journeyed to America in 1901 and in the '20s found steady employment as a dependable character actor on Broadway. In the early '30s, Travers went to Hollywood, where his kindly looks and twinkling eyes got him cast as benign old gentlemen. He won an Academy Award for Best Supporting Actor for his performance in 1942's *Mrs. Miniver.*

Frank Faylen, born Frank Ruf, who played Ernie the taxi driver, was a veteran character actor who appeared in many fine films. His credits include *The Grapes of Wrath* (1940), *The Lost Weekend* (1945), and *Funny Girl* (1968). An actor whose face was instantly recognizable, even if filmgoers couldn't remember his name, Faylen gained a certain level of fame and recognition playing Dobie Gillis' father in the 1959–62 television series *Dobie Gillis.*

Ward Bond (1903–1960), who played Bert the cop, was another character actor long in films. A member of John Ford's stock company, Bond appeared in such Ford-directed films as *They Were Expendable* (1945), *My Darling Clementine* (1946), *Fort Apache* (1948), *The Quiet Man* (1952), and *The Searchers* (1956). Bond's role in Ford's *Wagonmaster* (1950) led to his starring in the successful television series *Wagon Train.* The series, which ran for many years, made Bond a genuine star in his own right after years of excellent supporting performances. Unfortunately, his death from a heart attack in 1960 prematurely ended his newfound fame.

The other actors in Capra's large cast included members of his stock company and newcomers. H.B. Warner, who played Mr. Gower, the druggist, and Thomas Mitchell, who played the bumbling and forgetful Uncle Billy, were both in *Lost Horizon.* Sheldon Leonard (Nick, the bartender) played gangsters and hoods for years, finally becoming a television producer and hitting it big with *I Spy.* Beulah Bondi (Mrs. Bailey) seemed to have played old ladies of every kind for her whole career.

82   It's a Wonderful Life

Dimitri Tiomkin provided the music for Capra's paean to small-town virtues, and the score is another excellent contribution by the Russian-born composer. Tiomkin underscores the nightmarish scenes in Pottersville with music that is alternately somber or shrill. (For more on Tiomkin, see Chapter 9.)

The photography, by longtime Capra collaborator Joseph Walker, is gorgeous. Incredibly, in 1986, Earl Glick, the chairman of the Hal Roach Studio — in the forefront of black-and-white film colorization — claimed that Colorization Inc. *improved* on Joe Walker's work. Glick apparently has little appreciation for the subtlety of Walker's delicate shadings, from brilliant white to pitch black.

One of the reasons that *Wonderful Life*'s black-and-white photography is so important is that while the film is optimistic and reassuring on the surface, underneath its promise of brotherhood and support, it is really a *film noir*. Once one gets below this misleading surface, the film's underlying sense of frustration and denied self-realization becomes almost palpable. A number of critics — including Robin Wood, who noted the "disturbing influx of *film noir* into the world of small-town comedy" — have commented upon *Wonderful Life*'s dark core of despair.

George Bailey is trapped within what is to him a nightmare, a nightmare made explicit in the penultimate sequence in the film — his horrifying passage through the garish world made possible by his non-birth, through the hideous "Pottersville." For this disturbing sequence, Capra skillfully uses the cinematic language of *film noir:* flashbacks, low-key lighting, high contrast closeups, pulsating neon signs, odd camera angles, and heightened sound effects.

As in any *film noir*, there is no escape for George. He is a stranger to everyone he turns to: His friends and family not only don't recognize him, but are also frightened and repulsed by his overtures.

Capra told interviewer Richard Glatzer that the scene in which George and Mary are talking on the phone to Sam Wainwright is "one of the best scenes I've ever put on the screen. I love that scene. It's an offhand and offbeat way of playing a scene." Generally considered both comic and warm-hearted, the scene is perhaps unconsciously, bitterly revealing of George's losing battle with his small-town entrapment. Barbara Deming, in *Films in Review*, called the scene "as grim a sequence of hero resisting heroine as has ever been in the movies."

George, feeling himself being entombed even as he speaks, grabs Mary by the shoulders and in a frenzy shakes her. "Now you listen to me! I don't want any plastics and I don't want any ground floors, and I don't want to get married ever! I want to do what *I* want to do. . . .!" His face contorted and anguished, George hugs and kisses her, burying his face in her hair. As the heavenly voice-over notes, George "never does leave Bedford Falls."

George Bailey is an atypical Capra hero, facing not the hostile opposition of forces from without, but his own internal dissatisfactions and pressures. Unlike other Capra heroes who willingly embrace "martyrhood," George is forced by happenstance and the unwillingness of others to take responsibility for their own lives to forgo his dreams and ambitions for people who seem oblivious to his sacrifices. George's ultimate betrayal is not by an enemy, but by a member of his own family: the disastrously forgetful Uncle Billy, a cheerful incompetent whom he has kept on at the building and loan.

Until the very end of the film another family member, George's brother, is content to thoughtlessly allow George to continually put aside his own desires so Harry can first go to college and then move out of Bedford Falls to a well-paying job with a bright future.

Similarly, the run on the building and loan is smalltown selfishness and egocentric behavior at its worst. After George has helped the townspeople better their lives by allowing them to build their own homes and escape Potter's Field (a "potter's field" is literally a public burial place for paupers, unknown persons, and criminals), they repay his concern for their welfare by attempting to destroy the institution that has assisted them in achieving a decent standard of living.

As several perceptive critics of the film have noted, Potter — in addition to not really being George's direct antagonist — is the only person in the film who truly understands George. In a meeting between the two, Potter neatly sums up George's predicament, noting that George is probably the only man in town who hates the building and loan as much as he does.

Potter calls George "a young man who's been dying to get out on his own almost since he was born. A young man who has to sit by and watch his friends go places because he's trapped . . . trapped into frittering his life away playing nursemaid to a lot of garlic eaters." Potter then does what *no one else* in the film ever does — he offers George a chance to achieve some personal goals by taking a job with his firm for a high salary and generous perks.

George, of course, turns Potter down, but only at great cost to his peace of mind. After this incident, George learns that Mary is pregnant, and he is even more tightly bound to Bedford Falls. (George's wish at the old Granville house — to escape the town — never comes true; Mary's wish — to live there one day with George — *is* granted.)

When Clarence shows George what a "wonderful life" he has had, taking away his last chance of escape (by suicide), the angel does so by showing George what would have been had he not been born, and *not* what his life would have been like had he been born but left Bedford Falls after graduating from high school. That particular vision would have relieved George of his guilt over allowing the deaths of his brother, the child Mr.

Gower poisoned, and the men on board the transport not saved by Harry Bailey, and allowed George some measure of personal success.

But poor George has been sandbagged, this time by Clarence, for good: He has been revealed as the only glue holding the town of Bedford Falls together, and the guardian of the lives of a number of people who would otherwise be dead.

George now cheerfully accepts his imprisonment. Yet despite the warm and uplifting ending, nothing has really changed. George will pinch pennies for the rest of his life, bludgeoned into accepting his lot in life as inevitable and unavoidable. Mr. Potter and others like him will continue to oppose George and make his life difficult (Potter apparently even gets to keep the $8,000 Uncle Billy thoughtlessly gave him by accident!)

Capra's direction of *Wonderful Life* is nearly flawless. The film, a longish 129 minutes, never drags, never seems padded, as Capra keeps the overlapping flashbacks coming in quick succession.

Capra manages repeatedly to place the events in the context of real-life events. The film begins in 1919, and Mr. Gower gets a telegram informing him his son has died of influenza; 1919 was the year of a great influenza epidemic that killed millions of people. Later, when George Bailey is hoping to travel before going to college, Bert is seen holding a newspaper whose headline reads, "Smith Wins Nomination," identifying the year as 1928. George and Mary dance the Charleston at the high school dance. The war years are seen in a montage of brief scenes — tire drives, guarding the home front, and soldiers in uniform.

Capra's comic timing has never been better than in the scene where Ernie the cabbie welcomes George to his new home, the dilapidated old house at 320 Sycamore, on his wedding night. When Ernie leans back against the doorjamb, his hat goes up in front, as if he's tipping it, and he holds out his hand for a gratuity. A rain-soaked George just looks down at his palm and a stream of water from *his* hat pours into Ernie's hand.

Capra was capable of missteps as well. In George's Pottersville nightmare, Mary is a spinster librarian. But, unlike the Mary from George's life, *this* Mary, bound by the stereotype, needs to wear glasses! (Since she hasn't had a sex life which produced four children, Mary has apparently ruined her eyes by reading to sublimate her unmet desires.)

The acting in *Wonderful Life* is exceptional; everyone in the large cast was obviously carefully selected by Capra and given superb direction.

Although *Wonderful Life* was nominated for five Academy Awards — Best Picture, Best Director, Best Actor, Best Editing, and Best Sound Recording — it failed to take home a single statuette. The big winner that year was *The Best Years of Our Lives*, a Samuel Goldwyn–RKO production, which copped six Oscars and won in four of the categories in which *Life* was nominated.

A perennial Christmas classic, *It's a Wonderful Life* is a wonderful movie. I can think of no other film that can simultaneously delight and annoy me as it does. More than forty years after its release, it brings happiness and joy to those who have seen it a dozen times as well as to first-time viewers. Its magic is strong enough to withstand cutting, colorization, and remakes (1977's made-for-TV movie *It Happened One Christmas*, with Marlo Thomas in the Jimmy Stewart role).

Next Christmas, if you want a truly emotional viewing experience, tune in a TV station showing *Wonderful Life* or rent the videocassette. Watch it in its wonderfully pristine black-and-white original form, or in computer-added color—but watch it.

7. Jason and the Argonauts: Ancient Mythology

From every region of Aegea's shore
The brave assembled; those illustrious twins
Castor and Pollux; Orpheus, tuneful bard;
Zetes and Calais, as the wind in speed;
Strong Hercules and many a chief renowned.
On deep Ioclos' sandy shore they thronged,
Gleaming in armour, ardent of exploits;
And soon, the laurel cord and the huge stone
Uplifting to the deck, unmoored the bark;
Whose keel of wondrous length the skillful hand
Of Argus fashioned for the proud attempt;
And in the extended keel a lofty mast
Upraised, and sails full swelling; to the chiefs
Unwonted objects. Now first, now they learned
Their bolder steerage over ocean wave,
Led by the golden stars, as Chiron's art
Had marked the sphere celestial....
— From The Fleece, by John Dyer (1700–1758).

Released in 1963, *Jason and the Argonauts* is a wonderful fantasy film — full of heroic deeds, ignoble villainy, powerful yet petty gods, magical happenings, wondrous sights, and impressive monsters. The special effects are the work of Ray Harryhausen and are flawlessly integrated with the literate screenplay by Jan Read and Beverly Cross. Harryhausen himself has written that this film pleases him most.

Unfortunately for Harryhausen, producer Charles H. Schneer, and Columbia Pictures, this carefully crafted and expensive (between $3 and $3.5 million) example of the "ancient mythology" subgenre was released at the end of the cycle of low-budget, poorly made and poorly dubbed Italian epics loosely based on Greek and Roman legends that began with the superior *Hercules* (1957). Many moviegoers believed it just another muscle-bound, muscle-brained dud, and the film didn't find much of an audience in the United States (though it was one of the top ten grossers in Great Britain the year of its release).

86

This behind-the-scenes shot finds actor Niall MacGinnis, in his makeup and costume as Zeus, going over the script with Harryhausen's longtime producer and collaborator, Charles H. Schneer.

Harryhausen's Talos sequence is chilling and wonderful moviemaking, and his fight between Jason and seven sinister skeletons has never been equaled. As Ray wrote in his *Film Fantasy Scrapbook*, "Technically, it was unprecedented in the sphere of fantasy filming. [Realizing] there were seven skeletons fighting three men, with each skeleton having five appendages to move each frame of film, and keeping them all in synchronization with the three actors' movements, one can readily see why it took four and a half months to record the sequence for the screen." Sometimes, Harryhausen averaged only thirteen or fourteen frames a day—just a little over one-half second of screen time.

The Academy Award for Special Effects that year went to *Cleopatra*. Harryhausen was not even nominated; he has never won an Oscar for his technical wizardry. However, in 1981, the Museum of Modern Art in New York City held an exhibition of Harryhausen's work, honoring his contributions to fantasy and motion pictures.

Although *Jason* has achieved the status of cult classic, it was dismissed with mocking, almost brutal, notices by many of the critics of the day.

Time's review was typical of the savage reception American reviewers gave *Jason:* "The reflecting surface of the fish pond in Zeus' palace on Mount Olympus is a sort of giant-screen TV that brings in news shows from all over the Aegean. Zeus and Hera, who are just folks, watch it so much they must surely have to keep a six-pack of nectar and a frozen ambrosia dinner close at hand. But instead of astronauts they see Argonauts—a bearded body builder named Jason (Todd Armstrong) and his adventure-prone shipmates aboard the *Argo*. The straight story of Jason's exploits, told with magic and imagination and a minimum of studio trickery, might have been delightful. This version is more bull than Bulfinch."

Leo Mishkin of the *New York Morning Telegraph* was a bit kinder in his condemnation: *"Jason and the Argonauts* is strictly hot weather entertainment, suitable for keeping the children off the streets, perhaps, but hardly to be taken seriously by anybody beyond the age of puberty."

Jonathan Miller, in the *New Yorker*, wrote, *"Jason and the Argonauts*, a Hollywood adaptation of the classical myth, is another of those wine-dark-sea affairs. The Golden Fleece comes on as a tinselly rug that glows like some undreamed-of electric blanket from Norman Dine's Sleep Center. Seven-headed monsters and fighting skeletons still have a primitive, staccato action that brings back those jumpy little pieces by Georges Melies. In an age when practically anyone can bounce Khrushchev off a Telstar, film technicians should be able to do this standing on their heads. Back to the old drawing board is what I say." (Miller's, like most of the reviews, doesn't even mention or credit Harryhausen; actually, given his low regard for the film and the effects, that's probably for the best.)

Writing in the Catholic publication *America*, Moira Walsh at least allows as how the "kiddies" might enjoy the film. "If I had a few small fry clamoring to see a movie, I would be . . . inclined to take them to *Jason and the Argonauts* . . . a rather gruesome tale, complete with 'super-dynamated' mechanical monsters mixed in with its live actors. It is based loosely on a Greek legend that, in its original telling, would not be very suitable juvenile fare and in its present form may still make sensitive parents a little nervous. Still, it is moderately literate and intelligently acted and has some capacity to stir youngsters' imaginations in a constructive sense."

In his review in the *New York Times*, Howard Thompson wrote, "This absurd, unwieldy adventure—if that's the word—is no worse, but certainly no better, than most of its kind. The ingredients are the usual color, milling hordes of warriors, royal hanky-panky laced with historical or mythological footnotes, monsters, magic, and carefully exposed limbs and torsos. In one comic interlude Jason and his pals battle some rickety sword-swinging skeletons. How were they paid, Mr. Schneer—union scale?"

One reviewer, *Variety*'s "Tube.," eschewed showing off how funny and punny he could be and reviewed the film with the enthusiasm and dignity it deserved, crediting Harryhausen by name. Under a headline that read, "Diverting and ingeniously executed romp through Greek mythology. Solid moppet appeal makes it good summertime prospect." Tube. wrote, "Here's a choice hot weather attraction for the family trade—a sure delight for the kiddies and a diverting spectacle for adults with a taste for fantasy and adventure." Tube. went on to describe the film as "an impressive display of cinematic verisimilitude for which associate producer and special visual effects expert Ray Harryhausen rates at least the motion picture equivalent of two ears and a tail. Among the spectacular . . . characters brought to life through the ingenuity of illusionist Harryhausen . . . are a remarkably lifelike mobile version of the colossal bronze god, Talos; fluttery personifications of the bat-winged Harpies; [and] a batch of some astonishingly active skeletons who materialize out of the teeth of the Hydra. . . ."

Later writers and reviewers also recognized the quality of *Jason.* Leonard Maltin's *TV Movies and Video Guide, 1987 Edition,* gave the film three stars and mentioned both Harryhausen's effects and Bernard Herrmann's score.

In *The Motion Picture Guide: 1927–1983,* authors Jay Robert Nash and Stanley Ralph Ross wrote, "In *Jason and the Argonauts,* Harryhausen is at his most creative and brilliant. The stop-motion models of the monsters are sculpted with fine detail, and the rendering of their motion is outstanding in every scene. The technical ambition and brilliance of the final sword fight with the skeletons . . . is absolutely amazing. . . . A great film for kids, with enough 'adult' elements to please even the most discriminating viewer. A must-see."

At the bidding of Pelias (Douglas Wilmer), who seeks to overthrow Aristo, the king of Thessaly, an old soothsayer reads the ashes. He sees a Golden Fleece at the end of the world and foresees that Pelias' plot will succeed. The soothsayer warns, however, that one of Aristo's children will recover the crown. Pelias strikes, killing the royal family. While a soldier spirits away the infant Jason, Aristo's daughter prays to the goddess Hera. After killing the girl, Pelias is told by a mysterious woman—Hera in earthly form—that a man wearing one sandal will be his destruction.

On Olympus, home of the gods, Zeus and Hera (Niall MacGinnis and Honor Blackman) discuss earthly events, and he tells her that Jason has escaped. When she asks permission to help Jason, Zeus tells Hera she may help him five times—the number of times Aristo's daughter called for Hera's help.

Twenty years pass and Pelias, thrown from his horse into a river, is saved by a young man who loses one sandal in the process—Jason (Todd Armstrong). Jason reveals himself and his plans for revenge against the killer of his family, unaware he's speaking to Pelias. Pelias, knowing that the moment he kills Jason he himself will die, suggests that Jason build a ship, gather a crew, and sail in search of the Golden Fleece—only then returning to overthrow the king. To thwart Jason's chances at success, Pelias will send along his son, Acastus (Gary Raymond).

The old soothsayer changes into the god Hermes (Michael Gwynn) and takes Jason to Mount Olympus to speak with Zeus and Hera. When Jason refuses Zeus' offer of aid, Hera tells him to search for the Fleece in Colchis. Jason says he'll hold games to choose the strongest and the best for his crew. After the crew has been chosen, Hylas (John Cairney), a lad, is added when, by skipping his discus off the water, he throws farther than Hercules (Nigel Green).

Jason learns from Argus, the shipbuilder (Laurence Naismith), that his craft is ready, and he names the ship the *Argo* in the old man's honor.

Becalmed at sea under a burning sun, the Argonauts are running low on water. Jason speaks to the ship's figurehead (really Hera), and she tells him to steer north to the Isle of Bronze, where Hephaestus, the armorer of the gods, fashioned their weapons. She cautions they must take nothing but food and water.

Hercules and Hylas, chasing goats, discover an immense bronze figure cast in a crouching position—Talos. They enter a door in the statue's base and find giant jewels and treasures. Outside, after stealing a giant golden brooch pin, they watch in horror as Talos' head turns and stares down at them.

Talos pursues the sailors toward the *Argo*. Jason sets sail, but the passage out is blocked by Talos, who straddles the sea lane. Talos seizes the ship as if it were a toy and shakes it, tossing Argonauts into the sea and breaking off the ship's mast. When Jason asks Hera for help, she tells him to use his wits and "look to his ankles." The men draw Talos' attention while Jason hides and waits his chance. Seeing an immense screw in Talos' heel, Jason loosens it, and a fiery liquid gushes out. Talos stiffens as cracks appear in his body, and he falls, crushing Hylas.

Hercules searches for Hylas while the Argonauts repair the damage to the ship. Hercules stays behind to continue his search, and Acastus goads the men into refusing to leave without him. Hera then tells them that Hylas

Two harpies, harrassing the blind Phineas (Patrick Troughton). This scene, shot in the ruins of a real temple in Paestrum, Italy, called for careful planning to integrate the actions of the actor with the stop-motion harpies. (Photo courtesy of Ray Harryhausen.)

is dead and that Zeus has other plans for Hercules. She tells them to seek out the blind Phineas—he can guide them to the Fleece.

At a ruined temple, food is set out for Phineas (Patrick Troughton). But he is set upon by flying harpies who torment him and steal the food; he sobs in frustration as the harpies feast: "Lord Zeus, I was a sinner. I've never tried to deny it, but I didn't sin every day. . .why then do you punish me every day?"

When Jason and his men arrive, Phineas refuses to obey Hera and the gods, saying he'll speak only if Jason frees him from the harpies. After Jason and the sailor entrap the harpies in nets and cage them, Phineas tells them they must pass the Clashing Rocks and then sail for Colchis.

As they approach the narrow passage, they see another ship destroyed by falling rocks. Hera helps Jason by sending Triton, the sea god, to hold back the rocks long enough for the Argo to sail through.

The Argonauts rescue survivors of the destroyed ship, learning from one of them, Medea (Nancy Kovack), that they're from Colchis. When Jason tells the Argonauts he wants to scout the situation rather than attacking, Acastus fights him. Losing, Acastus dives overboard and escapes.

King Aeetes (Jack Gwillim) welcomes Jason and his men to a feast.

Later, saying he knows Jason has come for the Fleece, Aeetes has them disarmed, revealing he was warned by Acastus. Medea drugs the guards and helps free Jason and the Argonauts. A furious Aeetes, joined by soldiers, rushes to intercept Jason.

When Jason arrives at the tree which holds the Fleece, he sees the body of Acastus, held by a tail of the seven-headed Hydra which stands guard. Jason fights the Hydra, killing it by plunging his sword into its chest. After Argus, Phalerus (Andrew Faulds), and Castor (Gernando Poggi), appear and seize the Fleece, Aeetes follows and gathers the Hydra's teeth.

Aeetes' soldiers mortally wound Medea; Jason uses the healing powers of the Fleece to restore her to life and then faces Aeetes. Aeetes sows the Hydra's teeth, producing seven sword-wielding skeletons. Sending Medea away with Argus, Jason, Phalerus, and Castor stay behind to fight these "children of the Hydra." After his two loyal companions are killed, Jason escapes by leaping into the sea.

Zeus, watching Jason and Medea embrace, tells Hera that he was always "sentimental," but adds, "Let us continue with the game . . . another day."

Ray Harryhausen was born in Los Angeles on June 29, 1920. Early on, he exhibited an inordinate interest in dinosaurs and gorillas. In 1933, when he was 13, Ray and his mother received free tickets to the opening of *King Kong* at Grauman's Chinese Theatre in Hollywood from his aunt, a nurse who cared for Sid Grauman's elderly mother. Harryhausen had no idea what to expect, although he'd seen an ad in a local paper showing a huge gorilla. The film, and the floor show that preceded it, stunned him. Harryhausen called the experience, "the illusion of a lifetime."

The movies he'd seen to that time had featured men in gorilla suits, but he knew that neither King Kong nor the dinosaurs could have been done that way. Many months later, Harryhausen unearthed a *Look* magazine article that revealed that something called "stop-motion photography" was the means by which Kong and the dinosaurs had been brought to life.

Harryhausen took up the study of sculpture and anatomy in high school, and when he was a senior he made his first stop-motion film, animating a cave bear with a wooden skeleton and wooden ball-and-socket joints which he covered with a swatch from one of his mother's discarded fur coats—at least Harryhausen *thinks* it was a discard.

Through his friend Forrest J Ackerman, who later would create and edit *Famous Monsters of Filmland*, Harryhausen learned that others with interests similar to his had started the Los Angeles Science-Fiction Society. He began attending meetings at Clifton's Cafeteria. There, in the third-floor Little Brown Room, Ray met Ray—Harryhausen met Bradbury.

After his dream of becoming the world's greatest stop-motion animator was put on hold while he took acting classes at Los Angeles City College, Harryhausen realized he could "act" through his models and returned to his first love. Attending night film classes at USC, Harryhausen began his lifelong practice of always doing his film projects alone.

After meeting his idol, Willis O'Brien, in 1939 ("OBie" told the young man to study more anatomy after agreeing to look at Ray's models), Harryhausen was hired by George Pal for the producer's Puppetoon series. Harryhausen made $16 a week, not bad money for the time, and soon was making even more as his talent became apparent to Pal.

Drafted by the United States Army in 1942, Harryhausen wrangled his way into the Signal Corps, where he soon made several stop-motion films which caught Frank Capra's eye. Working for Capra's unit, Harryhausen stop-animated training films with titles like "How to Bridge a Gorge."

After the war, Harryhausen declined an offer to return to Pal's Puppetoon unit to work on his own projects, including a series of brief, animated fairy tales. By 1946, O'Brien, mired in extensive preproduction on *Mighty Joe Young*, remembered the young man who'd come to see him years before and hired him as his assistant. O'Brien was so preoccupied with his other responsibilities that Harryhausen ended up animating over 80 percent of the film.

Frenchman Eugene Lourie, hired to direct a low-budget film titled *The Monster from Beneath the Sea*, and producer Hal Chester had heard of a young animator who'd worked with Willis O'Brien. Their primary interest in O'Brien's protégé was the fact that they knew they could get him more cheaply than O'Brien (ironically, OBie's career was at a low point and he might not have been any more expensive than the novice Harryhausen).

Asked to look at the script by producer Chester, Ray Bradbury mentioned that it vaguely resembled a story of his in *The Saturday Evening Post*. Fearing a lawsuit, Chester sent Bradbury a check for $2,000 for the rights to the story and its title, "The Beast from 20,000 Fathoms." *Beast's* success led to other projects for Harryhausen, including his next effects job and first teaming with producer Charles Schneer: *It Came from Beneath the Sea*.

Harryhausen's body of work since *Beneath* has been impressive: *The Animal World* (1955), *Earth vs. the Flying Saucers* (1956), *20 Million Miles to Earth* (1957), *The Seventh Voyage of Sinbad* (his 1958 cult classic), *The Three Worlds of Gulliver* (1959), *Mysterious Island* (1960), *Jason and the Argonauts* (1963), *First Men in the Moon* (1964), *One Million Years B.C.* (1966, also directed by *Jason's* Don Chaffey), *The Valley of Gwangi* (1968), *The Golden Voyage of Sinbad* (1973), *Sinbad and the Eye of the Tiger* (1977), and *Clash of the Titans* (1981).

The Greek myth of "Jason and the Golden Fleece" (the film's original title) differs markedly from the screenplay by Jan Read and Beverly Cross, yet the changes Harryhausen and Schneer demanded reflect the difficulty the filmmakers would have had trying to bring the authentic legend to the screen.

Bulfinch's Mythology and other sources recount the story this way: King Aeson of Thessaly allows his brother Pelias to hold his crown until Jason, the son of Aeson, comes of age. Unwilling to yield the crown, Pelias suggests to Jason that he pursue the Golden Fleece in far off Colchis.

Jason's ship, the "Argo," was built by Argus to hold fifty men — an unheard-of number. Hercules and other great heroes were among the "Argonauts" who found the sage Phineas in Thrace. Phineas, freed by them from the torments of the harpies, instructed the Argonauts how to pass the Symplegades, or Clashing Islands. They followed closely behind a dove, though the closing of the islands behind them grazed their stern.

In Colchis, King Aeetes promised to give up the Golden Fleece if Jason would yoke to a plough two fire-breathing bulls and sow the teeth of the dragon which Cadmus had slain — from which would spring up a crop of armed men who would turn their swords against the sower. Jason accepted the challenge.

Having promised to marry Aeetes' daughter, Medea, Jason accepted a charm from her by which he could counter the deadly breath of the bulls and the weapons of the armed men.

When the bulls charged, Jason soothed them with his voice, petted them, and slipped on the yoke, forcing them to pull the plough, which he used to plant the dragon's teeth. When the armed men sprang up, Jason kept them at bay with his sword and shield until he could use the charm as Medea taught him. Seizing a stone, he tossed it in the soldiers' midst, and they turned upon each other until none was left alive. Jason then lulled to sleep the sleepless dragon with a preparation given him by Medea and seized the Fleece, fleeing to Thessaly and safety.

The changes from myth to film are profound, yet strangely minor in their effect upon the story. In the myth, Hercules leaves the expedition not because he was the cause of Hylas' death, but because Hylas, "a youth beloved by him," having gone for water, was captured and kept by nymphs of the spring. When Hercules did not return from his search, the *Argo* left him behind. Obviously, this interpretation would be difficult to justify in a family film.

Clashing Rocks seem inherently more dramatic than Clashing Islands, and following a dove through the strait lacks the visual excitement of seeing the giant sea god Triton holding open the passage, although some versions of the tale have the goddess Pallas Athene holding the rocks apart. (The whole tale, by the way, may be a corruption of the story of Noah and the Ark, a supposition given credence by the name *Argo* and by the incident of the dove.)

If critics found the skeletons amusing, what would they have made of

The actors playing the Argonauts in the foreground are real; Talos is actually a detailed model only a foot high and matted into the scene. (Photo courtesy of Ray Harryhausen.)

two fire-breathing bulls with brazen feet being sweet-talked by Jason until he could yoke them? And the skeletons, naysayers aside, are more sinister and frightening than mere armed men—somehow skeletons as the "children of the Hydra" make more story sense.

Talos, though he does appear in a few versions of the Jason myth, is mostly a Harryhausen creation. "In some stories, Talos was a bronze god about eight feet tall who sat in the fire until he got red hot, and then went around hugging the sailors and burning them to death," Harryhausen said. "Well, you could hardly do that for the screen."

The "sleepless dragon" became the Hydra—seven-headed, not nine-headed as in the legends. As it was, seven heads were plenty to animate. As Harryhausen told me at a conference in Houston in 1986, "It's very time-consuming and tiring work. You're in the midst of animating and photographing the model when the phone rings; when you return, you suddenly wonder which heads are going up and which are going down! Some of the fun is gone."

Harryhausen first interested the studio by developing the project through a dozen large drawings to show what was possible (his usual practice); only then was work begun on the script.

Schneer and Harryhausen first assigned Jan Read to write the screenplay. Later, Oxford scholar Beverly Cross (married to actress Maggie Smith, who appeared in Cross' and Harryhausen's *Clash of the Titans*) was hired to take over the script.

Cross' entry into screenwriting was purely a matter of chance. He was hired as an assistant to scriptwriter Robert Bolt for David Lean's Columbia production of *Lawrence of Arabia*. At the same time, Harryhausen and Schneer were preparing *Jason* for the studio. After meeting with Cross, Schneer hired him to take over the script; it was his first screenplay.

Cross' most difficult problems with the script came from trying to integrate the mythic elements with what was possible in terms of budget and animation time. In an early version of the script, Jason and Medea ventured into Hell, past Cerberus, the three-headed dog of the Underworld, in search of a potion to protect Jason from the Hydra. The Clashing Rocks sequence also called for stop-motion animation, but this too was scrapped; an actor dressed as Triton and placed in a miniature set was substituted.

Thanks to his scholarly background, Cross' script is unusually literate for a fantasy film and filled with intelligent dialogue. For instance, when Jason refuses Zeus' offer of help and a ship, Zeus says, "I did well to choose you, Jason. The gods are best served by those who want their help least." Later, as Jason approaches the roiling waters of the Clashing Rocks he says, "The gods of Greece are cruel—in time all men shall learn to do without them." Hera says to Zeus, "Jason dared to speak of the end of the gods, yet you let him live." Sagely, Zeus replies, "If I were to punish every blasphemy, I'd soon lose all loyalty and respect."

The location shooting, wrapped a whole year before Harryhausen was able to do the animation work, was originally planned for Yugoslavia but actually done in southern Italy, near the seacoast village of Palinuro—a site south of Naples featuring an incredibly blue ocean, white sandy beaches, and unique rock formations, all within a few miles of each other.

The temples used in the harpy sequence were actual temples in Paestum, Italy. The Italian government allowed the production to use the 3,000-year-old temples provided they did no damage. (Apparently, the Italians hadn't seen Harryhausen and Schneer's *20 Million Miles to Earth*, where the "Ymir" topples the Temple of Saturn!) The interiors were shot inside a studio in Rome.

Realizing that a model ship would be inadequate for the many long shots of the *Argo* at sea, Harryhausen and Schneer spent a quarter of a million dollars constructing Argus' heroic vessel atop an existing fishing boat. Equipping the craft with twin engines meant that director Chaffey could quickly move the ship into the correct position for each new set-up. The investment in authenticity was more than justified. The film has any number of lovely shots featuring the full-size vessel: the disk of the dying sun, hanging over the sea and framed by the ship's figurehead; a long shot

The full-scale *Argo*, which cost approximately $250,000 to build. (Photo courtesy of Ray Harryhausen.)

looking down at the *Argo* sailing into a narrow strait of intensely blue water as it approaches the Clashing Rocks. (One "take" of the *Argo* approaching the Isle of Bronze, however, was ruined when a replica of the *Golden Hind* from the television series *Sir Francis Drake* came sailing into the shot.)

  British director Don Chaffey, who began in films in 1944 as an assistant in the art department of Gainsborough Pictures and directed his first feature in 1950, was hired to helm *Jason*. He later directed Harryhausen's 1966 release, *One Million Years B.C.* (For more about Chaffey's other films, see the Appendix.)

  When *Clash of the Titans* was released in 1981, much was made of the fact that Harryhausen and Schneer finally had a cast that could match the effects in quality, including Laurence Olivier, Maggie Smith, Claire Bloom, Sian Phillips, Harry Hamlin, Judi Bowker, and Tim Pigott-Smith (Jack Gwillam, Aeetes in *Jason,* played Poseidon). While I don't dispute the star quality of this ensemble, I'd defend the actors in *Jason* against those in *Titans* or almost any fantasy film.

Todd Armstrong makes a brave and forceful Jason. He brings conviction to his role and, contrary to what one reviewer said — calling him a "body builder" — is simply lean and handsome. Unfortunately for his performance, Armstrong's all–American voice didn't mesh well with the British actors' and was dubbed over.

Laurance Naismith is a wonderful Argus, and Nigel Green's non-muscle-bound Hercules is a delight. Gary Raymond, who would become well known in the United States in the '60s for starring in television's *The Rat Patrol,* is properly treacherous as Acastus. Nancy Kovack's Medea is fine, but her character and the love interest she brings to the film come far too late into the adventure for her appearance to have much impact.

Niall MacGinnis, recognized by Lutherans everywhere for his forceful playing of *Martin Luther,* gives just as credible a performance as Zeus as Laurence Olivier gave in *Clash.* (For more about the actors and their other films, see the Appendix.)

A competent craftsman, Don Chaffey's direction of *Jason* is probably the best work of his long career in feature films. The same year *Jason* was released, 1963, also saw the release of a Disney picture he directed, *The Three Lives of Thomasina,* starring Patrick McGoohan. Chaffey's work must have impressed McGoohan, for he later directed several of the actor's *The Prisoner* episodes, including the first, "Arrival."

Of course, the real attraction of any Harryhausen film, no matter who the nominal "stars" are, is the special effects. To distinguish his stop-motion animation from cartoon animation, Harryhausen, beginning with *The Seventh Voyage of Sinbad,* has called his wizardry "Dynamation." (It's also been labeled Dynamation 90, as for *Jason,* and Dynarama for later releases.)

Harryhausen has been using his own split-screen techniques since *The Beast from 20,000 Fathoms.* His system uses mattes (see the *King Kong* chapter and Appendix) and the sodium-backing system to combine his miniature creations and live-action photography. Harryhausen also uses a rear screen onto which a specially constructed projector beams previously shot live-action footage one frame at a time. He then positions the stop-motion model — Talos, for instance — and aligns it with the rear screen image, carefully lighting it to match the live footage. If the color is properly balanced, the scene is ready to be photographed one frame at a time by Ray's camera.

Harryhausen and Schneer moved to London (Harryhausen literally—he's lived there since 1962) for the making of *The Three Worlds of Gulliver*. The old blue-screen method used in *The Seventh Voyage of Sinbad* had proved cumbersome and complex; if the elements in a composite shot are not aligned perfectly, mattes can easily be detected by "fringing" or "matte-line effect," an obvious halo around objects. English filmmakers, in contrast, had begun to use the more sophisticated sodium system, the so-called "yellow-backing" traveling matte system. Harryhausen found that the sodium method made an instantaneous matte in a split-beam camera. In *Jason*, actor Nigel Green was composited into the scene with Talos where the bronze giant turns his head and looks down at him through the sodium system. (See the Appendix for more on the sodium system.)

Harryhausen's goal is always to make his creations' actions as lifelike as possible, so it was especially difficult for the meticulous animator to deliberately make Talos move stiffly, in little jerks and stops, to emphasize that the statue is made of metal. Not surprisingly, some people criticized the sequence for that very reaosn. The beginning of the Talos sequence, whatever one thinks of the animation, is one of the most chilling moments in film: The massive head of the bronze god slowly turns and stares down at Hercules and Hylas. No matter how many times I've seen this scene, it always makes me shiver.

Because the live action is always shot first, Harryhausen was able to convincingly show Todd Armstrong's Jason plunging his sword into the body of the Hydra by having the actor go through the motions without a sword but as if he had one in his hand. Then, with his monster positioned before a miniature screen of the live footage, Harryhausen positioned a miniature sword from an overhead brace and frame-by-frame animated it entering and lodging in the Hydra's chest. In scenes where either Jason or Acastus was held by one of the Hydra's tails, the actor was replaced in long shots by a model—which Ray animated struggling and kicking its legs.

The overhead or aerial braces were also used in the shot where a harpy takes hold of Phineas' cloth girdle and pulls it from his body, rolling the blind prophet along the ground like a log. In the live-action shoot, the girdle was pulled from actor Patrick Troughton's body by wires and the actions of the harpy coordinated with the resulting footage.

The Triton sequence featured a non-actor, who, Harryhausen explained to Jeff Rovin in *The Fabulous Fantasy Films*, "was a professional swimmer, and that was one of the necessities of getting the part." Wearing water-repelling makeup—applied to his hair, beard, and moustache—the actor had to rise from and submerge back into the Shepperton Studios tank on cue. Studio technicians operated his mechanical tail which emerged, slapping the surface of the water, while the actor "held" the cliffs apart as the miniature *Argo* sailed through. As in all miniature water scenes, the

Jason (Todd Armstrong) battles the seven-headed Hydra, guardian of the Golden Fleece. (Photo courtesy of Ray Harryhausen.)

size of the water droplets (water cannot be "miniaturized") gave away the situation.

When Jason realizes he cannot defeat the skeletons, he runs to the edge of a cliff and leaps into the sea, closely followed by the persistent "children of the Hydra." A Greek stuntman, standing in for Todd Armstrong, executed this feat by leaping off a 90-foot-high platform into the sea closely followed by seven plaster skeletons hurled after him by crew members. For the close-up of the beginning of the leap, the "real" Jason jumped off a wooden platform onto a mattress a few feet below. When the footage is intercut, it is an exciting and realistic stunt.

The music for *Jason* was provided by one of Hollywood's premier film composers, Bernard Herrmann (1911–1975). Autocratic and demanding, Herrmann was quite selective about which films he would deign to score, often walking out of a screening and railing at the producer, "Why do you show me this garbage?" While he scored roughly 50 motion pictures, he is most often remembered for four: *All That Money Can Buy* (Academy Award, 1941), *The Day the Earth Stood Still* (1951), *The Seventh Voyage of Sinbad* (1958), and *Psycho* (1960).

Born in New York City, Herrmann took music lessons in grade school and at age 12 won a prize for a song he'd written. He attended New York University and was a fellowship student at the Juilliard School of Music. A professional musician by age 18, in 1933 he was composing and conducting

Jason (Todd Armstrong) and his two companions Phalerus and Castor (Andrew Faulds and Gernando Poggi) in a fight to the death with the seven sword-wielding skeletons spawned by the teeth of the Hydra. (Photo courtesy of Ray Harryhausen.)

for the Columbia Broadcasting System, where he met the young Orson Welles. At Welles' insistence, he wrote the score for the celebrated *Citizen Kane*. He won an Oscar for his very next score, *All That Money Can Buy*.

Active in radio and a popular New York concert conductor, Herrmann preferred the East to California and wrote no more than one film score a year for the next ten years. His experimental score of 1951's *The Day the Earth Stood Still* used no electronic instruments, yet suggested electronic music.

In 1955, Herrmann began a long and productive association with Alfred Hitchcock when he scored *The Trouble with Harry*. It was 1960's *Psycho* that is Herrmann's most famous link to Hitchcock, however. His brilliant score accompanies and amplifies the onscreen horror, especially his use of high-pitched and birdlike shrieking violins.

Beginning in 1958, with Schneer and Harryhausen's *The Seventh Voyage of Sinbad*, Herrmann scored a number of fantasy and science fiction films which allowed his musical imagination full rein. Herrmann's bold and clattering accompaniment to Sinbad's sword fight with the skeleton is brilliant motion picture composing and greatly enhances one of Harryhausen's most memorable sequences.

He followed *Sinbad* with *Journey to the Center of the Earth* (1959),

The Three Worlds of Gulliver (1960), *Mysterious Island* (1961), and, finally, *Jason* in 1963. Fearing typecasting, Herrmann refused other such films and returned to Hitchcock in 1964 for *Marnie*, a box-office dud whose failure studio executives used to pressure Hitch to hire someone else for *Torn Curtain*. The posthumous *Taxi Driver* and the Hitchcock-like *Obsession* (both 1976) marked the end of Herrmann's magnificent and idiosyncratic career.

Herrmann's score for *Jason* allowed his musical imagination great latitude and his rich, heroic themes support the onscreen action admirably. With its rich Greco-Roman texture, its attention to the machinations of the plot, Herrmann's score adds wit and charm to what might otherwise occasionally be too-solemn proceedings.

When I asked Ray Harryhausen if he planned future projects, he was evasive. For years, he's been rumored to be planning another Sinbad film, either one titled *Sinbad Goes to Mars*, or *Sinbad and the Seven Wonders of the World*. Given the growing hostility toward his later work by the editors and critics of some fantasy-oriented publications, perhaps Harryhausen is tired of the ordeals associated with his type of one-man moviemaking and may allow his long hiatus from films to grow into an unofficial retirement. Though he looks younger than his age and is in good health, Ray Harryhausen was born in 1920.

Perhaps he's worn out, unwilling to put in twelve-to-fifteen-hour days for little reward. Harryhausen's done it all — he's "seen the elephant" and may feel he has little left to prove to anyone, especially himself.

Ever the film magician, Harryhausen may also believe that the modern fantasy filmgoer knows too much about how his dazzling onscreen tricks are done. "I think there's far too much delving into, and analysis of, special effects," Harryhausen told *Cinefantastique*'s Dan Scapperotti. "It's a pity that too much is discussed about how it's done because it does destroy the illusion. And that's the business we're in, we're in the business of illusion, just like a magician."

Ray Harryhausen has produced an enviable body of work; he has given us film magic to take our breath away, to instill in cynical know-it-all hearts a sense of wonder. In *Jason and the Argonauts*, he used his magician's skills to bring the legends and myths of the Greeks to believable life and enliven a too-often juvenile and schlocky subgenre of the fantasy film.

8. King Kong: The Giant Monster

> And the Prophet said: "And lo! the Beast looked upon the face of Beauty. And it stayed its hand from killing. And from that day it was as one dead."
>
> —*"Old Arabian proverb."*

King Kong opened in New York City on March 2, 1933, at two major theaters simultaneously. Its Hollywood premiere was at Grauman's Chinese Theatre on Friday, March 24, 1933.

Mordaunt Hall's review in the *New York Times* said, "At both the Radio City Music Hall and the RKO Roxy, which have a combined seating capacity of 10,000, the main attraction now is a fantastic film known as 'King Kong.' Through multiple exposures, processed 'shots' and a variety of angles of camera wizardry the producers set forth an adequate story and furnish enough thrills for any devotee of such thrills."

William Troy, writing in *The Nation,* said, "At Radio City last week one was able to see the contradiction pretty dramatically borne out; an audience enjoying all the sensations of primitive terror and fascination within the scientifically air-cooled temple of baroque modernism that is Mr. Rockefeller's contribution to contemporary culture. But, unfortunately, it was thought necessary to mitigate some of the predominant horror by introducing a ho-hum, all-too-human, theme. 'It was not the guns that got him,' says one of the characters . . . 'It was Beauty killed the Beast.'"

After an "Old Arabian proverb" (see above) is shown, the film opens with a shot of New York Harbor. Two men discuss the voyage of a ship, the *Venture,* as being crazy. One of the men is Carl Denham, a filmmaker (Robert Armstrong).

Denham, Captain Engelhorn (Frank Reicher), and others discuss finding a "girl" for Denham's movie—the "love interest." Denham finds a starving Ann Darrow (Fay Wray) and buys her a meal. He tells her he wants her for a dangerous job involving "a long sea voyage that starts at six o'clock tomorrow morning."

103

A publicity shot of producer-director Merian C. Cooper presumably "dreaming up" a scene from *King Kong:* the fight between Kong and the Tyrannosaurus Rex.

Weeks pass aboard ship. Denham tests Ann's costumes before the cameras. Seeing Ann with a monkey, he says, "Beauty and the Beast." First Mate Jack Driscoll (Bruce Cabot) and Denham discuss Ann and how Jack is getting "sappy" about her.

For Ann's test, she dresses in her white "Beauty and the Beast" outfit. As some interested crewmen watch—in a phallically symbolic, vertically posed shot—Denham directs Ann to see something up high, something horrible, and to scream. . ."scream for your life."

Ashore on Skull Island, the landing party sees a massive wall and watches as gorilla-suited natives whirl in a ceremonial frenzy around a native girl, chanting, "Kong, Kong." The Chief spots Denham, brashly photographing the ceremony, and then Ann. The Chief offers to trade six of his women for this "woman of gold." The landing party makes a careful retreat, Denham whistling cockily.

That night, after Jack admits he loves Ann, she is kidnapped by the natives and tied to two poles inside the wall's gigantic gate. Ominous music, snarls, and the sound of trees being uprooted herald the coming of Kong. Ann's screams are for real as Kong picks up his prize and leaves before the arriving crewmen can rescue Ann.

Kong topples a number of the pursuing crewmen off a log across a deep ravine. Jack escapes by climbing down a vine to a safe spot on Kong's side of the ravine. Having survived Kong's rage, Jack and Denham speak across the ravine—Jack deciding to follow Kong while Denham returns to the ship for more men and guns.

Jack follows Kong to his cliff-edge aerie and, while the great ape battles a pterodactyl, helps Ann to escape. They race madly through the jungle toward the presumed safety of the village and wall.

Enraged at being denied his prize, Kong smashes through the gate to devastate the village, chewing and chomping natives until Denham hurls a gas bomb which knocks the ape unconscious.

In New York City, a sign proclaims "KING KONG—The Eighth Wonder of the World!" Denham has staged an exhibition of his subdued prize. A black-tie audience gasps as Denham raises the curtain on a chained (he appears to be crucified) Kong. But, angered by flashbulbs which seem to threaten Ann, Kong breaks free of the chains and, seizing Ann, escapes.

Finally ending up at the highest point in New York City, Kong climbs the Empire State Building as army biplanes are called out to attack him. Putting Ann down, Kong smashes one plane from the air, but at the cost of being struck many times by bullets. Kong admires Ann one more time; then, dying from his wounds, he falls to the street below.

Viewing the body of the great ape, Denham says, "It wasn't the airplanes . . . it was Beauty killed the Beast."

King Kong is a superlative fantasy film and the best of the "giant monster" movies. It seamlessly blends adventure, wonder, terror, exhilaration, and magical special effects to hold an audience spellbound in darkness. *Kong*, like all fantasy films, speaks to the child—the innocent—in all of us while mollifying the judgmental or adult part of our mind.

Kong is so unabashedly Freudian that to many it comes as a surprise to learn that Cooper and Schoedsack had nothing more meaningful in mind than a grand adventure movie that would entertain the audience while earning its producers—themselves—lots of money. Despite, or perhaps in addition to, their original intentions, Cooper and Schoedsack produced an almost mythic reaching out to the individual hidden in the mass consciousness of our shared symbolism. In ways we cannot fully understand, an 18-inch-high, rabbit-fur-covered model, through emotion-directing music and stop-motion animation, becomes more real than "reality" and speaks to our primitive "reptilian" brainstem of elemental fears.

Merian C. Cooper conceived the idea for *King Kong*, but Kong's father, the man who gave him motion and emotion, was Willis O'Brien—friends said OBie's expressions and body movements became Kong's. In many ways, O'Brien *was* Kong.

Willis Harold O'Brien was born to William and Minnie O'Brien on March 2, 1886 (exactly 47 years before *King Kong's* New York City premiere) in Oakland, California, where his father was the assistant district attorney. The young Willis, red-haired and blue-eyed, the fourth of six children, tried to run away from home several times. Bad investments impoverished his father when Willis was 11 years old, and he ran away "for good" when he was 14. Returning home at 17, he soon held a series of jobs, beginning as an office boy for an architect. He was then a sports cartoonist, a professional prize fighter, a Southern Pacific brakeman, a surveyor, and an assistant to the head architect for San Francisco's 1913 World's Fair.

O'Brien became interested in stop-motion animation at about this time. Stop-motion animation means positioning and readjusting objects by small increments and photographing the changes one frame at a time. When the individual frames are projected at sound speed, the animated objects seem to move on their own. Animated cartoons accomplish the same result by photographing thousands of drawings frame-by-frame and projecting them at 24 frames per second (sound speed).

OBie's interest led him to shoot a stop-motion test reel atop one of San Francisco's banks. Herman Wobber, a movie exhibitor, liked the test reel so much he gave OBie $5000 to produce *The Dinosaur and the Missing Link*. Thomas Alva Edison, impressed by the young filmmaker's talent, gave him a dollar per foot for the short and hired him to make other stop-motion shorts for his company's Edison Conquest Program of shorts and features. O'Brien made a series of films for the Edison company before it folded in 1917, his first being *R.F.D. 10,000 B.C.*

A pioneer film technician and cameraman, Herbert M. Dawley, gave OBie $3000 and three months to make a film based on his own script entitled *The Ghost of Slumber Mountain*. *Ghost*, released in 1919 by World Cinema Distributing Company of Fort Lee, New Jersey, grossed more than $100,000 and had a long run on Broadway at the Strang, proving OBie's stop-motion films could make money.

O'Brien and Watterson Rothacker joined forces to produce stop-motion novelty films. The men decided to make a feature film of Sir Arthur Conan Doyle's *The Lost World*, published in 1912. Seeking financing, Rothacker took the project to First National Pictures, where OBie worked with Fred W. Jackman, the head of the special effects department. OBie then was introduced to Ralph Hammeras, who had developed the glass (matte) shot—a way of combining painting on glass with live action, eliminating expensive sets (see the Appendix for more on mattes, glass shots, and traveling mattes).

Conan Doyle, in America to lecture on spiritualism, attended the annual meeting of the Society of American Magicians on June 2, 1922, taking with him a test reel of OBie's footage for the magicians. He would answer no questions concerning what they saw. A *Times* reporter who was present later wrote that Conan Doyle's "monsters of the ancient world or of the new world which he has discovered in the ether, were extraordinarily lifelike. If fakes, they were masterpieces."

First National premiered *World* at Broadway's Astor Theatre in February 1925. It was a hit and the first film to really integrate live-action and stop-motion techniques successfully. OBie's amazing climax showed London Bridge collapsing under the weight of a brontosaurus. "How was it done?" marveled a reporter for *The Boston Herald*. "How a naturally moving animal as big as a ship could chase real people down a real street and apparently break through a real bridge is too much for us. We'd better just believe it happened."

Strangely, O'Brien was not in demand after the release and success of *World* and was essentially unemployed until 1930, when RKO-Radio Pictures agreed to develop his next project, another prehistoric stop-motion picture called *Creation*.

With time on his hands, OBie set to work perfecting his method of split-screen matting. The result was a miniature rear projection system which could blend live-action, glass paintings, and miniature settings. Stop-motion dinosaurs could pass in front of live-action actors or sets as well as react to back-projected activities. OBie applied for a patent in 1928, and was granted the rights to his innovative new system in February 1933—just a month before the release of *King Kong*.

Producer-director Merian Caldwell Cooper was born in Jacksonville, Florida, on October 24, 1894. An adventurous young man, he left an appointment to the Naval Academy to work tramp steamers as an able seaman. Back on land, he was a reporter for the *Minneapolis Daily News*, then the *Des Moines Register-Leader*, and the *St. Louis Post-Dispatch*, which he left to join up with the Georgia National Guard chasing Pancho Villa in Mexico.

During World War I, Cooper went to France as a first lieutenant in the army aviation service and was shot down and taken prisoner by the Germans. Released from prison camp, he joined the Polish army in 1919 to fight the Bolsheviks and was again shot down and held prisoner.

Cooper went to work for the *New York Times* in 1921. Then Cooper and his friend Ernest B. Schoedsack, both weary of the routine of newspaper work, decided to make films together.

Ernest Beaumont Schoedsack, born in 1893, was a six-foot-five adventurer in the mold of Cooper. "Shorty" (as his friends called Schoedsack), Marguerite Harrison, and Cooper took two cameras and thousands of feet of film stock to Iran to film the annual migration of Baktiari tribesmen. After the three filmmakers edited their footage, it was released as a silent feature entitled *Grass* and became a major box office hit of 1925. Its success prompted another adventure film, *Chang*, in 1927.

Paramount was happily surprised by *Chang*'s success, and the studio quickly signed Cooper and Schoedsack to produce an adaptation of A.E.W. Mason's romantic adventure of cowardice and redemption, *The Four Feathers*. Cooper and Schoedsack shot background and "bridging" scenes in Africa. When they returned to Hollywood, the two adventurers used their African-shot footage to provide a realistic background for the romantic adventure plot filmed in the studios.

In addition to *King Kong*, *Son of Kong*, and *The Most Dangerous Game*, Cooper and Schoedsack teamed to make *The Last Days of Pompeii* (1935) and *Mighty Joe Young* (1949) with Willis O'Brien.

As a solo producer, Cooper was responsible for Fred Astaire and Ginger Rogers' first teaming in *Flying Down to Rio* (1933). Later John Ford and Cooper formed Argosy Productions and made a series of films together, most notably *She Wore a Yellow Ribbon* (1949) and *The Quiet Man* (1952). (See the Appendix for more Cooper and O'Brien films.)

If OBie could be considered to be "Kong," then surely Cooper is Carl Denham. Both Cooper and the film character Denham are particularly American types of entrepreneur-adventurers. Denham's talk of adding a girl as the love interest to his picture reflects the criticism of *Chang* offered by some movie executives and film critics. So, like Denham, in *King Kong* Cooper gives us Ann Darrow. Like Denham, Cooper will do what needs to be done to get his film made.

King Kong resulted from Merian C. Cooper's desire—obsession, almost—to make a film featuring a gorilla, a "Giant Terror Gorilla," as much as the influence of Douglas Burden's book, *The Dragon Lizards of Komodo*, and the stop-motion animation genius of Willis O'Brien. "To thrill myself," Cooper said in a 1933 press release explaining why he dreamed up *King Kong*. "To please the public, too, of course, but I also wanted something that I could view with pride and say, 'There is the ultimate in adventure.' It is beauty that kindles the spark of something the brute has never sensed before. He is amazed, he is subdued by this strange thing of beauty. So I decided it would be Beauty, personified by a girl, that would lead to King Kong's capture and, ultimately, to his death."

Late in 1931, RKO-Radio Pictures installed David O. Selznick (later

the producer of *Gone with the Wind*) as vice president in charge of production. One of Selznick's first acts was to hire Merian Cooper to evaluate prop-
erties RKO owned but which had not begun production. Cooper quickly
turned thumbs down on O'Brien's cherished project, *Creation*, telling
Selznick it didn't appear to be commercial enough to risk producing.

With *Creation* off the production schedule, O'Brien had to do
something fast. OBie had heard of Cooper's gorilla picture idea, so he and
artist Byron Crabbe painted a lurid scene showing a near-naked young
woman and a male adventurer threatened by a 12-foot gorilla. Intrigued by
OBie's ploy, Cooper reworked his ideas for the gorilla picture. For one
thing, he saw that he would need O'Brien's stop-motion animation techniques to make the film he wanted to shoot—he'd come to the realization
that using a real gorilla was out of the question.

Cooper took his ideas to Selznick, who allowed him to prepare a test
reel which would be shown to the board of directors, and to put O'Brien
on the payroll until the board made its decision. Until then, the film ten-
tatively went on the schedule as "Production 601."

For their showcase for the RKO bigwigs, Cooper and O'Brien chose
the sequences featuring Kong and the sailors at the log over the ravine, and
the Tyrannosaurus Rex. To guarantee the test footage would do the trick,
O'Brien and his crew made several hundred storyboard drawings visualiz-
ing each scene in the film. The test footage got its chance before the board
in 1932. The devouring of the sailors by the lizards and spiders at the bottom
of the ravine so impressed the executives that they immediately gave the
green light for Production 601 to proceed.

Cooper and O'Brien's gamble had paid off: They were going to make
their movie. Since O'Brien saw no reason to waste the time and hard work
that had gone into the *Creation* miniatures and animated sequences, he
convinced Cooper to work them into the new film's script.

Cooper and Schoedsack quickly signed Fay Wray, Bruce Cabot, and
Robert Armstrong to play the lead characters.

Cooper and Selznick discovered Bruce Cabot when the young actor
made himself up as Zaroff for *The Most Dangerous Game* and sent the
photographs to RKO. Cabot got the role of Jack Driscoll after proving to
Cooper that he could climb down the rope hanging from the log bridge on
Stage 11. Before his role in *King Kong*, Cabot had played a few bit parts as
Jacques de Bujac; his real name was Etienne Pelissier de Bujac. Born into
a wealthy French-Indian family in Carlsbad, New Mexico, in 1904, Cabot
attended New Mexico Military Academy, Swanee Military Academy, and
New Mexico University.

Although *Kong* was Cabot's first real film, its lengthy production
schedule meant that his second feature, *Roadhouse Murder* (1932), was
released first.

Top: This preproduction sketch shows the mighty ape shaking the pursuing sailors off the log bridge across the ravine. *Bottom:* This Mario Larrinaga preproduction sketch shows the horrifying fate of the sailors at the bottom of the ravine after they fall from the log bridge. The electrifying stop-motion animated scene was edited from the film. Rumors persist that the footage survives in Manila and in other private collections, but there is no proof of this.

Bruce Cabot was no actor at the time he made *King Kong,* but he is so right for his part that his lack of refined acting skills is irrelevant. Physically, he looks the role, and he's able to invest Jack Driscoll with an air of easy grace.

Robert Armstrong, born Donald Robert Smith in 1890, was attending law school at the University of Washington when he decided to forego law to join a touring vaudeville company. Armstrong is best known for his bravura playing of the role of Carl Denham, the man who stalks and captures Kong and has the movie's memorable last line. As Denham, Armstrong gave a strong performance — grand but never excessive.

Fay Wray, born in Canada in 1907, attended Hollywood High after her family moved to California. A bit player at the age of 16, she moved up to starring roles in Hal Roach comedies and Universal westerns and played the lead in Eric von Stroheim's *The Wedding March* (1928). Like Robert Armstrong, Fay Wray also appeared in *The Most Dangerous Game.* Her other genre films include *Doctor X* (1931), *The Vampire Bat* (1933), and *The Mystery of the Wax Museum* (1933), which was remade numerous times, most notably in 1953 in 3-D as *The House of Wax,* starring Vincent Price. (For more about the cast of *Kong,* see the Appendix.)

Edgar Wallace, a popular English writer, arrived in the United States in November or December of 1931 to write original scripts for RKO. Cooper, impressed by Wallace's fast and facile writing, arranged for Wallace to script his gorilla film. While Cooper favored the title *Kong,* Wallace suggested *King Ape.* Early RKO posters for *King Kong* bear the title *Kong.*

Wallace died of pneumonia on February 10, 1932, after having worked on the script for only two months. While little of his effort remains in the finished film, a 110-page copy of the scenario he prepared survives in England.

Cooper and Schoedsack next hired James Creelman to write the screenplay, but were soon dissatisfied with his efforts. The ideas he contributed to the story remain in the film, however.

In desperation, Cooper gave the script to Ruth Rose (Mrs. Ernest Schoedsack) to tackle. The daughter of a major theatrical producer and dramatist, Ruth Rose grew up with the theater. After a fling at stage acting, she joined the New York Zoological Society's tropical research station at Kartabo, British Guiana. Her theater background and knowledge of Broadway speech, combined with her familiarity with the dangers and rigors of life in tropical jungles, gave authority to her handling of the New York and expeditionary scenes.

One of Cooper's contributions to the screenplay was the "Old Arabian proverb" at the film's beginning.

The final shooting script, despite Edgar Wallace's well-publicized

The natives whirl in ceremonial frenzy outside the gates of the massive wall which
keeps Kong and the other prehistoric monsters on the other side from escaping.
Originally built for De Mille's *The King of Kings* in 1927, the wall perished as part
of the burning of Atlanta sequence in *Gone with the Wind.*

contributions and James Creelman's ideas, was the work of Ruth Rose.
Cooper later insisted that Edgar Wallace didn't write a word of *King Kong.*
Selznick wrote to Cooper saying, ". . . But the circumstances of [Wallace's]
death complicated the writing credits, and I think we were in agreement
that his name would be used and would indeed be helpful."

Most of *King Kong* was filmed in RKO's studios — no real jungle could
match the eerie correctness of the stage jungle, its strange and smothering
plant life enhanced by the many glass matte paintings contributed by Mario
Larrinaga and Byron L. Crabbe. Like *Forbidden Planet* (1956), set on an
alien world, *King Kong's* sense of wonder and displacement came not from
real locations dressed to look otherworldly but from a stylistic artificiality
that placed the film somewhere in a twilight zone of the imagination.

Apart from the beach scenes on Skull Island, which were filmed near
San Pedro, most of the live action was shot at the RKO-Pathé studio at
Grower Street and Culver City, built in 1918 by pioneer filmmaker Thomas
H. Ince and acquired by RKO in 1931. It was here that Cooper found the
standing skeleton of a monstrous gate Cecil B. De Mille had constructed
in 1927 for his life of Christ, *The King of Kings.* Here was Kong's wall and
gate already built but for the two immense doors in the center that the film

required. Cooper had the doors and sliding bolt constructed and built the native village in miniature in front of the wall.

Cooper was just as lucky in having the jungle he needed for *King Kong* handed to him on a platter: In May 1932, $200,000 was alloted to construct a vast jungle set on Stage 11 for the filming of Cooper and Schoedsack's *The Most Dangerous Game.*

Game was directed by Schoedsack, while both Cooper and Schoedsack received directing credit for *King Kong.* Since the films were in simultaneous production on Stage 11, Cooper had to direct most of *King Kong* between takes of Schoedsack's direction of *Game* and at night. The two productions also shared the acting services of Fay Wray and Robert Armstrong. Miss Wray had to switch from being a brunette in *Game* to being a blonde in *Kong.* Robert Armstrong often had to quickly change from wearing a tuxedo to sporting a safari jacket as he shuttled between the two productions.

Cooper's vision of Kong was that of a brute — a massive king in a kill-or-be-killed primitive world brought down by a fatal flaw: a weakness for beauty. Cooper directed the scenes of Kong crushing and chewing the natives. Both O'Brien and Schoedsack deplored this excessive violence, believing that Kong's cruelty lost him a measure of audience sympathy and identification. Indeed, most of the writers and critics who have praised Kong's sympathetic character have done so on the basis of viewing edited versions of the film. Kong's stompings and chewings, removed from the film's 1938 re-release, were not restored until Janus Films acquired *King Kong* and inserted the missing footage in 1971.

As co-director, Schoedsack encountered few serious problems during the shooting, but one of the more unpleasant involved Bruce Cabot. Cabot got drunk before he was to shoot the scenes aboard the ship where the crew searches for the kidnapped Ann Darrow. After Cabot performed a drunken jig in front of Schoedsack, the director twice slapped him hard across the face. Cabot soon sobered up and shooting resumed.

Willis O'Brien brought to *King Kong* his technical crew from *Creation.* Besides their marvelous glass mattes, Larrinaga and Crabbe also provided full "storyboards" visually detailing each camera shot to show the crew how each scene would look.

Carroll Sheppird checked the alignment of the various mattes and collected data on all exposed film so the effects footage would match the live-action plates. Orville Goldner kept the many miniature sets in good condition and saw that they were always ready for the day's shooting.

E.B. "Buz" Gibson was O'Brien's chief assistant animator, and Marcel Delgado the chief model maker. O'Brien had met Delgado in 1923 while attending night classes at the Otis Art Institute. O'Brien had offered the 20-year-old Delgado $75 a week to come to work for him. Delgado — for some reason that he has admitted escapes him — said no, even though at the time he was making only $18 weekly. O'Brien took Delgado to the studio and showed him the workshop and tools which would be his if he came to work for him. Finally, the young man accepted and spent the next several years making dinosaurs for *The Lost World*.

As the chief model maker on *King Kong*, it was Delgado who sculpted the two 18-inch-high, full-body models of the gorilla. Using clay sculpture as a guide, Delgado then constructed a steel armature based on OBie's design. The model maker next applied muscles, forming them from foam rubber and cotton. Over the musculature, Delgado built up layer upon layer of latex rubber for the dinosaurs and strips of rabbit fur glued onto the built-up muscles for the two Kong models.

Delgado had warned that the rabbit fur would cause animation problems. Each time the 18-inch-high Kong was touched, the animator's fingers left a mark or ripple on the fur. Thus while one of the model Kongs would be in front of the camera, filming, Delgado was tightening the screws in the second and grooming it for the next day's shooting.

At times, in the jungle for instance, the scale was one inch equals one foot, producing an 18-foot-tall Kong on screen. This was fine for the jungle but not nearly as impressive in the canyons of New York. For the city scenes, Cooper and Schoedsack reluctantly decided on a scale which made Kong appear to be 24 feet high. They hoped the audience would be too caught up in the film's headlong pace to notice the size difference.

For close-ups of Kong, OBie's technicians built a huge bust of the ape's head and shoulders. A frame of wood, metal, cloth, and wire was covered with rubber and the pruned skins of 40 bears. With three operators inside and three outside, the bust could be operated to make the eyes, eyelids, mouth, lips, and nose move in a thoroughly lifelike manner. For the close-up scenes of Ann in Kong's paw, a full-size arm and hand were built and mounted on a crane. Miss Wray would be placed in the hand, its fingers tightened around her, and the whole thing raised about ten feet in the air. Miss Wray would kick and struggle — apparently to be free, though in reality to *hang on* — until the fingers loosened to the point where the whole contraption had to be lowered to the studio floor and readjusted.

For the scene in which Kong gently peels off Ann's outer garments and sniffs them, a blending of the 18-inch-high Kong model and the full-size hand and arm was required. As previously shot footage of Kong going through the motions was played on a movieola, Cooper directed a stagehand to pull a series of nearly-invisible strings which held parts of Ann's clothing together. When the two pieces of film were combined optically, it appeared Kong was pulling the clothing off his terrified captive. The scene was written and animated by OBie. Wray, however, refused to end the scene nearly naked and wore underclothing to protect her modesty.

This composite shot shows Kong, a king atop his cliffside aerie, as he kills the pterodactyl which tried to carry off his prize—the cringing Ann Darrow.

To complement O'Brien's patented rear screen process, Sidney Saunders, supervisor of RKO's paint department, perfected a 16' × 20' flexible rear projection screen which produced an image 20 percent more brilliant while reducing "hot spot" tendencies by over 50 percent. The Dunn traveling matte process was used to combine foreground and background action. Simply stated, this means a blue object can be made to disappear when viewed through a blue filter or to stand out when viewed through a filter other than blue. Frank D. Williams' traveling matte process, perfected by mid-1932, was also used since it permitted white light to be used in the foreground action.

Kong's ascent up the side of the Empire State Building was animated by assistant animator Buz Gibson, who carefully positioned the miniature Kong for each frame-by-frame shot. Some critics (notably Steve Vertlieb in *The Girl in the Hairy Paw*) have written that this scene was accomplished by a man in an ape suit—Charles Gemora, veteran "chimp" actor, is the name mentioned most frequently. The truth is that *no* man in a "monkey suit" was ever used in any scenes in *King Kong*; O'Brien was too much the perfectionist to ever allow such heresy.

One marvelous miniature set reproduced a New York street complete with elevated train tracks, trains, and advertising posters trumpeting *Chang* and "Denham's Monster." The train engineer's point-of-view shot of Kong destroying the tracks was accomplished by putting the camera on a dolly and moving it toward the Kong model one frame at a time. Sophisticated computer-controlled effects cameras can achieve the same effect today, but it was invented by OBie, who first used it in *The Ghost of Slumber Mountain.*

Real navy biplanes from Floyd Bennet Field were filmed executing various dives and other attack manuevers, then skillfully intercut with models ranging in size from four to sixteen inches in wingspan and "flown" on piano wire. The flight commander and his co-pilot seen in close-up were Cooper and Schoedsack, who cast themselves after Cooper remarked, "We should kill the sonofabitch ourselves."

The special effects work in *King Kong* took over a year of hard work for O'Brien and his technical crew to execute. *Kong* was OBie's first sound stop-motion animated film, and the industry's standard of 24-frames-per-second film speed meant an increase of 50 percent in animation time over the old silent standard of 18 frames per second.

The marriage of music and image in *King Kong* gives the film a dimension lacking in many other fantasy movies. Critic Robert Fiedel, in *The Girl in the Hairy Paw,* argues that "Steiner's score . . . reaches our innermost feelings making us aware of Kong's soul, and thereby generates the great sympathy and audience identification which sets *KK* apart from the long legacy of prehistoric monster films. The score, in essence 'believes' in the screen narrative and conveys this 'belief' immediately to our own subconscious despite our intellectual objections."

Maximilian Raoul Walter Steiner was born in Vienna on May 10, 1888, and received his formal musical education at the Imperial Academy of Music, winning a gold medal for completing the course in only one year. Steiner arrived in America in 1914 and for the next 15 years worked as a conductor, arranger, orchestrator, and concert pianist. It was RKO's head of production, William Le Baron, who hired Steiner and brought him to Hollywood. Steiner arrived on Christmas day, 1929, and began working as an arranger in RKO's new music department for $450 a week. Between 1929 and 1936, when he left RKO to work at Warner Bros., he scored nearly 140 films.

While Steiner was excited about the musical possibilities for *Kong,* the studio bosses had little enthusiasm for anything about the film. Thinking that the gorilla looked phony and that the public wouldn't buy it, they told Steiner to use old tracks so they wouldn't have to put any money into the music. But Cooper approached Steiner, told him to write his best score, and offered to pay for the orchestra out of his own pocket.

In *Music for the Movies,* Tony Thomas notes, "Steiner took him at his word, he brought in an 80-piece orchestra and ran up a bill for $50,000. But it was worth every penny because it was his score that literally makes the film work. As soon as the audience hears that three-note theme—those three massive, darkly-orchestrated descending chords it knows it is in for a fantastic experience. The score . . . limns the frightful giant gorilla but it also does something else—it speaks for the streak of tenderness in the monster."

Cooper knew he got his money's worth from Steiner and arranged for the composer to get a bonus. Shortly before his death in 1972, Steiner fondly recalled *King Kong* as one of his favorite film scores.

Max Steiner's score has individual *leitmotifs* for Kong, Ann Darrow, and other characters and settings. The Kong motif is direct and powerful—it establishes Kong as the "Brute" Cooper perceived him to be. A descending "Ann Darrow" motif follows Kong's, reinforcing the Beauty and the Beast theme. At the film's climax, as Kong realizes his death is near, the "Ann Darrow" motif accompanies Kong's gentle handling of his love object. The score mourns for Kong's loss of love and life as he slips from the pinnacle of New York's tallest skyscraper. The music resolves Kong's fall and emphasizes his death. (For more about the music, see the Appendix.)

Murray Spivack, RKO's 31-year-old director of sound effects, had the job of giving voice to creatures that existed only on celluloid or in the dim past. For Kong's roar, Spivack recorded the roars of great cats at the Selig Zoo and then played them backward, slowing the tape down an octave, and finally recording them again. He took the peaks and pieced them together to get a sustained roar, because, as he noted, the roars of an animal that size had to be much longer than the sounds any real animal might make. Spivack also added a "tail" to the roar to make it fade naturally rather than cutting off abruptly as an artificial roar might do in less careful hands.

Spivack accomplished Kong's breast-beating by hitting assistant Walter G. Elliot on the chest with a tymp-stick while another assistant held a microphone to Elliot's back. For Kong's fight with the Tyrannosaurus, Spivack mixed the sounds of a compressed air machine, the screams of a puma, and his own throaty screeches to produce the "thunder lizard's" hissing cries. Spivack also supplied the horribly realistic screams of the sailors falling off the log. His unnerving cries were so effective that they were also used as the shrieks and moans of the shipwrecked sailors being devoured by sharks in *The Most Dangerous Game*.

The sound effects were added after filming had wrapped up. Fay Wray's screams—for which she became famous—were recorded in a single session and dubbed into the appropriate places on the soundtrack.

In *Film Comment*, critic Robin Wood discusses the link between films and dreams—"the embodiment of repressed desires, tensions, fears that our conscious mind rejects." Wood describes the "monster" in these films as reflecting society's basic fears and as a threat to the social norms of the heterosexual monogamous couple and the family.

In *The Dragons of Eden*, Carl Sagan muses that perhaps it was the terror induced by snakes, reptiles, and dinosaurs—the "dragons" of his title—

that helped bring about the evolution of human intelligence. Sleep began to play an important part in our ancestors' lives since to be awake and about at night would have been dangerous and frightening for the visually oriented primates whose functioning depended on the light of day.

Early in dreaming sleep, the dreamer may review the events of the day, but later, in the wee hours of the long night, dreams of snakes and dragons are astir in the brain. It is the time of nightmares. *King Kong* takes place almost entirely after the sun has left the world—the time of dreams and of things that go bump in the night. The entire movie may be viewed as a dream. It encompasses our fears of snakes; of falling; of being devoured, crushed, or suffocated.

King Kong has its own reality—a plastic one, in which time is compressed and expanded. Its errors of scale (Kong sometimes 18 feet tall, sometimes 24 feet tall) are characteristic of dreams, where objects may vary greatly in size. O'Brien's frame-by-frame animation gives Kong an air of unreality as his movements appear jerky. Even the film's "mistakes," such as the rippling of the miniature Kong's fur which caused Delgado and the RKO executives so much distress, contribute to the dreamlike state.

Movies affect the right hemisphere of our brain—where music, emotion, visual acuity, and most nonverbal functions reside—more than our verbal, analytical left hemisphere. Movies are emotional and right-hemisphere; logic is left-hemisphere.

King Kong, therefore, is a monster from the id. The viewer roots for him because the great ape does what so many of us would like to do: run amok, smash and destroy, be a giant gone berserk, taking revenge against civilization and its stifling rules of behavior. It is a canon of popular culture, however, that civilization must triumph over the impulses of the unrestrained libido. It wasn't the planes that got him; 'twas Society killed the Beast.

The novelization was published in 1933 by Grosset & Dunlap; the copyright was received in 1932 and assigned to Merian C. Cooper. The novel, an unremarkable work, was written by an old newspaper man and friend of Cooper, Delos W. Lovelace, from the screenplay.

The notable differences between the novelization and the film result from the book being written before the final release print of the film was ready. The novel, therefore, has scenes later trimmed from the film, including Cooper and O'Brien's original sequence of events at the log bridge. In the novel, the men are prevented from advancing across the log by Kong *and* from retreating by an angry triceratops—something not in the film. Also in the novel but missing from the film is the gruesome fate of the sailors, devoured by spiders, lizards, and giant centipedes—the most electrifying footage from OBie and Cooper's test reel.

To spare Ann a fate worse than death, the Jack Driscoll of the novel prepared to kill Ann with his knife should Kong threaten to recapture them. The novel's New York scenes have Kong going directly to the Empire State Building after his escape from the theatre.

An oddity, the novel lay forgotten and out of print until the publicity surrounding Dino De Laurentiis' ill-advised remake. Ace Books, a subsidiary of Grosset & Dunlap, issued a paperback edition with cover art by Frank Frazetta in 1976.

A sneak preview of *King Kong* was held in San Bernardino in late January 1933. The movie elicited all the excitement and enthusiasm Cooper could have hoped for, except for the scene with the spiders, centipedes, and lizards. The scene was so terrifying that many in the audience got up and left, while those who stayed were so affected by the graphic horror that they kept up a steady stream of comments for several minutes, completely forgetting about the plight of Fay Wray.

In *American Film*, Ron Haver quotes Cooper as saying, "It stopped the picture cold. So, the next day back at the studio, I took it out myself. OBie was heartbroken; he thought it was the best he'd done, and it was, but it worked against the picture so out it came."

King Kong had a half-million-dollar budget, but Cooper and Schoedsack brought the film in for just under $435,000. Once the studio accountants had tacked on all the usual studio "overhead," including all the *Creation* pre-production costs, the official cost rose to between $650–670,000.

NBC aired a 30-minute radio program on February 10, 1933, that announced the coming of *King Kong*. Apparently, it and all the other advertising gimmicks worked because, according to an ad in the trades: ". . . New York dug up $89,931 in four days (March 2, 3, 4, 5) to see 'King Kong' at Radio City, setting a new all-time world's record for attendance of *any* indoor attraction."

King Kong, more than a mere giant monster movie, has remained one of the world's favorite films. WWOR-TV in New York City plays it every Thanksgiving to high ratings. Prints of the film are in constant and wide circulation. A crisp new CAV-mode laserdisc release narrated by Ron Haver, with slow motion and background information on the special effects, has attracted the attention of film scholars and film buffs alike.

King Kong is so good that it almost lives up to Denham's boast: "KING KONG—The Eighth Wonder of the World!"

Long live the King.

9. Lost Horizon:
The Hidden Paradise

I believe that you will live through the storm. And after, through the long age of desolation, you may still live, growing older and wiser and more patient. You will conserve the fragrance of our history and add to it the touch of your own mind. You will welcome the stranger, and teach him the rule of age and wisdom; and one of these strangers, it may be, will succeed you when you are yourself very old. . . . I see, at a great distance, a new world stirring in the ruins, stirring clumsily but in hopefulness, seeking its lost and legendary treasures. And they will all be here, my son, hidden behind the mountains in the Valley of the Blue Moon, preserved as by a miracle for a new Renaissance. . . .

—*The High Lama to Conway, from the novel.*

Lost Horizon, both novel and film, holds a special place in the hearts and minds of many people. Millions have loved the novel; millions more have cherished the film since its release in 1937, when it won two Oscars.

Neither film nor novel is a great work of art, yet each is beloved. The reason for this particular fantasy's hold on us—the wistful dream of a secret Shangri-La—is its promise of a long and productive life spent far away from the cares and worries of the everyday world. All fantasies represent an escape from reality, of course; that is their nature and their function. But James Hilton's fantasy adventure, and the film based on it by Frank Capra, is so romantically persuasive that the very name of the mythical lamasery hidden high in the mountains of Tibet has entered our day-to-day language and become a generic term. (Until President Eisenhower renamed the presidential retreat in the mountains of Maryland "Camp David" after his grandson, F.D.R. had called it "Shangri-La.")

The difficulty with this particular fantasy is that it is a defensive one—perhaps even one with an air of fatalism about it. The High Lama wishes Robert Conway, the protagonist, to assume the leadership of Shangri-La (it's a benign dictatorship) and wait for the predicted new "dark ages." Then, when the outside world is ready for wisdom and the fulfilling of the "Christian ethic," Conway and his disciples will bring a new age of harmony to the war-ravaged world.

120

As appealing as this prospect sounds on the surface, it is a bomb-shelter mentality that prepares for the worst while doing little or nothing to achieve the best. A man of Conway's supposed talents ought, it seems, to be doing what he can to prevent the coming age of darkness, not preparing to eschew any involvement with our doomed civilization. There is a saying, "It is better to light one candle than to curse the darkness."

Lost Horizon is, despite its muddled philosophy, a human and humanist film. Like *It's a Wonderful Life* (see Chapter 6), it exhibits all the strengths and weaknesses of its famous director, Frank Capra. Capra's films were simultaneously praised and damned for the tribute they paid to the common man, a metaphorical "little man" who embodied our country's best — patriotism; loyalty to family, friends, and country; common sense, idealism, down-to-earthness; and a faith in the ability of love and honor to transform and ennoble even the lowest of the low.

Honored in 1982 by the tenth annual Life Achievement Award from the American Film Institute, Capra has nonetheless been dismissed as a panderer to populist sentiments — a spreader of empty platitudes. There is much more to Frank Capra than what his detractors see. For one, Capra, in the words of Richard Schickel, can be labeled a "premature auteurist" for his "One man, one film" theory of filmmaking. For another, Capra, no matter how corny his sentiments (especially in his 1930s films) may seem, was a true believer in the values his films espoused.

While *Horizon* is atypical of Capra's films of the 30s — with its non–American setting and hero (who is no anonymous "common man") — it offers him plenty of opportunities to stress favorite themes: brotherhood, moderation, and sanctuary. Capra's religious faith, present but only implied in his other pictures, is made explicit when the High Lama (in a passage taken directly from the novel) tells Conway, "Then, my son, when the strong have devoured each other, the Christian ethic may at least be fulfilled and the meek shall inherit the earth."

Frank S. Nugent's review in the *New York Times* was upbeat and supportive, calling *Horizon* "a grand adventure film, magnificently staged, beautifully photographed and capitally played. . . . There is no denying the opulence of the production, the impressiveness of the sets, the richness of the costuming, the satisfying attention to large and small detail which makes Hollywood at its best such a generous entertainer."

Variety's "Abel." was enamored of the film, but wondered if the production could turn a profit. "So canny are the ingredients, singly and in combination, that where credulity mayhap rears its practical head, audiences will be carried away by the histrionic illusion, skill, and general Hollywood legerdemain which have so effectively captured the best elements in this saga of Shangri-La.

"*Lost Horizon* can take its place with the best prestige pictures of

the industry. It is also a cinch for money, but with such an overhead Columbia can call Capra a miracle man, as well as 'genius,' if this one gets out from
under. However, *Horizon* will undoubtedly do much for the studio's program and therein is the presumed justification of the cost."

In *America*, T.J. Fitzmorris wrote, "[It is] a superbly photographed and
highly imaginative production, acted with sufficient art and warmth to
make its more fantastic qualities understandable and palatable to the ordinary moviegoer." (Who, Mr. Fitzmorris apparently thinks, is a dunce.)

Among the negative reviews was one by Mark Van Doren in *The Nation*: "A brilliant beginning and a great deal of wonderful photography
throughout do not conceal the fact that the message of the movie is
shamefully soft and false."

Another naysayer was John Mosher in *The New Yorker*: "There are
beautiful flying scenes in this film and there are wild and terrifying bits of
struggle on mountain peaks and crags. In general, though, James Hilton's
readable little fantasy seems somewhat longish and wearisome on the
screen. I thought the old lama would go on talking forever. Ronald Colman
is quite businesslike, [but] somehow I couldn't quite see him turning into
a lama before our eyes."

Otis Ferguson's review in *The New Republic* didn't mince words: "[T]he
Master's hand was not steady on the throttle because in diving off the deep
end he . . . landed on the horns of a dilemma and laid a pretty terrific
egg."

Graham Greene, writing in *The Spectator*, calls *Horizon* "a very long
picture . . . and a very dull one once the opening scenes are over."

The positive notices outweighed the negative ones, however, including
this one by *Time's* anonymous reviewer: "Director Capra . . . devised one
of the most magnificent sets in cinema history. He had the good judgment
to leave the story almost exactly as it was written and the skill to match
author Hilton's verbal talent with pictorial subtlety."

The film begins with this long introduction:

> In these days of wars and rumors of war—haven't you ever dreamed
> of a place where there was peace and security, where living was not a
> struggle but a lasting delight?
> Of course you have.
> So has every man since Time began. Always the same dream.
> Sometimes he calls it Utopia—Sometimes the Fountain of Youth—
> Sometimes merely "that little chicken farm."
> One man had such a dream and saw it come true. He was Robert
> Conway—England's "Man of the East"—soldier, diplomat, public hero—
> Our story starts in the war-torn Chinese city of Baskul, where Robert
> Conway has been sent to evacuate ninety white people before they are
> butchered in a local revolution.
> Baskul—the night of March 10, 1935.

Panic at the airfield. Robert Conway (Ronald Colman) is first seen carrying a little girl clutching a teddy bear. Conway sets fire to the hangar to light the way for more planes. While Conway and the others board, the pilot is overcome by an unseen person or persons.

Safely in the air, the plane's passengers are Conway and his brother George (John Howard); Alexander P. Lovett, a paleontologist (Edward Everett Horton); Henry Barnard, an American (Thomas Mitchell); and Gloria Stone, a postitute (Isabel Jewell).

In the morning, Barnard discovers that they're flying west, not east—away from Shanghai. Conway and the others now realize they've been hijacked by a Chinese or Tibetan pilot.

They land at a remote village and armed tribesmen refuel the airplane; they're off again in minutes. The plane climbs higher and higher—10,000 feet, 14,000 feet, above 21,000 feet.

The plane makes a rough high-altitude landing. After Conway finds a map on the pilot, killed in the crash landing, which shows that they're in Tibet, George reveals his hysterical side, telling the others they're going to die.

Mysteriously, a party of climbers led by a man called Chang (H.B. Warner) arrives. Chang asks about the pilot and gives the survivors suitable clothing. A long climb brings them to an opening in the peaks—Shangri-La, a remote valley, sheltered by mountains.

They arrive at the lamasery, a lovely structure surrounded by birds, flowers, gardens, and courtyards. Conway sees a young caucasian woman who laughs when he stumbles.

After they've changed clothes in the lamasery, a banquet is laid out for the visitors. Chang joins them and, apart from telling them radio reception is impossible, answers few questions. They learn from Chang that porters, who live 500 miles away, are the only link to the outside world. Later, Conway tells George that the whole kidnapping was a deliberate act to get them into this place.

Chang tells Conway they're in the Valley of the Blue Moon and discusses Shangri-La's founder, Father Perrault, a Belgian priest who arrived there in 1713. Father Perrault amputated his own leg before realizing his injuries would have healed in Shangri-La, a place of long life and perfect health. Chang says that climate, diet, and the lack of struggle all contribute to longevity; outside lives are shorter—a sort of "indirect suicide."

George meets a mysterious "Russian" woman named Maria (Margo), and Conway observes Sondra (Jane Wyatt), the girl he saw on arrival, playing a piano. Later, Conway sees Sondra go riding and quickly follows. Losing him, Sondra takes a nude swim, leaving her clothes on a bush. Conway approaches on foot and a squirrel alerts Sondra. She watches while Conway makes a stick figure of her clothing and leaves.

The survivors of the plane crash gather for a banquet at the mysterious lamasery of Shangri-La. From left to right around the table: Edward Everett Horton as Alexander P. Lovett, Isabel Jewell as Gloria Stone, John Howard as George Conway, Ronald Colman as Robert Conway, and Thomas Mitchell as Henry Barnard. (Servant is unidentified.)

Over dinner, Barnard reveals that he is really Chalmers Briant, a stock manipulator wanted by the police. George then blurts out that they're prisoners before rushing off with a revolver. Shooting wildly at a servant, George is knocked out by a blow from his brother. Conway confronts Chang—who tells him he was just on his way to take Conway to the High Lama.

The High Lama (Sam Jaffe) is an incredibly old man who has lost a leg and must rely on crutches; immediately, Conway realizes he is the still-living Father Perrault, now over 250 years old. The High Lama, admitting he's admired Conway for years, tells the younger man he belongs in Shangri-La where he will have a long and productive life.

Conway learns Shangri-La is a repository of art and knowledge and, after the dark times to come, will promote a life based on one premise: "Be kind." Conway, overcome, kisses the High Lama's hand and leaves with much on his mind.

In the valley, Conway sees the everyday, ordinary life of Shangri-La: sheep being sheared and driven, women doing laundry in the stream, oxen being led, and Sondra teaching class. Sondra tells him she was born just outside, then brought in and raised by Father Perrault himself. Conway tells her he senses he belongs in Shangri-La, and she in turn tells him that he's always been a part of Shangri-La. They fall in love with each other.

Lovett tells Chang the place is utopia and asks his permission to organize geology classes for the children. Meanwhile, Barnard wants to put in a modern plumbing system.

Talking to Chang, Conway learns that Maria arrived in 1888; if she left Shangri-La, she'd revert to looking her real age. George asks Barnard, Gloria, and Lovett to leave with him, but they all refuse.

Conway reveals George's frustrations to the High Lama, who tells him his brother is now *his* problem—he's placing the future and destiny of Shangri-La in Conway's hands. The High Lama, who reveals he's dying, says he's waited for the right replacement: Robert Conway. Shangri-La will revive and restore the world under his leadership.

Smiling, the High Lama gently dies. A breeze ruffles the curtains and the candle goes out, symbolizing the departure of the great man's soul. Conway sits solemnly, unsure what to do.

During the funeral procession for Father Perrault, George confronts Conway with his intention to leave immediately. Conway tells George the whole story—and is mocked for his "madness" in believing such a tale without real proof.

When Conway learns Maria has bribed the porters, he says she can't go because she'll age rapidly. George sadly informs him that Maria is only 20 and, furthermore, badly *wants* to go. Told she'll be left behind, Maria begs to go, calling Father Perrault insane. Further, she says Chang desires her and tells everyone she's old when she isn't.

Confused, his resolve faltering, Conway suddenly makes up his mind to leave with George and Maria. Chang watches impassively as they leave; Sondra, in tears, runs after them, calling Conway's name.

Outside, the porters daily get further and further ahead of the tired trio. Eventually, firing guns at the stragglers for amusement, the porters unleash an avalanche which sweeps them to their deaths. Suddenly, George sees that Maria's face is now the face of an old crone; horrified, he dashes off and falls to his death.

Conway, alone, makes his way down the mountains and is found, unconscious, by villagers. Newspapers trumpet the news: *Conway—Found Alive in Chinese Mission*. Conway, suffering from amnesia, is on his way home with Lord Gainsford. A wire from Gainsford then reveals that Conway recovered his memory and jumped ship in Singapore. Back in London's St. George Club, Gainsford tells of pursuing Conway for ten months and gives a long account of Conway's subsequent adventures.

A solitary figure high on a mountainside turns out to be the missing Conway. We see his frost-covered face light up with joy as he finally peers in at his elusive goal—Shangri-La.

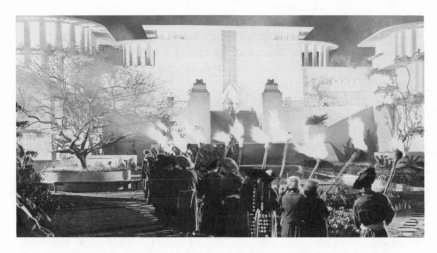

The nighttime funeral procession held for Father Perrault.

Frank Capra was born in Bisaquino, Sicily, in 1897. When he was six years old, on May 18, 1903, young "Cicco," his parents, and three of his six brothers and sisters were aboard the *Germania* on their way to Los Angeles and the promised land of America.

Young Frank stayed in school against the wishes of his family, but he worked hard nonetheless. His many jobs included two hours of early morning janitor work at school, playing a guitar at a local bistro, and "stuffing" copies of the *Los Angeles Sunday Times*.

After high school, Capra entered Caltech, in Pasadena, in 1915 (the school was then called Throop Polytechnic Institute). Again, because of his immigrant family's lack of money, young Frank worked long hours at a mind-boggling variety of part-time jobs while simultaneously pursuing his studies and winning the Freshman Scholarship Prize.

In 1917, Capra's equally hardworking father was killed when he was caught and crushed in the gears of his well pump. His death meant the loss of the family's farm and a return to city life for all of them.

Frank Capra graduated with a degree in Chemical Engineering in June 1918, and immediately enlisted in the United States Army. Instead of going to the front, Capra was assigned to teach mathematics at Fort Mason in San Francisco. After being released from the service, Capra couldn't find work as a chemical engineer and ended up doing odd jobs once again, this time including tutoring the son of a wealthy family.

For the next three years, Capra bummed his way across Arizona, Nevada, and California, selling photographs house-to-house, playing poker professionally, doing whatever was necessary to stay alive. These experiences would enrich and inform his later films about ordinary people.

By 1921, Capra, broke and disillusioned, drifted back to San Francisco. Then an incident worthy of any Frank Capra film occurred which changed the young man's life. Reading in a newspaper that a new movie studio was opening its doors, he went to the address given in the paper, only to find that the abandoned and ramshackle Jewish Athletic Club was the "studio's" site. Even more disheartening, the owner was a minor-league actor named Walter Montague, whose sincerest wish was to make a film of Kipling's "The Ballad of Fultah Fisher's Boarding House."

When Capra told the ham actor that he was from Hollywood, Montague assumed the young man meant he was a Hollywood director—a belief Capra did nothing to disabuse him of. Paid the magnificent sum of $75 to produce and direct Montague's one-reel film, Capra turned out a $1700 opus that not only worked, but also garnered respectable reviews ("...justified all claims made for it ... rapt attention ... all eyes on screen to the finish").

Next, Capra got a job in a film processing lab, a position he held until he was hired as idea man, editor, and gag writer for Bob Eddy comedies. Capra parlayed that into a job as comedy writer for Hal Roach's "Our Gang" series. When he stalled at that level, he jumped over to the Sennett studio as a writer and finally got his chance to direct when baby-faced comic Harry Langdon's regular director resigned in a dispute with the comedian. Capra directed two hit films in a row for Sennett and Langdon: *The Strong Man* and *Long Pants* (both 1926).

After the egotistical Langdon thought he could direct himself as Chaplin and Keaton did (he couldn't, because, as Capra pointed out, both those comic geniuses *created* their own screen personas), Capra struck out on his own, only to find he was blackballed after Langdon started the rumor that he, not Capra, had directed his films.

Capra finally accepted a job with Columbia Pictures, the "poverty row" studio headed by Harry Cohn. After churning out a number of profitable quickies for Cohn, Capra was given every director's dream: not only the money and time needed to make successful films, but also unprecedented artistic control. Cohn's theory was simple—if Capra wanted to trade salary and studio supervision for freedom, then Cohn would indulge him as long as his pictures were successful. In truth, Capra was more than merely "successful"; his string of comedy-drama hits established Columbia as a major studio to be taken seriously.

In 1934, working with a star who was being punished by Louis B. Mayer by being loaned out to a poverty-row studio (Clark Gable), Capra made one of his most popular and successful films, *It Happened One Night*. And one night in 1935, it happened that Capra's "road picture" won Oscars for Best Picture, Best Director, Best Actor (Gable), Best Actress (Claudette Colbert), and Best Screenplay (Robert Riskin).

It was while he was working on 1936's *Mr. Deeds Goes to Town* that Capra began pre-production on his next film—*Lost Horizon*.

Pocket Books' introduction to the forty-ninth paperback printing of the novel sums up the book's impact: "When *Lost Horizon* was first published in England, in 1933, James Hilton was an obscure author. His book had achieved only a quiet success. Then America's most influential critics read *Lost Horizon*. They fell in love with it. Readers rushed to buy. . . . In June, 1939, it became the first title in the first list published by Pocket Books, Inc. . . . For twenty-one and a half years it remained Pocket Book #1 through forty-six printings totalling nearly 2,000,000 copies."

The book was not generally available in the United States, however, until 1935. After its publication in America, the novel was touted by many critics, including Alexander Woollcott, who raved about its merits on his "Town Crier" radio program.

Harry Cohn invited Capra and others from the studio to attend a Stanford-U.S.C. football game in Palo Alto. Before boarding the train, Capra browsed through Union Station's newsstand for something to read. Spotting *Lost Horizon* and remembering Woollcott's laudatory review, Capra bought a copy and read it that night. By the morning, he was convinced that it would make a great film and asked Harry Cohn to buy it for him.

As Capra remembers in his autobiography, "I went on to tell [Cohn] that there was only one actor in the world to play the lead, Ronald Colman, and that the film would probably cost two million dollars. He dropped his fork."

Cohn appeased Capra by purchasing a six-month's option on the book, intent upon seeing how well *Mr. Deeds Goes to Town* did at the box office before commiting such an enormous sum on a fantasy. Since "*Mr. Deeds* went to town in a Brinks' money truck," as Capra put it, Cohn gave him the go-ahead—a courageous act considering that Cohn had to buck the studio's New York moneymen and no Columbia picture up to that time had cost more than $500,000.

The script would be written by Robert Riskin with, as usual, a great deal of collaboration by Capra. Riskin and Capra began their association on the Oscar-winning *It Happened One Night* and continued through *Mr. Deeds Goes to Town, Lost Horizon, You Can't Take It with You*, and *Meet John Doe*.

Capra talked about Riskin with Richard Schickel in *The Men Who Made the Movies:* "A director directs a writer by falling in love with and becoming friendly with him, and the two of them collaborate and the man becomes a part of a team. . . . And this was the case with Bob Riskin and I. We were great friends and loved each other. We were great audiences for each other. And we collaborated on all those stories we did with each

This shot shows some of the impressive architecture of Shangri-La. It's easy to see why art director Stephen Goosson won an Academy Award for his work on *Lost Horizon*.

other. . . . I can't say too much for Bob Riskin. He was the greatest screenplay artist that I've ever known—great ear for dialogue, and a great person to be around. And we had a symbiotic thing going between us. We created together. When that happens between a director and a writer, it is a wonderful thing for both."

Capra and Riskin settled in to begin the screenplay in a rented red-tiled adobe cottage at the La Quinta Hotel, near Indio, at the base of Santa Rosa Mountain. As Capra fondly recalled, "it was to be *our* Shangri-La. . . ."

Riskin and Capra reshaped the novel's story to add new dimensions to the characters and give them clear-cut reasons for their actions, including accepting or rejecting life at Shangri-La. Riskin added additional elements missing or in short supply in Hilton's novel, among them romance and humor.

To open up the novel (quite brief at 169 pages), Riskin (and uncredited collaborator Capra) added several characters not in Hilton's book. Hilton's obnoxious Mallinson was split into two characters: George Conway—Conway's selfish, cowardly, and impulsive younger brother—and Alexander P. Lovett, a fussbudget paleontologist.

One of Hilton's two female characters is the mysterious Lo-Tsen, who arrived in 1884 at the age of 18. Riskin and Capra kept Lo-Tsen's youthful appearance, and her (inexplicable) desire to escape Shangri-La, and gave that aspect of her to the script's newly created Maria. For the romantic side of Lo-Tsen (only vaguely developed in the novel), Riskin created the youthful (she's only 30) Sondra, Conway's love interest.

The other major character change from novel to film was changing the book's homely spinster Christian missionary, Miss Brinklow, into the glamorous, but consumptive, Gloria Stone — a prostitute.

The novel begins with a prologue (as did the film initially, until Capra threw out the first two reels) in London, where the strange story of a lost airplane carrying "glory Conway," is briefly discussed. Later, Rutherford, a novelist, tells the book's narrator a story about Conway being found. Conway had lost his memory but, in the presence of Rutherford, regained it.

Rutherford and Conway spoke for hours, and Conway told him an amazing story, which the writer committed to paper. Rutherford leaves the manuscript with the narrator for him to read. The manuscript tells Robert Conway's adventure.

Conway finally meets the High Lama in Chapter 7. The dialogue runs 21 pages — in which it is revealed that the High Lama is Father Perrault, and the purpose of Shangri-La is explained. Later, they meet again, and this time the High Lama tells Conway he is going to die and into Conway's hands will be placed "the heritage and destiny of Shangri-La."

Conway's story — and Rutherford's manuscript — end with Conway's, Mallinson's, and Lo-Tsen's escape from Shangri-La. In the epilogue, the narrator and Rutherford meet again. Rutherford tells him he never saw Conway again, or found any way into the mountains that might harbor Shangri-La. However, Rutherford reports finding a doctor who saw the woman who'd brought Conway to the hospital when he'd lost his memory. She was old, "most old of any one I have ever seen," the doctor reported.

In trying to remain true to Hilton's novel, Riskin and Capra produced a screenplay nearly 200 pages in length. While much new dialogue was added in the screenplay, Riskin and Capra were remarkably faithful to many of the book's original exchanges:

MALLINSON
We want to return to civilization as soon as possible.
CHANG
Are you so very certain that you are away from it?

After Conway asks Chang if there were never disputes about women, Chang says: "Only very rarely, because it would not be considered good manners to take a woman that another man wanted."

CONWAY
Supposing somebody wanted her so badly that he didn't care a damn whether it was good manners or not?

CHANG

Then, my dear sir, it would be good manners on the part of the other man to let him have her, and also on the part of the woman to be equally agreeable. You would be surprised, Conway, how the application of a little courtesy helps to smooth out these problems.

By the time production began, the lengthy script had been whittled down to under 180 pages. As filming proceeded, only a third of Riskin and Capra's script was actually shot, and additional scenes—both scripted and improvised (like Edward Everett Horton mugging into the mirror)—were added.

Unwisely, Riskin's original script faithfully kept the novel's long initial meeting between Conway and the High Lama. This 21-page sequence from the novel ran 16 minutes in the film until it was more than halved and an additional scene shot to provide the lost information with more brevity (more about this later).

While Riskin began adapting the novel to screenplay form, Capra began an enormous amount of research into the little-known land of Tibet, its people, and its lamaseries. Fortunately for the production, Capra was able to hire Harrison Forman, a famed explorer who had taken hundreds of photographs of Tibet, as *Horizon's* technical advisor. From these still pictures would come the sets, costumes, and musical instruments of Shangri-La.

The Tibetan musical instruments were loaned to the production by a California collector named Henry Eichman. The "Tibetans" who used them in the film were Pala Indians (since anthropologists believe American Indians crossed over to North America from Asia via a land bridge thousands of years ago). The small Tibetan horses seen in the film were "haired up" Shetland ponies, and the yaks were yearling steers covered by long-haired blankets.

Stephen Goosson was hired as art director, and it was he who designed and built the impressive sets. A full-scale Tibetan village was constructed outside Hollywood, at Lake Sherwood, in a natural basin that became the small lake—with a bridge across it—seen in the film.

While more than 140 workers labored to construct the village, Goosson oversaw the building of the lamasery exterior which was rising on the Columbia "ranch." Stills of this impressive set suggest an otherworldly atmosphere, yet a certain feeling of familiarity creeps into one's consciousness. If the lamasery seems like something we've seen before, it's because it is: Columbia artist Cary Odell based his drawings on the buildings of famed architect Frank Lloyd Wright.

This enormous set alone, including auxiliary buildings, cost nearly a quarter of a million dollars, and the main façade was an impressive 1,000 by 500 feet.

Robert Conway (Ronald Colman) meditates in the garden of the lamasery. This massive set was constructed outside Hollywood, at Lake Sherwood, and cost nearly a quarter of a million dollars.

Given the realism supplied by his expensive and impressive sets, Capra was concerned that his scenes aboard the hijacked airplane and in the mountain passes of Tibet be just as realistic. This meant seeing the actors' breath as they spoke their lines. But how to achieve that effect? Early attempts with tiny chips of dry ice contained in holders in actors' mouths turned out to be both dangerous and unconvincing.

Then Capra and assistant director Art Black discovered the Los Angeles Ice and Cold Storage Warehouse in the industrial heart of L.A. Capra was knocked out by what they found — an insulated cold storage facility 150 feet long, 75 feet wide, and 25 feet high. Inquiring about renting the warehouse, Capra discovered that it contained several artificial-snow machines, contraptions that took blocks of ice, ground them up into fine snow, and blew the snow over the fish stored there.

It cost the production $1,000 a day to rent the warehouse for the six weeks of shooting; the over-$40,000 cost was well worth it. All "cold" scenes were shot in the warehouse, over a period of six weeks, while outside Los Angeles sweltered in 90°-plus temperatures.

While the facility was comfortably large, its space was finite. For the mountain-climbing scenes, the actors would climb jury-rigged sets with certain backdrops for one take; then the crew would reassemble the sets and backdrops to make it appear in the next shot that the actors were further up or down the mountain.

The entire Valley of the Blue Moon had to be seen in several long shots, so Capra had the lamasery and its peaceful village constructed in miniature by E. Roy Davidson of Columbia's special effects department.

Other notable effects included scenes in the airplane where Conway goes from one side of the plane to the other, looking out and seeing mountains on both sides. This was accomplished by double rear projection.

The avalanche which swept the porters to their deaths was achieved by filling huge bins with artificial snow and ordinary cornflakes. A trapdoor would be opened on cue and down would come the "snow."

Capra had been impressed with Jack Dawn's skill in making the American actors in *The Good Earth* look Oriental, so the make-up artist was paid approximately $3,000 for making 43-year-old Sam Jaffe look like a centuries-old High Lama. The makeup took ten hours of work over several days of shooting, but much of Dawn's work was modified because, after seeing the first scenes shot, film editor Gene Milford opined that Jaffe looked like a monkey.

After cigarette paper, then dry oatmeal, then fish skin were utilized to give Jaffe the crinkly, wrinkly appearance of extreme old age, Dawn and his assistants cast the actor's face to get two built-in pieces, one for each side of the High Lama's face. Johnny Wallace and Charles Huber, the film's regular makeup artists, handled the chore of creating and applying old-age makeup to Jaffe's hands.

Capra, of course, had Ronald Colman in mind for the role of Robert Conway from the beginning, but casting the others was not as simple. Early newspaper clippings had Capra veteran Walter Connolly set for the High Lama's role as early as June 1935. Since Connolly had a prominent paunch, his casting as the High Lama would have been ludicrous. Instead, as Capra recalled, "I wanted Connolly to play the fugitive industrialist who had fleeced his stockholders, not the High Lama. But Connolly was committed to another assignment." (Columbia boss Harry Cohn did order tests shot with Connolly as the High Lama—wearing a beard which made him look like a jolly old Saint Nick or an aged Friar Tuck!)

Fritz Leiber was tested for the High Lama's role, as was a 90-year-old ex-theatre actor living in the San Gabriel Valley. The old man filmed a test with star Ronald Colman and was pronounced perfect as was—no makeup would even be necessary. When Capra phoned his home with the good news, the old gentleman's nurse-housekeeper was thrilled. An hour later she called back with the news that the old man had been so excited that Hollywood had finally beckoned that the shock of his good fortune killed him; he passed away with a smile on his face. (This was presumably A.E. Anson, but several sources, including Capra himself, are not clear as to his actual identity.)

Henry B. Walthall, the little colonel in Griffith's *The Birth of a Nation*, died before he could be tested. Capra next tested Sam Jaffe, a youngish actor originally on the stage. After recalling that the microphones straining to pick up Jaffe's words—he made his voice all but inaudible during the screen test—were also picking up gurgles from the crew's stomachs, Capra in his autobiography notes, "Jaffe's words were weak but the zeal behind them was strong—the last words of a prophet passing on his vision. We knew instantly we had found our High Lama."

Since Walter Connolly was committed to another project and unavailable to play the part of Barnard, the fugitive financier, the role went to veteran character actor Thomas Mitchell, a former reporter. Mitchell, who was just achieving recognition, would win an Academy Award for playing the drunken doctor in the classic western, *Stagecoach,* and lasting fame as Gerald O'Hara, Scarlett's father in *Gone with the Wind* (both 1939).

Edward Everett Horton was signed to play Lovett after Capra called him and assured him that the part, which didn't exist in the novel, was being written expressly for him.

John Howard (born John Cox) was cast as Conway's selfish and cowardly brother George, another role not in Hilton's novel.

The part of Sondra went to 24-year-old Jane Wyatt, making only her third film. Miss Wyatt gained stardom not as a film actress, but as Margaret Anderson in the quintessential family TV sitcom *Father Knows Best* (1954–1960). Later, she was to play Mr. Spock's human mother, Amanda, in both TV and film versions of the perennially popular *Star Trek*.

Spanish-born actress Margo (Maria Marguerita Guadelupe Boldao y Castilla), played the ill-fated Maria, whose lies convince Conway to leave Shangri-La against his better judgment.

H.B. Warner (Henry Byron Warner-Lickford), a British-born actor of immense dignity (he played Christ in the 1927 silent, *King of Kings)* was given the role of Chang, the High Lama's majordomo. He also appeared in Capra's *Mr. Deeds Goes to Town* and *It's a Wonderful Life.*

Another *Horizon* participant who would rejoin Capra for *Wonderful Life* was composer Dimitri Tiomkin. Born in St. Petersburg, Russia, Tiomkin was taught to play the piano as a small child and studied music at the St. Petersburg Conservatory of Music. He earned his first money accompanying silent films on piano in St. Petersburg theaters. After the Russian Revolution, Tiomkin moved to Berlin and moved in with a Russian pianist named Michael Kariton, forming a duo piano team which performed in Paris before sailing to America in 1925.

After marrying Albertina Rasch, who produced short ballet sequences for sound films in Hollywood, Tiomkin gave piano recitals in Los Angeles. One man who heard him play and was intrigued by him was Frank Capra.

Capra recalled Columbia's studio executives being adamantly opposed to using such an inexperienced composer for their expensive gamble. To hedge his bets, Capra hired *King Kong* composer Max Steiner to conduct Tiomkin's score, knowing that if Steiner found anything wrong with the score, he would not hesitate to rewrite it himself.

Tiomkin visited the set often during the months-long shooting schedule, constantly trying out themes and subtle variations. While the picture was being edited, Tiomkin even wrote music for the funeral procession sequence to a particular rhythm requested by editor Gene Milford.

Pleased by Tiomkin's score, Capra gave the Russian books filled with American music — spirituals, hymns, cowboy ballads — so that he could use the composer again on his resolutely American films. Going beyond the material Capra gave him, Tiomkin so thoroughly absorbed American music that he was not only able to write scores for Capra films like *Wonderful Life, You Can't Take It with You,* and *Mr. Smith Goes to Washington,* but also for many Westerns like *High Noon* and *Gunfight at the O.K. Corral.* Tiomkin's music for 1955's John Wayne–starrer, *The High and the Mighty,* won him an Academy Award.

When filming was completed, the thousands of feet of raw film were edited into a version running nearly three hours. After a projection room screening, scheduled mainly to see how Tiomkin's score worked, the executives in attendance were wowed by what they'd seen. Even Harry Cohn, famous for his wriggling during unendurable movies, kept his posterior firmly in his seat.

The first preview with an audience was held in Santa Barbara in November of 1936. During the first ten minutes, the audience began first to titter and then to laugh. Capra sweated blood while Cohn's rear practically oscillated. Rushing out for a drink of water, Capra met a fleeing audience member who remarked, "Did you ever see such a goddam Fu Manchu thing in your life? People who made it ought to be shot."

Three mornings later, after considerable soul-searching, thinking, and self-recriminations, Capra dashed to the studio and told editors Gene

Havlick and Gene Milford to eliminate the first reels, starting the picture with the exciting Baskul airport sequence. That done, Capra convinced a shaken Cohn to give the film another preview immediately.

The second preview took place in San Pedro and was an unqualified success. Capra learned a valuable lesson (one Stanley Kubrick also learned after seeing *2001* with a paying audience and then trimming the film)—no film is complete until it is viewed as it was intended, with an audience of ordinary moviegoers.

More cuts and trims were made over the next several months, necessitating reshooting some scenes and adding totally new ones. The first High Lama scene ran an agonizing 16 minutes, so Riskin and Capra wrote a scene between Chang and Conway in which Chang explains the origin of Shangri-La under its founder, Father Perrault. This three-minute, six-second scene, shot in December 1936, enabled Capra to trim the High Lama's first appearance in the film to a more acceptable six minutes, forty-five seconds. The High Lama's second scene, his death scene, runs only three minutes and fifteen seconds.

At *Horizon*'s March 3, 1937, premiere, its running time was 132 minutes, later shortened to 125 and then 118 minutes in general release. For years, the syndicated television version ran only 95 minutes. Finally, in 1986, Columbia Classics premiered a 132-minute restored version of the film at New York City's Museum of Modern Art. (For more about such cutting and restoring, see the Appendix.)

Lost Horizon holds up surprisingly well, given its advanced age. Its photography, by the great Joseph B. Walker, is stunning and intelligent; its magnificent sets have rarely been equaled, let alone surpassed; its direction is crisp and knowing; and its acting is generally outstanding. Its special effects, however, apart from the ice house scenes, no longer seem very special; the plane crash is especially phony-looking.

Ronald Colman (1891–1958) is perfect for his role as the world-weary man of diplomacy and action, and his scenes with both H.B. Warner's Chang and Sam Jaffe's High Lama are powerfully effective—all the more so for his quiet way of expressing deep feeling. Close-ups of Colman capture his emotions as his face either glows with hope and inspiration, or darkens with doubt and despair. This is screen acting—acting for the camera—at its best. Colman's Conway inspires trust; one can readily accept the High Lama's conclusion that Robert Conway is the one man to take his place.

As the High Lama, the 250-year-old Father Perrault, Sam Jaffe (1893–1984), with his halo of wispy white hair and gentle voice, is wonderful. Like Conway, the High Lama must project sincerity, in addition to wisdom born of many years of experience. Jaffe's inspired performance is one of his many great film roles, including the heroic waterboy in *Gunga Din* (1939) and Professor Barnhardt in *The Day the Earth Stood Still* (1951).

After a long but relatively anonymous film career, Jaffe found himself famous for playing Dr. David Zorba on the popular television series *Ben Casey* (1961–1966).

H.B. Warner's (1876–1958) Chang helps hold the center of the film together, and his conversations with Colman are delightful for their low-intensity verbal dueling.

Both Edward Everett Horton (1886–1970) and Thomas Mitchell (1892–1962) are fine as, respectively, Lovett and Barnard, but they have relatively minor parts. (For more on the actors and their films, see the Appendix.)

Perhaps the major flaw of the film (and it comes directly from the novel — which Riskin and Capra followed too slavishly at times) is the series of newspaper headlines detailing Conway's post–Shangri-La travels and adventures and the dull, talky, and totally uncinematic scene in the St. George Club where we hear second-hand what we should have seen with our own eyes. Seeing Conway's shock at re-encountering "civilization" would have vindicated his choice to return to his hidden paradise.

A further discomforting aspect of the film is its unconscious and (one hopes) unintended racism and sexism — from the opening written narration informing us Conway was sent to Baskul to rescue not 90 Europeans but 90 "white people," to its identifying Sondra as a "white girl," to the dialogue between Chang and Conway over a man taking another man's woman. The inhabitants of the Valley of the Blue Moon are seen as cheerful servants and hard-working peasants. But all these lapses are probably more indicative of the mores of the time than any hostility toward other races or toward women on the part of Riskin and Capra.

Shangri-La is just one in a long series of fictional utopias. The word "utopia," which was created by Sir Thomas More for his City of God in 1516, literally means "no place." These impossible paradises reflect the longings and the prejudices of the people who envision them. There have been utopian novels, plays, and films which see the perfect society as one in which all men and women are equal, or sexually liberated; in which there is freedom from want or envy; in which socialism or Darwinism or capitalism or nudism or any "ism" you can imagine has finally triumphed. The opposite of a utopia, like the hideous worlds of *1984* and *Brazil*, is called a dystopia.

Real-life attempts to create utopias have led to experimental, and usually unsuccessful, societies like the Shaker communities or hippie communes. At its most extreme, this hunger for a perfect order has resulted in tragedy — the murderous Charles Manson family of the 1960s, or Jim Jones' cult's suicides in 1978 in Guyana.

Lost Horizon is a superior and engaging fantasy. If it offers an escape from the "real" world, well then, so much the better. As a character in the film says, we all *want* to believe in Shangri-La, and the promise of a place without struggle or envy. Shangri-La stands for many things—for as many wishes and dreams as there are wishers or dreamers. *Lost Horizon* embodies one of the most potent of all fantasies: the fantasy of an idyllic, fulfilling, and long life.

If we can just find Shangri-La, Robert Conway is sure to be waiting to greet us—after all, he's still a relatively young man, isn't he?

10. Popeye:
The Comic Strip Hero

Popeye was a nice fairy tale with a loving spirit to it, and I think most
people — especially movie critics — were expecting a combination of *Superman* and a Busby Berkeley musical. . . . In the end, I think that what
Altman got was a very gentle fable with music and a lot of heart.
— *Robin Williams, in his* Playboy *interview.*

The Paramount-Disney production of the Jules Feiffer–scripted,
Robert Altman–directed *Popeye* is a fabulous fantasy film. Eagerly anticipated, it was Paramount's Christmas 1980 release. *Popeye*, it was hoped,
would garner critical and popular raves, and do "boffo" box-office business,
drawing in kids and their parents through the holiday season and well into
the new year. Alas, it was not to be. Although *Popeye* generated rentals of
just over $24,500,000, its approximately $20,000,000 production costs
meant that while the picture was not a bomb, it was also far from the roaring
success Paramount-Disney executives had hoped for.

Popeye was far more successful with children than with adults, but the
smaller admission prices paid by the under-12 crowd meant that full
theaters didn't translate into respectable grosses.

That children liked *Popeye* more than their elders is somewhat surprising, given the film's muted colors and dark emotional tone. One might think
that children, fed a steady stream of Saturday morning cartoons, would
prefer the animated Popeye — a rock'em, sock'em, rubber-limbed whirling
dervish devoid of any but the most basic and surface emotions. True to the
original E.C. Segar comic strips, writer Jules Feiffer's Popeye is a well-
developed and totally "round" character. Emotionally open and sensitive,
Popeye's initial kindness and strength of character only deepen as he adopts
Swee'pea, the orphan "infink," falls in love with Olive Oyl, and is reunited
with his long lost Pappy.

A likely explanation for most adults' rejection of Feiffer and Altman's
Popeye is that they — not children — are the ones who most remember and
prefer Fleischer's animated Popeye. The Fleischer cartoons, in "old-
fashioned" black-and-white, are now shown infrequently, but when most of

139

today's adults were growing up, Popeye could be viewed before and after school, and almost any time on Saturdays and Sundays.

Young children, never exposed to the violent and simplistic cartoon Popeye, responded to the warmth and humanity in the film. Adults, including critics, wanted the "real" Popeye.

The reviews for *Popeye* were almost unanimously bad. Some critics, perhaps, were waiting for a chance to stick a fork into director Altman to see if he was "done." Yet, in reading all the reviews in their entirety (not just the excerpts quoted here), one senses that most of the reviewers genuinely wanted to like *Popeye* and were therefore all the more disappointed in the final product.

David Sterritt's review in the *Christian Science Monitor* was relatively mild, and he was supportive of the effort the filmmakers had put forth. "*Popeye* itself is an odd duck of a movie. Its visual ideas are often unappealing, and a lot of its jokes fall flat. Still, it has enormous energy, and it's fascinating to see the adventurous Robert Altman try his hand at an old-fashioned Christmastime entertainment."

In *Film Quarterly*, Barbara Quart, another critic whose review was generally supportive, wrote, "The biggest surprise is that *Popeye* has turned out to be so winning, for all its flaws. *Popeye* in its small off-key way is a heartening start to a year the prospects of which do little to raise the spirit."

Less taken with the film was Edwin Kephart. Writing in *Films in Review*, he said, "Out of a setting that looks part Charles Dickens, part John Millington Synge and part Disneyland, Robert Altman has directed a version of the Popeye story that simply never gets off the ground. I sat watching *Popeye* with an audience of children; it was only Baby Swee'pea's ad libs that held their fascination and elicited some response."

In the *New Leader*, Robert Asahina writes, "Jules Feiffer's meandering script and Harry Nilsson's lifeless songs reduce an alleged musical comedy to a tuneless bore."

John Coleman, writing in *New Statesman*, makes an interesting point in his review: "Altmanesque quirks abound—overlapping voices, zany characters doing mad little 'bits' on the fringes, everything very busy—but kids may wonder where *their* Popeye went. This one *hates* spinach."

David Denby's *New York* review is mixed but ends on a downbeat note: "Working on a large scale for the first time, Robert Altman has made a crankily personal movie, every bit as individual as a small Altman picture like *McCabe and Mrs. Miller* or *Thieves Like Us*. Watching this movie, I couldn't shake the feeling that Altman had devised intricate bits of business for his large stock company in order to keep them occupied but had never asked himself how any of it would work for the audience. The movie is personal all right, but it's not very expressive. It sits there on the screen in joyless, eccentric pride, a long, long way from us.

Archer Winston, of the *New York Post*, found the film to be "boring almost beyond endurance," but pronounced the sets "marvelous."

In *Newsweek*, David Ansen found the whole thing a strange undertaking. "This is high-risk chemistry, and the results are bizarre. The bulging forearms and corncob pipe are in place, but this Popeye hates spinach. The plot hinges on his Oedipal search for his Pappy . . . and this gruff icon of pugnacious, all–American goodness has been set adrift on an abstract isle that can best be described as back-lot Ionesco. *Popeye*'s air of alienated whimsy makes for an odd 'family movie' indeed."

Further mining this vein, Richard Schickel, in *Time*, outright calls *Popeye* "one of the most grievously miscalculated movies in recent memory, claustrophobic in manner, mean in spirit, downright grotesque to look at. *Popeye* will bore children and offend adults who fondly remember the original. It is a travesty to hear Williams warble the classic 'I yam what I yam' line in one of Harry Nilsson's many witless songs. 'I'm not the man I was' would be a more appropriate lyric. Or maybe, 'What have they done to me?'"

The film opens with a brief glimpse of the cartoon Popeye before switching to live action in the midst of a raging storm at sea. We see a small figure in a boat on the tossing waves. The darkness gives way to daylight and the people of the seacoast town of Sweethaven sing "Sweethaven" as, through individual "bits," they're introduced to us.

Popeye (Robin Williams), the figure from the boat, arrives and is immediately assessed fees by the Taxman (Donald Moffat). As Popeye wanders through the small town, people point and stare at him, avoiding making any contact with this (gulp) *stranger*.

Meeting Nana Oyl (Roberta Maxwell), Popeye learns the Oyls have a room for rent. Inside, he meets the rest of the Oyl family—Cole (MacIntyre Dixon), Castor (Donovan Scott), and the lovely Olive Oyl (Shelley Duvall). Unfortunately, Popeye and Olive get off to a poor start as she shows him to his room.

Dinner at the Oyls. Olive is engaged (it's her fourth time) to Bluto, who, we learn, runs the town for the mysterious and never-seen Commodore.

While Popeye muses about his long-lost Pappy, the hulking Bluto (Paul L. Smith) announces the nine o'clock curfew from his boat, the *Vile Body*. All Popeye has to remember his Pappy from is a blank picture frame ("Me Poppa," it says inside where the picture should be).

A new day begins with the customers of the Rough House Cafe singing "Food, Food, Food (Everything is Food)." Still mostly ignored, Popeye talks about his long-lost Pap and his search for him to an uninterested Wimpy (Paul Dooley), who only stays with the sailor because Popeye's given him a burger to eat. The Rough House gang insults Popeye and beats up some townspeople. Feeling a "sense of humiligration," Popeye teaches them better manners.

Popeye goes to Olive's engagement party and is totally ignored; frustrated, he leaves. Meanwhile, Olive, dressing, sings a song about Bluto, her intended: "He's Large." Clearly, Olive, whose ex-fiancees include Ham Gravy, is planning to run out on Bluto as well.

Olive, with a basketful of belongings, bumps into Popeye on the wharf. At the Oyls', Bluto waits impatiently for Olive's appearance while she and Popeye continue their conversation. Popeye speaks of his Pappy while a mysterious figure switches baskets with Olive. After it makes a "rattlesnake" noise, Popeye lifts the lid and finds a baby boy (Wesley Ivan Hurt).

Furious at being stood up, Bluto sings "I'm Mean" while totally destroying the Oyls' house. Popeye and Olive turn up with the child, and Bluto knocks an apologetic Popeye off the porch, down the street, and through the pier.

The Taxman confiscates what little of the Oyls' property remains intact. Popeye tells Olive he's naming the "infink" Swee'pea — "I found him in Sweethaven, dat is why he is me Swee'pea."

Castor Oyl, hoping to earn $15 and ten days' tax exemption for his mom and pop, will try to spend one round in the ring with Oxblood Oxheart, "the dirtiest fighter alive." When the Oyls, Popeye, and Swee'pea show up at the fight, they see Castor easily beaten and literally knocked out of the ring. Taking up the challenge, Popeye cocks his fist and kayos Oxblood Oxheart (Peter Bray), winning the prize money.

As Popeye and Olive feed Swee'pea, they sing "Sail with Me," and begin to feel an attraction for each other. Later, Olive says Swee'pea "told" her that Popeye would not only survive in the ring but also win. Overhearing this, Wimpy gets the idea to take Swee'pea to the horse races to help him pick winners.

Learning that Wimpy won 120 "samoleons," Olive's indignation turns to greed, and she wants to use Swee'pea's talent to win money for the destitute Oyls. An angry Popeye says, "Wrong is wrong, even if it helps you," sings "I Yam What I Yam," and takes Swee'pea away.

Concerned for Swee'pea's upbringing, Popeye moves out and sets up house on the wharf. After Popeye pushes the Taxman into the sea, the townspeople cheer and sweep Popeye away from Swee'pea, who's taken by Wimpy to Bluto. While Popeye worries over Swee'pea, Olive, now smitten for the sailor, sings "He Needs Me."

Watching through a telescope as Bluto takes Swee'pea to the Commodore, Wimpy inadvertently reveals his part in the kidnapping to Olive. Talking to Bluto ("I got millions of enemies — and you is 10 or 12 of them"), the Commodore (Ray Walston) is obviously . . . ta da! . . . Popeye's Pappy!

Robin Williams as Popeye. His "squinty eye" was achieved by gluing a small piece of latex onto Williams' right eyelid.

He sings "It's Not Easy Bein' Me" as Bluto ties him up and takes Swee'pea to find the Commodore's treasure.

Told the whereabouts of Swee'pea and his Pappy, Popeye shows up as Bluto slips away with the baby. Face to face with his own son, the Commodore denies he's anybody's Pappy, but 'fesses up when Popeye reveals he doesn't like spinach.

Seizing Olive as well, Bluto escapes by boat to Scab Island, where Pappy's treasure is hidden. Pappy and Popeye are in hot pursuit and Pappy sings "Kids." After firing a "warning shot" that disables his target, Pappy rams Bluto's boat.

As the boats sink, Bluto escapes in a rowboat and dives for the treasure. Popeye arrives, and he and Bluto duke it out in the sea. Unfortunately for Popeye, the Oyls throw a life preserver and inadvertently pin the sailor's arms. Trying to throw Popeye a cutlass, Cole throws it to Bluto! Popeye snatches up another cutlass and the battle is joined. Bluto and Popeye's furious sword fight continues underwater while an octopus threatens Swee'pea. Pappy saves the "infink," and the octopus goes after Olive.

Pappy's "treasure" chest is full of baby toys, a "Me Son" empty picture frame, and . . . cans of spinach. After Pappy throws a can of spinach to Popeye and he refuses to eat it, Bluto forces the green stuff down the sailor's throat. A giant arm—Popeye's—knocks out Bluto and the sailor man kayos the octopus as well. Bluto, now literally all yellow, swims off while Popeye sings "I'm Popeye the Sailor Man" and dances on top of the water.

On January 17, 1929, E[lzie] C[risler] Segar's popular "Thimble Theater" cartoon strip introduced the character who was to become its star, Popeye the Sailor. In Segar's strip, Castor Oyl (Olive's brother) hires a sailor and his boat to take him to Dice Island to gamble. Asked if he's a sailor, Popeye replies, "Ja think I'm a cowboy?" In short order, "Thimble Theater" became "Thimble Theater Starring Popeye the Sailor," and then simply "Popeye."

When E.C. Segar died at age 44 in 1938, Popeye and the artist's other creations—Olive Oyl, Bluto, Alice the Goon, the Jeep, and the Sea Hag—continued their popularity in a slew of movie and television cartoons.

Max Fleischer produced more than 250 Popeye cartoon shorts for Paramount Studios. Later shown on television, these crude, rude, and generally enjoyable exercises in cartoon violence proved so popular that King Features produced a whole series of Popeye cartoons made expressly for the tube. Featuring the omnipresent cans of spinach, Popeye's unique "pronunskiation," and most of the characters from the earlier Fleischer black-and-white theatricals, the toned-down remakes were successful but lacked the originals' vulgar energy and wit.

In 1977, producer Robert Evans attended a performance of the smash Broadway musical *Annie*. Emerging from the theater with the sound of the audience's applause still ringing in his ears, he resolved to attain the rights to a film version. Then affiliated with Paramount (for whom he'd produced *Chinatown* and *Marathon Man*, among others), he stayed in the bidding until the asking price passed $10,000,000. With *Annie* out of his grasp, Evans cast about for another project.

According to Bridget Terry, in *The Popeye Story*, Marvin Cane, of Famous Music Corporation, which owned the rights to "I'm Popeye the Sailor Man," told Evans that the song earned Famous and Paramount $75,000 a year. Cane asked, "Why don't we make *Popeye?*"

Evans quickly secured the rights from King Features Syndicate and, on the phone to the actor, got Dustin Hoffman to agree to portray the world-famous sailor man. An executive producer friend of Evans then suggested that Jules Feiffer be hired to write the script.

Feiffer, a playwright and cartoonist, was initially reluctant to get involved with Evans, a man whom he considered the epitome of the "slick Hollywood producer" type. After Evans met with Feiffer and told him that he could ignore the rough-and-tumble Popeye of the cartoon shorts in favor of Segar's original strips, the writer agreed to do the script.

In *American Film*, producer Evans revealed that he and Feiffer agreed that *Popeye's* theme should be the sailor's own espoused credo: "I yam what I yam (and that's all that I yam)." "That's what I wanted to get across in the story—that one line," Evans said. "People are individuals. They are what they are."

So enamoured—and in awe—of the original Segar strips was Feiffer that, initially, the only way he could begin writing the screenplay was to call Popeye and Olive by different names—Sam and Celia. As he grew comfortable with the idea of writing Popeye and Olive's story, Feiffer discarded his ruse and soon produced a 150-page script.

Evans loved the script, but Hoffman began to exhibit some reluctance. When Evans bravely stuck with his writer, Hoffman walked away from the picture. "With Dustin," Evans recalled in an unsigned *American Film* article, "I had a go from Paramount. Without Dustin, I had nothing but a script."

With a script he liked, but no star, Evans considered and then rejected actor after actor. Finally, late in 1978, the whole project on hold, Evans told his friend Michael Eisner (later the head of Disney) that it wasn't necessary to find a major star to play the role because *Popeye* was the star. Spotting Robin Williams on *Mork and Mindy*, Evans off-handedly remarked, "For Chrissakes, even, uh . . . Robin Williams . . . could play it." Said and done: Williams was quickly signed for his first film role.

With his "Popeye" now safely signed to a contract, Evans began a long and wearying campaign against the studio for the director he wanted for the project—Robert Altman, the brilliant but controversial director of such films as *M*A*S*H, McCabe and Mrs. Miller*, and *Nashville*. After a string of flops, including *Buffalo Bill and the Indians, Quintet, A Perfect Couple*, and the unreleased *Health*, Altman needed a hit. Looking askance at Altman's recent track record, Paramount deemed the director "unbankable." Evans remained adamant that Altman was his one and only choice, and when the producer got Robin Williams to back him, the studio gave in and hired Altman.

Born in Kansas City, Missouri, in 1925, Robert Altman began his career as a magazine and radio writer. After working on a number of industrial films, he made his first feature, the low-budget *The Delinquents*, in 1955. He made a number of marginally successful films before his fifth feature, the anti-war black comedy *M*A*S*H*, propelled him into the top tier of directors. It was a precarious position, and his failures left Altman anxious to prove himself again with an unqualified success. Altman's vehicle back to the top was to be *Popeye*, a big, splashy, commercial Hollywood film.

With Altman on board, things began moving again and Evans hired pop composer-singer Harry Nilsson to write the music. While Nilsson retreated to his home to begin composing songs, Robin Williams began preparing for his first starring film role. Williams had high hopes *Popeye* would do for him what *Superman* had done for his friend Christopher Reeve. As Williams told interviewer Lawrence Linderman in his October 1982 interview in *Playboy*, "When I was training for *Popeye*, I thought, This is it, this is MY *Superman*, and it's gonna go through the fuckin' roof!"

Since Feiffer's script was based on Segar's original strips, Williams pored over them for inspiration, but also watched hours of Popeye cartoons as well. With a pipe sticking out of the right side of his mouth, Williams practiced speaking from the left side of his mouth—something which helped him to keep his right eye shut in Popeye's characteristic squint. Dancer Lou Wills, Jr., was hired to give Williams tap-dancing lessons.

"Yes, I learned how to tap-dance," Williams said in *Playboy*, "and I worked hard on my one song in the film, and I often practiced Popeye's speaking voice, which sounded like a frog farting under water." Williams also worked out daily with a punching bag. "Just using the punching bag," he noted in *American Film*, "helped a little for speed, to keep you tight and moving. Popeye's a fast dude—constant, quick movements."

With Robin Williams set as Popeye, Evans and Altman needed to find the right Olive Oyl. Paramount executives fruitlessly pursued Gilda Radner of NBC's *Saturday Night Live* for the pivotal role of Olive Oyl. Meanwhile, Altman, who'd discovered Shelley Duvall in Houston, Texas, and cast her in *Brewster McCloud*, wanted Duvall for the role from the start.

When Duvall returned from making *The Shining* in London with Stanley Kubrick, Altman hustled her into a recording studio with Nilsson to record Olive Oyl's big number in the film, "He Needs Me." Dubbing Duvall's cut over a clip of Duvall scenes from other films (he did the same for Paul L. Smith's "I'm Mean" number), Altman baited his trap.

When Paramount executives, including Gulf & Western chairman Charles Bludorn and his wife, arrived at Altman's Lion Gate Studios for a party, Altman played the clips. When Mrs. Bludorn remarked how much Duvall looked like Olive Oyl, Altman knew his favorite actress had the role.

When she was growing up, other children had taunted the skinny Duvall, calling her "Olive Oyl." But, as an actress, she found the comparison a compliment.

Duvall had no preconceived ideas on how to approach playing Olive Oyl. "I work from the gut," she explained in *American Film*. "I didn't know what Olive would sound like or talk like or walk like until several weeks after I got there."

Paul L. Smith, an actor in spaghetti westerns, was hired to play Popeye's nemesis, the hulking Bluto. The six-foot, four-inch, 320-pound Smith had acted mainly in Europe and was best known for playing the cruelly sadistic jailor in *Midnight Express*. If Shelley Duvall was fated to play Olive Oyl, then the same was true of Paul L. Smith and Bluto. Smith told Bridget Terry, the publicist who wrote *The Popeye Story* (a "making of" book), that "as a kid, when we played Popeye, I always played Bluto."

Altman regular Paul Dooley was cast as Wimpy despite the efforts of Evans and Paramount to get Altman to accept a bigger star, someone like

Even though Olive Oyl (Shelley Duvall) says "Phooey" to Popeye, it's clear he's fall-ing for her angular charms.

Buddy Hackett or Dom DeLuise. Dooley's roles in Altman films like *A Wed-ding, A Perfect Couple,* and *Health* didn't impress the studio. However, Dooley's performance that summer in *Breaking Away,* a box-office smash, coupled with the fact that Feiffer wanted him in the role as well, helped him land the part.

Olive's mother, Nana Oyl, was played by Roberta Maxwell (*Psycho III*), who at the time had appeared in only one other film, *The Changeling,* with George C. Scott.

MacIntire Dixon (*Alice's Restaurant, Reds*) was signed to play Cole Oyl, Olive's father, and Donovan Scott (*1941*) was cast as Castor Oyl, Olive's brother.

Fresh from a funny role in *The In-Laws,* Richard Libertini became Geezil, while Allan Nichols (*Nashville*) was chosen as Rough House. The Taxman was played by British-born Donald Moffat (L.B.J. in *The Right Stuff*).

Wesley Ivan Hurt, born March 5, 1979, and Altman's grandson, was cast as Swee'pea. Wesley's face was partially paralyzed — a condition which specialists said would disappear in a few years — giving the little boy an un-canny resemblance to an "infink" Popeye.

The role of Poopdeck Pappy was one Evans wanted to be played by Jason Robards. But Robards' agent wanted approximately $1 million for his client to play the part, and Evans declined. Ray Walston, told that Pappy was a "mean old sonofabitch," was finally chosen as Popeye's missing pappy. In makeup, Walston looked remarkably like his "son," and, like Robin Williams, had played a visiting extraterrestrial in *his* hit sitcom of the 1960s, *My Favorite Martian.*

Costume designer and associate producer Scott Bushnell helped with the casting, seeking out dancers, circus performers, street performers, and others with experience with "physical" acting. Most of those hired this way would become the citizens of Sweethaven and be given individual "bits" to do in the film.

Harry Nilsson, who wrote the music, is best known for singing "Everybody's Talking (at Me)," the hit song from *Midnight Cowboy,* and for writing, narrating, and singing *The Point,* which was both a record and an animated TV special. His other albums include *Nilsson Schmilsson, Son of Schmilsson,* and *A Little Touch of Schmilsson in the Night.*

For *Popeye,* Nilsson's Malta musicians were the Falcons: Ray Cooper, Doug Dillard, Van Dyke Parks, Klaus Voorman, and featuring The Mysterious Karsten at the organ. After Nilsson and the Falcons recorded the music, a track with Nilsson's vocal of the song would be added to the mix, and the actors involved in the song would then get a cassette so they could learn the words and music.

Among the songs Nilsson wrote for *Popeye* were "I Yam What I Yam," "He Needs Me," "Swee'pea's Lullaby," "Sweethaven," "Blow Me Down," "Sailin'," "It's Not Easy Being Me," "I'm Mean," "He's Large," and "Kids." "Din We" (Barnacle Bill's lament), didn't make it into the film, and another, "Food, Food, Food," was written for Wimpy and Geezil but sung in the Rough House by everybody. "I'm Popeye the Sailor Man," from the cartoons and heard only at the film's conclusion, was written by Sam Lerner.

Evans and Altman chose Malta as the perfect site to shoot the film. The 122-square-mile Republic of Malta consists of five islands with a combined land area smaller than Philadelphia. It's strategic location just 97 kilometers (approximately 60 miles) south of the southeastern tip of Sicily allowed the British to use it as a fixed-locale aircraft carrier and submarine base from which to attack the Axis forces in the Mediterranean during World War II. Before it was invaded by actors and technicians from Hollywood, Malta had been occupied by the Phoenicians, the Greeks, the Carthaginians, the Romans, the French (under Napoleon), and finally the British.

Two things made Malta the perfect location for the film. First, it had one of the best special effects water tanks to be found outside Hollywood or London (it had been enlarged by Lord Lew Grade for the filming of his titanic bomb, *Raise the Titanic).* Secondly, and perhaps more importantly (at least to director Altman), it was thousands of miles away from second-guessing studio executives.

Wolf Kroeger, a Canadian production designer born in Germany, scouted Malta's coastline and, at Anchor Bay, discovered a good site to construct the town of Sweethaven. With Malta and Anchor Bay confirmed as the location, Kroeger began building a marvelously detailed 8' × 10' model of Sweethaven to guide the carpenters and crew who would shortly begin putting up the actual sets.

Instead of the typical Hollywood buildings used on most films — façades with little behind the front but supporting timbers — Sweethaven's houses and businesses were real buildings, complete with four walls and roofs. Since Malta is essentially treeless, Kroeger was forced to import nearly eight million linear feet of wood from as far away as Taiwan. Needing just the right shingles for the roofs and some exterior walls, he had several tons shipped in from Vancouver, Canada. Despite all this attention to detail, only the Oyls' house and the Rough House Cafe would be used for interior filming.

A three-masted sailing ship, called the *Black Pearl*, that Kroeger rented to moor in the town's harbor sank during a storm before filming began. Rather than raise her, Altman and Evans decided to leave the ship half sunk, deciding that it added to Sweethaven's barren and hopeless atmosphere.

In December 1979, before shooting began, Walt Disney Productions signed a coproduction pact with Paramount Pictures. Disney's deal meant that, while Paramount would distribute the film in the United States, Disney — still a potent name overseas — would be the distributor in foreign markets.

In the first few days of shooting, after Robin Williams began to improvise Popeye's muttered asides, Feiffer grew annoyed that his script was not being religiously followed and complained about Williams' improvisations to director Altman. Altman then complained about Feiffer's "interference" to Evans. Agreeing to back off, Feiffer stayed with the production, often rewriting entire scenes overnight as Altman rethought the story and each character's contribution.

For the people of Sweethaven, the actors in the small but important supporting roles, Altman worked with the performers to develop what he called "pick-a-tic," finding an appropriate quirk that would be unique to that character.

Popeye's half-closed eye was achieved by gluing a small piece of latex onto Williams' right eyelid. The weight and feel of this small appliance was just apparent enough to the actor to remind him to keep his eye clamped shut during shooting.

Popeye's distinctive bulgy forearms were another matter. Nothing seemed to work, and the production was three weeks underway before makeup supervisor Giancarlo Del Brocco licked the problem. His seamless rubber arms were molded in foam rubber and covered with lifelike latex skin. Implanted with hair for a realistic look, the arms also came with and without hands.

Williams told *Playboy* interviewer Linderman that it took him about an hour and a half to be made up. "And after that, they'd strap on the latex arms: they tied me off almost as if I were a junkie. In some of my fight scenes," Williams recalled, "I'd lose all the circulation in my arms and they'd lock up, so we'd have to stop shooting . . . and they'd untie me." Once the circulation returned to Williams' arms, shooting would resume for another half hour or so until the problem reoccurred.

Among the special effects required for *Popeye* were pipes that could spin or squirt water, pipes that could collapse or blow smoke, and pipes that could function as periscopes. Only a few of these specialized pipes were finally utilized in production.

The larger special effects were created by a Los Angeles company known as Cosmekinetics. Apart from a pelican and a "stunt" Swee'Pea, the firm's major contribution was to be the creation of a large, hydraulically operated octopus called Slimy Sam. The stunt baby was rarely used because on screen it failed to look like a real baby. The pelican was used in several scenes, but the device was stiff and unrealistic as well.

As for Slimy Sam, Robin Williams complained in *Playboy* that the rubber-tentacled octopus couldn't *do* anything. Disney "had half investment in *Popeye,* and if anyone had let them know that the octopus couldn't even manipulate its arms, I think they would have sent over a couple of guys and we would've had an octopus that could blink, wink, blow bubbles and smoke underwater." Williams complained that poor Shelley Duvall had to create the illusion that Slimy Sam was grappling with her by wrapping the inert arms about her and then acting as if she were struggling to escape its grasp. (See the ending of a truly awful Edward D. Wood film, 1956's *Bride of the Monster,* for a similar scene: The aged Bela Lugosi is trapped by his own killer octopus and must also create the illusion that the cheap rubber prop is attacking him.)

Robin Williams was hoping for a big "boffo" ending, but Paramount pulled the plug on the overbudget, overschedule production and ordered everyone home. As Williams moaned to *Playboy,* "I'd pictured Popeye flying through the air, sort of like the cartoon thing in which he becomes a tornado with his legs spinning at warp four."

Although *Popeye* didn't lose money, it failed to generate much, if any, initial profit (though its recent videocassette sales and pay-cable exposure have surely pushed it into profitability). The reasons for *Popeye*'s lackluster box-office performance are many. One major factor in the film's less-than-rousing reception by audiences is probably that it—like *Dragonslayer,* a later Paramount-Disney production also doomed to failure—was a Genrebuster. *Popeye* failed to deliver the genre goods.

Film critic and scholar Mark Roth, refuting critic John Baxter's argument that the dance numbers in musicals are—and ought to be removable—argues in "Some Warners Musicals and the Spirit of the New Deal" that "they are no more expendable than chanting in religious services or Greek tragedy. They function as part of the fabric to raise the work to a poetic or mythic level...."

But in *American Film*, before the film's release, Robin Williams was quoted as saying, "*Popeye*'s more of an unmusical, really. For better or worse, there won't be a full-blown dance number." Later, after *Popeye* had been mauled by the critics and ignored by audiences, Williams' words came back to haunt him. As he told *Playboy*, "When we were making the movie ... I could feel what was missing. For instance, we needed a couple of slam-bang musical numbers that really tore the tits off the place."

Robin Williams, having had a long time to ponder *Popeye*'s weak reception by audiences, is right on the mark. The film has no real dance numbers as such. Given *Popeye*'s relatively (for a fantasy) realistic plot, it needed the contrast to its somber tones that could have been provided by big Hollywood-style production numbers.

Newsweek's David Ansen was one of many critics who noted *Popeye*'s musical-genre shortcomings: "The songs and minimal dances are designed for singers who can't sing and dancers who can't dance...."

Further, the film went to incomprehensible lengths for "authenticity." In *Saturday Review*, Judith Crist rightly observed that "adults may well ponder the purpose of it all—let alone the complex structure of the town of Sweethaven, built in Malta, featuring 19 four-sided structures made of wood imported from Austria, with 'hand-split' cedar shingles from British Columbia, and none of it magical or amusing."

All Hollywood movies are fantasies, in their own way, and few producers have ever felt the need to construct fully realized structures. One wonders what Altman, Evans, and production designer Wolf Kroeger believed this misplaced—and presumably expensive—realism would contribute to the film's success.

If *Popeye*'s false notes and missteps are easy to pinpoint, so are its many successes. Robin Williams is brilliant as the squinty-eyed sailor. If *Popeye* wasn't the giant success for Williams that *Superman* was for Christopher Reeve, it's just as difficult to conceive of another actor playing Popeye as it is to imagine someone other than Reeve as the "Man of Steel."

Williams' many fractured muttered asides are gems—if you can hear them (Altman's soundtrack is too cluttered and too low). At one point, in the racetrack/house of ill-repute, Popeye looks around and notes one could get "a venerable disease." Williams' scenes with Poopdeck Pappy are marvelously realized and acted. And, Feiffer's objections aside, Altman ought to have allowed Williams to improvise *more*, not less.

Shelley Duvall is just as wonderful as Olive Oyl. Her love song number, "He Needs Me," is made even more appealing by her gawky yet graceful movements. For that brief, touching moment, *Popeye* is magical as actress and character meld to become one.

Many of Feiffer's lines, the ones we *can* hear, are funny and true to Segar's original and off-center strips. When Nana Oyl first meets Popeye, she asks him to come in, "Before you catch your death of mud." At one point, speaking ill of another character, Geezil says, "Next to Wimpy, I hate him the best." A sign at the prizefight ring reads, "First man who is dead, loses."

Bluto's character never seems to come alive, and one doesn't know whether the fault is Altman's, Feiffer's, or Paul L. Smith's. Still, Bluto is given some amusing dimensions: He makes odd bull- or steerlike noises, and he's constantly circled by buzzing flies.

One of Feiffer's and Altman's funniest sight gags occurs when Popeye is given the cold shoulder at Olive's engagement party. Not only does everyone fall silent when he enters, but a fur stole lifts its muzzle and snarls at him!

When *Popeye* gives in to duplicating animated effects—Popeye punching out one of the Rough House toughs, or being knocked for a literal "loop" by Bluto—the old cartoon magic works.

An inventive, imaginative, funny, and heartwarming fantasy film, *Popeye* nonetheless failed to reach a wide audience because of its genre illiteracy. Seen today, shorn of the high expectations that greeted it upon its release, *Popeye* remains a wonderful family film—a film for children of all ages.

Like many another film in this book, *Popeye* will grow in stature over the years, and will be appreciated by more and more people. As Robin Williams told Lawrence Linderman, "I recently found out that a lot of people are buying video tapes of *Popeye* and their kids watch it four or five times a month. That makes me feel good...."

11. Superman: The Super Hero

"This is no fantasy. . .no careless product of wild imagination."
— *Jor-El, in* Superman

"Look! Up in the sky! It's a bird! It's a plane! It's. . .SUPERMAN!"
From The Adventures of Superman *television series.*

In 1978, one of America's great superheroes came to the screen in a lavishly mounted fantasy film that both exceeds and confounds expectations. After a long period of nonheroic heroes in film, Americans were looking for protagonists strong enough to confront and defeat powerful enemies. In Superman, they found a hero from the 1930s — an earlier era beset by doubt and national malaise — and an all-but-indestructible answer to the nation's prayers.

All over the place, both dramatically and in terms of its story, *Superman* is seemingly two or three different films in one. It is an origin-of-Superman story, an adventure-plus-love story, and a slapstick comedy, complete with a bumbling henchman so inept as to invalidate the air of menace generated by his master-criminal employer.

Still, in its long middle section, in the sequences where Clark Kent becomes Superman, alternately romancing Lois Lane and rounding up bad guys, *Superman: The Movie* (as it was sometimes called) soars and carries its audience to new heights of fantasy film fulfillment. It's a fantasy film for our time, a fable for both children and adults who haven't forgotten what it's like to be a child.

Variety's review was enthusiastic: "Magnify James Bond's extraordinary physical powers while curbing his sex drive and you have the essence of *Superman,* a wonderful, chuckling, preposterously exciting fantasy guaranteed to challenge world box office records this time round, and perhaps with sequels to come."

Jenny Craven, in *Films and Filming,* was more critical, saying, "The film is a disappointment because it is unfinished." Still, Ms. Craven enjoyed the second half of *Superman,* noting that "casting, performances, and witty dialogue combine to infuse this portion of the film with a spirit of fun."

The *New York Times'* anonymous reviewer wrote, "*Superman* is good, clean, simple-minded fun, though it's a movie whose limited appeal is built in. There isn't a thought in this film's head that would be out of place on the side of a box of Wheaties."

In *Newsweek*, Jack Kroll wrote that "*Superman* turns out to be a surprisingly infectious entertainment, nicely balanced between warmth and wit, intimacy and impressive special effects, comic-strip fantasy and several elements that make the movie eminently eligible for Deep Thinking about rescue fantasies, cherubic messiahs and other pieces of popcorn metaphysics."

Time enthused, "Not since *Star Wars*, the alltime champ, has there been such an entertaining movie for children of all ages. It has a few flaws, but *Superman* is nonetheless two hours and 15 minutes of pure fun, fancy, and adventure."

Stanley Kauffmann's *New Republic* piece, while not the only negative review, was among the few to skewer the film. Kauffmann wrote, "I hardly need to note that the result [of the several scriptwriters] is blah. Not only blah but occasionally inexplicable...for instance, the entrance to the villain's headquarters seems to be far under Grand Central Terminal in New York but the interior seems to be in the terminal itself."

Summing up the upbeat reviews, Jim Beaver, in *Films in Review*, opened his piece by noting, "'Sometimes the magic works, and sometimes it doesn't.' In *Superman*, the magic works." Beaver concluded, "Though '78's *Superman* is not a great film, it is the most enjoyable film of the year for all ages."

Krypton leader Jor-El (Marlon Brando) charges General Zod (Terence Stamp) and his two accomplices Ursa and Non (Sarah Douglas and Jack O'Halloran) with plotting to overthrow the government. Jor-El and the Council elders vote the trio guilty. General Zod says Jor-El and his heirs will bow down to him some day. The criminals are frozen inside a pane of glass and sent into space.

After Jor-El warns the Council that Krypton will soon explode, he and his wife Lara (Susannah York) send their son to Earth, launching the space craft as the planet destroys itself. As he travels through space for three years, the infant hears the teachings of Jor-El. The crystal craft lands in a Kansas wheatfield and the child is found by Jonathan and Martha Clark Kent (Glenn Ford and Phyllis Thaxter), who keep the boy and raise him as their own, naming him Clark.

The teenage Clark (Jeff East) is the equipment manager of the football team. Not invited to join a group of teens that includes Lana Lang, a red-haired cheerleader, a frustrated Clark kicks a football out of sight. Later, Clark races a speeding train and even beats his "friends" home.

Jonathan Kent tells Clark that he's "here for a reason," before suffering a fatal heart attack. A mysterious green-glowing crystal leads Clark to the Arctic. Throwing the crystal as far as he can, Clark watches as it grows to a "Fortress of Solitude." It is here that the image of Clark's real father, Jor-El, continues his education for twelve years. Clark, now 30, returns to Earth as Superman.

New York City. . .er. . .Metropolis. Inside the busy *Daily Planet* offices, newly hired Clark Kent (Christopher Reeve) meets reporter Lois Lane (Margot Kidder) and photographer Jimmy Olsen (Marc McClure) in the office of Perry White (Jackie Cooper). Later, a gun-wielding stickup man forces Clark and Lois into an alley. When Lois resists, the man fires. Shielding Lois, Clark catches the bullet and pretends to faint. Revived, Clark somehow describes the exact contents of Lois' purse.

After an undercover cop trails Otis (Ned Beatty), the moronic henchman of Lex Luthor, down into the bowels of Grand Central Station, the evil master criminal hurls the cop into the path of an oncoming train. Secluded 200 feet below Park Avenue with his mistress, Eve Teschmacher (Valerie Perrine), Luthor (Gene Hackman) spends his time planning a gigantic real-estate swindle. (He plans to buy up property along the eastern edge of California, then by means of nuclear missiles, trigger a grand earthquake that will cause California to break away from the continent. Voila! New beachfront property!)

A helicopter taking Lois from the roof of the *Daily Planet* building to meet the incoming Air Force One crashes and hangs precariously over the edge of the building. Clark changes into Superman and flies to the rescue, catching the falling Lois and returning her and the helicopter unharmed to the roof. He tells Lois that he's "a friend."

Superman's big night: After collaring a cat burglar crawling up the side of a building, Superman catches several robbers, gets a little girl's cat out of a tree, and saves Air Force One after the plane loses an engine. Excited TV news reporters show scenes of Superman's exploits.

Lois gets a note asking her to meet "a friend" at 8 P.M. at her apartment. Superman arrives and gives Lois an exclusive interview. After revealing that he can't see through lead, Superman tells Lois that he's "here to fight for truth, justice, and the American way." Then Superman takes Lois on an exhilarating flight above the city.

Lois now names the thus-far nameless super hero: "I Spent the Night with Superman," reads the bold headline in the next day's *Daily Planet.* Reading Lois' revelations that Superman is from the planet Krypton and cannot see through lead, Luthor devises a plan to kill Superman with a meteorite from Krypton.

While Lois and Jimmy are on assignment near Boulder Dam, Luthor, Otis, and Miss Teschmacher penetrate a military convoy and change the coordinates on two nuclear missiles. As the missiles are launched, Superman follows a high-frequency transmission from Luthor to its source and learns of Luthor's plans to trigger an earthquake. Tricked into thinking Luthor is hiding the detonator inside a lead-lined box, Superman opens it to find a Kryptonite necklace, which Luthor slips around Superman's neck.

After Miss Teschmacher learns that the second missile is heading toward her mother's home in Hackensack, New Jersey, she frees Superman on the condition he save her mom first. After Superman deflects the first missile into space, the other one strikes and triggers an enormous earthquake. Superman repairs the fault, then saves a school bus dangling over the edge of the Golden Gate Bridge.

Moments after Boulder Dam bursts, Superman rescues Jimmy Olsen and creates an avalanche that blocks the floodwaters. But Lois is smothered and crushed in her car. Pulling her out, Superman mourns over her dead body. With a cry of rage and anguish, Superman flies into space and reverses the Earth's rotation—reversing time itself and preventing Lois' death.

Superman flies Luthor and Otis to a prison to await a fair trial.

In 1933, Jerry Siegel and Joe Shuster, two Cleveland teenagers, came up with what they believed to be a sure-fire idea for a comic strip: an American version of Friedrich Nietzsche's *Ubermensch* (Overman) to be called Superman. Since the two young men were unsuccessful in their attempts to sell their idea as a comic strip, they turned to comic books.

Siegel and Shuster's Superman, a refugee from the doomed planet Krypton, was introduced in *Action Comics #1*, June, 1938. Besides featuring the origin and first appearance of Superman, that fateful issue also contained Marco Polo, Tex Thompson, Pep Morgan, Chuck Dawson & Scoop Scanlon, and the introduction to Zatara. A copy of *Action Comics #1* in mint condition can now bring as much as $15,000 from a collector (its original cover price was ten cents). By the summer of 1939, the character's popularity led to his getting his own magazine, *Superman. Superman #1* reprinted the first four *Action* stories, plus four pages accidently omitted from *Action Comics #1.*

Although Superman later became a near god, the early Superman's powers came chiefly from his reaction to earth's atmosphere and lesser gravity. Superman did not fly, per se; he *leaped*—that's where the memorable phrase "Able to leap tall buildings in a single bound" came from. Later, more detailed explanations of Superman's powers clarified the origin of his invulnerability: His atoms, more tightly packed, render him impervious to harm and give him superhuman strength.

Siegel and Shuster were strongly influenced by Philip Wylie's 1930 SF novel *Gladiator*, in which a midwestern scientist transformed his son into a pre–Superman superman. He was impervious to gunfire, constructed his own fortress, and battled for "good" in World War I. The young authors probably got their hero's first name of Clark, and the idea of a Fortress of Solitude in the icy North, from Doc Savage, "The Man of Bronze."

In *The Great Comic Book Heroes*, Jules Feiffer wrote, "The particular brilliance of Superman lay not only in the fact that he was the first of the super-heroes, but in the concept of his alter ego." To Feiffer, the decision to give a godlike figure a fake identity—a weakling with eyeglasses who fainted at the sight of trouble—was a stroke of genius. As Feiffer notes, "His fake identity is our real one." Clark Kent, then, allows us to imagine ourselves as Superman—saying enough's enough, taking off our glasses, tearing open our shirts to reveal the S underneath, and then putting bureaucrats, bosses, and bullies in their place.

Superman became one of the greatest success stories of all time. Unfortunately, Jerry Siegel and Joe Shuster had signed a standard comics-industry contract and lost the copyright to DC Comics. Years later, legally blind, Shuster was reduced to working as a stock boy and messenger, and Siegel, troubled by heart ailments, found employment in a Los Angeles post office.

In a *Newsweek* article at the time of the film's release, Siegel said, "The only sad thing is tht Joe and I aren't getting anything from the movie. It does feel strange that there's so much prosperity around 'Superman' and Joe and I are just getting by." Shuster, the model for mild-mannered Clark Kent, was more ebullient, saying, "I'm very happy about the movie. I'm delighted to see our creation on the screen." Shuster added: "Chris Reeve . . . really *is* Superman."

Over the years, DC Comics, once the giant in the field, grew fat and complacent. The hungry kid on the block, Marvel Comics, introduced "new and improved" superheroes to the comics field and became the acknowledged leader of the comics industry. Realizing that they had not only allowed Superman to be pulled this way and that in other universes and dimensions, but also allowed his various spin-offs—*Superboy, Supergirl, Superman's Girlfriend Lois Lane, Superman's Pal Jimmy Olsen, et al.*—to muddy the once-clear image comic book readers had of Superman, DC Comics discarded many of these superfluous elements and began anew in 1986 with a six-part series called *The Man of Steel*.

This limited series written and drawn by John Byrne and Dick Girdano reestablished and redefined the Superman story. While most of the familiar elements of the myth remain the same—Jor-El and Lara send their son in a rocket to Earth before their planet of Krypton destroys itself—Byrne and Girdano have wrought subtle changes. Unlike the "old" Clark Kent of the

Superman battles for "truth, justice, and the American way."

comics and the films, a clumsy high school "nerd" who keeps his powers hidden, the modern version is a popular football star and all-around athlete at Smallville High.

Once the series ended—after involving Superman with old flame Lana Lang, invoking his uneasy friendship with Batman, introducing Lex Luthor, and revealing to Superman his origins—*Superman* resumed monthly publication.

On February 12, 1940, *Superman* premiered as a thrice-weekly radio program on the Mutual Network. Starring Clayton "Bud" Collyer, the Kellogg's Cereals–sponsored program introduced a viable threat to the otherwise indestructible Man of Steel: Kryptonite.

With Bud Collyer continuing to play the voice role, *Superman* came to movie screens in 1941 as a series of 17 lavishly produced, fully animated color cartoons produced by Fleischer Studios and released by Paramount. As Superman, Collyer spoke in a deeper, more resonant voice than as Clark Kent. The first in the cartoon series, *Superman* (AKA *The Mad Scientist*), was followed by *Destruction, Inc.*, *Terror on the Midway*, *Jungle Drums* (with embarrassing racial sterotypes), *The Mummy Strikes*, *The Bulleteers*, and such World War II propaganda pieces as *The Japoteurs*.

In the mid '40s, producer Sam Katzman, known for quickie, low-budget productions, purchased the film rights to the *Superman* comic. After both Universal and Republic rejected Katzman's proposed Superman serial, he turned to Columbia Pictures. Columbia and Katzman hired the versatile Kirk Alyn to play Clark Kent/Superman, thereby forever typecasting the young actor.

The 1948 serial, fittingly titled *Superman*, was notable for several things. It not only introduced Noel Neill as Lois Lane, but also gave the Man of Steel the power of flight in place of giant leaps. The well-made fifteen-parter was so successful (reportedly the highest-grossing serial ever) that it was followed two years later by the inevitable sequel, *Atom Man vs. Superman*.

In 1951, Superman returned to the screen in a feature film called *Superman and the Mole Men*. Starring George Reeves as the Man of Steel, this successful effort, directed by Lee Sholem, served as a pilot for the long-running TV series. The low-budget Lippert production was later incorporated into the television show as episodes 25 and 26, "The Unknown People." The "Mole Men" were midgets, the best known being Billy Curtis.

George Reeves, the star of *Superman and the Mole Men*, portrayed the caped superhero for five seasons (1953–57) in the syndicated *The Adventures of Superman*. After Phyllis Coates played Lois Lane for the initial season, Noel Neill reprised her role as the enterprising reporter. The other regulars were John Hamilton as Perry White, Jack Larson as Jimmy Olsen, and Robert Shayne as Inspector Bill Henderson.

The 104 episodes established George Reeves (no relation to Christopher Reeve) as the definitive Superman in the minds of those who grew up watching the series. Reeves, an excellent film actor (he was one of the Tarleton twins in 1939's *Gone with the Wind*), became as typecast as Superman as had Kirk Alyn earlier. Finally, in 1959, despondent and alone, unable to find other roles, Reeves committed suicide at age 45.

It's a Bird! It's a Plane! It's Superman! was a 1960s Broadway musical by Charles Strouse and David Newman. In 1975, with David Wilson in the title role, the musical appeared as a TV movie on ABC.

In 1974, the father-son producing team of Alexander and Ilya Salkind purchased the film rights to Superman from Warner Communications for

$6.5 million. The younger Salkind (Ilya) had convinced his father that people were in desperate need of "a hero." Ilya Salkind was surprised that Superman's proprietors gave up such a valuable property so easily. "Warners thought *Superman* was dated, past its prime," he said. Later, after changing its corporate mind, Warners bought back into the distribution rights.

The Salkinds first hoped that the film could be made for a relatively modest $15 million in six months. But costs began escalating from day one, when they signed Mario Puzo, author and co-screenwriter of *The Godfather* and *The Godfather, Part II*, to write the script. Puzo demanded—and got—a lot of money for his elephantine script, reportedly over 500 pages long.

While Puzo was laboring on the screenplay, Pierre Spengler was assigned the producer's role, and he began making plans for the film to be shot in Cinecitta Studios in Rome. Cinecitta's stages and technicians, however, were not up to such a potentially daunting special effects extravaganza, and the Salkinds and Spengler looked elsewhere—but only after numerous sets had already been constructed in Italy.

Guy Hamilton, a veteran of several James Bond movies, had been hired as *Superman's* director. However, after the Salkinds and Spengler moved the production to England, Hamilton, a British citizen, could not remain as director because of tax reasons. Casting about frantically, the Salkinds hired Richard Donner, a workmanlike director who'd recently had a huge success with the supernatural *The Omen*.

Born in New York City, Richard Donner originally wanted to be an actor, not a director. While Donner did manage to land a number of small roles on the stage, his acting career was less than spectacular. Martin Ritt directed Donner in a television drama and asked him to become his assistant. Reasoning that he didn't have much of an acting career to give up, Donner agreed and quickly moved from assistant director to director. After directing industrial films, television commercials, and a number of documentaries, Donner ventured west to Hollywood.

Producer Ed Adamson noticed a Westinghouse commercial Donner directed and asked him if he could work with a young actor named Steve McQueen for a Western series to be called *Wanted: Dead or Alive.* Donner laughed and told Adamson that he and McQueen had been stage actors together in New York. Donner was hired to direct several shows, and began a career as a television director, helming episodes of series like *The Twilight Zone* and *The Fugitive*.

Donner's first feature, the semi-documentary *X-15* (1961), was followed by a number of forgettable films. Donner finally scored a box-office and critical success with *The Omen* in 1976 and came to the attention of the Salkinds.

In *Cinefantastique*, Donner called Puzo's original script "well-written" but also "ridiculous," because of its 550-page length. Most shooting scripts, Donner noted, average 110 pages in length. Even allowing for the fact that Puzo had written two movie scripts in one, the original screenplay was over 300 pages too long.

Puzo's script, which Salkind called "very heavy," was reworked by the team of Robert Benton and David Newman, who'd written the 1960s Broadway musical version. They succeeded all too well in taking Puzo's doom and gloom in the opposite direction, adding such jokey touches as Superman, looking for Lex Luthor, flying down to a bald man in the street and discovering he's grabbed Telly Savalas (then popular as *Kojak*)—who says, "Who loves ya, Baby?"

After Benton and Newman's first draft, Benton left the project and was replaced by Newman's wife, Leslie, who was especially helpful in molding Lois Lane into a spunky-yet-vulnerable foil for Clark Kent/Superman.

Hired in January 1977, director Donner, hoping to find a middle ground between Puzo's high seriousness and Benton and Newman's high camp, brought in writer Tom Mankiewicz as a "creative consultant." Working closely with Mankiewicz, Donner and the 35-year-old writer sought "verisimilitude," attempting to keep the framework of the comic book yet not make a joke or parody out of it, *à la* TV's campy *Batman* series of the mid-'60s.

British designer John Barry was hired to design the sets and create *Superman*'s "look." Born in 1935, Barry had designed Stanley Kubrick's *A Clockwork Orange* (1971) and George Lucas' *Star Wars* (1977). (Barry later died suddenly and unexpectedly during the production of *Star Wars*' 1980 sequel, *The Empire Strikes Back*.)

Cinematographer Geoffrey Unsworth was hired as the director of photography. A superb cinematographer, the talented Unsworth's previous films included *A Night to Remember* (1958), *Becket* (1964), *2001: A Space Odyssey* (1968), and *Cabaret* (1972). Unsworth died shortly after *Superman* was completed. He received screen credit for *Superman II* and won a posthumous Academy Award for his photography for Roman Polanski's *Tess* (1979).

Academy Award–winning actor Marlon Brando was signed—for a reported $3.7 million dollars—to play Superman's Krypton father, Jor-El. While the amount of money the Salkinds paid Brando for a few minutes of screen time was mocked and criticized at the time, his signing gave the project instant respectability—which was the producers' intent.

According to an *American Film* interview, Donner learned from Jay Kanter, an agent and a friend of the actor's, that Marlon Brando wanted to portray Jor-El as a green suitcase, using only his voice in the film. Donner called Francis Ford Coppola to see if Brando could possibly be serious. Coppola told Donner that the actor talked a lot, wonderful talk. "But just let him talk," Coppola advised, "because he'll always talk himself out of anything you don't want him to do."

Thus prepared, Donner went to Brando's house. Ever elusive and playful, Brando then suggested playing Jor-El as a bagel. But, since Brando had earlier told a story about one of his children to make a point about how bright kids are, Donner trapped him by agreeing with him that kids are pretty sharp and aware of things.

Pointing out that most kids knew what Jor-El looked like from reading the comic books, Donner forced Brando to admit that they'd know that Superman's father was neither a green suitcase nor a bagel. After confessing that he'd "hung" himself, Brando simply said, "Show me my costume."

After being hired to replace Guy Hamilton, Donner had only 11 weeks lead time before shooting was scheduled to begin. He made every minute count: working on the script with Mankiewicz, scouting locations in Canada and the United States, preparing the London sets, and hiring actors.

While all this was going on, the Salkinds were looking for someone to play the Man of Steel. Their first choice, incredibly, was Robert Redford. Redford, however, wanted a reported $6 million up front and a piece of the action. He was turned down and the search continued; Clint Eastwood and Kris Kristofferson were among the many others considered for the part.

Donner finally decided to take a chance on a young, too-skinny, essentially unknown actor named Christopher Reeve. Reeve, the son of F.D. Reeve, a Yale professor and novelist, grew up a serious young boy who read classic plays and novels for entertainment, in place of the movies he and his brother were forbidden to attend until they were teenagers.

Reeve attended Cornell University, where he majored in English and music theory, and the Juilliard School, where he studied acting. After graduation, he joined the Circle Repertory Company in New York City and found steady work playing Ben Harper on *Love of Life*, a television soap opera.

To build up his body for his new role, Reeve lifted weights for two hours daily and was allowed to eat anything he wanted for his four meals. Learning to "fly" was a bit more complicated. The 25-year-old Reeve spent several hours a day, for ten weeks, bounding on a trampoline to practice taking off and landing. Reeve admitted that learning to land on his feet after coming in from 75 feet at roughly the same speed as a parachutist was a time-consuming and dangerous experience. But, after he'd grown confident of his ability to pull off his landings and takeoffs, Reeve confessed that he felt as unbeatable and invulnerable as the superhero.

The cast of *Superman* is one of the most star-studded ever assembled for a fantasy film. Besides Marlon Brando, the other actors included Gene Hackman as Lex Luthor, Glenn Ford as Pa Kent, Jackie Cooper as Perry White (replacing Keenan Wynn), Phyllis Thaxter as Martha Kent, Ned

Beatty as Otis, Susannah York as Lara, Valerie Perrine as Miss Teschmacher, Trevor Howard as the First Krypton Elder, Margot Kidder as Lois Lane, Terence Stamp as General Zod, and Harry Andrews as the Second Krypton Elder.

The sets, designed by John Barry, were constructed at Pinewood Studios. Some work was done at Pinewood initially, before Barry was hired, and then the production moved to Bray Studios, to Rome, to Shepperton Studios, and finally back to Pinewood after Donner was hired as director.

The Krypton sets, among the first built, were constructed with hydraulics underneath to move and shake them as if in an earthquake. A number of half-ton crystals were mounted on hydraulic lifts so that they could smash up through the breakaway floors in the scenes in which the planet Krypton destroys itself. Derek Meddings constructed the crystal towers of Krypton out of fiberglass and plaster, occupying an entire sound-stage with the enormous miniature.

Meddings' other "miniatures" included a 60-foot-high model of the Golden Gate Bridge and a 40-foot-high model of Boulder Dam. Meddings' Golden Gate Bridge was built outside, so the sky could be used for a natural backdrop. This exterior set also allowed Donner to play with the concept of "flying" a stuntman from a 300-foot crane hundreds of feet behind the miniature, in an attempt to put an in-scale Superman into the same picture. The idea was dropped when it proved unconvincing and difficult to bring off.

The bridge miniature was constructed on a moveable foundation so that the structure could be shaken and swayed to simulate a massive earthquake.

Calling Derek Meddings the "maestro," director Donner later fumed that producer Spengler, underestimating the shooting schedule required for the film, failed to secure Meddings' services for the duration of the project, losing him to a James Bond film. Thus while Meddings was responsible for the excellent Boulder Dam miniature, the reverse end of that miniature, the little town that is inundated by the burst dam's flood water, was done by someone else. Meddings is sorely missed: That sequence is one of the worst examples of special effects miniature work ever to find its way into a major motion picture.

Superman's first appearance, the scene in which he rescues Lois from the falling helicopter, was a combination of live-action shots integrated with models and full-size special effects shooting. First, a real helicopter was filmed landing on the top of the Citibank building on Wall Street in New York. Then two tops of the *Daily Planet* building were constructed, one full-size and one miniature.

Colin Chilvers and the effects crew purchased the remains of a crashed helicopter and rebuilt it to their own specifications. Suspended from a

45-ton crane, the full-size helicopter—its blades turning—was filmed spinning out of control atop the skyscraper. The crash shots were particularly difficult and dangerous because the 3000-pound helicopter not only had people inside it, it also had a camera crew hanging off its side.

After the helicopter was filmed dangling over the edge of the full-size set in Pinewood, miniatures of both the helicopter and the building were utilized for the scenes of the aircraft falling down the building's side. After Superman caught both Lois Lane and the falling helicopter, several cranes lifted the full-size, rebuilt helicopter back onto the top of the set, cementing the illusion of Superman effortlessly replacing the aircraft on its landing pad.

Chilvers and crew also used hydraulics and a very old camera trick to create the illusion that Superman is pushing a huge rock off a mountainside to initiate an avalanche that will halt the flood waters. An eight-foot-tall, half-ton foreground miniature boulder was placed on a mock-up of the mountainside, and Christopher Reeve stood on a platform some feet behind it. The camera alignment makes it appear that Superman pushes the hydraulically propelled rock—which falls with the gravity and slowness of the real rock that it is—off the mountainside.

The ultimate special effect in the film was to prove the most difficult to achieve: flying. A variety of methods were tried to make Christopher Reeve fly in a realistic-looking and convincing manner. Most attempts failed miserably. Director Donner knew only one thing before he began: He was not going to use back projection. A few attempts to use traveling mattes with blue backing were made, but Donner was never pleased with the results.

After actually flying Reeve on a crane, with poor and nonrepeatable results, Chilvers and the other special effects technicians tried suspending the actor on wires from several tracks embedded in the soundstage ceiling. With the wires painted to make them disappear against the background, Reeve was pulled along by stagehands. More than once Reeve ended up in a safety net placed at the end of the track to keep him from hitting the studio wall.

Superman finally used a sophisticated front-projection system invented by Zoran Perisic, a Yugoslavia-born cinematographer who'd moved to England and worked as an animation photographer for Stanley Kubrick's *2001*. Perisic later founded his own company in England, Courier Films Ltd., producing numerous television programs and commercials.

As Perisic explained in a 1977 article in *American Cinematographer*, his "Zoptic" (Zoom + optic) special effects device permitted a subject to seem to "move 'in depth' while its real position relative to the camera remains unchanged . . . making objects or people appear to fly or simply grow and shrink."

Superman's flying scenes were achieved by using a Neilson-Hordell front matte projector equipped with a Zoptic system device to project the background scene. The model or subject was positioned in front of this projected background. Then, with the projector showing a small background scene, the lens was zoomed to a longer focal length to cause Superman to seem to fly forward while the background remained stationary.

Reeve did all his flying in front of a blue screen, held in place by a fourteen-foot pole-arm colored blue to disappear against the background. To eliminate the pole from the shot altogether, body molds were taken of Reeve's body in all the positions he would be seen flying. Depending upon the mold attached to the pole, Reeve could fly on his back, his left or right side, or on his stomach. For closeups, a smaller version of the pole-arm, a gimbal, was used.

Christopher Reeve, who had experience flying gliders, tried to capture that feeling in his flying scenes. Realizing that it wouldn't work on camera, Reeve objected when stuntmen took his place in the more dangerous flying equipment and only his face was photographed in closeups. As he told interviewer David Barry in *Moviegoer*, "Technically it would all be correct, but something was missing from my eyes—a sense of where I was, of being fulfilled by it; a sense of airspeed, of what I was looking at, where I was going, and how it felt." Reeve replaced the stunt men.

Even though Reeve/Superman wasn't really flying, his cape had to swirl and flutter realistically. But wind machines failed to make the cape perform as it should when Reeve flew in front of the process screen, so other methods had to be employed. Les Bowie, in charge of matte painting, built a radio-controlled system of rods, remarkably similar to ordinary fishing rods, which manipulated lines attached to Superman's cape. With this system in place, Superman's cape behaved as it should—finally.

While most of the sets were constructed at Pinewood, the production did location shooting in New York City and in Canada. Just as the Citibank building's rooftop helipad doubled for the *Daily Planet*'s, the *New York Daily News* became the *Daily Planet* itself. In New York, the production had to put up with curious crowds, a midsummer heat wave, and, on July 13, a citywide power blackout.

Director Donner needed vast fields of waving wheat, and locations in Calgary and Alberta, Canada were selected for Smallville, Clark Kent's hometown in Kansas, because the United States wheat crop would already be harvested at the time of the location lensing. Other locales included British Columbia, Canada, and Gallup, New Mexico.

Superman's music was written by John Williams, the composer who is the closest to a modern equivalent of those earlier producers of stirring film scores, Erich Wolfgang Korngold *(The Sea Hawk)*, Miklos Rozsa *(The Thief of Bagdad)*, and the incomparable Max Steiner *(King Kong)*.

A flying sequence with Lois (Margot Kidder) from *Superman II.*

Before winning acclaim and Academy Awards for his scores for *Jaws* (1975) and *Star Wars* (1977), Williams had written the music for 43 films over a period of 17 years. Having begun in Hollywood as a studio pianist in 1956, Williams was fortunate actually to work with Alfred Newman, Franz Waxman, Dimitri Tiomkin, and Max Steiner. Sadly, Williams was learning his lessons from these masters of romance and adventure just as the romantic era in film scores seemed to be over. Gritty, "realistic" movies and scores became the vogue.

Young film auteur George Lucas, realizing his rollicking space adventure movie *Star Wars* needed a suitably larger-than-life score in the grand romantic style, turned to Williams. Using a 104-member orchestra, Williams restored the heroic tradition to films with his beautiful soundtrack.

Fresh on the heels of his *Star Wars* triumph, Williams agreed to write *Superman*'s score. *Superman*'s main title overture is as thrilling and heroic as *Star Wars*', and Williams' music helps the film soar by alternately being sad or exhilarating, spiritual or triumphant.

The acting in *Superman* is mostly top drawer. But Brando, once considered the world's greatest film actor, had begun walking through his film roles by the time of *Superman*. Although he had only a few scenes, Brando insisted on using cue cards to help him remember his lines. Brando's rationale for refusing to learn his lines was that the cue cards provided his characterization with spontaneity: Jor-El would seem to be searching for words.

Brando's "spontaneous" performance at least has the value of being sincere. But his mildly hammy presence, in a Gorgeous George wig, adds little to the film, and his Jor-El could have been played by anyone.

Gene Hackman, who shot to fame with *Bonnie and Clyde*, 1967's blood-bag ballet, gets all the mileage possible out of the confusing character of Lex Luthor. While never taking himself too seriously, Hackman also never allows his characterization to deteriorate into high camp—a very real possibility when one must play off a Beagle Boys–stupid henchman like Ned Beatty's Otis.

Margot Kidder, who possesses a slightly sexy, slightly hookerish appeal, is attractive without being especially pretty. Yet her Lois is as vulnerable as she is tough, and needs reassurance just as much as she needs a good dictionary. Kidder's spunky, no-nonsense performance as the go-getter reporter validates her selection for the role.

Kidder works well with Reeve, and her line readings are among the best in the film ("How big are you . . . How *tall* are you?" "Do you . . . eat?"). Unfortunately, Kidder has to deliver a sappy voice-over narration ("Can you read my mind?") as Lois flies with Superman. The narration puts into words what the images, the moving pictures, are already showing; it's an unnecessary and embarrassing sequence.

Original scriptwriter Mario Puzo told *American Film:* "I think that Christopher Reeve makes that picture more than anyone else. He's the perfect guy for that part." Puzo's assessment is correct; it is all but impossible to imagine another actor in the dual role. Not only did Reeve have to live up to our expectations as Superman, the Man of Steel, he also had to be just as convincing as Clark Kent, Superman's alter ego.

Before beginning work on *Superman IV*, Reeve told *Starlog* he believed his decision to agree to play Superman was one of the most courageous acts of his career since Superman was a joke to many people. "I remember feeling that the odds were very much against trying to pull off that first movie," Reeve said. He added that he hoped he would "be able to make a character out of this and make it romantic rather than macho — make it funny rather than pompous or one-dimensional."

Reeve appeared as an ensign in *Gray Lady Down* in 1977. In addition to the *Superman* sequels, he has starred in *Somewhere in Time* (1980), *Deathtrap, Monsignor* (both 1982), *The Aviator* and *The Bostonians* (both 1984), *Street Smart* (1987), and *Switching Channels* (1988).

One of the film's great sequences, both for its technical audacity and its flawless acting, is the scene in which Superman flies from Lois' balcony as she walks to her front door to admit Clark Kent. The shot is accomplished without a cut, and audiences are always amazed and thrilled by this delightful bit of movie magic. After Superman leaves (probably a blue-screen process shot), Clark arrives. While Lois is out of the room, Clark momentarily takes off his glasses, straightens up, and becomes ... *Superman.*

Superman is a strange and wonderful amalgam of disparate elements—the Superman myth, a Christian allegory, mind-boggling special effects, accomplished acting, shoddy reasoning, slapstick humor, and near-camp lines and situations.

The parallels with the Christ story have been noted by a number of critics and observers. Jor-El sends his only son to far-off earth, promising to be with him always, saying, "The son becomes the father and the father the son." Later, when Jor-El, a holographic image, reveals himself to his son, Jor-El speaks of the earthlings: "They only lack the light to show them the way. For this reason above all, their capacity for good, I have sent them you—my only son."

Living a normal, nondescript life with his earthly parents Jonathan and Martha Kent (Joseph and Mary), the young messiah is instructed by his heavenly father and sent out to perform acts (miracles) beyond the abilities of normal people.

In their romantic flight, the earthy and sex-obsessed Lois goes so far as to marvel that she's "holding hands with a god." Later, in love with Lois (Mary Magdalene), Superman even alters the space-time continuum to raise her from the dead.

Of course, when Superman "turns back the clock," the film leaves us wondering what happened to the little town that he saved after the dam burst. When Jimmy Olsen appears, his comments reveal that Superman *did* save him at the dam, so what was the fate of the town while the Man of Steel was saving Lois?

There are similar lapses in logic in the film, and just plain silly decisions. For instance, that stylized "S" on Superman's costume, the symbol that he is Superman, is worn by Brando's Jor-El at the beginning of the film. Was that Donner's decision? Was it in the screenplay? Did costume designer Yvonne Blake conceive of it? Whatever, it makes no sense.

Lex Luthor quickly deduces that the radioactivity of a meteorite from Krypton would harm or kill Superman. In a word, *why?* Why should a piece of Superman's home planet have such a fatal effect upon him?

As limned by Gene Hackman, Lex Luthor is a hammy delight. But it seems far-fetched and preposterous that such a criminal "genius" would have as his primary assistant such a knuckleheaded bumbler.

The scenes of Jor-El dispatching the trio of General Zod, Ursa, and Non to an eternity of imprisonment inside a mirror-like crystal have absolutely nothing to do with the rest of the film, and the time devoted to this puzzling sequence makes no sense. It was only after *Superman II* opened that moviegoers understood the inclusion of that sequence in the original film. (*Superman* was to have ended with the trio's release from confinement and murderous attack on the moon base that later occurred in the first sequel, but Donner decided against ending the film with a cliffhanger.)

During *Superman*'s production, Donner reportedly shot most of the sequel. After a falling out with producer Spengler, Donner was replaced as director of *Superman II* by Richard Lester. Lester had to reshoot a lot of footage that involved Jor-El because Brando was suing the Salkinds for a percentage of the gross coming to him from *Superman*. Scrapping Brando's scenes meant scrapping most of the Donner-directed footage, and cost the production company millions of dollars.

There are wonderfully comic moments in *Superman*, as when Clark Kent, needing a phone booth in which to change into Superman, notices the open, streamlined phone cubicles of the 1970s and does a perfectly delivered "take." Superman's and Lois' scenes together are sparked by taut sexual and comic tension worthy of the classic couple of Tracy and Hepburn. Valerie Perrine's scenes with Hackman and Reeve stand with the best work she's done, but unfortunately, she really doesn't have much to do.

Superman took the modern film's obsession with credits to ridiculous heights (just look in the Appendix if you don't believe me). The opening credits unrolled for four minutes, and the closing credits for seven and a half—meaning that eleven and a half minutes of the film's total of 143 were given over to listing anyone who even walked by the set.

The closing credits dedicate the film to Terry Hill and John Bodimeade, two stuntmen killed during shooting, and to Cinematographer Geoffrey Unsworth, who died shortly after the production wrapped.

The final cost for *Superman* is difficult to assess accurately since its costs are intertwined with the (partially) simultaneously shot *Superman II*. Ilya Salkind told *Time* that the film cost $35 million, but other figures range from $25 million to as high as $50 million. *Screen International*, published at the Cannes Film Festival, put the combined cost of the two films at $109 million. Assuming that's a fair assessment (a large assumption), and figuring in the interest charges which could not be repaid until *Superman II* opened two years after its production, the Salkinds paid heavily to bring the comic book superhero to the screen.

Superman was a big hit at the box office. According to *Variety*, the film earned nearly $83 million in U.S. and Canadian rentals (making it the fifteenth-highest all-time rental champ in *Variety*'s January 1987 listing), and did quite well overseas. *Superman II* earned rentals of $65 million, and *Superman III* only $37 million. *Superman IV* was released in 1987.

Superman is a fine fantasy film, a marvel of innovative special effects and a well-intentioned—and mostly successful—effort to bring America's favorite super hero to the screen.

12. The Thief of Bagdad: Arabian Nights

"Where have you come from?"
"From the other side of time . . . to find you."
"How long have you been searching?"
"Since time began."
"Now that you've found me, how long will you stay?"
"Till the end of time."
— *The Princess' and Ahmad's first meeting in the garden.*

The Thief of Bagdad is one of the best fantasy films ever made. Some would call it the best, and it surely ranks in the top three. Nearly 50 years after its release, few films have approached its incredible photography, color, and sets. While its acting ranges from merely competent to brilliant, its literate and witty script is remarkably adult for a "child's" fantasy. Imaginative, compelling, and intricately structured, *Thief* remains a viewing treat to this day, and the finest "Arabian Nights" fantasy ever filmed. (For a listing of other Arabian Nights films, see the Appendix.)

Georges Perinal's Technicolor photography won him the Academy Award for cinematography. Lawrence Butler and Jack Whitney's wizardry won them the Oscar for special effects, and Vincent Korda's Academy Award was for the Best Color Interior Decoration.

Like many a film which has achieved the aura of a classic or a masterpiece over the years since its release, *The Thief of Bagdad* was not well liked by the critics of the day. Otis Ferguson's review in *The New Republic* was typical of *Thief*'s harsh reception: "*The Thief of Bagdad*, an extravaganza in full color, fabulous sets, and processed devices of many wonderful kinds . . . is a picture for children of all ages up to six. Beyond six, to all except cases of retarded development and Swahili who are seeing their first magic lantern show, its numerous defects will very quickly become apparent.

"But the thing that even children will get vaguely restless over is that here are the means and money to make come true some of the world's stored treasures of the imagination; and here, in all its empty splendor, is a movie walking flatfooted among them without any use of the imagination."

Variety's "Walt" was somewhat less derogatory in his review, but still less than enthused: *"The Thief of Bagdad* is one of the most colorful, lavish, and eye-appealing spectacles ever screened. It's an expensive production, accenting visual appeal, combining sweeping panoramas and huge sets, amazing special effects and process photography, and the most vividly magnificent Technicolor yet. These factors insure its b[ox] o[ffice] success, and completely submerge the stolid, slow, and rather disjointed fairy tale which lacks any semblance of spontaneity in its telling."

Bosley Crowther, writing in the *New York Times,* was one of the few contemporary reviewers who admired the film. "It is all too seldom that the films, in their headlong quest of 'escape,' invade the happy realm of legends and fairy tales [yet] *The Thief of Bagdad* . . . ranks next to *Fantasia* as the most beguiling and wondrous film of this troubled season. So the least one can do is to recommend it as a cinematic delight, and thank Mr. Korda for reaching boldly into a happy world."

As the years passed, critics and film writers began to better appreciate *Thief*'s qualities. Basil Wright called it "The true stuff of fairy tale," and, in 1969, one film journal called the film "both spectacular and highly inventive." "Magical, highly entertaining, and now revalued by Hollywood moguls Lucas and Coppola," stated *Time Out* in 1980. Leonard Maltin, film historian and author of *TV Movies,* gives the film his highest rating: four stars. Leslie Halliwell, the hard-to-please author of *Halliwell's Film Guide,* calls *Thief* a "marvelous blend of magic, action and music, the only film to catch on celluloid the overpowering atmosphere of the Arabian Nights."

The busy seaport of Basra. Ahmad (John Justin), a blind beggar with a dog, cries out for alms. Ahmad is taken to the palace by Halima (Mary Morris), a beautiful agent of Bagdad's evil ruler, Jaffar. Ahmad explains to Halima and other young harem dwellers that he was once a king, Ahmad the Caliph of Bagdad, and his dog was Abu the thief. Ahmad tells them the story of how he and Abu came to their present state. (As Ahmad tells his story, it unfolds before our eyes in the following flashback.)

While witnessing an execution, Ahmad is told by his Grand Vizier Jaffar (Conrad Veidt) that he must keep his subjects in line. Jaffar suggests that Ahmad go among his people incognito and learn the truth of their natures. Ahmad learns that, because of Jaffar's cruelty, he is despised and hears of a prophecy of a liberator to come from "the lowest of the low."

Jaffar has Ahmad arrested and thrown in prison, where he meets a young thief named Abu (Sabu). Ahmad and Abu are sentenced to die in the morning, but Abu has stolen the key to their cell.

The two escape to the river, where they steal a small boat and sail to Basra. After Abu steals food to eat, they see the palace of a Sultan who owns a thousand toys. There is confusion and panic as the Sultan's soldiers clear the way for his beautiful daughter. It is death to look upon the unwed Princess (June Duprez). Defying the ban, a smitten Ahmad watches the beautiful Princess enter atop a pink elephant and vows to see her again. Her maidens tell the Princess of a Djinni in the garden pool. Curious, she looks and sees Ahmad's reflection — he's above her in a tree. After she talks to him, believing him a Djinni, Ahmad swings down and reveals himself to be a man. Calling himself "your slave," Ahmad falls in love with the lovely Princess.

They promise undying love, and kiss. Ahmad vows to return the next day. "Tomorrow," he says. "And all tomorrows," the Princess whispers after he leaves.

The next day Jaffar visits Basra and the Sultan's palace, viewing the old man's many toys. Jaffar reveals a new wonder he has brought with him: a mechanical flying horse. When the Sultan (Miles Malleson) says he *must* have it, Jaffar promises it to him . . . in return for the Princess' hand in marriage; he has seen her beauty in his crystal. Overhearing the conversation, the Princess insists she'll never marry Jaffar and rides into the desert.

The Sultan's men, searching for the Princess, find Ahmad and Abu. When Ahmad attempts to explain who he is to the Sultan ("My eyes have been witness to his treachery"), Jaffar causes him to go blind and turns Abu into a dog before the young thief can give voice to his claim that Jaffar is a usurper.

Ahmad's tale over, he learns from Halima that the Princess is in the palace but in a magical sleep. Taken to her, Ahmad wakes her and tells her he is no dream. After learning Ahmad is blind, the Princess is tricked into going aboard Jaffar's ship, which immediately sails. Jaffar reveals his presence and has Abu the dog thrown overboard.

Jaffar comes to the Princess ("Jaffar," he says, "it is always Jaffar") and tells her he found and rescued her from the desert, and kept her while she slept. He also tells her that the same moment that he holds her in his arms, Ahmad will see. "Take me in your arms," the Princess says, and Ahmad cries out in joy and pain. His vision has been restored — but he knows the cost of his sight. Abu, who has climbed up on the docks as a dog, is also transformed back to his old self.

Jaffar now has the Princess' body but not her love or her soul. Trying to throw herself into the sea, she spots Ahmad and Abu following in a small boat. "Wind!" cries Jaffar and a wall of water overturns the small skiff, tossing Ahmad and Abu into the sea. Later, Abu washes up on a deserted beach near the wreckage of their boat; there is no sign of Ahmad.

The Princess then asks to return to Basra, where she tells her father, the Sultan, that she doesn't want to go to Bagdad with Jaffar. "No, never, never, never . . . never while I live," the old Sultan declares while Jaffar looks on.

Jaffar now gives the toy-crazed Sultan a fatal gift—a beautiful six-armed silver mechanical doll. When Jaffar promises that "her embrace will thrill you as no other woman ever has . . . or will," the Sultan is encircled by her arms—and killed when she drives a spike into the back of his neck.

Abu finds a bottle and opens it, releasing a giant Djinni (Rex Ingram). "Freedom!" cries the Djinni. "Free after 2000 years. Two thousand years ago King Solomon, master of all the Djinn, imprisoned me within that bottle." He intends to kill Abu despite being released by him. After Abu tricks him back into the bottle, he refuses to free the Djinni again until he is granted three wishes.

Abu's first wish is for sausages like his mother used to make. Then the Djinni and Abu fly off in search of the All-Seeing Eye in the forehead of the Goddess of Light in the Temple of the Dawn. "And now, my little master," says the Djinni, "You can be a thief *and* a hero all in one." The Djinni places Abu inside the temple and blows him to the Goddess' base.

Abu begins his climb to the forehead, ascending a huge web. Far below awaits an octopus pit; above, the giant spider of the web. Abu sees skeletons entombed in the grip of the web and then spots the spider. Warding off the monstrous arachnid with his sword, Abu cuts the strand of web holding the spider, and it falls into the octopus pit.

Climbing out onto the Goddess' face, Abu removes the Eye. Abu then looks into the Eye, sees Ahmad wandering in desert canyons, and uses his second wish to be taken to Ahmad.

Ahmad sees the Princess in the Eye, watching in anguish as she inhales the essence of the Blue Rose of Forgetfuness. Despairing and angry, Ahmad wishes he'd never met Abu; he wishes he were in Bagdad. An angry Abu wishes Ahmad were there, too—alas, it's his third wish and the Djinni flies off after granting it.

Jaffar is telling the Princess that she has loved—and will always love—him. But Ahmad materializes and the spell is broken. Ahmad is overpowered by Jaffar's guards and imprisoned facing his beloved Princess.

Seeing all this in the Eye, Abu wishes he could help them. Frustrated, he smashes the Eye—and is transported to the Land of Legend, where he is welcomed as a Prince by an old King (Morton Selten). The King tells him they have been waiting for him "twice 2000 years."

Abu is to be the old King's successor, and is presented with a magic crossbow: "Aim this only at injustice," the old King tells him, "and you cannot fail." All is to be his, except a magic carpet, "which flies when it is bidden 'Fly, carpet,'" and which is to carry the old King to Allah.

Later, as the old King watches unseen but approvingly, Abu apologizes to Allah for stealing the carpet to help his friends and then uses it to fly to Bagdad.

The Djinni, released from his bottle, holds a terrified Abu in his hand.

As Ahmad is about to be beheaded, the Storyteller (Allan Jeayes) is again telling the populace of the legend: "A wise man . . . gave comfort to them with a prophecy, saying in the fullness of time a liberator shall come upon them. . . . One day in the blue, you shall see a boy, the lowest of the low, mounted on a cloud. . . ."

Then Abu arrives, and the city dwellers watch in wonder as the prophecy is fulfilled. Abu shoots the executioner with the crossbow. The people rise in revolt and overpower Jaffar's guards. As Jaffar tries to escape on the mechanical horse, Abu kills him with the Arrow of Justice.

Ahmad is restored as Caliph and marries the Princess. He tells the people that Abu will be schooled and trained so that one day he might become his Grand Vizier. Wanting none of that, Abu flies off on the carpet seeking "some fun and an adventure at last."

Alexander Korda (1893–1956), eldest of the three talented Korda brothers, was born Sandor Kellner in a small Hungarian town. The mogul-to-be became a journalist for a Budapest newspaper when he was 20. After contributing an essay on movies to his paper, Korda was surprised to find himself hailed an expert in the young and quickly expanding field. Fluent in German, French, and English, Korda was asked to translate the titles of foreign-made pictures into Hungarian. Soon, with the aid of a battered, used movie camera, he was making his own films — writing, producing, and directing them himself to save money.

After this modest beginning, Korda became a director for Sasha Films in Vienna, and moved to the UFA Studios in Berlin in 1923. With his first wife Maria Corda, he struck out for Hollywood in 1926. *The Private Life of Helen of Troy* was his first of ten films for First National Pictures, and he was soon making $100,000 a year.

After moving around from studio to studio, Korda tired of Hollywood and his treatment at the hands of the moguls who ran things. Besides, he wanted to be his own boss. Packing his bags, he returned to Europe, settling in London.

After making one film for Paramount, *Service for Ladies* (1932), Korda and two friends, writer Lajos Biro and French movie salesman Stephen Pallos, created London Films. Korda made a few forgettable films to put money in the till, then sent for his brother Vincent, who joined the compay as art director.

The persuasive Korda convinced Charles Laughton to portray the title role in *The Private Life of Henry VIII* for London Films and distributor United Artists. The film was an immediate success and made the homely Laughton an even bigger international star, as well as winning him an Academy Award as Best Actor. Better yet, from Korda's point of view, the film cost a mere £60,000 and earned London Films £500,000. Korda's success encouraged a new wave of British filmmaking, and Korda is considered by many to be one of the fathers of the modern British film industry. (For Korda's other films, see the Appendix.)

Korda's 1937 production of *Elephant Boy* was directed by Robert Flaherty and propelled its young Indian lead to stardom. Sabu Dastagir was an elephant stable boy for the Maharajah of Mysore when he was spotted by Flaherty. New scenes were added to take advantage of Sabu's natural flair for acting, and the teenager was flown to London to shoot the additional footage.

After the success of *Elephant Boy,* Korda cast his new young star in a color adaptation of an A.E.W. Mason story about an Indian prince whose knowledge of British army drum signals saves a British regiment from an ambush. *The Drum* (released as *Drums* in the United States) was another hit for Korda and Sabu.

Korda knew he couldn't keep finding similar vehicles for his young star, so he cast about for something different for Sabu to play.

Korda was seated across a banquet table from Douglas Fairbanks following the London premiere of *Drums* discussing the athletic actor's 1924 Arabian Nights hit, *The Thief of Bagdad.* The more the two talked, the more Korda realized that a remake of Fairbanks' black-and-white silent film was just what he was looking for. Korda asked Fairbanks if he would sell the rights to his film's title so that he could create an entirely new story more appropriate to his young star. To Korda's delight, Fairbanks agreed.

Korda hoped that *Thief* would firmly establish him as a major international filmmaker, successful on both sides of the Atlantic.

Douglas Fairbanks' 1924 production of *The Thief of Bagdad* ranks as one of the great silent fantasy films. The story concerns the transformation of a professional thief (Fairbanks at his best) after he sees a beautiful Princess. To prove himself worthy of her, he undergoes a series of adventures and, ultimately, saves his Princess and Bagdad from a Mongol invader. (Korda's *Thief* split Fairbanks' adventures and love interest into two parts, giving the action scenes to Sabu and the romantic element to John Justin.)

Fairbanks' fantasy adventure is imaginative and wonderfully photographed, if a bit long at 140 minutes. Dircted by Raoul Walsh, the film boasts awesome sets and magical special effects.

William Cameron Menzies was hired by Fairbanks to design the production for the Arabian Nights fantasy (a task he would repeat for Korda's version 16 years later). Menzies was one of the foremost art directors in Hollywood in the '20s, '30s and '40s; in 1928 he won the first Academy Award for art direction (or "interior decoration" as it was called then) for *The Dove*. Later, Menzies was a major contributor to the look of 1939's *Gone with the Wind*, drawing nearly 3000 detailed sketches for the camera to follow. Seeking a name for what Menzies contributed to *GWTW*, art director Lyle Wheeler and producer David O. Selznick devised the title "Production designer." (For more about Menzies, see the Appendix.)

Korda believed a fantasy which appealed to both adults and children was what the public wanted—and he intended to give it to them. He further intended to recapture the sweep and imagination of silent film, believing that "talkies" had virtually destroyed the fantasy genre.

Korda wanted his fantasy to dwarf all that had gone before, with huge, lavish sets lovingly photographed in Technicolor, a costly and difficult process to work with—so much so that each production which utilized it was assigned a special consultant by the company itself to offer expertise.

Korda hired his brother Vincent as the film's production designer and signed his favorite photographer, Georges Perinal, to capture the visual excitement on film. June Duprez recalled that, while Vincent Korda designed the sets, William Cameron Menzies designed the film as a whole and was responsible for all the direction on the miniature work.

The special effects, doubly difficult because the film was to be in color, were handled by American Lawrence Butler and his British crew. Butler, an expert on providing full-sized mechanical effects, had worked with fellow American Ned Mann on Korda and Menzies' *Things to Come*.

Butler and Mann's American optical effects expert Jack Thomas returned to the States in 1938, and his place was taken by Tom Howard. Howard, today one of Britain's top effects men *(tom thumb, 2001: A Space*

Rex Ingram, as the Djinni, standing in the miniature exterior set of the Temple of the Dawn.

Odyssey), has been credited with the invention of the traveling matte process in color. He later recalled doing at least a hundred traveling matte shots for *Thief* and said that Englishman Johnny Mills was responsible for all the hanging miniatures, yet neither Howard nor Mills was credited on the film. Lawrence Butler, who Howard recalled as a supervisor, received the screen credit . . . and the accompanying Academy Award.

When Korda was unable to sign Jon Hall for the role of Ahmad, he cast John Justin, a young British stage actor and Hall look-alike in his first film role. The part of the Princess was not quite right for Korda's wife, Merle

Oberon, so Vivien Leigh was set to play the part. Unfortunately for Korda, Leigh followed her beloved Laurence Olivier to Hollywood, where he was filming *Wuthering Heights*. When David O. Selznick spotted her, he tested her and ultimately signed her to play Scarlett O'Hara in *Gone with the Wind*. How different Hollywood history would be had Vivien Leigh played the Princess in *Thief* rather than going to America and starring in *GWTW!*

In place of Leigh, Korda used one of his young contract players, the lovely June Duprez. June Duprez had played the only female part in Korda's 1939 film version of *Four Feathers*. She recalled that her role was "the perfect vehicle for someone new. The part was too small for someone established and too important to cast with just anyone."

The 15-year-old Sabu was, of course, already under contract to Korda, and the producer cast another of his regular players in the part of the evil Vizier, the silky Conrad Veidt. Veidt gained international stardom playing the part of the somnambulist Cesare in the 1919 German silent, *The Cabinet of Dr. Caligari*. That vivid portrayal typecast him for years.

Black actor Rex Ingram had been a doctor before making his first film, *Hearts in Dixie*, in 1929. He joined the cast of *Thief* as the Djinni after two triumphal screen appearances: as De Lawd in 1936's all-black film *The Green Pastures*, and as Jim in the 1939 release of *Huckleberry Finn*.

Mary Morris played both Halima, Jaffar's beautiful agent, and the Silver Maid, the deadly toy which, after a dramatically choreographed "dance," kills the old Sultan. Like co-star Conrad Veidt she had appeared in Korda and Powell's *The Spy in Black* in 1939. (For more about the actors and their films, see the Appendix.)

The intelligent screenplay, almost totally devoid of either plain, unadorned "see Spot run" prose or inflated heroic speeches, was crafted by screenwriter, actor, and playwright Miles Malleson, based on Korda crony Lajos Biro's "scenario." Malleson and Biro were apparently strongly influenced by Powys Mathers' translation of *The Thousand and One Nights*.

Malleson, familiar to moviegoers from his many film roles, such as the executioner in *Kind Hearts and Coronets* or Canon Chasuble in *The Importance of Being Earnest*, also played the toy-infatuated Sultan in *Thief*.

As Korda's crews began to construct Vincent Korda's huge sets on the lot at Denham, tensions were mounting in Europe, and there was fear that war could erupt at any time. As Vincent's son Michael wrote in *Charmed Lives*, "Spy scares were frequent. My father, who had gone to Cornwall to shoot exterior footage for *The Thief of Bagdad* with a camera crew consisting largely of Central European refugees and exiles, was summarily arrested and charged with photographing destroyers at sea." At the time of this arrest, Vincent Korda and his camera crew were shooting the scene where Sabu finds the bottle and releases Rex Ingram's Djinni. Fortunately for the Kordas, the king interceded and Vincent was released.

This backstage shot shows Conrad Veidt looking at a page of the script (note the monocle in his right eye) as director Michael Powell looks on. Smiling up at Powell is June Duprez, who played the film's beautiful princess.

As hints of war increased, Alexander Korda responded patriotically to his adopted country's needs, pulled his technicians off *Thief* and quickly threw together a low-budget film about the R.A.F. called *The Lion Has Wings*. (Its cast included Duprez and Malleson.)

Korda turned his attentions back to *Thief* and hired German-born Ludwig Berger to direct his extravagant fantasy. Korda soon discovered that while Berger was fine in the intimate love scenes, his inability to handle the spectacle of flamboyant sets peopled by rainbow-costumed extras and exotic animals was all too apparent.

Top: Abu rides to Ahmad's rescue on the Flying Carpet. *Bottom:* The Sultan rides Jaffar's gift of a flying mechanical horse.

When Berger resisted Korda's entreaties to remove himself from the film, the producer hired Tim Whelan and Michael Powell to shoot the sequences Berger was incapable of properly staging. Later, when the two men disagreed over how certain scenes should be filmed, Korda fired Berger.

Michael Powell, who'd begun his film career in France in the 1920s, always insisted that his contribution to *Thief* was minor—that it was a producer's film, not a director's. Nonetheless, Powell brought much to the picture, including his working experience with Conrad Veidt on 1939's *The Spy in Black*.

Tim Whelan, *Thief*'s third credited director, was an American who spent much of his early career in England. Not well remembered today, he is best known for directing *Q Planes* (1939) and *Thief*. (For more about Powell's other films, see the Appendix.)

Much of *Thief* had already been completed when the war made it impossible to continue filming in Europe or Africa, where Korda hoped to shoot the exteriors needed for the last third of the picture.

Korda briefly considered moving the production to Canada, but he soon discovered that wartime Canada lacked the facilities for a film of *Thief*'s magnitude and complexity. As much as he resisted the idea of returning to Hollywood, Korda realized it was the one place which had everything he needed to complete his ambitious fantasy. As Vincent Korda struggled to rebuild many of the massive sets on the General Services Studio backlot, his producer brother exhorted him to make the rebuilt sets even larger than the sizeable originals. Size, Alexander wanted *more* size— bigger sets, bigger crowd scenes . . . BIGGER.

Even Alexander Korda had to be satsified with one of his new locations: America's Grand Canyon. Scenes with Abu, Ahmad, and the Djinni were filmed at Hopi Point and along the Colorado River.

Not too far from the Grand Canyon, Korda found another exterior location unavailable anywhere else in the world: the Painted Desert, which represented the "Land of Legend" in the film. Associate producers Zoltan Korda and William Cameron Menzies directed the American location sequences.

The picture's stirring score was the work of Miklos Rozsa, born in Budapest in 1907. As a child, Rozsa could read music before he could read words, and his mother, against the wishes of his industrialist father, saw to it that he was given violin lessons at the age of five.

A prize-winning music student in secondary school, he dropped out of the University of Leipzig to enroll in that city's Conservatory of Music. Moving to Paris after he graduated, Rozsa wrote several compositions which marked him as a young composer to watch.

Rozsa moved to London in 1936 and met French film director Jacques Feyder, who tried to convince the young man to write music for motion pictures. Feyder introduced Rozsa to Marlene Deitrich, who was starring in an Alexander Korda picture called *Knight Without Armour*. Feyder told Korda that Rozsa was a close friend of his brother Vincent — though Rozsa had never met either Korda before.

Hired by Korda, Rozsa bought a book on film scoring and went to the movies to see how it was done, only to be appalled at the quality of the (mostly American) scores.

Before scoring *Thief*, Rozsa scored *Knight Without Armour*, *The Squeaker*, *The Divorce of Lady X*, and *The Four Feathers* for Korda. Since *Thief*, had to be completed in America, Rozsa found himself in Hollywood in the spring of 1940 writing the music for a major international production.

Miklos Rozsa's magnificent score has faint echoes of Rimsky-Korsakov's *Scheherazade* but is entirely original. Rozsa developed themes for the Princess and the Djinni, a song for Sabu (which is also his leit-motif) called "I Want to Be a Sailor," Jaffar's leit-motif, the flight of the Djinni, and wondrously dramatic and powerful passages for the Silver Maid's (arm) dance of death and the flight of the Flying Horse.

Three designers were responsible for *Thief*'s colorful costumes: John Armstrong, who'd been under contract to Korda since *The Private Life of Henry VIII*; Oliver Messel, who'd done the costumes for Korda's *The Private Life of Don Juan* in 1934; and Frenchman Marcel Vertes.

Reminiscing with John Kobal in the wonderful *People Will Talk*, June Duprez could only sigh when recalling Korda's extravagance: "Korda just went on spending and spending, because this was personal project, and time and money were no object." *Thief*, however, is one film where the enormous sums of money spent for its production show up on the screen.

Vincent Korda's magnificent sets, and William Cameron Menzies' overall design, give *Thief* the necessary mixture of realism and impossibility a good fantasy needs. The palace exteriors are imposing and grand, while the brightly lit interiors are the size of airplane hangars and come with wonderfully improbable highly polished floors.

Eyes (and sight) are central to *Thief*. The very first shot is of a giant eye painted on the bow of Jaffar's junk, quickly followed by a closeup of Jaffar's icy blue-gray eyes. Later, when Ahmad tells his story in the harem, revealing that his dog was once Abu the thief, the camera closes in on the dog's alert eyes and then cuts to a closeup of Abu's brown eyes scanning a marketplace.

Mary Morris' Halima is most often seen with her knowing eyes the only visible feature of her properly veiled face. When the same actress, playing the beautiful pale-blue Silver Maid, is activated at Jaffar's command, her closed eyes open and widen in anticipation of her deadly role.

Ahmad is blind for the first third of the film — only figuratively at first (to the perfidy of his Grand Vizier and to the injustices the people suffer), and then literally when Jaffar blinds him. Ahmad sees the forbidden princess with his own eyes, while the magician Jaffar sees her in his crystal.

Later, Jaffar tells the Princess, after Ahmad's sight has been restored, "For a man with eyes, the world is full of women."

After Abu steals the All-Seeing Eye from the Goddess of Light, the Djinni says, "Not for 2000 years will she grow another. . . . For a hundred generations of men, she will not know their doings."

After seeing the Princess inhale the essence of the Blue Rose of Forgetfulness in the Eye, a despondent Ahmad inadvertently causes Abu to use up his last wish transporting the deposed King back to Bagdad.

Sight of a different kind also plays a role when Abu is transported to a magical place ruled by an old King who has long waited for him: "This is the Land of Legend, where everything is possible when seen through the eyes of youth."

Miles Malleson's literate screenplay, which approaches poetry at times, is another of *Thief*'s major strengths. It ranges from low, but effective, comedy (citizen of Basra to Ahmad and Abu: "Now out of my way, you masters of a thousand fleas. Allah be with you—but I doubt it!"), to humorous insight into human behavior (the Djinni to Abu, after his third wish: "You're a clever little man, little master of the universe, but mortals are weak and frail. If their stomach speaks, they forget their brain. If their brain speaks, they forget their hearts. And if their hearts speak . . . ha, ha, ha . . . they forget *everything!*").

Malleson's dialogue between Abu and the old King is wonderful, and gives the fantasy a powerful moral underpinning: "We are the remnants of the Golden Age; golden because gold was nothing—no more than the sand beneath your feet or the stone that we became."

When Abu asks, "How did you become stone?" The old King replies, "We were petrified with horror at the evil done among men, when they ceased to be children and to believe in the beauty of the impossible. Whenever the heart of a child returns to us, and comes in to us, we live again. And so, as that child, you are to be my successor."

When Jaffar presents himself to the Princess after imprisoning her on his junk, he says, "Yes, Jaffar. It's always Jaffar. Since you left your palace I have kept you safe. When you rode hopeless and lost in the desert, who guided you? When you were sold in the slave market, who bought you? Always Jaffar. It was in my house that you were cared for to sleep your sleep . . . and dream to its end your first dream of love."

Rarely has a villain been given such dimension, such human qualities; one can almost feel sorry for Jaffar—he loves the Princess almost as much as Ahmad does and will do anything to have her. He even restores his rival's sight to feel the Princess in his arms.

Veidt is convincing in his obsessive desire for the love of the Princess, especially so when one considers that 20-year-old June Duprez was the same age as his daughter, whom Duprez spent much of her free time talking to. Duprez recalled that the older actor seemed to regard her as a child, refusing to discuss their roles or scenes; any passion he portrayed, she says, was acting talent and nothing more.

Conrad Veidt's performance is the best in the picture, spellbinding and made up of many consciously controlled gestures. Unfortunately, this fine actor — cast as Nazis and human monsters in American films, but more sympathetically in British pictures — died in 1943 at age 50.

Sabu's performance, especially in his scenes with Rex Ingram's Djinni is second only to Veidt's. Much as Judy Garland's innocence and belief in the fantastic happenings around her give validity to *The Wizard of Oz*, so too does Sabu's enthusiasm and sincerity imbue *Thief* with "the heart of a child" the old King spoke of.

Rex Ingram's performance as the Djinni is, appropriately, larger-than-life and full of infectious good humor. Ingram delivers his lines with gusto and clearly enjoys his battle of wits with Sabu's impish thief.

June Duprez, as the Princess, has little to do but look alternately wistful and lovesick, then repelled and fearful. Her exotic features, heightened by makeup, and her creamy-skinned beauty make her a believable object for obsessive worship.

John Justin, in his film debut, is appropriately handsome and dashing, looking rather like a youthful — and skinnier — Errol Flynn. Justin's Ahmad is convincing first as a callow and distant ruler, and then as an enlightened and compassionate potentate. For a man who, at the film's beginning, is said to have 365 wives, Justin's Ahmad delivers his vow of love to the Princess with total sincerity: "For me there can be no more beauty in the world but yours."

Mary Morris's dual performance, as Halima and the Silver Maid, is made more chilling for the distant beauty of her finely chiseled features. Her *danse de mort* as the homicidal mechanical doll is erotically compelling, and her fatal embrace seems almost worth the price to be held in her many arms. For Miles Malleson's wonderful, blustering Sultan, no more appropriate death could be conceived of than to perish at the hands of a deadly "toy."

Today, decades after its initial release, *Thief* has the power to transport us to an ancient world of fable and fantasy, a world that never existed and could never exist. Its color, its sets, its marvels of screen magic, have been copied, but never with as much success as the unique original.

A few modern critics fault some of the film's special effects (and some *are* admittedly cheesy, like the shots of the immobile dummy meant to represent the Djinni's flight over the roof of the world), but never had so many cinema tricks been called for in a Technicolor film of *Thief*'s complexity.

As the first color film to make use of many of the effects seen in *Thief*, the production broke new ground. As John Brosnan notes in his book *Movie Magic*, the Flying Horse scene, which has been faulted for being cartoonish, "was not achieved through cartoon animation but was in fact an early and complicated example of a traveling matte filmed in color and, when viewed today, appears relatively effective."

See *Thief* uncut and in color, and show it to your children.

And remember: "Everything is possible when seen through the eyes of youth."

13. Time Bandits: Child as Hero

I think the purpose of the fairy tale is to give a rather frightening experience. Kids come out of it at the other end, all right, but it says . . . that
there's evil out there, there's dangerous things. . . .

                                                        — *Terry Gilliam on* Time Bandits

Time Bandits was released in the United States in late 1981, to reviews
ranging from lauditory to outright hostile. Apparently, as with *The Wizard
of Oz,* some critics found it too scary, too dark, and too unfunny. Kids,
however, loved it, and the film had no difficulty attracting appreciative audiences. Terry Gilliam himself has confirmed the film's similarity to—and
borrowings from—*The Wizard of Oz, Snow White,* and *Alice in Wonderland.*

    Time Bandits is admittedly a dark and sometimes scary film, perhaps
too intense for really small children. But for older children, it presents a
wonderful conceit: A young boy named Kevin is its hero, its level-headed
leader and moral center. Whenever the dwarfs, adults who are Kevin's size
or *smaller,* get into a pickle, it is Kevin's ingenuity that saves the day—at
least until the *deus ex machina* appearance of Sir Ralph Richardson as the
Supreme Being at the end.

    Kevin is a throwback kid to an earlier, sweeter age: He reads books
while his parents, lumpy British couch potatoes, watch cruel and inane TV
game shows.

    David Sterritt's review in the *Christian Science Monitor* noted, "It's not
surprising that a children's film should be successful at this time of the year,
but *Time Bandits* is no ordinary children's film." Sterritt concluded his
lengthy piece by calling *Time Bandits* "a flawed and quirky movie, yet one
that may be remembered after more expensive and more ephemeral enter-
tainments have faded from the screen for good."

    In the *Los Angeles Times,* Sheila Benson observed that "*Time Bandits*
has every virtue, including unexpectedness. To explain the elaborate
premise of its story makes it sound massive and cumbersome, yet on the
screen it sorts itself out in a twinkling, and what emerges is marvelous.

186

Time Bandits . . . fairly bristles with wit, invention, a wry and fey intelligence and a conjuror's chest of dazzling effects."

Archer Winston's *New York Post* review called *Time Bandits* "an imaginative, historical fantasy . . . totally original, always stimulating and fairly good fun if the sheer Anglicism of the humor doesn't elude you. The production values are grand."

In *Newsday*, Joseph Gelmis wrote, "*Time Bandits* is a delightful romp for children of all ages . . . a curious combination of bizarre humor and fabulous adventure seen from the subjective child's-eye view of its young dreamer."

Newsweek's David Ansen enthused, "What you get in *Time Bandits* is true invention, a fecund imagination at play. The sheer technical accomplishment—sets, costumes, special effects—is dazzling, but it's more than icing on a cake, it's part of [Terry Gilliam's] unified vision."

Richard Corliss, writing in *Time,* was one of the naysayers, calling the film "a nasty fantasy, an antiepic, a revisionist fable." Turned off by what he saw as Gilliam and Palin's odd ideas, poor comic timing, and laborious pacing, Corliss asks, "Who can care about six dwarfs when they're all Dopey?"

In *New York*, David Denby argued that the film's "inventiveness has gone into the imagery, but the roughhousing grows tiresome after a while, and nothing so gauche as a human emotion ever takes shape. It's possible that some of today's kids will love *Time Bandits* as much as their grandparents loved *The Wizard of Oz,* but I'm not sure I'm prepared to love those kids very much."

Finally, the *Village Voice*'s Carrie Rickey called the film ". . . a Hardy Boys wet dream. . . . Who wouldn't want to hobknob with one's favorite heroes (regrettably this is boys' stuff—no heroines) able to time-travel to all the exciting ages . . . ?" Rickey ended her piece by observing, "Thank God there's no place like home, *Time Bandits* seems to say. It's the first movie I've seen [recently] that made me feel kidlike, made me want to live in it."

Middle-class parents are watching television in their consumer-culture, appliance-loaded home as their young son Kevin (Craig Warnock) reads by himself. That night, as he lies in bed, he hears noises from his wardrobe. Suddenly, an armored knight on horseback smashes out into the room. After wheeling about, he jumps his horse over Kevin and disappears.

Kevin's mother (Sheila Fearn) and father (David Daker) are a consumer goods–crazed couple; mom is always talking about the latest consumer products her friends have acquired that her family now must have to keep up. She tells Kevin's father about her friends' microwave oven, which can turn "a block of ice to Boeuf Bourguignon in eight seconds."

Ignoring his parents' prattle, Kevin goes to bed early the next night—to be ready with his flashlight and instant camera—and dozes off as he waits. Kevin's wardrobe door opens and six dwarfs step out. Attacking Kevin, they stop once they see he's not someone they call the Supreme Being but just a kid.

Suddenly the wall pushes away down a corridor. The giant face of the Supreme Being appears and Kevin follows the fleeing dwarfs. "Return the map," intones the disembodied head. The corridor ends and all seven fall into a void . . . and land in a farmyard in eighteenth-century Italy during an invasion by Napoleon.

Amidst scenes of carnage, the dwarfs tell Kevin they're master criminals and are planning a robbery. Their intended victim is Napoleon himself (Ian Holm), who's watching a puppet show. The puppeteer is suddenly killed by a stray bullet, but the show must go on. Hearing that Napoleon likes "little things," the dwarfs take the stage to sing "Me and My Shadow." Napoleon loves their act and makes them all his new generals.

After a drunken banquet, the dwarfs and Kevin escape with their loot into a convenient time hole, emerging in Sherwood Forest. Sheepishly, Randall (David Rappaport) and Fidgit (Kenny Baker) admit to Kevin that it was their first heist. Randall tells Kevin they stole the map, which shows the holes in time, from the Supreme Being. Kevin takes their picture, including the map.

After encountering Vincent and Pansy (Michael Palin and Shelley Duvall), they're trapped by Robin Hood's men and taken to Robin's camp. Robin (John Cleese) says, "Call me Hood," before confiscating their ill-gotten gains for the poor.

Evil (David Warner) watches the dwarfs' progress from the Fortress of Ultimate Darkness. Exiled in the fortress, Evil seeks a way to escape and rule the universe.

When the floating head of the Supreme Being reappears, Kevin escapes by himself through a time doorway into ancient Greece, saving King Agamemnon's life as the ruler battles a bull-headed warrior.

Agamemnon (Sean Connery) returns to his court with Kevin, who, not wanting to go back to the dwarfs, eagerly settles in. The king adopts Kevin and holds a feast. During the celebration, the dwarfs appear and, in the guise of magicians, rob the king and take Kevin with them.

The group materializes on the doomed ocean liner *Titanic* and encounters later versions of Vincent and Pansy. Trying to cool Kevin's anger over being snatched back, Randall tells him of the Time of Legends and of the Fortress of Ultimate Darkness—which may harbor a great fortune. "Waiter, more champagne . . . and plenty of ice," Randall orders.

Suddenly, CRASH! Evil snatches them from the ocean and deposits them in the Time of Legends. An Ogre (Peter Vaughan) and his wife

The six dwarfs pose for Kevin's camera with their greatest prize, a map showing the holes in time.

(Katherine Helmond) are passing in a ship and net the lot. The Ogre is nasty but suffers from a bad back. After telling him that stretching will help, Kevin tricks the Ogre into allowing himself to be seized by the dwarfs, who toss him and his wife overboard.

They sail off, but their triumph is short-lived as the ship rises from the water—it's a hat atop a giant, who strides ashore. Inside the ship, Kevin has the others drug the giant by injecting a sleeping potion into his scalp. Drowsy, the giant sits down, takes off his hat, and they escape from the ship.

Kevin and the dwarfs wander through a wasteland of sand and skeletons. After they collide with an invisible barrier, the others rebel against Randall, who throws a skull and accidently smashes a way into the Fortress of Ultimate Darkness.

Inside, they encounter a complex maze which is part of a game show featuring Kevin's mom and dad. After the emcee asks for and receives the map, he turns into Evil, and Kevin's parents are revealed as Evil's minions, Benson and Robert.

Kevin and the others are enslaved in cages suspended over a bottomless pit. After Kevin recalls that his group photo also shows the map, they plan an escape through the nearest time hole. The dwarfs swing Strutter (Malcolm Dixon) over to the next cage and then to a ledge. The rest quickly follow.

Kevin insists they steal the map back. And they do—pursued by Evil and his ghouls, tall wraiths with horns who shoot fireballs from their eyes. Kevin and Og (Mike Edmonds) now a pig, confront Evil and threaten to burn the map.

Evil uses his powers to seize the map, but help arrives: Randall in a tank, knights on horseback, archers, cowboys on horseback, and a spacecraft piloted by Wally (Jack Purvis). Lassoed by the cowboys, Evil spins and throws them off. Then his cloak inflates, stopping the arrows launched at him by the archers. He makes the arrows fly back and kill the bowmen.

Things get worse. The knights are no match for gas; neither is Randall's tank, nor Wally's spaceship. In the confusion, a heavy stone column falls on Fidgit, killing him.

The Supreme Being (Sir Ralph Richardson) finally shows up after turning Evil to stone and saving the day. He restores Og to human form and orders the dwarfs to tidy up. Almost as an afterthought, he brings Fidgit back to life, saying that death "is no excuse for laying off work."

The Supreme Being says he was just testing his handiwork—Evil turned out rather well. In the cleanup, a tiny piece of concentrated Evil is overlooked. As the Supreme Being and the dwarfs depart, he says that Kevin must stay behind.

Smoke. Kevin wakes up in his smoke-filled house and is saved by firemen—one of whom is Sean Connery. Kevin's parents continue to bicker and worry about their possessions as their toaster oven is brought out. Inside is the missing piece of Evil, which efficiently blows up Kevin's parents, leaving him standing alone amid the rubble of his house.

Terry Gilliam was born on November 22, 1940, in a rural hamlet near Minneapolis, Minnesota, the son of a traveling Folger's Coffee salesman. As a child, Gilliam devoured every comic book and humor magazine he could lay his hands on, especially *Mad, Humbug, Trump,* and *Help!,* which featured the work of Harvey Kurtzman.

After a childhood spent in this bucolic setting, Gilliam attended Occidental College. Inspired by Kurztman and other comic-book artists, Gilliam became a cartoonist for the school's humor magazine, and before graduation he began sending samples of his work to humor magazines. One of the publications he targeted was Harvey Kurtzman's *Help!*

Kurtzman liked what he saw in the samples Gilliam had submitted. So, when a position unexpectedly opened up at *Help!,* Gilliam was hired. During his three-year stay at the magazine, he learned a great deal about layout, design, and using cut-outs and photographs for illustrating amusing stories. Kurtzman and *Help!* used "Fumettis"—black-and-white live-action photographs of professional actors—in lieu of drawn cartoon figures, and Gilliam was responsible for casting and laying out many of them.

At the conclusion, the Supreme Being (Sir Ralph Richardson) arrives to save the day and the map. He listens gravely as Randall (David Rappaport), the dwarfs' leader, tries to explain.

John Cleese was in New York in 1964 for the run of *Cambridge Circus*, a satiric review that had just finished touring New Zealand. Meeting Cleese, Gilliam convinced him to appear in what is now one of *Help!'*s better-remembered fumettis, "Christopher's Punctured Romance," in which the lanky actor portrayed a suburbanite who developed a yen for a Barbie doll.

Cleese told George Perry in *The Life of Python*, "I liked [Gilliam] enormously and I think that he thought that I was good at mugging, which is supposed to be a sort of compliment."

With the Viet Nam war looming large on Terry Gilliam's horizon in the form of the draft, he joined the National Guard. After his brief stint was over, Gilliam decided against returning to *Help!* and spent several months hitchhiking through Europe. When his savings were exhausted, Gilliam took a job at *Pilote*, a Paris magazine.

Gilliam returned to New York and, after living for a short time in Harvey Kurtzman's attic, he ventured west to Los Angeles. After brief spells in free-lance illustration and in the advertising business, he moved to London for good.

John Cleese and Graham Chapman tried to help Gilliam find work, introducing him to producers. Finally, in 1968, Gilliam was hired to produce caricatures for the television comedy show *Do Not Adjust Your Set*. His next show, *We Have Ways of Making You Laugh*, featured Michael Palin, Terry Jones, and Eric Idle. The others were not sure what to make of this strange young American artist and writer.

By the time the BBC allowed the six young men to write and appear in the show that was eventually called *Monty Python's Flying Circus* (other proposed titles included *Owl Stretching Time; Bunn, Wackett, Buzzard, Stubble, and Boot;* and — getting warmer now — *Gwen Dibley's Flying Circus*), they'd agreed that Gilliam's contribution, at least initially, was to be animation, including the show's opening titles. Gilliam's wacked-out graphics were set to John Philip Sousa's rousing *Liberty Bell March*, and the tune and animation became the group's readily identified signature.

Gilliam duplicated pictures from art magazines, then cut them up and animated them by moving the cut-outs about and photographing them a frame at a time. Compared to normal animation, done with drawings, it was cheap and fast, if a great deal of work. The Pythons were harsh critics of their own material — often altering and rewriting each other's sketches — but the back-breaking schedule of animating that Gilliam adhered to allowed no one else to edit his work. Often his animated linking segments were finished just hours before the program aired, making last-minute revisions impossible.

Monty Python's Flying Circus appeared on BBC-1 in three limited series between October, 1969, and January, 1973. The show returned for one season on BBC-2, minus John Cleese, between October, 1974, and December, 1974. Their 45 half-hour shows became a worldwide phenomenon, making the six Pythons international celebrities.

Terry Gilliam's inspired and crazed cut-out animation, as marvelous as it was, left the young man nowhere to go artistically. So, after the Pythons gained the clout to completely control their own work, they decided that Gilliam and Terry Jones would share the directorial reins on their first non-skit feature film, *Monty Python and the Holy Grail*.

Finding the arrangement less satisfactory than did Jones, Gilliam decided to develop his own feature film, 1977's *Jabberwocky*. Gilliam co-scripted the screenplay with Charles Alverson. *Jabberwocky*, starring fellow Python Michael Palin, was not well received, perhaps because of its fondness for filth and its utterly bleak medieval setting.

After *Jabberwocky*, Gilliam came up with the idea of doing something for kids. In just seven pages, Gilliam laid out the basic *Bandits* plot.

After Michael Palin agreed to write the screenplay with him, Gilliam approached producer Denis O'Brien and acted out the idea. Since Gilliam's Python animations never had to be "sold" to the group like everyone else's ideas and skits, he often lamented that he lacked the necessary skills to pitch his work. In this instance, however, Gilliam was so convincing that O'Brien immediately gave the project his backing.

Gilliam started with one basic idea—a "kid" would be the main character, and the story would be told at a child's level. Gilliam added the dwarfs when he realized they were the only way of surrounding his main character, Kevin, with interesting characters who were adults yet kidsized.

Once Gilliam had worked out the story (although he still lacked an ending), he handed things over to Michael Palin. Palin then wrote the actual script, turning Gilliam's ideas and concepts into workable scenes, complete with dialogue. Gilliam also relied on Palin to flesh out his spare characterizations, giving the story's characters depth and believability.

After Palin had put the story into script form, the two men sat down together and talked over what they'd wrought. Then, armed with Gilliam's suggestions, additions, and other feedback, Palin again went away to write. After the script returned to Gilliam, it was his turn to rewrite it. Finally, the two Pythons had something they both liked and felt was workable.

Gilliam's and Palin's script had a scene that read, "Greek warrior takes his helmet off, revealing him to be none other than Sean Connery. . . ." The two writers mentioned Connery's name as a suitable "heroic" type of actor, not actually expecting that they would end up casting the former James Bond. But their executive producer, Denis O'Brien, read the script and thought the idea a fine one. O'Brien asked the actor if he'd play the part and, to Gilliam's astonishment, Connery said yes.

With all but the ending decided, Gilliam began storyboarding *Bandits* shot for shot. This careful blueprinting of his films' shots is one of the reasons Gilliam can produce such lush and expensive-looking features on minuscule (by Hollywood standards) budgets. Gilliam, having observed the waste in other films' overconstructed sets, builds his sets to fill the shot and no more. He has noted that if the camera were to pan a foot or so in any direction, the set would be nonexistent.

Gilliam's films call for outstanding special effects, things which often make an audience gasp, yet the effects are always secondary to the story and not thrown in for cheap effect. Gilliam uses modern techniques when he needs to, but he's aware that, often, "old fashioned" stuff works just as well or better.

The giant sequence, involving the strangely tatooed giant who emerges from the sea wearing the ship containing Kevin and the dwarfs on his head as a hat, was accomplished by high-speed photography and camera angles. The actor playing the giant was just 5 feet 8 inches tall because Gilliam knew that a taller man would look unnaturally elongated. The relatively short "giant" looked perfect when Gilliam filmed him with a camera with a wide angle lens shooting up.

Gilliam went to Morocco for several of his exteriors—those set in Agamemnon's Greece, and in the Time of Legends. Other exteriors, including Ragan Castle, were filmed in Wales.

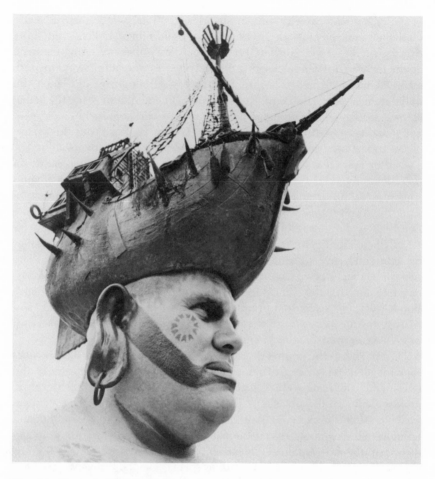

The ship Kevin and the dwarfs are aboard turns out to be a hat worn by a giant covered in curious markings.

Even as filming progressed, Gilliam had no ending for *Bandits*. Finally, he remembered that Sean Connery had suggested that he come back as a fireman. That fitted in with the scene Gilliam had already shot of the firemen coming in and pulling Kevin from his smoky room. When Gilliam asked for Connery back to shoot the additional scene, there was some foot-dragging. Gilliam all but threw a tantrum to get Connery back for an hour.

With a fire truck waiting in the studio's parking lot, Connery showed up, got into his fireman's costume, delivered his line ("Say, you're a lucky fellow"), got in the truck and winked, and drove off. End of scene. Gilliam had his ending—albeit one that was later to prove controversial.

Sean Connery was the film's major star and selling point to distributors, despite his limited onscreen time. Made world-famous and rich from his playing of James Bond in seven hugely successful films, Connery was looking for a change-of-pace role. He gladly signed to play King Agamemnon in *Bandits* because it was a rare opportunity for the virile Scots actor to play a father-type role. Agamemnon's relationship with Kevin is a warm and caring one, and Connery's and Craig Warnock's scenes together have a tenderness rare in Python films and rarer still in Terry Gilliam films.

Connery is wonderful in his brief role, and he makes a hugely appealing father figure. Indeed, Connery's Agamemnon is so caring and so unlike Kevin's real father that the lad wants nothing more than to be able to stay in ancient Greece as the king's adopted son. This understandable desire is thwarted, however, by the untimely appearance of Randall and the other dwarfs.

As the pint-sized Willie Suttons whirl and dance for the king, Kevin realizes who they really are and resists being "saved" by them. Agamemnon, however, is tickled by their performance and gladly allows Kevin to step forward and join in the dwarfs' all-too-real disappearing act. Connery's acting in this scene is amazing and totally natural. His open face reveals his childlike delight as this kindly, trusting man waits futilely for Kevin and the dwarfs to reappear with his crown and other valuables.

Sean Connery was born Thomas Connery in Edinburgh, Scotland, on August 25, 1930. The son of lower-middle-class parents, Connery dropped out of school to join the Royal navy when he was just 15. After stints as a lifeguard and a coffin polisher, he turned to body building and soon found himself in demand as a model for swimming trunks.

He began his acting career by singing in the chorus of a 1951 production of *South Pacific*. After a few stage roles he appeared in his first film in 1956, *No Road Back*. He appeared in Disney's *Darby O'Gill and the Little People, Tarzan's Greatest Adventure,* and *The Longest Day* before playing suave secret agent James Bond in the 1962 film *Dr. No*.

His post–Bond films have included *Zardoz, The Man Who Would Be King, Robin and Marion* (he played Robin Hood, a role his son Jason would later play on British television), *Outland, The Name of the Rose,* and *The Untouchables* for which he won an Oscar as Best Supporting Actor.

In an equally small *Bandits* part, giving an equally splendid performance, John Cleese plays Robin Hood. Tall and urbane, Cleese's Robin Hood appears before the startled little people's eyes and introduces himself, saying, "Hello, I'm . . . Hood." Later, Cleese mutters, "Oh, me, there's *so* much wealth to redistribute."

Several British critics noted the presumably intentional similarities between Cleese's unctious Robin Hood and members of the Royal Family. Cleese's Hood cheerfully separates the dwarfs from their ill-gotten gains and distributes it to the poor. Although he is outwardly cordial, he mutters, "What awful people," after the small band moves on.

John Cleese (1939–) has appeared in a number of non–Monty Python films, including *Privates on Parade* (1982) and *Silverado* (1985), but he is best known outside the Python television series for a limited-run series called *Fawlty Towers*. Cleese and his wife at the time, Connie Booth, created a wonderfully realized innkeeper called Basil Fawlty. The series was enormously popular and successful, but Cleese grew bored with it after only 12 episodes.

Gilliam was pleased that Palin, his writing partner for *Bandits*, agreed to play Vincent, Pansy's unlucky suitor, whose awkward advances are thwarted by the untimely "dropping in" of Kevin and the dwarfs. The first incident takes place in Sherwood Forest, moments after Palin's Vincent tells Pansy that his personal problem is solved: He no longer has to wear his "special thing." Then the dwarfs appear, upsetting everything.

Palin's second incident takes place aboard the ill-fated *Titanic*. This time the dwarfs knock poor Vincent's toupee off, revealing his pasty-white scalp to a shocked Pansy.

As Pansy, Shelley Duvall is appropriately fluttery and wide-eyed, but she really has little to do but react to Palin's comic distress.

David Warner's Evil is surely that, if not especially scary. Warner's classic British delivery—deadpan straight, with no hint of playing things for laughs—of Palin's and Gilliam's lines gives them extra comic punch.

Born in 1941, David Warner has been in films since his appearance in *Tom Jones* in 1963. His 1966 starring role in *Morgan* made him a low-magnitude star and internationally famous. Rarely out of work, Warner drew special notice for his chilling portrayal of Jack the Ripper in the time-travel fantasy film, *Time After Time*.

Other notables in the cast included Sir Ralph Richardson as the Supreme Being (see Chapter 4 for more on Sir Ralph); Peter Vaughan as the Ogre and Katherine Helmond as his wife (both would reappear in Gilliam's next film, the controversial *Brazil*); Ian Holm as Napoleon; Kenny Baker (R2-D2, from *Star Wars*) as Fidgit; and David Rappaport as Randall. Rappaport's polished performance drew attention and he found himself in demand—a "little person" who could act. In 1986, Rappaport got his own short-lived CBS television series, *The Wizard*.

Mike Moran wrote the music score for the film, and it admirably supports Gilliam's onscreen images and situations. However, several others contributed songs and music as well.

Trevor Jones, who wrote the music score for Jim Henson's *Dark Crystal* (see Chapter 3), wrote the Greek dance music used in the scenes in Agamemnon's court.

Not every executive producer gets a chance to write music for the film he's overseeing, but not every executive producer is a world-famous musician like ex–Beatle George Harrison, one of the principals behind Handmade Films, the production company which made *Bandits*. While written expressly for *Bandits*, his music is clearly recognizable as the Harrison style.

Although Milly Burns was the *Bandits* production designer, Norman Garwood the art director, and Jim Acheson and Hazel Cote the costume designers, any Gilliam film has his fingerprints all over it. Gilliam was inspired by the works of Hieronymous Bosch, and that interest was reflected in the design of the costumes for the fireball-shooting ghouls. The realistic muck and mire are also clear giveaways that the film is in the patented Gilliam mold.

Time Bandits cost a mere $5 million—a figure that's difficult to believe, given the film's fabulous effects, first-rate photography, and exotic locations. According to *Variety*'s January 14, 1987 issue, *Bandits* earned North American rentals of approximately $19.5 million, meaning that the film did quite well financially for Handmade Films and its American distributor. Avco Embassy picked up the American distribution rights to the completed film after all the major United States studios and distributors passed on buying them—most studio executives calling the film "unfunny" and "too English."

While simply a delightful kids' film on the surface, *Bandits* clearly has depths lacking in most fare aimed squarely at children. Gilliam has stated on several occasions that his intention in making *Bandits* was to produce something for children that recognized that kids can be more clear-minded, ruthless, and open-minded than the adults who too often produce overly romanticized and condescending material for them.

While there is violence in *Bandits*, it's often cartoonish stuff and not to be taken too seriously: An arm wrestler in Robin Hood's camp has his arm torn off, various ghouls and minions of Evil are "blown up real good," a puppeteer is shot and killed, Fidgit is crushed to death (but the Supreme Being restores him to life), and Kevin's parents are blown up at the end.

Apparently, it was this unusual ending for a kids' film ("Oh, Auntie Em, there's no place like home"—KERBOOM!!) that rankled a number of critics, including some of those who otherwise gave the film a high rating. Handmade Films wasn't sure about the seemingly nihilistic ending, citing commercial resistance to such a "down" conclusion. Others felt that the onscreen death of the young hero's parents might be threatening to kids, especially younger ones.

The latter concern did give Gilliam second thoughts. "I'm really pro-kid, you know!" Gilliam told David Sterritt of the *Christian Science Monitor*. "So we screened it for lots of people before it was released, and we found that kids weren't bothered at all."

If the violence didn't bother kids, perhaps more threatening are the film's darker, less accessible revelations about the disillusioning process of growing up into a world where good and evil are less clearly defined than youngsters expect them to be. After beginning his journey as magically as Dorothy did in *The Wizard of Oz*, Kevin finds many of his childhood heroes to be less heroic than he had imagined. The pictures hanging in Kevin's room include Napoleon. Kevin's encounter with the diminutive emperor reveals him to be a height-obsessed drunkard, more a candidate for a treatment program than for enshrinement in a hall of heroes. And while Robin Hood clearly does rob from the rich to give to the poor, one of his men also hands out a brutal punch to the jaw of each recipient.

The realistic and semi-hallucinogenic scenes of destruction in war-torn Italy show Kevin that his romantic visions of battle are just that, not the grime and pain of real life (before he sets off on his adventures, Kevin says enthusiastically, "The ancient Greeks could kill people 27 different ways").

Kevin finds in Agamemnon the perfect father; his own self-absorbed parent is too concerned with material things and with the boob tube to be much of an inspiration. (Asked if he wants to return to his "own mother and father," Kevin emphatically says, "No!") Unfortunately, Kevin is "rescued" from this harmonious life and restored to the real world once again.

Ultimately, the lesson Kevin learns from the confrontation between Good and Evil (the one represented by God and the other created by Him) is that free will sets men and women adrift in a vast and uncaring universe. (There's a touching — and cruelly humorous — scene in which the cottage of a tiny troll family is crushed under the foot of the ship-wearing giant; there is nothing vicious in the giant's action: he's unaware that he's stepping on someone's home and family.)

What Kevin learns is that, ultimately, he can count on no one but himself — a frightening idea, but one everyone learns in the process of growing up. By the film's end, the brave, intelligent, and morally strong Kevin has moved a little closer to becoming an adult.

Not all of *Bandits* is so heavy or thought-provoking. There are many marvelous moments of fun to be found in the film and in Gilliam's and Palin's script. For example, Kevin's parents don't watch just *any* inane game show, they view a program called "Your Money or Your Life," which takes its title seriously. And when Robin Hood relieves the dwarfs of the loot they've stolen from Napoleon, Leonardo's *Mona Lisa* can be briefly glimpsed among the candlesticks and gold plates.

Palin and Gilliam view modern technology with suspicion, if not outright hostility. As Evil says, "God is not interested in technology. . . . He knows nothing of the potential of the microchip or silicon revolution. Look at what He spends His time on: butterflies, daffodils, 43 species of parrot. Nipples . . . for men! When I understand computers, *I* shall be the Supreme

Being." Besides seeking an "understanding" of digital watches, Evil would
have "*started* with lasers, eight o'clock on day one!"

The Ogre and Mrs. Ogre are marvelous characters: His name is
Winston, and he's got a bad back; she's a domestic whiz who has a dozen
or so human feet hanging about her kitchen on large hooks.

More than once the film seems to recall *The Wizard of Oz*. While Evil
may not have the Wicked Witch's flying monkeys, he watches the progress
of Kevin and the dwarfs in his own version of a crystal ball. In another example, just as *The Wizard of Oz* has the threatening floating head of the powerful wizard to terrify and impress the travelers, *Bandits* has the imposing
visage of the Supreme Being. And just as the wizard in *Oz* is revealed to be
less impressive than his sham floating head—a little man in a waistcoat—so,
too, is the Supreme Being shown to be less imposing in person. When the
Supreme Being appears and saves the day, he's none other than Sir Ralph
Richardson in a three-piece suit, mumbling vague homilies about good and
evil and free will.

Successful financially and critically, *Time Bandits* has earned a place
among the great fantasy films. It meshes adventure, slapstick comedy, sly
word play, and thought-provoking ideas into a singular entertainment. For
children, it offers a young hero they can admire and envy. It shows them
that books and imagination have more to offer than the stale formulas of
television.

So many films have been called a new *The Wizard of Oz;* I think *Time
Bandits*—at least for the '70s and '80s—can honestly claim that distinc-
tion.

14. Topper:
The Ghost Story

Topper, one of the comedy hits of 1937, was released during the summer as a delicious ghost comedy in the tradition of *The Ghost Goes West* (1936). *Topper*'s success made possible many of the best-known and best-remembered "screwball" comedies of the '30s, a few of them, like *Topper*, starring Cary Grant: *The Awful Truth* (1937), *Bringing Up Baby* (1938), and *My Favorite Wife* (1940).

Topper pleased critics as well as audiences. Writing in *America*, T.J. Fitzmorris said, "There is a mixture of realism and fantasy in this brittle comedy which gives it an interest beyond the ordinary. . . . The bright dialogue is splendidly handled . . . and it is literate enough to satisfy the demands of sophisticated adults."

The American Legion Auxiliary called *Topper* ". . . fantastic, gay, witty. Excellent cast. Mature." *Newsweek* said *Topper* was "Expertly produced by Hal Roach and spiced with some of the cleverest camera tricks to date. . . . [It] achieves bright and airy comedy with none of the gruesome overtones inherent in the subject matter."

Stage said, "Thorne Smith's wild, ribald tale" was "shaved of its lustier moments but still retaining in some measure the flavor of the book. Some honestly funny moments and some that are a little drawn out."

Topper opens with George and Marion Kerby (Cary Grant and Constance Bennett) whizzing down a country road in a sporty convertible George is steering with his feet. They're on their way to see their banker, Cosmo Topper (Roland Young). More than 12 hours early, they drive to Topper's National Security Bank, park, and go to sleep.

Just getting up is Cosmo Topper—a middle-aged banker with a domineering wife (Billie Burke) and a haughty butler named Wilkins (Alan Mowbray). Onlookers laugh and gawk at George and Marion, asleep in their car, as Topper arrives at his bank. George wakes up and he joins a meeting of the board (he's the largest stockholder) after Topper has already begun and doesn't hide his boredom. Marion wakes up, steps into Topper's private office, and settles in on the couch.

Topper comes in and calls George Kerby a nitwit, unaware that Marion is there. She just laughs in a flustered Topper's face and sits in his chair, teasing him. George comes in looking for a bottle of booze and the two Kerbys leave. Topper daydreams of Marion, calling her a "blonde angel."

Later, speeding down the road, George gets something in his eye and the car runs off the road into a tree. The Kerby's ghostly selves then step out of their bodies, and they talk, unaware that they're dead. Realizing their condition, they aren't sure what to do next—a good deed, perhaps.

Cosmo is next seen discussing the deceased Kerbys with Mrs. Topper. Topper receives the Kerby's repaired convertible to sell; his domineering wife tells him that it's too much car for him. The henpecked man, fed up with his wife's rigidity, angrily takes the car for a spin. Topper is a terrible driver, and a flat tire finally forces him off the road before he wrecks the car.

Contemplating his fix, Topper hears the voices of the Kerbys and watches them materialize; he faints. As an invisible George changes the tire, the revived Topper talks with Marion.

Later, at the Kerbys' penthouse hotel apartment, George and Topper drink wine and talk. Topper tells George he hasn't beaten his wife . . . yet.

Among other shenanigans, Marion pops the elevator boy in the eye and leaps off a piece of furniture into a drunken Topper's arms. The Kerbys carry the passed-out Topper outside; awaking, he starts a fight that involves cabbies and the police, and ends before a judge, who promptly fines him $100.

At breakfast, Mrs. Topper reads, "Banker and Babe in Brawl." She tells a contrite Topper they're finished socially. But later a *grande dame* of society asks the Toppers to dinner. Before Cosmo's newspaper escapades, she thought the Toppers were too stodgy for her and her friends.

At the bank, everyone gapes approvingly at Topper—he's an unexpected swinger. Marion materializes and Topper takes her "shopping." She tucks a pair of women's panties into Topper's pocket, and they fall out when he gets home. Mrs. Topper flees upstairs in tears. After Topper moves out, butler Wilkins says, "And lo the worm turns." Later, Wilkins advises Mrs. Topper to wear more glamorous clothing—and to allow Topper to wear the pants.

At Topper's hotel, Casey the house detective (Eugene Pallette) is suspicious when he hears a woman's voice from inside Topper's single room. Marion takes a shower and materializes fully dressed by the time Casey and the manager demand to search Topper's room for the "woman" they heard outside. The manager apologizes to Topper when they find no one.

Marion and Topper dance in the hotel's night club until George appears to tell Marion to behave herself and Cosmo to go home to his wife. George makes a chair follow Topper around the lobby of the hotel, and the

Cosmo Topper (Roland Young) is understandably frightened by the ghostly reap-
pearance of his two dead acquaintances, Marion and George Kerby (Constance
Bennett and Cary Grant).

guests become understandably upset. Several policemen arrive to search
for the "phantom" trying to wreck the hotel. George causes mischief while
the cops link arms to corral the phantom.

Topper escapes in his convertible and, with George driving, the car
crashes in the fatal spot as before. Slightly transparent as he steps from the
wreckage—he's unconscious—Topper reluctantly reenters his body as an
ambulance arrives.

Topper awakens in his own bed. George and Marion are up on the roof
talking, and Marion calls George her "little angel." At Topper's bedside,
Mrs. Topper tells him he's a dear. When Topper tells her that he loves her
too, she shows him her new lingerie. An upside down George and
Marion—they're still on the roof—look into the room and tell "Toppy"
they're leaving for good now.

Wilkins looks in at Mr. and Mrs. Topper and says, "Bless our happy
home."

While *Topper*'s "man must wear the pants" theme is dated today, the
film is surprisingly fresh and undated in most other respects. Its characters
are mature human beings with a variety of human needs, desires,
weaknesses, and surprising strengths.

The fantasy elements in *Topper* are achieved through special effects and a willing suspension of disbelief. The audience accepts the Kerbys as ghosts almost as quickly as George and Marion themselves do. This is a particular strength of the fantasy film—this willingness of the audience to accept what is happening on the screen, however phantasmagorical, because after all, seeing is believing. (The first audiences to see a steam locomotive coming directly at the camera in a nickelodeon ran away in panic.) Thus, filmmakers begin with an advantage: The viewer is already on their side.

In *Topper*, George and Marion Kerby's astonishing transformation into "ghosts" is casually alluded to with a vague reference to "ectoplasm" and their need to conserve it by not becoming visible too often.

One role of popular culture is to explain and defend popular values, especially establishment values, and life after death is a pillar of both mass culture and Christian theology. Heaven is not mentioned directly in the film—though Marion calls George her "little angel"—but its existence is implied.

Movies teach us how to live . . . or how we think we *ought* to live. George and Marion show Topper that a too-orderly and "respectable" life is as wrongheaded as one that is too rebellious and undisciplined. Coddled and henpecked, restrained by iron bars of habit and regularity, Cosmo Topper is a man who must be taught how to live. The crazy Kerbys, though just what Topper needs, are role models to be followed just so far. They live life to the fullest and are not bound by routine or schedules, but they're also immature, selfish, and shallow. The viewer laughs at George driving his convertible with his feet while sitting atop the seat back, but it is an uneasy laugh. A drunken free spirit careening down the highway behind the wheel of a speeding car is not as funny today as it was in 1937.

Some of the other values in *Topper* have undergone a revolution as well. Women today may bristle when Mrs. Topper (she's *Mrs.* Topper throughout the film save for one time when Cosmo calls her by her first name) is advised—by a male—to dress up in frilly things for her husband and to allow him to "wear the pants" in the family. It's always unfair, however, to use current cultural and social standards to judge those of a different era. Today's fantasy films will likewise reveal to future viewers some social values which they will find repugnant or puzzling; we are all products of our time.

Thorne Smith (1892–1934), a writer for the popular men's magazine *Esquire*, published his novel *Topper* in 1926, 11 years before the film's release. Even though the novel was a product of the 1920s, it was still too sexually sophisticated and risque in 1937 for the nation's screens. It was up to screenwriters Jack Jevne, Eric Hatch, and Eddie Moran to capture the essence of the novel while downplaying its sexual content. Given this handicap, it isn't difficult to understand why the film bears no more than a superficial resemblance to the novel.

The novel begins with Marion and George Kerby already dead for three months. Topper is described as "nearly forty and acquiring flesh," and his position at the bank is not as lofty as in the film. The Toppers have no butler in the novel, but do have a maid and a cat named Scollops.

The book's version of Topper discovers the ghostly Kerbys when, out for a spin in their convertible, he is accused by George of sitting on the invisible Marion's lap. Whereas in the film Topper and the Kerbys go to the spirits' hotel apartment, the setting in the novel is an abandoned inn. There Topper tells George, "If Mrs. Topper should walk into the room right now I'd be forced to speak to her quite pointedly to keep her from raising a row. But I've never beaten her . . . not yet, I haven't." As in the film, Marion jumps down into Topper's arms; she remarks, "A fat man has his uses."

After a fight with villagers (not the film's cabbies), Topper attends a court scene similar to the film's, but the novel has Mrs. Topper there; she writes the Justice a note saying Topper is "either drunk or crazy." "'Thanks,' he [Topper] called out with a terrible smile. 'You are very helpful, my dear. The Justice thanks you, too.'"

Rather than gaining stature by his misdeeds — as he does in the film — Topper is shamed in his small town. But, fortunately, his bank has not heard of his "exploits."

Topper asks for an extended vacation and, while George goes off to haunt Europe, he and Marion travel together. In a scene too frank for a '30s film Marion and Topper share a bed together several times. An exasperated Topper says, "Do you mean to tell me . . . that in spite of all the beds in this house you're so depraved as to insist on sleeping with me?" Marion blandly replies, "I just thought it would be more fun."

Marion and Topper join forces with a ghostly trio: the Colonel; the Colonel's lover, Mrs. Hart; and a partially visible dog named Oscar. While they camp by a lake, Topper grows lean and tanned, realizing that "loose living and large thinking could get along quite comfortably together, that they were in fact boon companions."

Topper's idyllic holiday ends when George returns to reclaim Marion. He and George have a clamshell duel that George wins by knocking Topper unconscious. Contrite for nearly killing Topper, George drives them back to the old tree and again wrecks the car.

Mrs. Topper professes her love for Topper and all seems well. Though glad to have his wife's affections again, Topper knows that "somewhere out there between the wind and the stars Marion Kerby was drifting, drifting farther and farther away." It is a poignant ending for such a high-spirited book.

Topper made use of a number of well-established effects, such as rear

Taken to their penthouse hotel apartment by the ghostly George and Marion, a
slightly sloshed Cosmo convinces Marion to leap into his waiting arms.

projection for scenes in the car, and reverse action to show Topper's clothes
rearranging themselves and his hair being combed invisibly.

For the scene where the Kerbys materialize on a log and amaze Topper, the two "ghosts" entered the right side of the set at the same time
Roland Young crossed to the left. Grant and Bennett waited a few moments
after sitting on the log, then played the scene. With extra footage of the
empty set shot from the same camera set-up, an optical printer combined
the footage with Bennett and Grant already seated on the log. They were
faded in while the empty set was faded out.

To show Cary Grant invisibly changing a flat tire on the convertible,
simple mechanical effects were employed. One assistant, out of sight inside
the car, opened the door while another assistant hidden under the car made
the jack operate. The tires being changed were manipulated by wires; stop-
motion animation was also briefly used when the wires couldn't convincingly manipulate the tires.

For the scene in which Topper checks into a hotel and signs his name
only to have "and me" added by the invisible Marion, stop-motion animation
was again employed. The tip of the pen was attached to the blotter under
the registration card and moved a fraction of an inch and a single frame of
film exposed. When projected at sound speed, it appeared the pen was
writing by itself.

To show an invisible Marion taking a shower in Topper's hotel room, black velvet and a high-pressure air hose made it appear the water was hitting a shapely but invisible body. The blast of air caused the water to spray outward—as it would when hitting a torso. An optical printer then printed in soap, steam, and the shower stall. The rotating hot and cold water handles were operated by an assistant behind the shower stall.

Topper's producer, Hal Roach was born in 1892 and began his career in movies by working as a $5-a-day extra with a friend who was to become one of the great silent comedians: Harold Lloyd. When Roach inherited several hundred dollars from a relative, he used it to realize his ambition to produce comedies.

After Roach had made a few pictures, Pathé offered him a producer's position if he could sign several stars, including Lloyd, to contracts. Roach's offer of $50 a week lured Lloyd away from Keystone and into a series of one-reelers for Pathé featuring a character called "Lonesome Luke." In 1919, Roach started making two-reelers for Pathé, including *Bumping into Broadway*.

Among the comedians Roach worked with in silent films were Stan Laurel and Oliver Hardy and the kids of the *Our Gang* shorts. His films were noted for the fast and furious pace at which gags were hurled at the audience. Roach's approach to making those movies was simple: Make 'em laugh!

In addition to *Topper*, Roach's sound films include *Fraternally Yours* (1933), *Way Out West* (1936), *Of Mice and Men, Turnabout,* and *One Million B.C.* (all 1940), and *Topper Returns* (1941).

Harold Lloyd, in Kevin Brownlow's *The Parade's Gone By . . . ,* recalled Roach this way, "He really wasn't a very good director. He had fortitude, he had drive, and he had worlds of confidence. . . . Roach was very creative, he was a very good gag man, and he had great courage." When no one else in Hollywood would give the great silent director D.W. Griffith a job, Roach hired him to do various production duties for *One Million B.C.* in 1940.

Hal Roach selected Norman Z. McLeod (1898–1964) to direct *Topper*. McLeod had started out as an animator, then wrote screenplays (including *Skippy*, 1931), and eventually got into directing. He had a special forte for zany comedy and directed the Marx Brothers in *Monkey Business* (1931) and *Horse Feathers* (1932). McLeod directed Cary Grant as the Mock Turtle in 1933's star-studded *Alice in Wonderland,* and Grant was less than thrilled to learn that McLeod would be his director in *Topper*.

McLeod's other films as director include *It's a Gift* (1934), *The Secret Life of Walter Mitty* (1947), and *The Paleface* (1947).

McLeod's direction always emphasized the visual, and he drew thumbnail sketches in the margins of his scripts—his own version of storyboards. In *Topper*, he never lets the witty dialogue overpower the visual side of the film. His deft sense of timing moves the film along, although the first fifteen minutes of *Topper* are perhaps too slowly paced. He gets a marvelous performance from Roland Young as Topper. McLeod did have his problems with Cary Grant, however. McLeod and Roach wanted Grant to have to court his wife all over again since their marriage contract included the phrase "till death do us part." Grant would have none of it, flatly telling Roach that "I'm not going to run after Constance Bennett." McLeod, fortunately, had no such difficulties with the other actors in the film.

Constance Bennett's role in *Topper* was one she played on screen and off for over 40 years—sophisticated, beautiful, sexy, slightly spoiled, and glamorous. Born in New York City on October 22, 1905, she was the first of three daughters of sometime matinee idol Richard Bennett and Adrienne (Mabel) Morrison. Her sisters were Joan and Barbara Bennett.

In 1920, her father helped Bennett get extra and bit parts in several one-reel comedies filmed on Long Island. After Constance eloped with the first of five husbands in 1922, she was offered a bit part in Ralph Ince's *Reckless Youth*. In her next film, *What's Wrong with the Women* (1922), Miss Bennett's performance as a modern, fun-seeking, rich young woman was praised by the New York critics.

Her vivacious personality—not her acting ability—got her noticed in her first Hollywood movie, *Cytherea*. Again typecast, she played a devil-may-care flapper in James Cruze's *The Goose Hangs High* (1925). Hardly a dedicated, ambitious, and hardworking actress, Connie Bennett freelanced in films so long as they didn't conflict with her full social life.

Louis B. Meyer signed Bennett to a seven-year contract, adding a provisio that allowed her to appear in other films when MGM wasn't using her.

This Thing Called Love (1929) was her first talking film, and, in 1931, she worked with her father for the first time in *Bought*. Constance Bennett's next film, David O. Selznick's *What Price Hollywood?* (1932), made her a much-sought-after actress. It was her role in *Ladies in Love* (1936), however, which led to her landing the lead in *Topper*, perhaps her best-remembered film. The success of *Topper*, with Connie Bennett playing the same character as always, made her "box-office once again, and she was nearly as successful with *Merrily We Live* (1938), another Roach-produced comedy.

After a small role in *It Should Happen to You* (1953), Bennett dropped out of films to devote herself to other business interests and to her fifth and last husband, army colonel John Theron Coulter, whom she'd married in 1946.

Cary Grant was born Alexander Archibald Leach in Bristol, England, on January 18, 1904, the son of a textile worker. At age 10 he was sent to the Fairfield Academy in Somerset after the death of his mother. At age 13

George and Marion try to convince Topper that everything is going to be all right.

he ran away for the first time, joining an acrobatic troupe. His father found him after four weeks and returned him to school. He ran away for good two years later and became a regular member of the acrobatic troupe. It was interesting training for an actor-to-be: he danced, tumbled, stilt-walked, and appeared in comedy skits. After the troupe appeared in New York in 1920, the young Leach decided to remain in the United States.

Success did not come quickly or easily. He supported himself by working as a stilt-walker advertising a Coney Island amusement park, by hand-painting and selling ties, and by playing small-town vaudeville circuits as a mind-reader.

After three years he returned to England and appeared as a bit player in musicals. Somehow, he wrangled a screen test for Paramount Pictures — which rejected him because "his neck is too thick and he has bowed legs." However, after supporting an actress in *her* screen test, he was spotted and signed to a contract with Paramount — whose first demand was that he change his name. Fay Wray suggested that the young Leach take the name of a character he'd played: Cary. The studio changed his last name to Grant and thus "Cary Grant" was born.

Paramount signed him a few weeks before his twenty-eighth birthday, and he was soon making $450 a week to appear in his first film, *This Is the*

Night (1932), with Thelma Todd and Roland Young. After Grant made a few now-largely-forgotten films, Mae West convinced Paramount to cast Grant as her leading man in *She Done Him Wrong* (1933). A grateful Grant later said, "I learned everything from her. Well, not everything, but almost everything."

Free of his Paramount contract in 1937, Grant became one of the first major free-lance actors in Hollywood, and he negotiated a four-picture deal with Columbia which would guarantee him $50,000 per film for the first two pictures and $75,000 per film for the final two.

Since he was not to start filming until May 1, he had time to make a little film Hal Roach had suggested he star in—*Topper*. At first Grant said Roach couldn't afford him, claiming he could get $50,000 for a Columbia film. Not one to give up, Roach kept after the reluctant Grant until he not only agreed to play George Kerby, but also agreed to allow Constance Bennett to receive top billing.

Grant's first film for Columbia was directed by Leo McCary and called *The Awful Truth* (1937). It made Grant a major star and all but guaranteed he would not return for any sequels to the successful *Topper*. His next film, with Katharine Hepburn, is one of the best-remembered screwball comedies of all: *Bringing Up Baby* (1938), in which he played a befuddled paleontologist sparring with an uninhibited young woman whose "baby" is a tame leopard.

Grant's other films include *Gunga Din* (1939), *His Girl Friday* (1940), *Arsenic and Old Lace* (1944), *Mr. Blandings Builds His Dream House* (1948), *To Catch a Thief* (1955), *North By Northwest* (1959), and *Walk, Don't Run* (1966), his last film.

In *Topper*, Grant brings grace and sophistication to a role which could have made the character look a boor were it not for his charm and acting skills. Grant is underappreciated in *Topper* for the same reason his roles in other films were often underappreciated—he makes it look too easy. It doesn't look like he's acting, but he is. And in *Topper*, today's film buffs can see Cary Grant in one of his first and best starring roles.

The 82-year-old Cary Grant died of a stroke in 1986. He had been in Davenport, Iowa, to make a public appearance at a tribute when he became ill and died almost immediately—as quick and graceful an exit as one could wish for.

Roland Young (1887–1953) began acting on the British stage and made his first film appearance in *Sherlock Holmes* in 1922. In addition to the two *Topper* sequels, his other films include *The Man Who Could Work Miracles* (1936), *The Philadelphia Story* (1940), and *And Then There Were None* (1945). Young most often played henpecked or ineffectual types.

In *Topper*, Young displays his skill at comedic acting—a challenging blend of timing and movement. Cosmo Topper must be believable or the center of the movie collapses. Young holds the film together with his droll mannerisms and his unusual way of speaking, his British accent giving him an air of upperclass twitism.

Slightly dated today, *Topper* can still wring laughs from a modern audience. Its irreverence is timeless, and its special effects, though no longer startling, are crisply executed and effective. Its performances, effects, and adult humor make *Topper* one of the great fantasy films of the 1930s.

The ghost in literature is the obvious forerunner to the ghost in movies. Mankind has long been fascinated by the supernatural and by the strange "life after death" that ghosts represent. That one might continue his existence as a ghost is both reassuring and frightening: The continuance of the self is appealing—but at what price?

Among the earliest-known examples of the "Gothic novel"—works full of madness, murder, ghosts, and grotesque horror—are Horace Walpole's *The Castle of Otranto* and Matthew Lewis' *The Monk*. Walpole and Lewis were followed by Edgar Allan Poe and Nathaniel Hawthorne. Poe and Hawthorne's horror fantasies were built upon elaborately constructed sentences which used the reader's own imagination to build to a crescendo of terror and a suffocating fear of the unknown and the supernatural.

Many early silent films were horror films, but they were filled with madmen and monsters, not ghosts. Indeed, with few exceptions—such as Griffith's *The Avenging Conscience* (1914)—most movie ghosts, like the jovial George and Marion, were fun-loving, misunderstood, the victims of family curses, or ordinary characters sent back to Earth to earn their way into Heaven by doing good deeds for mortals. It was not until the British-made *Dead of Night* (1945) that the ghost picture became horrific.

The success of *The Ghost Goes West* (1936, starring Robert Donat) and *Topper* prompted a slew of ghost films, including *Hold that Ghost* (1941, with Abbott and Costello), *The Canterville Ghost* (1944, with Charles Laughton as the victim of a centuries-old curse), *Blithe Spirit* (1945, with Rex Harrison), and *The Ghost and Mrs. Muir* (1947, with Rex Harrison again). *Topper* itself spawned two sequels minus Cary Grant: *Topper Takes a Trip* (1939), in which Marion helps Topper save his wife from a Riviera philanderer, and *Topper Returns* (1941), in which a girl helps Topper solve her own murder. (For more on the ghost in films, see the Appendix.)

15. The Wizard of Oz: The Fabulous Journey

> For nearly forty years this story has given faithful service to the Young in Heart; and Time has been powerless to put its kindly philosophy out of Fashion.
> To those of you who have been faithful to it in return . . . and to the Young in Heart. . .
> We dedicate this picture.

With those words begins one of the most beloved motion pictures ever made, a film as much a part of childhood as Santa Claus or the Easter Bunny. Parents, remembering the unalloyed joy of discovery they felt when they first saw the movie, eagerly await the chance to introduce their own youngsters to its pleasures.

Shown annually on television, *The Wizard of Oz* is the most successful fantasy film of all time, and its characters — the Tin Man, the Scarecrow, the Cowardly Lion — among the most recognizable figures in American popular culture.

Oz is so successful, in fact, that people often tend to overlook the fact that the picture didn't turn a profit until it was rereleased in 1948. And with ten scriptwriters, four directors, two Tin Men, and musical numbers filmed, cut, put back in, and cut again, the fact that the resulting film is anything but a mishmash is a miracle!

Although *Oz* is considered a classic today, it was not universally or immediately hailed as one by the critics and film reviewers of 1939. Indeed, it was sometimes compared unfavorably with Disney's *Snow White and the Seven Dwarfs* and its "vaudeville" flavor derided.

Frank S. Nugent's review in the *New York Times* of Friday, August 18, 1939, was typical of the many positive notices the film got. "Not since Disney's *Snow White* has anything quite so fantastic succeeded quite so well. . . . Mr. Lahr's lion is fion [and] it is clear enough that Mr. Dawn, the make-up wizard, Victor Fleming, the director-wizard, Arnold Gillespie, the special effects wizard, were pleased as Punches with the tricks they played. They have every reason to be."

211

The reviewer for the *Boston Transcript* said, "I like *Oz* . . . there is warming fantasy in its conception, lovely color in its execution, and there should be an Academy Award, even if a special award has to be created, for Bert Lahr."

The *Christian Science Monitor*'s reviewer called the film "two splendid hours [sic] of melody and magic in Technicolor. The technical trickery is perhaps even more impressive than the story itself."

Not all critics found *Oz* to be a stunning success, however. The *New Yorker*'s reviewer wrote, "I sat cringing before *Oz* which displays no trace of imagination, good taste, or ingenuity. . . . The vulgarity of which I was conscious all through the film is difficult to analyze."

Otis Ferguson's review for the *New Republic* was almost as harsh: "It has dwarfs, music, Technicolor, freak characters, and Judy Garland. It can't be expected to have a sense of humor as well — and as for the light touch of fantasy, it weighs like a pound of fruitcake soaking wet."

Variety's reviewer, however, spoke for the majority of critics when he wrote, "Occasionally a film rates the designation 'great' and this is such an occasion. It outshines any fantasy heretofore attempted, the only comparable picture in its class being *Snow White*, with which it will compete for world grosses, critical and popular applause."

When the mixed reviews for *Oz* are read today, we must remember that the film's contemporary reviewers were seeing the film as adult men and women. As Aljean Harmetz* notes, later generations of critics first saw the film not as grownups but as children or adolescents. Their reactions to the film are far different than the mature critics who first wrote about *Oz*. While almost no contemporary reviewer mentioned either Margaret Hamilton's Wicked Witch or the Winged Monkeys, if you ask any child what in the film made the most impression on him, he's sure to name both.

The film opens in Kansas, where we meet 11-year-old Dorothy (Judy Garland), her dog, Toto (Terry), her Aunt Em (Clara Blandick) and Uncle Henry (Charley Grapewin), and three farmhands — Hunk, Zeke, and Hickory (Ray Bolger, Bert Lahr, and Jack Haley). Feeling unappreciated after Aunt Em and Uncle Henry agree that nasty Miss Gulch (Margaret Hamilton) has the right to take Toto to the sheriff for biting her, Dorothy and Toto run away.

Dorothy meets up with a traveling, self-styled mindreader named Pro-

*Although I've relied on many sources, the best, most informative, most exhaustive, and best-written source of information is Aljean Harmetz's wonderful 1977 book *The Making of the Wizard of Oz* (Alfred A. Knopf). She's especially informative concerning the technical side — special effects, etc.

fessor Marvel (Frank Morgan), and he convinces her she's needed at home.
A tornado sweeps across the plains and forces everyone at the farm into a
storm cellar. Dorothy is alone in the house when the storm picks it up and
deposits it whole in a fabulous land called Oz—where Technicolor replaces
Kansas' drab sepia.

Dorothy learns from Glinda, a good witch (Billie Burke), that her house
has fallen on the Wicked Witch of the East and killed her. The little people
of the land, the Munchkins, sing 'Ding Dong, the Witch Is Dead' and make
Dorothy a national hero. But suddenly the Wicked Witch of the West
(Margaret Hamilton) arrives to claim her sister's ruby slippers—which
Glinda transfers to Dorothy's feet.

After the Wicked Witch vows revenge and disappears in a ball of flame,
the good witch, Glinda, sees Dorothy, who wants to go home, off down the
Yellow Brick Road to find the great and terrible Wizard of Oz, who perhaps
can send her back to Kansas. Soon she meets up with a talking Scarecrow.
Wanting brains, he joins Dorothy to see the Wizard. They soon come upon
a Tin Man, rusted in place from a sudden rainstorm. After they oil him, he
too joins their quest since he would like to receive a heart from the Wizard.

The trio meets up with a Cowardly Lion who wants courage from the
Wizard and so follows along. The travelers are threatened by the Witch,
and she makes the flesh-and-blood members of the party fall asleep in a field
of poppies. But Glinda intervenes, sending a snowstorm, and they awaken
to march into the Emerald City.

In the Emerald City, the intrepid travelers see wonders like the Horse
of a Different Color before being ushered into the presence of the Wizard.
The Wizard, a massive, floating, stone-faced head, says he will grant their
wishes if they will bring back the Wicked Witch of the West's broomstick.

The Wicked Witch sends an army of Winged Monkeys to capture
Dorothy and Toto and bring them back to her castle. Toto escapes,
however, and leads the others to the Witch's castle. Once inside, they free
Dorothy, only to be surrounded by the Witch's snarling guards. The Witch
sets the Scarecrow's arm on fire. Dorothy, trying to put it out, throws water
on the fire and, inadvertently, on the Wicked Witch. The Witch begins to
melt and shrink until there's nothing left of her. The guards, relieved she's
dead, readily give Dorothy the broomstick.

When the group tries to get the Wizard to make good his promises, he
attempts to put them off. While the others cower before his anger, Toto
pulls back a curtain to reveal an ordinary man standing before a microphone
and throwing switches—the Wizard is a fake and a humbug. Still, he gives
the Scarecrow a diploma, the Tin Man a heart-shaped watch, and the
Cowardly Lion a medal for bravery. To fulfill Dorothy's wish, the Wizard

Glinda and Dorothy stand in the middle of the main Munchkinland set, built on
Stage 27 by MGM carpenters and the 80-man crew of Henry Greutert, head of the
sculpture department. It was designed by Cedric Gibbons, head of the art department, and his associate, William A. Horning.

attempts to fly her home in his hot air balloon, but accidently takes off
without her.

Glinda appears and tells Dorothy she can go home simply by clicking
the heels of the ruby slippers together and saying, "There's no place like
home" three times. Dorothy does, and is transported back to Kansas (and
black-and-white). Surrounded by her family and friends, she vows never to
leave home again.

Lyman Frank Baum was born in upstate New York on May 15, 1856,
and died on May 6, 1919 — just 11 days shy of his sixty-third year. After a brief
and unsuccessful stint as an actor under the name of George Brooks, he was
a salesman for his father and later tried acting again. He took up
playwriting, and his first play, The Maid of Arran, was a success, although
his later efforts were not.

Baum married Maud Gage in 1882, and they immediately began a
family. Although Baum wanted a daughter, his first child was a boy: Frank
Joslyn Baum. Baum's father, concerned that his son might not be able to

support his children, gave Baum a string of theaters. Through no fault of his own, Baum lost the theaters, and his life entered a dark period which was to last ten years.

After becoming a successful traveling salesman, Baum took up writing again, and W(illiam) W(allace) Denslow illustrated Baum's *Father Goose, His Book*. Baum then began a book for children which he first called *The Emerald City*, then *From Kansas to Fairyland, The Fairyland of Oz, The Land of Oz*, and, finally, *The Wonderful Wizard of Oz*. Baum conceived of calling his magical land Oz after looking at a filing cabinet and seeing a drawer labeled O-Z.

The Wonderful Wizard of Oz was published on August 1, 1900. The book was an immediate success, and Baum made a musical play from it in 1902, which opened in Chicago and moved to Broadway in 1903.

As successful as Baum's fantasy was, it was rarely to be found on library shelves. Writer Ray Bradbury believes librarians of the time mistrusted *all* fantasy, believing that it would "turn your brain to mush." A devoted fan of the book, Bradbury called it "a fabulous trip, a marvelous journey," on the PBS special *The Whimsical World of Oz*.

In 1919, the year Baum died, *Glinda of Oz*, the last Oz book he wrote, was published. After his death, Maud Gage Baum—who was to survive L. Frank by 34 years, dying at the age of 92 in 1953—commissioned a young woman named Ruth Plumly Thompson to continue producing the ever-popular Oz adventures. Thompson wrote one Oz book a year for the next 19 years.

In 1914, Baum created the Oz Film Manufacturing Company and produced his first Oz films: *The Patchwork Girl of Oz* and *His Majesty, the Scarecrow of Oz*, which he wrote and directed (a 1910 production entitled *The Wizard of Oz* was written and directed by Otis Turner for the Selig company). In 1925, a silent film titled *The Wizard of Oz* was made featuring a portly Oliver Hardy as the Tin Man. An animated version of *The Wizard of Oz*, written by Baum's son, Colonel Frank Baum, was released in 1933.

In 1934, the ever-shrewd Samuel Goldwyn bought the film rights to *Oz* for $40,000, hoping to transform the book into a vehicle for Eddie Cantor. After Disney's amazing success with his animated *Snow White and the Seven Dwarfs* in 1937, other studios tried to buy the rights to *Oz* from Goldwyn. Eager to get his hands on a hot property, MGM studio head Louis B. Mayer paid Goldwyn $75,000 for the rights to the book in June of 1938 after a series of lengthy negotiations. Mayer then assigned Mervyn LeRoy to produce the film with the assistance of Arthur Freed. The film's budget was set at slightly over $2 million, indicating that MGM, Mayer, and LeRoy had enough faith in the property's ultimate success to designate it, not only as an "A" film, but also as a major—and possibly prestigious—undertaking.

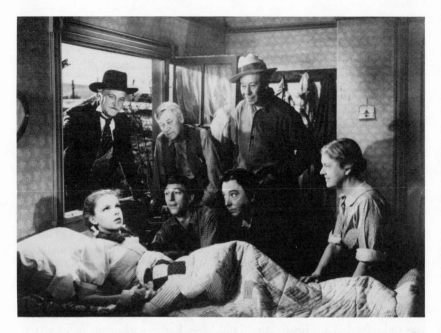

"There's no place like home." Dorothy awakens from her "dream." Clockwise from the top left: Professor Marvel (Frank Morgan), Uncle Henry (Charlie Grapewin), Zeke (Bert Lahr), Auntie Em (Clara Blandick), Hickory (Jack Haley), Hunk (Ray Bolger), and Dorothy Gale (Judy Garland). Not pictured — "Terry," who played Dorothy's dog, Toto.

Herman J. Mankiewicz, today famous as the co-writer with Orson Welles of the script of *Citizen Kane*, was the first writer to work on *Oz*'s script. He began working on his draft in February 1938, after MGM had optioned the book but before it had been purchased. While Mankiewicz spent little time on the project, his script called for the Kansas sequences to be shot in black and white and Oz to be filmed in color.

After Ogden Nash tried his hand at a treatment, Noel Langley was brought in in March to render yet another version. While other writers replaced Langley, much of what the gangly 26-year-old writer invented remained in the finished film. It was Langley who invented Hunk and Hickory, the two Kansas farmhands, and Miss Gulch — who was to reappear in Oz, and in children's nightmares, as the Wicked Witch of the West.

In June 1938, Langley, having substantially created the framework for the *Oz* we know today, was replaced by Herbert Fields. Fields' reign was brief, however, and he in turn was replaced by Samuel Hoffenstein. Less than a week after that, Florence Ryerson and Edgar Allan Woolf were given the assignment. Ryerson and Woolf's screenplay added the ploy of having the Scarecrow be seemingly destroyed several times only to be restored to wholeness. They also suggested that the "Wizard" be quadrupled by having the actor playing him also appear as the gateman, the driver of the Horse of a Different Color, and as the guard.

After Ryerson and Woolf's departure, Noel Langley was again assigned to the film, and he immediately proceeded to restore as much of *his* version as he could. Lyricist E.Y. ("Yip") Harburg then polished the Ryerson/Woolf/Langley script, only to be followed by yet another writer, Jack Mintiz. Mintiz gave way to Sid Silvers, who worked on the script the week after the film had begun production. Finally, veteran screenwriter John Lee Mahin (*Red Dust, Treasure Island,* and *Captains Courageous*) worked on *Oz* from October 1938 to January 1939.

Although a total of ten writers worked on the screenplay, the final credits for *The Wizard of Oz* would read: "Screenplay by Noel Langley, Florence Ryerson, and Edgar Allan Woolf. Adaptation by Noel Langley."

In today's Hollywood, the actors—the *stars,* more precisely—call many of the shots. More and more their own production companies are intimately involved in the films they deign to participate in, often for a fee of several million dollars up front and a piece of the picture's profits. They may do only one picture every two years, or even more infrequently. They pick and choose their projects carefully. In the Hollywood of the '30s and '40s, things were different.

Ray Bolger, a Broadway star, signed a long-term MGM contract for $3,000 a week in 1936. Bolger's casting in *Oz* was simple. Mervyn LeRoy called the dancer into his office and informed him he was to play the Tin Man. End of discussion.

Also under contract at MGM at that time was Buddy Ebsen. The six-foot-three-inch tall Ebsen not only looked like a scarecrow because of his thin frame, he was already Langley's choice for the part of the film's Scarecrow. Ebsen could see that *Oz* was going to be a major production, perhaps a star-making one. He just wanted to be a part of it, no matter what the role, so he readily agreed to switch parts with Bolger, who wished to play the Scarecrow.

Ten days after principal filming had begun, Buddy Ebsen went home and began to relax from a hard day's shooting. "After dinner I took a breath and nothing happened," he later recalled in *The Best of M-G-M: The Golden Years: 1928–1959,* by James Robert Parish and Gregory Mank. After Ebsen had spent two weeks in Los Angeles' Good Samaritan Hospital, MGM realized that his condition—later diagnosed as an allergic reaction to the aluminum powder used in his makeup—meant he was lost to the picture. The studio borrowed Jack Haley from 20th Century–Fox to take over the role of the Tin Man.

According to Parish and Mank, Wallace Beery desperately wanted to play the part of the Wizard, hoping that it would impress his young adopted daughter. Unfortunately for Beery's chances, his career at MGM was at a low point, and he was reduced to plugging away in "B" films. Producer LeRoy wanted comedian Ed Wynn for the part of the Wizard and offered him the role. Wynn promptly turned him down, disdaining a role he felt was too insignificant for someone of his stature.

Freed and Harburg argued for W.C. Fields, and surely his Wizard would have been an interesting one. He, too, initially felt the part too small for a star of his magnitude. Still, he agreed to take the role for $100,000; MGM offered him $75,000, and Fields declined. Frank Morgan, like Buddy Ebsen, could see *Oz*'s promise. He actively went after the role of the Wizard and succeeded in landing it after demonstrating his familiarity with the screenplay.

Thirty-six-year-old Margaret Hamilton was chosen to be Miss Gulch/the Wicked Witch. Although she never formally signed a contract, her tenure on the production lasted four months. Margaret Hamilton is today so identified with the role of the Wicked Witch that it comes as quite a shock to learn that producer LeRoy at first wanted to cast beautiful Gale Sondergaard in the part, envisioning her as darkly seductive as well as evil. As Miss Sondergaard later told *Film Fan Monthly:* "Mervyn LeRoy had a sudden thought . . . to make a glamorous witch instead of an ugly witch. We actually did the costumes — a high, pointed hat, but of sequins, a very glamorous sequined gown. She was to be the most glamorous, but wicked sort of witch. And we got into testing for it, and it was absolutely gorgeous. And then, I suppose, Mervyn got to remembering that this was a classic by now, and the children who read it, and grownups too, were going to say, 'That isn't the way it was written!' And everybody agreed you could not do that to *The Wizard of Oz.*"

According to John Lahr, in *Notes on a Cowardly Lion*, Bert Lahr, the burlesque comedian, was chosen to play the Cowardly Lion at lyricist Yip Harburg's suggestion. Harburg could do perfect imitations of Lahr's unique vocal style, and he began ad-libbing lines to the producers. "'Put up your dukes! Put up your paws!' Can you imagine Bert doing that?" LeRoy and Freed readily agreed to sign Lahr because they thought he was funny. Harburg had other ideas, believing that Lahr would bring a warmth and humanity to the picture — even under all that makeup!

Studio head Mayer originally hoped that ten-year-old Shirley Temple would play the part of Dorothy, but Twentieth Century–Fox refused to lend her out. When the studio sought the loan of Deanna Durbin, Universal emphatically said no. Mayer then made do with a young actress already under contract: Judy Garland. She was signed to play the role for a mere $500 a week — only Terry, the female Cairn terrier who played Toto, received less than Garland at $125 a week.

After MGM's first choice for Glinda, Metro contract player Helen Gilbert, played hooky from the studio on a romantic fling, the rather fey Billie Burke was an almost unanimous choice to play the good witch. Charley Grapewin and Clara Blandick were signed to play Uncle Henry and Aunt Em.

In a way, the hardest roles to cast were the Munchkins. Somehow, the production had to find over a hundred little people to play the diminutive residents of Munchkinland. Casting director Bill Grady contacted Leo Singer of Singer's Midgets. Most of Singer's little people were acrobats, singers, and assorted circus performers.

The midgets joined the production in mid–November of 1938 and their sheer numbers — over 124 of them — made them a major headache. However, contrary to countless Hollywood myths and legends, the midgets were *not* a bunch of drunken, fun-loving, and hard-to-handle little troublemakers (as they were portrayed in the truly terrible 1981 film *Under the Rainbow*, which starred Chevy Chase and Carrie Fisher). (For more about the actors and their films, see the Appendix.)

Principal photography began on October 12, 1938. Richard Thorpe was in the director's chair the first day of shooting and gone twelve days later. Producer LeRoy hated Thorpe's work and that was that. Buddy Ebsen's exit from the film due to his illness came a day or so after Thorpe's, and many in the cast and crew, not knowing what had happened to him, assumed he had been fired as well.

Ebsen's makeup included powdered aluminum which was liberally applied to his face and head since, at the time, doctors assumed pure aluminum dust was harmless. Haley was more fortunate: The aluminum was made into a paste and rubbed on. Even so, Haley suffered an eye infection from the paste.

After Thorpe's dismissal, George Cukor was the director of *Oz* for all of three days. It was Cukor who removed Judy Garland's blonde wig and cherubic makeup, correctly believing it made her look too artificial. Cukor was relieved to be off the picture. Parish and Mank quote him as later saying, "I was brought up on grander things. I was brought up on Tennyson."

Next up was Victor Fleming, who directed most of *Oz*. The 55-year-old Fleming was considered a man's director after having helmed such red-meat productions as *Red Dust* (1932) and *Captains Courageous* (1937). As Andrew Sarris notes in *The American Cinema*, his "most popularly remembered films, *Gone with the Wind* and *The Wizard of Oz*, seem extraneous to his career...."

When Clark Gable asked that "man's director" Victor Fleming replace "woman's director" George Cukor on *GWTW*, King Vidor stepped in to direct *Oz* for the final ten days of shooting. Vidor directed the film's Kansas sequences and hence was responsible for staging the film's most famous and memorable moment: Judy Garland singing "Over the Rainbow." As Vidor recalled during an episode of the television series *The Men Who Made the Movies:* "Victor Fleming was a good friend, and he took me around to all the sets that had been built and went through the thing. He left that night and I took over. It was, as I remember, about two and a half weeks—three weeks possibly, which included the 'Somewhere Over the Rainbow.' It's run all the time, and whenever I hear it, I get a tremendous kick out of knowing I directed that scene. . . . I did some of the cyclone scenes, and 'We're Off to See the Wizard.' . . . But I did not want any credit, and, as long as Victor was alive, I kept quiet about it."

E(dgar) Y. Harburg and Harold Arlen were hired in May of 1938 to write the film's music and lyrics, producing a marvelously plot-advancing score. MGM house composer Herbert Stothart was credited with *Oz's* "Musical Adaptation."

William Horning, the art director, and the MGM wardrobe department followed, as closely as they could, W.W. Denslow's original illustrations for Baum's book.

Gilbert Adrian was the man behind the "Costumes by Adrian" credit. Adrian was born in Connecticut in 1903 and died in 1959. After beginning with the DeMille Studios, he moved to MGM in 1928 and remained there until 1942. In 1939, he designed the costumes for Lubitsch's *Ninotchka* as well as for *Oz.*

Makeup artist Jack Dawn achieved subtle characterizations in designing the Cowardly Lion and the other fantasy characters by using appliances rather than masks. ("Appliances" are individual facial parts—noses, ears, etc.—applied to the actor's face, not covering it totally and immobilely like a mask.) After Dawn's skillful work on Bert Lahr, it was hard to believe that no one had ever noticed how much he looked like a lion.

Charles Schram, who also worked on *Oz,* was responsible for Bert Lahr's daily makeup. Piece by piece—the turned-up nose and split in his upper lip, the false whiskers—the rubber appliances had to go on. (The effect which most delights children was relatively simple to achieve: A fishline attached to the Lion's tail was controlled by a technician overhead with a fishing pole, who manipulated its wags and swishes.)

Haley's makeup as the Tin Man, after the Ebsen fiasco, was carefully considered. Dawn added laundry bluing to the silver to achieve the correct look through the camera. But it was Ray Bolger, as the Scarecrow, whose makeup Dawn considered the most challenging. Dawn made a plaster cast of Bolger's face and then cast his appliances in foam rubber.

After Dawn and Schram had made a life mask of Margaret Hamilton's face, molds were formed to match the contours of her nose and chin. The appliances were glued to her face with spirit gum and then a special grease with a green foundation was spread on. Near the end of the picture, Hamilton discovered that she still maintained a greenish tinge after removing her makeup—it had gradually sunk into her skin, and it was months before she was totally free of the greenish cast.

With his appliances in place, Lahr could only sip his lunch through a straw. The studio bigwigs thought the made-up actors looked too grotesque to eat in the commissary, so they ate in their dressing rooms.

Technicolor was not a new process in 1939, but the film stock used on *Oz* was. As director of photography Harold Rossen told Aljean Harmetz, "Technicolor came out with a new film that was speeded up." A "fast" speed number for film stock means it needs less light than a "slow" speed number; even so, Rossen and his lighting crew "had to use every light we could get our hands on." (If you look closely, in the Scarecrow's early scenes, Ray Bolger can be seen blinking rapidly and often—probably a reaction to the blinding candlepower of the lights.)

The intense lighting meant the actors had to work—in their heavy costumes and pore-closing makeup—in incredible heat. As Jack Haley told John Lahr, "Each day Judy had to go to school. Her tutor—an old woman—would come onto the set and someone would yell 'School Time!' We used to long for that sound—it meant we had an hour's rest." Fleming would have the powerful lights turned off and the massive stage doors opened so the actors could hurry outside in the relatively cool California midday air. The doors remained open until the baking sets cooled down.

Jack Haley, who felt the production was an unpleasant experience given the makeup and the heat from the lights, also felt that whatever he and his fellow sufferers did, it was *not* acting: "It was all movement. We were running all the time. We were always afraid. We were running all over the joint—putting out fires, chopping down doors, cutting the rope that held the Witch's chandelier," he recalls in *The Making of the Wizard of Oz*. Haley also had an idea how the Tin Man and Scarecrow ought to speak to Dorothy. "I said [to director Fleming] 'I want to talk the way I talk when I'm telling a story to my five-year-old son.' And he said, 'Give me an example.' I started with, 'Well, there was this big frog. And he had great long legs.' Sort of breathless. And then I said the Tin Man's first speech in that same voice. 'Well, a long time ago I was standing here, and it started to rain. . . .' And he said, 'That's it.' And then Bolger followed my key."

In his son's book, Bert Lahr later said of the director: "Vic Fleming had never experienced guys like us. Some legitimate directors can't imagine anybody thinking about something else and when he yells, 'Shoot,' just going in and playing. We'd kid around up to the last minute and go on. You could see he got mad and red-faced. Some actors try and get into the mood. They'll put themselves into the character. I never did that. I'm not—let's say—dedicated."

Victor Fleming was a veteran director, and he knew he had his hands full with the young Garland and three experienced troupers who'd seen it all. Haley told John Lahr that "Fleming had a wonderful understanding of people. He knew that the makeup was wearing on us. . . . In order for us not to lose interest in the picture, to try to keep our animation, he would call the three of us together and say, 'Fellahs, you've got to help me on this scene.' Well, I knew this guy was a big director, and he didn't need actors to help him. He'd say, 'You guys are Broadway stars, what do you think we should do here?'" But Fleming's interest paid off when Lahr convinced him — in the poppy field scene when Glinda has made it snow — to allow the Lion to say, "Unusual weather we're havin', ain't it?" The line never fails to generate a huge laugh.

It was Judy Garland's acting, under the sure hand of Fleming that carried the picture. As Haley said to John Lahr, "You believed she *really* wanted to get back to Kansas."

The filming was beset by a number of minor — and not so minor — accidents. An example of the former was the time one of the Witch's castle guards stepped on Terry, the little dog playing Toto. More serious was Margaret Hamilton's fiery exit from Munchkinland. The special effects crew were to quickly drop her through a trap door in the stage as smoke billowed up and was immediately followed by jets of flame. It looked impressive and was considered a safe "gag." After a perfect take, Fleming called for another one, "for insurance." Unfortunately for Miss Hamilton, the smoke and flames were triggered too quickly and she was enveloped in fire. Although she felt a warmth on her face, Hamilton didn't know that her hat and broom were on fire. She was badly burned on the right side of her face and her right hand had the outer layer of skin burned off.

The green in her makeup was toxic because it contained copper, and it had to be immediately removed from her burned skin with alcohol. Although the pain was excruciating, Hamilton, the ultimate professional, did not scream. Margaret Hamilton left to go home — and didn't return to the set for six weeks. When she finally did return, she had to wear green gloves because her hands were not completely healed.

When Margaret Hamilton refused to have anything more to do with any shots requiring fire, stunt person Betty Danko agreed to sit atop a pipe disguised to look like the Witch's broomstick for the skywriting sequence. On the third take, the pipe exploded, and Betty Danko spent 11 days in the hospital.

A. Arnold ("Buddy") Gillespie, *Oz*'s special effects wizard, came to Hollywood in 1922 and proceeded to spend the next eight months working 12 to 14-hour days in Cecil B. DeMille's Paramount art department. He later moved over to the Goldwyn Studio, which became part of MGM. Gillespie worked on the original *Ben Hur* in Italy, then returned to Hollywood in

1924 to serve as an art director under Cedric Gibbons until he joined the special effects department in 1936.

Since *Oz* was shot entirely on soundstages, the production made use of Stages 14, 15, 25, 26, 27, and others. The cornfield where Dorothy finds the Scarecrow and most of the other sets were surrounded by huge canvas paintings—cycloramas, masterpieces of movie illusion in which rocks, cornstalks, trees, and mountains seem to retreat into a distant horizon (Gillespie was to make use of cycloramas again in 1956 for the studio-bound SF masterpiece *Forbidden Planet*). The sets were so huge that some scenes in *Oz* utilized as many as nine cameras, all shooting simultaneously, to catch the flow of Munchkins or Winged Monkeys.

The matte paintings used in *Oz*, including shots of the distant Emerald City and the grim landscape surrounding the Wicked Witch's castle, were not rendered in the usual manner. Instead of oil on glass, they were crayon pastels on four-foot-wide pieces of black cardboard.

The tornado that sweeps Dorothy, Toto, and their house off to Oz was one of the first and best twisters ever captured on film. Not an optical effect—something created in the camera—or animation, the cyclone was a massive "miniature": a 35-foot muslin wind sock. As a gantry carried the muslin tornado across the floor of a miniature set—complete with miniature farm buildings and cornfields—fuller's earth and compressed air were forced up through its bottom to emerge at its base, its crown, and through the porous muslin itself. The fuller's earth provided two illusions: First, it helped blur the motion of the spinning muslin. Second, it created the cloud of dust that any whirling, digging, and biting tornado creates as it sweeps across dusty plains.

The Winged Monkeys attacking Dorothy and her friends were a combination of actors in suits and six-inch-high miniatures hung from the gantry by piano wire. As the gantry moved across the stage, the miniature monkeys appeared to fly—although not very convincingly, since they looked rigid and lifeless. For the live action, the monkey-suited actors' wings were made to go up and down by small windshield wiper motors.

The impressive floating head of the Wizard that terrifies Dorothy and the others was simply a filmed image front-projected onto a cloud of steam. Similarly, the images in the Witch's crystal ball were also simple film projections. The hollow glass ball contained a translucent screen onto which Buddy Gillespie projected the desired image—Aunt Em dissolving into the gloating face of the Witch as Dorothy awaits her execution, for instance.

Ironically, the most impressive effects are often the simplest to create. To show the melting of the Wicked Witch after Dorothy douses her with a bucket of water, Gillespie made use of a hydraulic elevator and dry ice. Recalling the illusion in *Film Tricks*, by Harold Schechter and David Everitt, Gillespie said, "It was so doggone simple. We had her [Margaret

The leader of the Flying Monkeys and the Wicked Witch glare into her crystal ball—which in this shot is reflecting the studio's lighting equipment. In the film, a process projector and a mirror were used to project images onto a small translucent screen inside the hollow ball.

Hamilton] on a little hydraulic lift and just lowered her down through the floor. Her black costume was fastened . . . to the floor. We had a little dry ice that came out to make it look as though she were melting. And she went down and down and down! Her black hat stayed on the floor, and her costume just spread out and covered up the hole."

Principal photography on *Oz* was completed on Thursday, March 16, 1939. After 22 weeks of shooting, and at a final cost of more than $2,700,000, MGM's prestige picture was in the can. All that remained, after additional effects shooting, cutting the film, and laying in the music track, was to preview the final product.

Not until the San Bernadino preview in June 1939 did Louis B. Mayer see the film which had cost him so much time and trouble. Aljean Harmetz notes that Harburg and Arlan's "musical elaboration of 'We're Out of the Woods' was dropped as was most of a song—'Lions and Tigers and Bears'. . . . The music surrounding Dorothy's triumphant return to the Emerald City after the Witch's melting was cut along with that whole sequence."

Subsequent to the first sneak preview, Mayer decided to remove Judy Garland's ballad "Over the Rainbow," calling the song "too sad." Harburg,

Arlen, and Freed argued vehemently to keep the song in, and Mayer reluctantly relented. Also trimmed after the first preview was the Scarecrow's lengthy dance after he first meets Dorothy. As Ray Bolger told Aljean Harmetz, "It was a fantastic dance that didn't mean anything to the picture."

Oz was previewed for a second time on Tuesday, July 18, 1939 at the Westwood Village Theatre. It was after this preview that the decision to cut a major number was made. "The Jitter Bug," a number which centered around Lahr's Lion, was eliminated because, as Harburg later put it, the studio "began to worry that 'The Jitter Bug' might date the picture."

Harold Arlen took color home movies of the filming of "The Jitter Bug" number, and when that footage is viewed with a recording of the song, one can get a pretty good idea of how the sequence went. Dorothy and the Scarecrow dance alone and with each other, and the Lion and the Tin Man dance with each other as the surrounding trees sway and reach out for them. (Other Arlen footage shows Margaret Hamilton in full makeup as the Wicked Witch and *smiling* broadly at the camera.)

In the finished film, all that remains of five long and hard weeks of filming is the line the Wicked Witch delivers to Nikko, her head Winged Monkey, before she orders the monkeys to attack the travelers in the Haunted Forest and carry off Dorothy: "I'll send a little insect on ahead to take care of them."

Since *Oz* had cost just over $2.7 million and grossed $3 million, after the costs of distribution and the theatre owners' shares were subtracted, the film lost MGM $1 million during its initial release. It moved into profitability, albeit marginally, when it was rereleased in 1948. However, not until the film was shown on CBS in November of 1956 did the picture really begin to return substantial profits. (According to *Variety*'s list of All-time U.S./Canadian Rental Champs, *Oz* has returned rentals of $4 million over the years; hence the film, simply on the basis of its North American rentals, *has* earned profits on its theatrical distribution.)

After CBS paid a mere $225,000 for two broadcasts, the licensing fee for subsequent broadcasts kept inching up until CBS (NBC owned the rights between 1968 and 1976) was paying MGM $800,000 a year for the rights between 1976 and 1980.

A new videocassette version with Hi-Fi sound was released in 1986 and was immediately popular, selling hundreds of thousands of copies. (For information about the film's awards and nominations, see the Appendix.)

In 1960, *The Shirley Temple Show* presented *The Land of Oz* on television with Miss Temple playing Tip/Ozma.

An animated 60-minute television version called *Return to Oz* was aired in 1963.

In 1969, a 72-minute film called *The Wonderful Land of Oz* and based on the book *The Land of Oz* was released by Childhood Productions.

A *Wizard of Oz* on-the-set conference. From left to right: Ray Bolger (in the Scarecrow's costume); Victor Fleming, the director; Bobby Connolly, the dance director; and Mervyn LeRoy, the producer.

Judy Garland's daughter, Liza Minnelli, provided the voice of Dorothy for a 1974 animated Oz film titled *Journey Back to Oz*. This uninspired sequel without the Wizard was originally made in 1964 and released ten years later. Other voices in the cast included Mickey Rooney as the Scarecrow, Milton Berle as the Cowardly Lion, Danny Thomas as the Tin Man, and Margaret Hamilton as Aunt Em.

In 1976 an Australian rock-and-roll version, simply titled *Oz*, was released. (In *Variety*'s unique parlance, Australia itself is referred to as "Oz.") The film was "suggested" by *The Wizard of Oz* and released under the title *20th Century Oz* in the United States.

Critic David Stratton, in his book *The Last Wave*, wrote, "The concept of Dorothy as a persistent little groupie who fends off incipient rape on the highways of Victoria so as to sleep with the greatest rock star of all is an ingenious one, and her final realization that 'fame really fucks you up' is a marvellously cynical '70s variation on the original Dorothy's realization that 'there's no place like home.'"

After *The Wiz*, an all-black musical version of *The Wizard of Oz*, became a Broadway hit, Universal acquired the film rights and turned a 1975 stage success into a 1978 film flop. One of Universal's many miscalculations was casting an obviously-too-old Diana Ross as Dorothy. Hoping to get around this anomaly, the producers had the screenwriters turn Dorothy into a lonely schoolteacher in her mid-twenties. The Emerald City was, in this strange reworking of the material, New York City below 125th Street—an area Dorothy/Diana had never left Harlem to explore . . . uh huh.

Michael Jackson (best known then as one of the Jackson Five) played the Scarecrow, Ted Ross the Lion, Nipsey Russell the Tin Man, and Richard Pryor was the Wiz himself. While the sets were impressive, the overall effect was limpid and dreary, and the film returned rentals of only $12,381,241 after costing an estimated $24,000,000.

Walt Disney owned the film rights to all the Oz stories and books, and in 1957 his *Mickey Mouse Club* Mouseketeers did a black-and-white, song-and-dance, mini-version of a planned Oz production called "Rainbow Road to Oz." The two numbers filmed appeared on the *Disneyland Fourth Anniversary Show* on September 11, 1957. Perhaps fearing high production costs and unflattering comparisons to the Judy Garland version just beginning its TV run, Disney never went any further with the idea of a big-budget, live-action version of *Rainbow Road to Oz*.

Finally in 1985, the Disney studio did get around to making their own Oz film, *Return to Oz*, based on the second and third books in Baum's series, *The Marvelous Land of Oz* and *Ozma of Oz*. Unfortunately, the film was one of 1985's most expensive disasters. Although *Return to Oz* cost $28,000,000 to produce and release, it returned rentals of only $4,450,000.

Critics charge that the film was all technical wizardry without any emotional wonder. Naysayers also note that the first 20 minutes of the film, where Dorothy is taken to a quack doctor specializing in "electrical cures," is dark, somber, and terrifying to young children (sound familiar?).

Return to Oz, admittedly a dark and scary film, admittedly a non-musical, probably had no chance. The Judy Garland singing and dancing version, so established in our minds and hearts, is just too powerful an icon to tamper with. Given our sentimental attachment to Bolger's Scarecrow, Lahr's Lion, and Haley's Tin Man, the fact that *Return*'s versions are truer to John R. Neill's character illustrations for the books is an empty accomplishment. I believe, however, that *Return*, despite its emotional hollowness, will grow in stature over the years, gaining grudging admission to its rightful place in the hierarchy of great fantasy films, just a rung or two below its celebrated forerunner.

To view *The Wizard of Oz* today is to visit an old friend. Those of us in our thirties and forties have grown up with the annual television showings. It's hard to remember a time when we didn't know the lyrics, didn't look forward to seeing the strange sights that greet Dorothy inside the cyclone, and didn't marvel at *the* moment—that fabulous instant when Dorothy opens the door to Oz and to Technicolor. The film is such a showcase for the original three-strip Technicolor that seeing those vivid, patently unreal colors today (such as Dorothy's red hair and the Witch's green face and hands) makes one mourn the loss of that expensive but long-lasting process.

The music swells under Leo the MGM Lion, and the credits roll by in black and white. The film takes care to establish Dorothy and her life on the farm with Aunt Em, Uncle Henry, and the three farmhands. Kansas is seen as such a drab, colorless place that—at the film's conclusion—we wonder why Dorothy is so eager to return. Also, in Kansas the pace of the film is deliberate; it's only when we get to Oz that the film seems to gallop from one incredible sight or production number to another.

Frank Morgan, as Professor Marvel, is a delight, and the twister, spinning across the open fields, is an ominous, unstoppable force of nature. Inside the cyclone comes the film's first great shock: seeing Miss Gulch, on her bicycle, turn into the Witch seated on her broomstick.

The film's nearly horrific (for small children) moments are offset by the obvious good humor and dazzling production numbers. The score and the songs are great, and I defy anyone to view the film and not have snatches of lyricist Harburg's songs floating unbidden through his or her head for days afterward.

Actor-singer-dancers Haley, Bolger, and Lahr provide the vim and verve and vaudevillian energy, but, as Jack Haley observed, it was Judy Garland's sincerity which carried the picture and provided its heart. Only a stone-hearted cynic would deny the power of Dorothy's heartfelt "He got away, he got away!" when Toto escapes from the Witch's castle.

As a child, I found the revelation of the Wizard's real identity disorienting and disappointing: That little guy is really the Wizard? (Oz shares this element with Star Trek—The Motion Picture: Both the Wizard and V'ger are revealed to be much less than they first appeared. "Don't look behind that curtain" is not all that different from "Don't look at that little gismo atop the miles-long space machine.")

That all Dorothy has to do to go back to Kansas is to tap her ruby slippers together seems a bit of a cheat after all she's been through. And seeing Lahr, Bolger, and Haley as mere humans once again is a shock—they're so much more convincing as a lion, a scarecrow, and a tin man.

The film disappoints in another way at its conclusion, as well. We're meant to see that it was all a dream, not a real adventure, and that Dorothy is better off back in plain, cruel Kansas—where, presumably, Miss Gulch waits again to take away Toto.

As Danny Peary notes in Cult Movies, "the 1939 film makes this 'no place like home' nonsense the picture's major theme, the conclusion Dorothy somehow draws from her dream experiences in Oz. And it is nonsense. The Dorothy we see in the opening scenes is an unhappy little girl who is lonely because there seem to be no children about, who has no parents and lives with a very unsupportive, elderly uncle and aunt on a very barren gray farm." (In the books, Dorothy finally has the good sense to settle permanently in Oz.)

The Wizard of Oz is a superior fantasy film and child's adventure. What makes the film unique among the great fantasy films, dominated by males and male fantasies, is that its core, its human heart, is a little girl. Dorothy Gale, L. Frank Baum's loving creation, is courageous, warm-hearted, spunky, and resolute—an adolescent heroine who offered other little girls (and boys) someone to admire and identify with.

Baum's books, while aimed at all children, were especially appealing to little girls, who could read about intelligent, resourceful, and brave female characters. Little boys got a hair-raising shock when, at the conclusion of *The Land of Oz*, the masculine hero Tip (called "small and rather delicate in appearance") turned out to be a (gasp!) *girl*—Ozma, the rightful ruler of Oz.

Oz is an adventure, a magical journey we eagerly anticipate taking again. It's a return to innocence—as personified by the young, still-unspoiled Judy Garland singing "Over the Rainbow"—that we know we cannot easily regain in any other way. We approach *Oz* like the small child who wishes to experience his or her favorite fairy tale over and over: "Read it to me again, Daddy!"

Filmography

BEAUTY AND THE BEAST (LA BELLE ET LA BÊTE). An Andre Paulve Production. Discina International/Lopert Films. Black and White. 1946 (U.S.A. 1947). 90 min. (8100 feet). Opened December 23, 1947, at the Bijou, New York City. *Producer:* Andre Paulve. *Story, dialogue, and direction:* Jean Cocteau. From a fairy-tale by Mme. Leprince de Beaumont. *Art director:* Christian Berard. *Technical advisor:* Rene Clement. *Settings:* Rene Moulaert & Carre. *Costumes:* Escoffier & Castillo. Made by Paquin. *Music:* Georges Auric. *Orchestra director:* Roger Desormiere. *Director of photography:* Henri Alekan. *Cameramen:* Henri Tiquet, Foucard, & Letouzey. *Stills:* Aldo. *Makeup:* Arakelian. *Script girl:* Lucile Costa. *Supervising editor:* Claude Iberia. *General manager:* Roger Rogelys. *Production manager:* Emile Darbon. Filmed at St. Maurice Studios. G.M. Film Laboratories. *Sound:* Jacques Lebreton & Jacques Carrere. *Assistants:* H. Girbal & P. Gaboriau. *English sub-titles:* Francis Howard.

Cast: Jean Marais (Avenant, The Beast, The Prince), Josette Day (Beauty), Mila Parely (Adelaide), Nane Germon (Felicie), Michel Auclair (Ludovic), and Marcel Andre (the Merchant).

CONAN THE BARBARIAN. A Universal Release. A Dino De Laurentiis presentation. An Edward R. Pressman production. 1982. Technicolor. Todd-AO. Running time: 129 min. (11,610 feet). [Also 123 & 115 min.] *Executive producers:* D. Constantine Conte & Edward R. Pressman. *Producers:* Buzz Feitshans & Raffaella De Laurentiis. *Director:* John Milius. *Screenplay:* John Milius & Oliver Stone. Based on the character created by Robert E. Howard. *Director of photography:* Duke Callaghan. *Production designer:* Ron Cobb. *Special effects supervisor:* Nick Allder. *Associate producer:* Edward Summer. *Special visual effects:* Frank Van Der Veer. *Animated visual effects:* Visual Concepts Engineering & Peter Kuran. *Editor:* Tim O'Meara. *Co-editor:* Fred Stafford. *Music:* Basil Poledouris. *Sound:* Jim Willis. *Supervising sound editor:* Fred J. Brown. *Second unit director:* Terry Leonard. *Costume designer:* John Bloomfield. *Art directors:* Pierluigi Basile & Benjamin Fernandez. *Animated opticals:* RGB Opticals & James R. Hagedorn. *Animation:* Katherine Kean, Len Morgantt, & Susan Turner. *Special effects makeup supervisor:* Carlo De Marchis. *Makeup and hair supervisor:* Jose Antonio Sanchez. *Special effects chief:* Antonio Parra. *Special effects sculptor:* Peter Voysey. *Special effects technician:* Roger Nichols & John McGoldrick. *Set dresser:* Giorgio Postiglione. *Assistant set dresser:* Francesca De Laurentiis. *Production supervisor:* Alfredo De Laurentiis. *Production manager:* Vicente Escriva Jr. *Model maker:* Emilio Ruiz Del Rio. *Construction manager:* Aldo Puccini. *Wardrobe supervisor:* Franco Antonelli. *Makeup artists:* Jose Quetglas & Carlos Paradela. *Property master/buyer:* Julian Mateos. *Property master:* Graham Sumner. *Assistant director:* Roberta Cirla. *Stunt coordinators:* Terry Leonard & Juan Majan. *Second assistant director:* Victor Albarran. *Production assistant:* Barbara Back. *Assistant art director:* Jose Maria Alarcon.

Draughtsman: Luciano Arroyo. *Sword master:* Kiyoshi Yamasaki. *Headdress maker:* Michael Jones. *Sword maker:* Tim Huchthausen. *Title design:* Ron Cobb. *Technical advisor:* L. Sprague de Camp. *Spiritual advisor:* Dr. Fred L. Rexer. *Production research:* Michael B. Gladych. *Animal handler:* Francisco Ardura. *Snake trainer:* Dr. Yves De Vestel Tiva. *Serpents expert:* ITI Ophiology.

Cast: Arnold Schwarzenegger (Conan), James Earl Jones (Thulsa Doom), Sandahl Bergman (Valeria), Ben Davidson (Rexor), Cassandra Gaviola (Witch woman), Gerry Lopez (Subotai), Mako (the Wizard), Valerie Quennessen (Princess Yasimina), William Smith (Conan's father), Max Von Sydow (King Osric), Franco Columbu (Pictish warrior), Gary Herman (Osric's sergeant), Nadiuska (Conan's mother), Sven Ole Thorsen (Thorgrim), Luis Barboo (Red Hair), Jorge Sanz (Young Conan), Akio Mitamura (Japanese general), Kiyoshi Yamasaki (Sword master), Tony Brubaker (Black pitfighter), Ron Cobb (Haga vendor), Cathy Valerie (girl at pillar), Leslie Foldvary (Sacrificial snake girl), Erik Holmey (Turanian officer), Celia Milius (Snake princess).

THE DARK CRYSTAL. A Henson Organization Ltd. Production for ITC Entertainment Ltd. Distributed by Universal Pictures & Associated Film Distribution Corporation, 1982. Technicolor. Panavision. 94 min. (8460 feet). *Producers:* Jim Henson & Gary Kurtz. *Directors:* Jim Henson & Frank Oz. *Screenplay:* David Odell. *Story:* Jim Henson. *Executive producer:* David Lazer. *Conceptual designer:* Brian Froud. *Production designer:* Harry Lange. *Photography:* Oswald Morris, B.S.C. *Editor:* Ralph Kemplen. *Music:* Trevor Jones. *Associate producer:* Bruce Sharman. *Special visual effects:* Roy Field & Brian Smithies. *Supervising art director:* Charles Bishop. *Art directors:* Terry Ackland-Snow, Malcolm Stone & Brian Ackland-Snow. *Set decorator:* Peter Young. *Construction manager:* Alan Booth. *Assistant art directors:* Richard Dawking, Fred Evans & Katherina Kubrick. *Operating cameraman:* Derek Browne. *Property master:* George Ball. *Property supervisors:* Eddie Francis, Ray Perry & Denis Hopperton. *Associate producer for Jim Henson:* Duncan Kenworthy. *Production manager:* Philip Kohler. *Choreography & Mime training:* Jean-Pierre Amiel. *First assistant director:* Dusty Symonds. *Continuity:* Cheryl Leigh. *Production coordinator:* Bi Benton. *Sound editor:* Nicholas Stevenson. *Music editors:* Michael Clifford & Dina Eaton. *Re-recording:* Bille Rowe. *Production sound:* Peter Sutton, Don Wortham & Bob Taylor. *Music recording:* John Richards & Eric Tomlinson. *Orchestrations:* Peter Knight & John Coleman. *Conductor:* Marcus Dodds. *Special sound effects:* Ben Burtt. *Music performed by:* The London Symphony Orchestra. *Synthesized electronic sounds:* David Lawson, Brian Gasgoigne, David Firman & Trevor Jones.

Creature Development: *Creature and Costume Design:* Brian Froud. *Creative supervisor:* Sherry Amott. *Creature design and fabrication/Gelfling:* Wendy Midener. *Skeksis:* Lyle Conway, Sarah Bradpiece. *Mystics:* Sherry Amott & Tim Clarke. *Garthim:* Fred Nihda. *Aughra and Urskeks:* Lyle Conway. *Landstriders:* Valerie Charlton. *Pod People and Slaves:* Sherry Amott. *Environmental Creatures:* Tim Miller & John Coppinger. *Fizzgig:* Rollin Krewson. *Associate Costume Designers/Skeksis:* Sarah Bradpiece & Steven Gregory. *Mystics:* Shirley Denny & Diana Mosley. *Gelfling and Pod People:* Polly Smith, Barbara Davis & Ellis Duncan. *Costumers:* Val Jones & Lesia Liber. *Wardrobe supervisor:* Betty Adamson. *Wigs and hair:* Stuart Artingstall. *Special mechanical design:* Leigh Donaldson, Tad Krzanowski, John Stephenson & Bob Baldwin. *Foam latex supervisor:* Tom McLaughlin. *Radio control design:* Faz Fazakas. *Second-unit director:* Gary Kurtz. *Miniature effects unit director:* Brian Smithies. *Mechanical effects supervision:* Ian

Wingrove. *Optical printing supervision:* Richard Dimbleby. *Matte paintings:* Mike Pangrazio & Chris Evans. *Titles:* Graphmation. Made at EMI Elstree Studios, Hertforshire, England.

The Character Performers: Jim Henson (Jen), Kathryn Mullen (Kira), Frank Oz (Aughra), Dave Goelz (Fizzgig).

The Skeksis: Frank Oz (Chamberlain), Dave Goelz (General/Garthim-Master), Jim Henson (High Priest/Ritual-Master), Steve Whitmire (Scientist), Louise Gold (Gourmand), Brian Muehl (Ornamentalist), Bob Payne (Historian/Scrollkeeper), Mike Quinn (Slavemaster), Tim Rose (Treasurer).

The Mystics: Brian Muehl (Urzah and Dying Master), Jean-Pierre Amiel (Weaver), Hugh Spight (Cook), Robbie Barnett (Numerologist), Swee Lim (Hunter), Simon Williamson (Chanter), Hus Levant (Scribe), Toby Philpott (Alchemist), Dave Greenaway & Richard Slaughter (Healer), Hugh Spight, Swee Lim & Robbie Barnett (Landstriders), Kiran Shah, Mike Edmonds, Malcolm Dixon, Sadie Corre, Deep Roy, Gerald Stadden, Mike Cottrell, Abbie Jones, Natasha Knight, Lisa Esson, Peter Burroughs, Jack Purvis & John Ghavan (Addition performers), Kiran Shah (stunts).

Character Voices: Stephen Garlick (Jen), Lisa Maxwell (Kira), Billie Whitlaw (Aughra), Percy Edwards (Fizzgig). *The Skeksis:* Barry Dennen (Chamberlain), Michael Kilgarriff (General), Jerry Nelson (High Priest and Dying Emperor), Steve Whitmire (Scientist), Thick Wilson (Gourmand), Brian Muehl (Ornamentalist), John Baddeley (Historian), David Buck (Slavemaster), Charles Collingwood (Treasurer). *The Mystics:* Brian Muehl (Dying Master), Sean Barrett (Urzah), Miki Iveria, Patrick Monckton, Sue Westerby, Barry Dennen (Pod People), Joseph O'Conner (urSkeks and Narrator).

DRAGONSLAYER. A Paramount Pictures release. A Walt Disney/Barwood-Robbins production. 1981. Panavision. Metrocolor. Dolby Stereo. 108 min. (9720 feet). Opened June 1981 at the Baronet Theatre in New York. *Executive producer:* Howard W. Koch. *Producer:* Hal Barwood. *Director:* Matthew Robbins. *Screenplay:* Hal Barwood & Matthew Robbins. *Director of photography:* Derek Vanlint. *Music:* Alex North. *Production designer:* Elliot Scott. *Editor:* Tony Lawson. *Associate producer:* Eric Rattray. *Assistant director:* Barry Langley. *Art director:* Alan Cassie. *Supervisor of special mechanical effects:* Brian Johnson. Photographic effects produced at Industrial Light & Magic, Inc. Marin County, California. *Supervisor of special visual effects:* Dennis Muren. *Dragon action props:* Danny Lee & Walt Disney Studios. *Halo Crane:* Nick Allder, Dennis Low & Ray Evans. *Travelling matte consultant:* Dennis Bartlett. *Period music:* Christopher Page. *Choreography:* Peggy Dixon. *Sound design:* Dale Strumpell. *Sound:* Anthony Dawe, Andrew Aaron, Douglas Hemphill & (music) Eric Tomlinson. *Sound editors:* Terry Eckton, Jay Boekelheide & Tim Holland. *Supervising re-recorder:* Mark Berger. *Re-recorders:* Walter Murch & Dale Strumpell. *Production sound recordist:* Anthony Davis. *Music recordist:* Eric Tomlinson. *Music editor:* June Edgerton. *Music coordinator:* Sidney Sax. *Set decorator:* Ian Whittaker. *Scenic artist:* Ernie Smith. *Matte painting supervisor:* Alan Maley. *Animation supervisor:* Samuel Comstock. *Graphics:* David Bunnett. *Draughtsmen:* Ted Ambrose (supervisor), Peter Childs & Frank Walsh. *Miniature/Optical effects supervisor:* Dennis Muren. *Miniature set designer:* Dave Carson. *Special effects production supervisor:* Thomas Smith. *Special effects production coordinator:* Laurie Vermont. *Special effects editor/coordinators:* Arthur Repola & Howard Stein. *Special effects technicians:* David Watkins, Philip Knowles, Neil Swann, John Gant, P.W. Hutchinson & Andrew Kelly. *Pyrotechnics:* Thaine Morris.

234   Filmography

Dragon supervisors: Phil Tippett & Ken Ralston. *Dragon designer:* David Bunnett. *Dragon movers:* Christopher Walas, Tom St. Armand, Stuart Ziff, Gary Leo & Jon Berg. *Closeup dragon:* Christopher Walas. *Dragon set designs:* Dave Carson. *Dragon consultant:* Dave Berg. *Optical photography supervisor:* Bruce Nicholson. *Optical coordinator:* Warren Franklin. *Visual effects editors:* Arthur Repola & Howard Stein. *Matte painting supervisor:* Alan Maley. *Matte photography:* Neil Krepela. *Chief sculptor:* Derek Howarth. *Sculptures:* Arthur Healey & Brian Muir. *Makeup:* Graham Freeborn & Jane Royle. *Hair:* Barbara Ritchie & Bobbie Smith. *Costume designer:* Anthony Mendleson. *Wardrobe master:* John Hilling. *Wardrobe mistress:* Dorothy Edwards. *Boom operator:* Nicolas Dunn. *Dialogue editor:* Leslie Shatz. *Aerial photography:* Continental Camera Systems. *Pilot:* Clay Lacy. *Continuity:* Pamela Davies. *Unit production manager:* Donald Toms. *Production secretary:* Norma Garment. *Location manager:* Rita Davison. *Production accountant:* John Sargent. *Casting:* Deborah McWilliams & Deborah Brown. *First unit camera operator:* Eddie Collins. *Chief Electrician:* Bert Bosher. *Second unit director:* Peter McDonald. *Property master:* Barry Wilkinson. *Stunt coordinator:* Terry Walsh. *Magic advisor:* Harold Taylor. *Latin advisor:* Eric Watts. Made at Pinewood Studios, London, England, and on location on the Isle of Skye, Scotland, and in North Wales.

Cast: Peter MacNichol (Galen), Caitlin Clarke (Valerian), Ralph Richardson (Ulrich), John Hallam (Tyrian), Peter Eyre (Casiodorus Rex), Albert Salmi (Greil), Sydney Bromley (Hodge), Chloe Salaman (Princess Elspeth), Emrys James (Simon), Roger Kemp (Horsrik), Ian McDiarmid (Brother Jacopus), Ken Shorter & Jason White (Henchmen), Yolanda Palfrey (Dragon victim), Douglas Cooper, Alf Mangon, David Mount, James Payne, Chris Twinn (Urlanders).

THE 5,000 FINGERS OF DR. T. Columbia Pictures. A Stanley Kramer Company Production. Opened June 19, 1953, at the Criterion Theater in New York City. Technicolor. 1953. Running time: 89 min. (8010 feet). *Producer:* Stanley Kramer. *Director:* Roy Rowland. *Screenplay:* Dr. Seuss & Alan Scott. *Story and Conception:* Dr. Seuss. *Production designer:* Rudolph Sternad. *Director of photography:* Frank Planer, A.S.C. *Color:* Technicolor. *Technicolor color consultant:* Francis Cugat. *Music:* Frederick Hollander. *Musical director:* Morris Stoloff. *Lyrics:* Dr. Seuss. *Choreographer:* Eugene Loring. *Miss Healey's gowns:* Jean Louis. *Art director:* Cary Odell. *Editorial supervisor:* Harry Gerstad. *Production manager:* Clem Beauchamp. *Film editor:* Al Clark, A.C.E. *Set decorator:* William Kiernan. *Assistant director:* Frederick Briskin. *Hairstyles:* Helen Hunt. *Makeup:* Clay Campbell. *Sound engineer:* Russell Malmgren.

Cast: Peter Lind Hayes (August Zabladowski), Mary Healy (Mrs. Collins), Hans Conried (Dr. Terwilliker), Tommy Rettig (Bart Collins), John Heasley (Uncle Whitney), Robert Heasley (Uncle Judson), Noel Cravat (Sergeant Lunk), Henry Kulky (Stroogo).

JASON AND THE ARGONAUTS. Columbia Pictures. A Charles H. Schneer Production. Eastmancolor by Pathé. United States/Great Britain. 1963. Opened August 7, 1963, at Loew's State in New York City. Running time: 104 min. (9360 feet). *Producer:* Charles H. Schneer. *Director:* Don Chaffey. *Associate producer:* Ray Harryhausen, creator of special visual effects. *Screenplay:* Jan Read & Beverly Cross. *Photographer:* Wilkie Cooper. *Music:* Bernard Herrmann, conducting the Royal Philharmonic Orchestra. *Production designer:* Geoffrey Drake. *Production executive:* John Dark. *Unit managers:* Leon Lenoir, Jimmy Komisar & Paul Maslansky.

Editor: Maurice Rootes. *Camera operator:* Harry Gillam. *Art directors:* Herbert Smith, Jack Maxstead & Tony Sarzi Braca. *Continuity:* Phyllis Crocker. *Sound recordists:* Cyril Collick & Red Law. *Sound editor:* Alfred Cox. *Assistant director:* Dennis Bertera. *Title designer:* James Wines.

Cast: Todd Armstrong (Jason), Nancy Kovack (Medea), Gary Raymond (Acastus), Laurence Naismith (Argus), Niall MacGinnis (Zeus), Michael Gwynn (Hermes), Douglas Wilmer (Pelias), Jack Gwillim (King Aeetes), Honor Blackman (Hera), John Cairney (Hylas), Patrick Troughton (Phineas), Andrew Faulds (Phalerus), Nigel Green (Hercules), John Crawford (Polydeuces), Douglas Robinson (Euphemus), Gernando Poggi (Castor).

KING KONG. RKO-Radio Pictures. 1933. Black & white. 100 min. (9000 feet). NYC Premiere March 2 at the new Roxy & the Radio City Music Hall. *Producers/directors:* Merian C. Cooper & Ernest B. Schoedsack. *Screenplay:* Ruth Rose & James Creelman. *Idea conceived by:* Merian C. Cooper. *Original story:* Merian C. Cooper & Edgar Wallace. *Executive producer:* David O. Selznick. *Chief technician:* Willis H. O'Brien. *Music:* Max Steiner. *Technical staff:* E.B. Gibson, Marcel Delgado, Fred Reefe, Orville Goldner & Carroll Shepphird. *Art technicians:* Mario Larrinaga & Byron L. Crabbe. *Art directors:* Carroll Clark & Al Herman. *Photographers:* Eddie Linden, Vernon L. Walker & J.O. Taylor. *Construction technician:* W.G. White. *Technical artists:* Juan Larrinaga, Zachary Hoag & Victor Delgado. *Associate/sound effects:* Walter G. Elliot. *Makeup supervision:* Mel Burns. *Set decorations:* Thomas Little. *Supervising art director:* Van Nest Polglase. *Costumes:* Walter Plunkett. *Assistant to Merian Cooper:* Zoe Porter. *Painting technician:* Peter Stich. *Camera aircraft pilots:* Duke Krantz & George Weiss. *Technical advisors:* Dr. J.W. Lytle, Dr. O.A. Paterson & Dr. Harry C. Raven. *Art titles:* Pacific Title Co. *Sound system:* RCA Photophone.

Cast: Fay Wray (Ann Darrow), Robert Armstrong (Carl Denham), Bruce Cabot (John [Jack] Driscoll), Frank Reicher (Captain Englehorn), Sam Hardy (Weston [the agent]), Noble Johnson (native chief), Steve Clemento (witch king), James Flavin (second mate Briggs), Victor Wong (Charley the cook), Paul Porcasi (Socrates), Russ Powell (dock watchman), Sandra Shaw (hotel victim), Ethan Laidlaw, Blackie Whiteford, Dick Curtis, Charles Sullivan, Harry Tenbrook, & Gil Perkins (sailors), Vera Lewis & Leroy Mason (theatre patrons), Frank Mills & Lynton Brent (reporters), Jim Thorpe (native dancer), George MacQuarrie (police captain), Madame Sul-te-wan (handmaiden), Etta MacDaniel (native woman), Ray Turner (native), Dorothy Gulliver & Carlotta Monti (girls), Barney Capehart, Bob Galloway, Eric Wood, Dusty Mitchell, & Russ Rogers (navy pilots), Reginald Barlow (engineer), Merian C. Cooper (flight commander), Ernest B. Schoedsack (chief observer), and King Kong, the Eighth Wonder of the World.

LOST HORIZON. A Frank Capra Production. Columbia Pictures. 1937. Black & white. Opened March 3, 1937, at the Globe Theatre in New York City. Running time: 132 min., later 125 min., and 118 min. (10,620 feet). *Producer/director:* Frank Capra. *Executive producer:* Harry Cohn. *Screenplay:* Robert Riskin. From the novel by James Hilton. *Director of photography:* Joseph B. Walker, A.S.C. *Music:* Dimitri Tiomkin. *Musical conductor:* Max Steiner. *Aerial photography:* Elmer G. Dyer, A.S.C. *Art director:* Stephen Goosson. *Costumes:* Ernest Dryden. *Film editors:* Gene Havlick & Gene Milford. *Special camera effects:* E. Roy Davidson & Ganahl Carson. *Choral music:* Hall Johnson Choir. *Assistant directors:* C.C. Coleman & Milton Carter. *Sound engineer:* Edward Bernds. *Additional photography:* Henry Freulich, A.S.C. *Camera operators:* Victor Scheurich & George Kelley. *Assistant cameramen:*

Alfred S. Keller, William Jolly, Irving Klein, Roy Babbitt & Sam Rosen. *Set designer:* Cary Odell. *Interior decorator:* Babs Johnstone. *Technical advisor:* Harrison Forman. *Costume designer:* Dan Sayre Groesbeck. *Musical director:* M.W. Stoloff. *Microphones:* Buster Libbott. *Dialogue director:* Harold Winston. *Ice house engineer:* Regis Gubser. *Property master:* Jack Wren. *Set dressers:* Ted Dickson & Fay Babcock. *Makeup:* Johnny Wallace & Charles Huber (uncredited: Jack Dawn). *Tibetan musical instruments:* Henry Eichman.

Cast: Ronald Colman (Robert Conway), Jane Wyatt (Sondra Bizet), John Howard (George Conway), Margo (Maria), Thomas Mitchell (Henry Barnard), Edward Everett Horton (Alexander P. Lovett), Isabel Jewell (Gloria Stone), H.B. Warner (Chang), Sam Jaffe (the High Lama), Hugh Buckler (Lord Gainsford), David Torrence (the Prime Minister), Noble Johnson (Head porter), Val Durand (Talu), Milton Owen (Fenner), Richard Loo (Airport official), John Tettener (Montaigne), and with Victor Wong, Willie Fung, John Burton, John Miltern, Dennis D'Auburn, John T. Murray, & Lawrence Grant.

IT'S A WONDERFUL LIFE. An RKO-Radio Picture. A Liberty Films Production. 1946. Black & white. 129 min. (11,610 feet). Opened December 21, 1946, at the Globe Theatre in New York City. *Producer/director:* Frank Capra. *Assistant director:* Arthur S. Black. *Screenplay:* Frances Goodrich, Albert Hackett, & Frank Capra, based on Philip Van Doren Stern's story "The Greatest Gift." *Additional scenes:* Jo Swerling. *Cinematographers:* Joseph Walker & Joseph Biroc. *Art director:* Jack Okey. *Set decorator:* Emile Kuri. *Editor:* William Hornbeck. *Musical score written and directed by:* Dimitri Tiomkin. *Sound:* Richard Van Hessen & Clem Portman. *Costumes:* Edward Stevenson. *Special effects:* Russell A. Cully. *Makeup:* Gordon Bau.

Cast: James Stewart (George Bailey), Donna Reed (Mary Hatch), Lionel Barrymore (Mr. Potter), Thomas Mitchell (Uncle Billy), Henry Travers (Clarence), Beulah Bondi (Mrs. Bailey), Frank Faylen (Ernie), Ward Bond (Bert), Gloria Grahame (Violet), H.B. Warner (Mr. Gower), Todd Karns (Harry Bailey), Samuel S. Hinds (Mr. Bailey), Mary Treen (Cousin Millie), Frank Albertson (Sam Wainwright), Virginia Patton (Ruth Dakin), Charles Williams (Cousin Eustace), Sarah Edwards (Mrs. Hatch), Lillian Randolph (Annie), William Edmunds (Mr. Martini), Argentina Brunetti (Mrs. Martini), Bobbie Anderson (young George Bailey), Ronnie Ralph (young Sam Wainwright), Jean Gale (young Mary Hatch), Jeanine Anne Roose (young Violet), Georgie Nokes (young Harry Bailey), Sheldon Leonard (Nick), Frank Hagney (Potter's bodyguard), Ray Walker (Joe, in luggage shop), Charles Lane (Potter's rent collector), Carol Coomes (Janie Bailey), Karoline Grimes (Zuzu Bailey), Larry Sims (Pete Bailey), Jimmy Hawkins (Tommy Bailey), Charles Halton (Bank examiner), Tom Fadden (Tollhouse keeper), Harry Holman (Principal of high school), Edward Kean (Tom, at B&L), Stanley Andrews (Mr. Welch), Hal Landon (Marty Hatch), Carl "Alfalfa" Switzer (Freddie, rival at dance), Bobby Scott (Mickey), Harry Cheshire (Doctor Campbell), Ed Featherstone (Bank teller), J. Farrell MacDonald (Owner of house), Garry Owen (Bill poster), Marian Carr (Mrs. Wainwright), Ellen Corby (Miss Davis), Almira Sessions (Mr. Potter's secretary).

POPEYE. Paramount Pictures Corporation and Walt Disney Productions. 1980. Metrocolor. Technovision. 114 min. (10,260 feet). Filmed in Malta in collaboration with Malta Film Facilities. *Producer:* Robert Evans. *Director:* Robert Altman. *Screenplay:* Jules Feiffer. *Executive producer:* C.O. Erickson. *Music and Lyrics:*

Harry Nilsson. *Photographer:* Giuseppe Rotunno, A.S.C. *Production designer:* Wolf Kroeger. *Supervising editor:* Tony Lombardo. *Costume designer:* Scott Bushnell. *Additional score:* Tom Pierson. *Assistant art directors:* Reg Bream & Stephan Reichel. *Choreography (dance):* Sharon Kinney. *Choreography (circus):* Hovey Burgess. *Robin Williams' dance numbers:* Lou Wills. *Associate producer:* Scott Bushnell. *First assistant directors:* Bob Dahlin & Victor Tourjansky. *Sound:* Robert Gravenor. *Location manager:* Robert Eggenweiler. *Film editors:* John W. Holmes, A.C.E. & David Simmons. *Additional editing:* Raja R. Gosnell. *Assistant editors:* Paul Rubell, Stephen Tucker, Eric Whitfield & Bob Lederman. *Supervising re-recording mixer:* Michael Minkler, C.A.S. *Scoring and music re-recording mixer:* Dan Wallin. *Re-recording engineer:* Steve Brimmer. *Supervising sound editor:* Sam Gemette. *Sound effects consultant:* Rodney Holland. *Sound editors:* Sam Shaw, John Larson, Larry Singer, Bill Phillips, Michael Ford & Hal Sanders. *Sound effects editors:* Teresa Eckton & Andy Patterson. *Supervising music editor:* Ted Whitfield. *Music editor:* Richard Whitfield. *Assistant music editor:* Leslie A. Whitfield. *Post production coordinator:* Suzanne Hines. *Post production sound and editorial facilities:* Lion's Gate Sound. *Camera operators:* Giovanni Fiore & Gianfranco Trasunto. *Assistant operators:* Luigi Bernardini, Mauro Merchetti & Gian Maria Majorana. *Underwater camera operator:* Lorenzo Battaglia. *Camera assistants:* Robert Reed Altman & Maurizio Zampagni. *Gaffer:* Rudolfo Bramucci. *Key grips:* Miro Salvatore & Alberto Emidi. *Boom man:* Don Merritt. *Recorder:* Doug Shulman. *Location engineer:* Randy Honaker. *Special effects coordinator:* Allen Hall. *Assistant:* Robert Willard. *Technical advisors:* RJ Holman & Steve Foster. *Stunt coordinator:* Roberto Messina. *Wardrobe supervisor:* John Hay. *Wardrobe construction:* Kate McDermott. *Wardrobe mistress:* Yvonne Zarb Cousin. *Property master:* Stephen Altman. *Property men:* John Bucklin & Tony Maccario. *Set decorator:* Jack Stephens. *Construction coordinator:* Stephane Reichel. *Construction manager:* Alvaro Belsole. *Makeup supervisor:* Giancarlo Del Brocco. *Makeup artist:* Alfredo Tiberi. *Assistants:* Gilberto Provenghi & Alvaro Rossi. *Chief hairdresser:* Maria Teresa Corridoni. *Hairdressers:* Aldo Signoretti & Gabriella Borzelli. *Assistant:* Rita Innocenzi. *Script supervisor:* Luca Kouimelis. *Talent coordinator:* Rick Sparks. *Publicist:* Bridget Terry. *Publicity assistants:* Rita Galea & Cathy Keller. *Unit photographer:* Paul Ronald. *Unit manager:* Paulo Lucidi. *Unit coordinators:* David Levy & Peter Bray. *Title design:* Patty Ryan. *Opticals:* Cinema Research. *Executive assistant to Mr. Evans:* Barbara Kalish. *Assistants to Mr. Evans:* Cathy Chazan & Stephanie Aranas. *Assistant to Mr. Williams:* Mark Ruttenberg. *Auditor:* Richard Dubuque. *Assistant accountant:* Luciano Tartaglia. *Controller:* Tim Engel. *Master carpenters:* Gaetano Miranti & Bert Bowers. *Master painter:* Gugliemo Modestini. *Sculptors:* Angelo Marta, Angelo Zaccaria & Michael Stroud. *Draftsman:* Lester Smith. *Animated artifacts created by:* Cosmekinetics, Ellis Burman & Bob Williams. *Physical therapist:* James A. Rumsey, R.P.T. *Caterer:* Mickey Chonos. *European production manager:* Frederick Muller. *Transportation captain:* Bill Turner.

    Cast: Robin Williams (Popeye), Shelley Duvall (Olive Oyl), Ray Walston (Poopdeck Pappy), Paul Dooley (Wimpy), Paul L. Smith (Bluto), Richard Libertini (Geezil), Donald Moffat (Taxman), MacIntyre Dixon (Cole Oyl), Roberta Maxwell (Nana Oyl), Donovan Scott (Castor Oyl), Allan Nicholls (Rough House), Wesley Ivan Hurt (Swee'pea), Bill Irwin (Ham Gravy, the old boyfriend), Robert Fortier (Bill Barnacle, the town drunk), David McCharen (Harry Hotcash, the gambler), Sharon Kinney (Cherry, his moll), Peter Bray (Oxblood Oxheart, the fighter), Linda Hunt (Mrs. Oxheart, his mom), Geoff Hoyle (Scoop, the reporter), Wayne Robson (Chizzelflint, the pawnbroker), Larry Pisoni (Chico, the dishwasher), Carlo

Pellegrini (Swifty, the cook), Susan Kingsley (La Verne, the waitress), Michael Christensen (Splatz, the janitor), Ray Cooper (Preacher), Noel Parenti (Slick, the milkman), Karen McCormick (Rosie, the milkmaid), John Bristol (Bear, the hermit), Julie Janney (Mena), Patty Katz (Mina), Diane Shaffer (Mona), Nathalie Blossom (Blossom), Dennis Franz (Spike), Carlos Brown (Slug), Ned Dowd (Butch), Hovey Burgess (Mort), Roberto Messina (Gozo), Pietro Torrisi (Bolo), Margary Bond (Daisy), Judy Burgess (Petunia), Saundra MacDonald (Violet), Eve Knoller (Min), Peggy Pisoni (Pickelina), Barbara Zegler (Daphne), Paul Zegler (Mayor Stonefeller/Official), Pamela Burrell (Mrs. Stonefeller), David Arkin (Mailman/Policeman), Klaus Voorman (Von Schnitzel, the conductor), Doug Dillard (Clem, the banjo player), Van Dyke Parks (Hoagy, the piano player), Stan Wilson (Oscar, the barber), Roberto Dell'Aqua (Chimneysweep), Valerie Velardi (Cindy, the drudge). Jack Mercer is the voice of Popeye in the animated prologue.

SUPERMAN. A Warner Brothers release. An Alexander and Ilya Salkind Production. 1980. Panavision 70. Technicolor. Dolby Stereo. 143 min. (12,870 feet). *Producer:* Pierre Spengler. *Director:* Richard Donner. *Executive producers:* Ilya Salkind & Alexander Salkind. *Associate producer:* Charles F. Greenlaw. *Screenplay:* Mario Puzo, David Newman, Leslie Newman & Robert Benton. *Additional script material:* Norman Enfield. *Story:* Mario Puzo. *Based on the D.C. Comics Inc. characters created by:* Jerry Siegel & Joe Shuster. *Cinematographer:* Geoffrey Unsworth. *Production designer:* John Barry. *Supervising film editor:* Stuart Baird. *Music:* John Williams, conducting the London Symphony Orchestra. *Creative consultant:* Tom Mankiewicz. *Title design:* Denis Rich. *Makeup supervisor:* Stuart Freeborn. *Makeup artists:* Philip Rhodes, Basil Newall, Kay Freeborn, Graham Freeborn, Nick Maley, Sylvia Croft & Connie Reeve. *United States makeup artist:* Louis Lane. *Canadian makeup artist:* Jamie Brown. *Casting:* Lynn Stalmaster. *Casting associate:* Lou De Giamo. *English casting:* Mary Selway. *Chief script supervisor:* Elaine Schreyeck. *Script supervisors:* Kay Rawlings & Doris Martin. *United States script supervisor:* Betty Norton. *Production executive:* Geoffrey Helman. *Second unit directors:* David Tomblin, John Glen, John Barry, David Lane, Peter Duffel & Robert Lynn. *Film editor:* Michael Ellis. *Supervising sound effects and dialogue replacement editor:* Chris Greenham. *Samuel Goldwyn Studios sound supervisor:* Don Rogers. *Dolby Stereo consultant:* Max Bell. *Production mixers:* Roy Charman, Norman Bolland & Brian Marshall. *United States production mixers:* Charles Schmitz & Dick Ragusa. *Canadian production mixer:* Chris Large. *Sound engineers:* Michael Tucker, George Rice, Keith Pamplin & Des Edwards. *Scoring mixer:* Eric Tomlinson. *Dubbing mixer:* Gordon K. McCallum. *Music recording:* Anvil Films Ltd. *Sound:* Samuel Goldwyn Studios & Pinewood Studios. *Stunt coordinators:* Alf Joint & Vic Armstrong. *New York stunt coordinator:* Alex Stevens. *Main titles:* Steve Frankfort Communications, R/Greenberg Associates Inc. *End Titles:* Camera Effects Ltd. *End title cinematography:* Roy Pace & Sheldon Elbourne. *Louma camera crane technical advisers:* Jean-Maria Lavalou & Alain Masseron. *Poem "Can You Read My Mind":* John Williams & Leslie Bricusse. *Performed by:* Margot Kidder. *Orchestration:* Herbert W. Spencer & Arthur Morton. *Aerial camera equipment:* Wesscam Camera Systems. *Visual effects designer:* Dennis Rich. *Optical effects supervisor:* Roy Field. *Matte and composites director:* Derek Meddings. *Process cinematography:* Denys Coop. *Zoptic effects:* Zoran Perisic. *Process unit director:* Andre de Toth. *Visual effects editor:* Pete Watson. *Visual effects coordinators:* Ernest Walter & Michael Campbell. *Flying unit coordinator:* Dominic Fulford. *Miniature cinematography:* Paul Wilson & Jack Atcheler. *Additional miniature cinematography:* Darryl A. Anderson. *Assistant visual* *effects editor:* Russell Woolnough. *Flying systems and process projection:* Wally Veevers & Jan Jacobson. *Process systems:* Charles Staffell. *Travelling matte supervisor:* Dennis Bartlett. *Matte artists:* Doug Ferris & Ray Caple. *Wire flying effects:* Derek Botell & Bob Harman. *Special optical effects:* Camera Effects Ltd. *Special optical cinematography:* Roy Pace & Sheldon Elbourne. *Special optical sequences:* Howard A. Anderson Company & Continental Camera Systems Inc. *Optical effects:* Oxford Scientific Films Ltd., Peter Parks, Sean Morris, National Screen Service Ltd., Gillie Potter Productions Ltd., Delecluse Realizations, Cinema Research Corporation, Peter Donen, Joe Wallikas, Rocky Mahoney, Charles Colwell, Van der Veer Photo Effects, Frank van der Veer, Greg van der Veer & Rank Post Productions Ltd. *Star ship designer:* Ed Gimmell. *Mechanical effects director:* Colin Chilvers. *New York and Canadian mechanical effects supervisor:* John Richardson. *New Mexico mechanical effects supervisor:* Robert A. MacDonald. *Production supervisor:* Tim Hampton. *North American production supervisor:* Timothy Burrill. *Location manager:* Chris Coles. *New York location manager:* David Lane. *Assistant directors:* David Tomblin, Dominic Fulford, Vincent Winter, Michael Dryhurst, Allan James & Gareth Tandy. *United States assistant directors:* Jerry Grandey, Michael Rauch & Bud Grace. *Production coordinator:* Michael Duthie. *Script clerk:* Katya Kolpaktchy. *Additional cinematographer:* Alex Thomson. *New Mexico additional cinematographer:* Robert E. Collins. *Alberta additional cinematographer:* Reginald Morris. *New York additional cinematographer:* Sol Negrin. *Aerial cinematography:* Peter Allwork. *Camera operators:* Peter MacDonald, John Harris, Jimmy Devis, John Morgan, Michael Fox, Gordon Hayman, Geoff Glover, Ken Coles, Ronnie Fox Rogers, Ginger Gemmell, Roy Ford, Jack Lowen & George Pink. *United States camera operators:* Lou Barlia, Jim Contner, Michael Chevalier, Jack Courtland & Howard A. Anderson III. *Canadian camera operator:* Rod Parkhurst. *Wesscam cinematography:* Ronald Goodman. *New Mexico helicopter pilot:* Marc Wolfe. *New York helicopter pilot:* Al Cerullo. *Music editor:* Bob Hathaway. *Assistant music editor:* Ken Ross. *First assistant film editor:* Bob Mullen. *Sound effects editors:* Peter Pennell, Stan Fiferman & John Foster. *England and New York supervising art director:* Maurice Fowler. *Canada and New Mexico supervising art director:* Bill Brodie. *Art directors:* Harry Lange, Norman Dorme, Norman Reynolds, Ernest Archer, Tony Reading, Les Dilly & Stuart Craig. *United States art directors:* Gene Rudolf, Philip Bennet & Stan Jolley. *Set designers:* Tony Rimmington, Reg Bream, Ted Ambrose, Dennis Bosher & Alan Cassie. *Set decorator:* Peter Howitt. *United States set decorator:* Fred Weiler. *Production illustrators:* Ivor Beddoes, Roy Carnon & Reg Hill. *Modelers:* Janet Stevens & Peter Voysey. *Scenic artists:* Ernest Smith & Bill Beavis. *Decor and lettering artist:* Norman Hart. *Unit publicist:* Gordon Arnell. *Still photographers:* Robert Penn & Douglas Luke. *Crane grip:* Roy Van Buskirk. *Costume designer:* Yvonne Blake. *Additional costume designers:* Betty Adamson & Ruth Morley. *Lee electric gaffer:* Maurice Gillett. Dedicated to Terry Hill and John Bodimeade.

  Cast: Christopher Reeve (Clark Kent/Superman), Marlon Brando (Jor-El), Gene Hackman (Lex Luthor), Margot Kidder (Lois Lane), Ned Beatty (Otis), Jackie Cooper (Perry White), Glenn Ford (Jonathan Kent), Trevor Howard (First Krypton council elder), Valerie Perrine (Miss Teschmacher), Jack O'Halloran (Non), Maria Schell (Vond-Ah), Terence Stamp (General Zod), Phyllis Thaxter (Martha Kent), Susannah York (Lara), Jeff East (Teenage Clark), Marc McClure (Jimmy Olsen), Sarah Douglas (Ursa), Harry Andrews (Second Krypton council elder), Vass Anderson (Third Krypton council elder), John Hollis (Fourth Krypton council elder), James Garbutt (Fifth Krypton council elder), Michael Glover (Sixth Krypton council elder), David Neal (Seventh Krypton Council elder), William Russell (Eighth Krypton council elder), Penelope Lee (Ninth Krypton council elder), John Stuart (Tenth Krypton council elder), Alan Cullen (Eleventh Krypton council elder), Lee Quigley (baby Kal-El), Aaron Smolinski (Baby Clark Kent), Diane Sherry (Lana Lang), Jeff Atcheson (Football coach), Brad Flock (First football player), David Petrou (Football team manager), Kathy Painter (Young Lois Lane [girl on train]), Noel Neill (Mrs. Lane), Kirk Alwyn (Mr. Lane), Billy J. Mitchell (First *Daily Planet* editor), Robert Henderson (Second *Daily Planet* editor), Larry Lamb (First *Daily Planet* reporter), James Brockington (Second *Daily Planet* reporter), John Cassady (Third *Daily Planet* reporter), John F. Parker (Fourth *Daily Planet* reporter), Antony Scott (Fifth *Daily Planet* reporter), Ray Evans (Sixth *Daily Planet* reporter), Su Shifrin (Seventh *Daily Planet* reporter), Miguel Brown (Eighth *Daily Planet* reporter), Vincent Marzello (First copy boy), Benjamin Feitelson (Second copy boy), Lise Hilboldt (First *Daily Planet* secretary), Leueen Willoughby (Second *Daily Planet* secretary), Jill Ingham (Perry White's secretary), Pieter Stuyck (Window cleaner), Rex Reed (Rex Reed), Weston Gavin (Mugger), Stephen Kahan (First policeman), Ray Hassett (Second policeman), Randy Jurgenson (Third policeman), Matt Russo (News vendor), Robert Dahdad (News customer), Colin Seaping (Helicopter pilot), Bo Rucker (Pimp), Paul Avery (Television cameraman), David Baxt (Burglar), George Harris (Officer Mooney), Michael Harrigan (First hood), John Cording (Second hood), Raymond Thompson (Third hood), Oz Clarke (Fourth hood), Rex Everhardt (Desk sergeant), Jayne Tottman (Little girl), Frank Lazarus (Air Force One pilot), Brian Protheroe (Air Force One co-pilot), Lawrence Trimble (First Air Force One crewman), Robert Whelan (Second Air Force One crewman), David Calder (Third Air Force One crewman), Norwich Duff (First newscaster), Keith Alexander (Second newscaster), Michael Ensign (Third newscaster), Larry Hagman (Missile convoy major), Paul Tuerpe (Sergeant Hayley), Graham McPherson (Missile convoy lieutenant), David Yorston (Missile convoy petty officer), Robert O'Neill (Mission Control admiral), Robert MacLeod (Mission Control general), John Ratzenberger (First mission controller), Chief Tug Smith (Indian chief), Norman Warwick (Superchief driver), Chuck Julian (Assistant Superchief driver), Colin Etherington (Power company driver), Mark Wynter (Power company technician), Roy Stevens (Prison warden), Stunts, Inc., Alf Joint, Vic Armstrong, Alex Stevens, Terry Hill, John Bodimeade, Paul Weston, George Cooper, Wendy Leech, Bill Weston, Stuart Fell, Ellen Bry, Martin Grace, Dick Butler & Richard Hackman (Stunt persons).

THE THIEF OF BAGDAD. An Alexander Korda Production. London Films. Distributed by United Artists. 1940. Technicolor. 106 min. (9540 feet). Opened December 5, 1940, at Radio City Music Hall. *Producer:* Alexander Korda. *Associate producers:* Zoltan Korda & William Cameron Menzies. *Directors:* Ludwig Berger, Michael Powell, Tim Whelan (and, uncredited, Zoltan Korda, William Cameron Menzies & Alexander Korda). *Screen Play and Dialogue:* Miles Malleson. *Scenario:* Lajos Biro. *Production designed in color by* Vincent Korda. *Cinematographer:* Georges Perinal. *Associate Cinematographer:* Osmond H. Borradaile. *Musical score and songs:* Miklos Rozsa. *Musical director:* Muir Mathieson. *Sound supervisors:* Anthony W. Watkins & Jack Whitney. *Sound:* Denham Studios & General Service Studios. *Supervising film editor:* William Hornbeck. *Film editor:* Charles Crichton. *Art directors:* Vincent Korda & William Cameron Menzies. *Assistant art director:* Elliot Scott. *Associate art directors:* Frederick Pussey & Ferdinand Pullen. *Assistant to the producer and second unit director:* Andre de Toth. *Assistant directors:* Geoffrey Boothby & Charles David. *Second assistant director:* Jack Clayton. *Cos-*

tume designers: Olive Messell, John Armstrong & Marcel Vertes. *Makeup:* Chris Mueller. *Technicolor director:* Natalie Kalmus. *Camera operator:* Robert Krasker. *Production manager:* David B. Cunynghame. *Aerial sequences:* Paul Mantz. *Aerial cinematographer:* Elmer Dye. *Matte artists:* W. Percy Day & Wally Veevers. *Travelling mattes:* Thomas Howard & Stanley Sayer. *Miniatures:* Johnny Mills. *Mechanical effects:* Lawrence Butler. *Scenic backgrounds:* Percy Day.

Cast: Conrad Veidt (Jaffar), Sabu (Abu), June Duprez (the Princess), John Justin (Ahmad), Rex Ingram (Djinni), Miles Malleson (Old Sultan), Morton Selten (the Old King), Mary Morris (Halima/the Silver Maid), Bruce Winston (the Merchant), Hay Petrie (Astrologer), Adelaide Hall (Singer), Roy Emerton (Jailer), Allan Jeayes (the Story teller).

TIME BANDITS. An Avco-Embassy Pictures release. A Handmade Films Production. 1981. Technicolor. Dolby Stereo. 116 min. (10,440 feet). *Producer/Director:* Terry Gilliam. *Screenplay:* Michael Palin & Terry Gilliam. *Executive producers:* George Harrison & Denis O'Brien. *Associate producer:* Neville C. Thompson. *Director of photography:* Peter Biziou. *Editor:* Julian Doyle. *Production designer:* Milly Burns. *Art director:* Norman Garwood. *Costumes:* Jim Acheson in association with Hazel Cote. *Hairdressing and Makeup:* Maggie Weston & Elaine Carew. *Music:* Mike Moran. *Songs and additional material:* George Harrison. *Music producer:* Ray Cooper. *Casting director:* Irene Lamb. *Camera operator:* David Garvath. *Continuity:* Penny Eyles. *Production manager:* Graham Ford. *First assistant director:* Simon Hinkly. *Second-unit director:* Julian Doyle. *Sound mixer:* Garth Marshal. *Special FX senior technician:* John Bunker. *Construction manager:* Peter Verard. *Location manager:* Patrick Cassavetti. *Production assistant:* Linda Bruce. *Producer's assistant:* Rachel Neale. *Second assistant director:* Coy Travers. *Third assistant directors:* Mark Cooper & Chris Thompson. *Focus puller:* Bob Stilwell. *Clapper/Loader:* Simon Fulford. *Grip:* Freddie Fry. *Boom operator:* Bob Doyle. *Sound maintenance:* Philip Chubb. *Production buyer:* Karen Brookes. *Assistant art director:* Celia Barnett. *Draughtsman:* Steve Cooper. *Modelmaker:* Val Charlton. *Assistant modelmakers:* Carol De Jong, Jean Ramsey, Alix Harwood & Behira Thraves. *Sculptors:* Geoff Rivers Bland & Laurie Warburton. *Assistant costume designer:* T. Stephen Miles. *Wardrobe mistress:* Dorothea Smylie. *Wardrobe assistants:* Gilly Hebden, Tony Williams & Dai Murch. *Costumiers:* Richard Cattermole & Dorothy Williams. *Assistant makeup:* Sue Frear. *Wigs and beards:* Kenneth Lintott. Optical effects: Kent Houston, Paul Whitbread, assisted by Tim Ollive, Dennis De Groot, Peerless Camera Company, LTD, London. *Matte paintings:* Ray Caple. *Special FX technician:* Ross King. *Special FX consultants:* Chris Verner & Andy Thompson. *Special FX modellers:* Chris Overs & Lewis Coleman. *Special FX runner:* Chris Ostwald. Fortress of Ultimate Darkness by Westbridge Studios. *Models photographer:* Julian Doyle. *Stunts:* Peter Brayham & Terry Yorke. *Wingman:* Bob Harman. *Puppet show:* John Styles. *Trolls:* Ray Scott. *Greek dance music:* Trevor Jones. *Greek dance choreographer:* Tom Jobe. *Music production sound effects:* Andre Jacquemin. *Other music:* Music De Wolfe & Ready Music. *Percussion sequences:* Ray Cooper. *Music director:* Harry Rabinowitz. *Sound engineer:* John Richards. Music recorded at CTS Studios. *Foreign location travel:* Moving Movies. *Camera equipment:* Joe Donton Cameras. *Lighting equipment:* Lee (Electric) Lighting. "Og the Pig" supplied by Mike Hearst. "Benson the Duck" supplied by John Woodgate. *Second-unit focus puller:* Brian Herlihy. *Second-unit clapper/loader:* Simon Haveland. *Second-unit grip:* Tony Andrews. *Assistant editor:* Rodney Glenn. *Second assistant editor:* Adam Unger. *Dubbing mixers:* Paul Carr & Brian Paxton. *Dubbing editor:* Stanley Fiferman. *Dialogue editor:* Mike Hopkins. *Footsteps editor:* Dino Di Campo. *Property master:* Peter Grant. *Standby props:* John Cole & Dave Newton. *Dressing props:* Ray Perry. *Prop dresser:* Steve Wheeler. *Drapes:* Ron Cowan. *Supervising carpenter:* Len Day. *Carpenter:* Mickey Fisher. *Best boy:* Chuck Finch. Ragan Castle used by permission of The Ancient Monuments Branch, Welsh Office. Filmed at Lee International Studios and on location in England, Wales, and Morocco.

Cast: Sean Connery (King Agamemnon/Fireman), John Cleese (Robin Hood), Ian Holm (Napoleon), Craig Warnock (Kevin), Shelley Duvall (Pansy), (Sir) Ralph Richardson (The Supreme Being), David Warner (Evil), Michael Palin (Vincent), Peter Vaughan (Ogre), Katherine Helmond (Mrs. Ogre), David Rappaport (Randall), Kenny Baker (Fidget), Mike Edmonds (Og), Tiny Ross (Vermin), David Deaker (Kevin's father), Sheila Fearn (Kevin's mother), Jim Broadbent (Compere), John Young (Reginald), Leon Lissek (First refugee), Brian Bowes (Stunt knight/Hussar), Myrtle Devinish (Beryl), Terence Baylor (Lucien), Preston Lockwood (Neguy), David Leland (Puppeteer), Charles McKeown (Theatre manager), John Hushman (the Great Rumbozo), Derrick O'Connor (Robber leader), Neil McCarthy (Second robber), Declan Mulholland (Third robber), Peter Jonfield (Arm wrestler), Jerrold Wells (Benson), Derek Deadman (Robert), Roger Frost (Cartwright), Marcus Powell (Horse Flesh), Martin Carroll (Baxi Brazilla III), Ian Muir (Giant), Winston Dennis (Bull-headed warrior), Del Baker (Greek fighting warrior), Juliette James (Greek queen), Mark Holmes (Troll father), Andrew MacLachian (Fireman), Chris Grant (Voice of TV announcer), Tony Jay (Voice of Supreme Being), Edwin Finn (Supreme Being's face).

TOPPER. A Hal Roach Production. Released by MGM. Black & white. Running time: 97 minutes (8730 feet). *Producer:* Hal Roach. *Director:* Norman Z. McLeod. *Associate producer:* Milton H. Bren. *Screenplay:* Jack Jevne, Eric Hatch, & Eddie Moran. *Based on the novel by:* Thorne Smith. *Photographer:* Norbert Brodine, A.S.C., *Photographic effects:* Roy Seawright. *Film editor:* William Terhune. *Sound:* William Randall. *Art director:* Arthur I. Royce. *Set decorator:* W.L. Stevens. *Gowns:* Samuel M. Lange. *Musical director:* Marvin Hatley. *Musical arranger:* Arthur Morton. *"Old Man Moon" music & lyrics by* Hoagy Carmichael.

Cast: Constance Bennett (Marion Kerby), Cary Grant (George Kerby), Roland Young (Cosmo Topper), Billie Burke (Mrs. Topper), Alan Mowbray (Wilkins, the butler), Eugene Pallette (Casey, the house dick), Arthur Lake (Elevator boy), Hedda Hopper (Mrs. Styvesant), Virginia Sale (Miss Johnson), Theodore van Eltz (Hotel manager), J. Farrell McDonald (Policeman), Elaine Shepard (Secretary), Doodles Weaver & Si Jenks (Rustics), & the "Three Hits and a Miss."

THE WIZARD OF OZ. A Victor Fleming Production. Released by MGM. Technicolor. Running time: 101 minutes (9090 feet). *Producer:* Mervyn LeRoy. *Director:* Victor Fleming. *Screenplay:* Noel Langley, Florence Ryerson & Edgar Allan Woolf. *Adaptation:* Noel Langley. *Based on the novel by:* L. Frank Baum. *Musical adaptation:* Herbert Stothart, Robert Stringer, Roger Edens & Van Alstyne. *Lyrics:* E.Y. Harburg. *Music:* Harold Arlen. *Associate conductor:* George Stoll. *Orchestra and vocal arrangements:* George Bassman, Murray Cutter, Paul Marquardt, Roger Edens & Ken Darby. *Musical numbers staged by:* Bobby Connolly. *Photographer:* Harold Rosson, A.S.C. *Associate:* Allen Davey, A.S.C. *Technicolor color director:* Natalie Kalmus. *Associate:* Henri Jaffa. *Sound:* Douglas Shearer. *Art director:* Cedric Gibbons. *Associate:* William A. Horning. *Assistant art directors:* Randall Duell & Malcolm Brown. *Set decorator:* Edwin B. Willis. *Special effects supervisor:* A. Arnold Gillespie. *Assistant:* Warren Newcomb. *Special effects:* Marcel Delgado, Jack McMasters, Franklin E. Milton, Glen Robinson & Hal Millar. *Production mixer:* Conrad Kahn. *Assistant sound supervisor:* Wesley C. Miller. *Assistant to the producer:* Arthur Freed. *Costumes:* Adrian. *Character makeup:* Jack Dawn. *Makeup:* Jack Young, Charles Schram, Howard Smit, William Tuttle, Josef Norin, Gustav Norin, Emile La Vigne, Jack Kevan & Lee Steinfield. *Editor:* Blanche Sewell. *Property master:* Billy H. Scott. *Casting:* Billy Grady, Henry Kramer & Leonard Murphy. *Publicity supervisors:* Howard Dietz & Howard Strickling. *Unit publicist:* Mary Mayer. *Vocal coach:* Roger Edens. *Production manager:* Joseph S. Cohn. *Unit manager:* Keith Weeks. *Assistant director:* Al Shoenberg. *Wardrobe:* John B. Scura, Marie Wharton, Marian Parker, Sheila O'Brien, Rose Meltzer, Vera Mordaunt & Marie Rose. *Camera operator:* Henry Imus. *Scenic supervisor:* George Gibson. *Scenic artist:* Ben Carre. *Dog trainer:* Carl Spitz.

Cast: Judy Garland (Dorothy), Frank Morgan (Professor Marvel), Ray Bolger (Hunk/Scarecrow), Bert Lahr (Zeke/Cowardly Lion), Jack Haley (Hickory/Tin Man), Billie Burke (Glinda), Margaret Hamilton (Miss Gulch/Wicked Witch of the West), Charley Grapewin (Uncle Henry), Pat Walshe (Nikko, the chief Winged Monkey), Clara Blandick (Auntie Em), Terry (Toto), and the Munchkins.

Appendix

Beauty and the Beast

Live-Action Fairy Tale Films. *The Pied Piper of Hamlin* was a 1917 German silent film (also known as *Der Ratenfanger/The Ratcatcher*) directed by and starring Paul Wegener, who later starred in *The Golem.*

An all-star version of *Alice in Wonderland* was released by Paramount in 1933. Directed by Norman Z. McLeod (*Topper*), this interesting effort starred W.C. Fields as Humpty Dumpty, Cary Grant as the Mock Turtle, Gary Cooper as the White Knight, Edward Everett Horton as the Mad Hatter, Charles Ruggles as the March Hare, and Ned Sparks as the Caterpillar.

Danny Kaye was the star of Samuel Goldwyn's 1952 biopic, *Hans Christian Andersen.* A drama with songs, this production was directed by Charles Vidor and featured truncated versions of several of the Danish storyteller's tales. Another version of *The Pied Piper of Hamlin*, directed by Bretaigne Windust and starring Van Johnson and Claude Rains, was a 1957 made-for-television movie.

tom thumb was a 1958 George Pal production starring Russ Tamblyn as the 5½″ hero. The film had the considerable talents of Peter Sellers and Terry-Thomas and a host of stop-motion animated puppet characters. Tom Howard's optical printing won him an Academy Award.

A lesser effort was 1961's *Snow White and the Three Stooges*, starring a miscast Carol Heiss, of ice-skating fame. Even the physical schtick of the Three Stooges couldn't save this Walter Lang–directed stinker.

The Wonderful World of the Brothers Grimm was a 1962 George Pal–Cinerama production that starred Laurence Harvey and Karl Boehm as the fairy tale–writing brothers. The film, directed by Henry Levin and George Pal, presents a number of delightful fairy tales featuring Arnold Stang, Yvette Mimieux, Jim Backus, Terry-Thomas, and Buddy Hackett, among others.

A Technicolor version of *Beauty and the Beast* starring Joyce Taylor and Mark Damon was released in 1963. This dreadful picture, directed by Edward L. Cahn, is best forgotten.

Walt Disney's 1964 hit *Mary Poppins* might not be a classic "fairy tale," but its merits are undeniable. Starring Julie Andrews (in an Oscar-winning performance) and featuring the marvelous Dick Van Dyke, this magical film is a treat for children of all ages. Disney "house director" Robert Stevenson captures the magic of P.L. Travers' book about a "practically perfect" nanny who can fly.

Yet another version of *The Pied Piper* was released in 1972. Director Jacques Demy's version is well done if a bit grim. This British production starred Donovan, Donald Pleasence, Michael Hordern, Jack Wild, Diana Dors, and John Hurt.

Alice's Adventures in Wonderland, a 1972 British film, was a valiant but generally unsuccessful effort, by writer-director William Sterling to capture the essence of the Lewis Carroll novel. It featured Michael Crawford as the White Rabbit, Dudley Moore as the Dormouse, Peter Sellers as the March Hare, and Ralph Richardson as the Caterpillar.

The Slipper and the Rose, starring Richard Chamberlain, Gemma Craven, and Annette Crosbie, and directed by Bryan Forbes, was a 1976 British musical version of Cinderella. A bit long at 146 minutes, it was edited down to 128 minutes for United States release.

The Blue Bird, a 1976 U.S.A./U.S.S.R. coproduction, was directed by George Cukor and starred Elizabeth Taylor, Jane Fonda, Ava Gardner, Cicely Tyson, and Robert Morley. This ill-conceived venture cost millions and earned less than $1 million in American rentals.

Animated Fairy Tale Films. Walt Disney's 1937 version of Snow White and the Seven Dwarfs established the Disney studio as a Hollywood major and inspired L.B. Mayer to make the live-action The Wizard of Oz. A treat for children and adults, this beautiful example of the animator's art is a timeless joy.

Some animation aficionados prefer the Disney Studio's almost flawless 1940 version of Pinocchio. This glorious film introduced Jiminy Cricket singing the gooey-but-classic "When You Wish Upon a Star," which won an Academy Award for Best Song.

By 1950, some of the zip was gone from Disney full-length cartoon films, but Cinderella is still a satisfying fairy tale. While it didn't win, the song "Bibbidy Bob-bidy Boo" was nominated for an Academy Award. The film is populated with cute animal characters; the mice overshadow Cindy and her blandly handsome Prince Charming.

Uncle Walt got back on the right track with 1951's marvelously bizarre Alice in Wonderland. But by 1959, the Disney Studio's The Sleeping Beauty revealed that the Disney touch was fast fading. In "Technirama 70," this dry version of the fairy tale seemed lifeless when compared to the joyous and imaginative Disney gems of the '30s and '40s.

Pinocchio in Outer Space, a 1964 U.S.A./France co-venture, featured the voice of Arnold Stang and less-than-memorable tunes.

Films by the Stars and Crew of Beauty and the Beast. The films of Jean Cocteau are: Le Sang d'un Poete/The Blood of a Poet (writer-director, 1930), La Comedie du Bonheur (writer, 1940), Le Baron Fantome (w, 1943), Les Dames du Bois de Boulogne/Ladies of the Park (w, 1945), La Belle et la Bête (1946), Ruy Blas (w, 1948), L'Amore (w, episode, 1948), L'Aigle a Deux Tetes/Eagle With Two Heads (w-d, 1948), Les Parents Terribles/The Storm Within (w-d, 1948), Les Noces de Sable (w, 1949), Les Enfants Terribles/The Strange Ones (w-d, 1950), La Corona Negra (w, 1952), Les Testament d'Orphee/The Testament of Orpheus (w-d, 1960), La Princesse de Cleves (w, 1961), Thomas l'Imposteur (w, 1965), and many 16 mm shorts.

Among the films of Jean Marais (Jean Alfred Villain-Marais): L'Empevier (1933), Le Scandale (1936), Le Pavillon Brule (1941), L'Eternel Retour (1943), Carmen (1943, released 1945), La Belle et la Bête (1946), Ruy Blas, L'Aigle a Deux Tetes, Les Parents Terribles (all 1948), Le Secret de Mayerling (1949), Orphee (1950), Julietta (1953), Dortoir des Grandes (1953), Si Versailles M'etait Conte (1954), Le Comte de Monte-Cristo (1955), Le Notti Bianche (1957), Le Testament d'Orphee (1960), La Princesse de Cleves (1961), Ponsio Pilato (1962), Le Masque de Fer (1962), Fantomas (1964), Le Saint Prend l'Affut (1966), Fantomas contre Scotland Yard (1967), Le Paria (1968), Peau de'Ane/Donkey Skin (1971), others.

Among the films of Josette Day (Josette Dagory): La Pocharde (1919), Le Barbier de Seville/The Barber of Seville (1934), Club de Femmes (1936), L'Homme du Jour

(1938), *La Fille de Puisatier* (1941), *La Belle et la Bête* (1946), *Les Parents Terribles* (1948), *Swiss Tour* (1949), *La Revoltee* (1949), others.

Conan the Barbarian

Sword and Sorcery. *The Sword and the Dragon,* a 1956 Soviet film directed by Alexander Ptushko and starring Boris Andreyev, was a fine entry in the S&S subgenre.

Jack the Giant Killer was a 1962 tale of sorcerers and giants, wizards and heroes. A stop-motion animated film starring Kerwin Matthews of *Sinbad* and *Gulliver* fame—and featuring Torin Thatcher—*Jack* was believed by many fans to be a Harryhausen film. The effects, however, were handled by sometime Harryhausen collaborator Jim Danforth. This often-overlooked little film was directed by Nathan Juran.

Another 1962 film, *The Magic Sword,* directed by Bert I. Gordon, was a superior entry from the usually cheapjack Gordon. Starring Gary Lockwood as Sir George, it featured stellar supporting performances by old pros Basil Rathbone and Estelle Winwood.

Monty Python and the Holy Grail was the madcap British comedy group's irreverent treatment of the search for the Holy Grail. Directed by Pythons Terry Gilliam and Terry Jones, this 1974 film featured such wackiness as the "holy hand grenade" and the Knights Who Say "Nik."

The delightful *Excalibur* was 1981's superior version of the King Arthur legend. Directed by John Boorman, it featured outstanding performances by Nicol Williamson as Merlin, Helen Mirren as Morgana, and Nigel Terry as Arthur.

1980's *Hawk the Slayer* was a mild British production directed by Terry Marcel, and starring Jack Palance. John Terry was "Hawk."

Lee Horsely was no Arnold Schwarzenegger as "Talon," but the actor did a pretty good impersonation in 1982's low-budget *Sword and the Sorcerer,* directed by Albert Pyun. Featuring George Maharis as the nasty sorcerer of the title, this fun-filled actioner actually beat *Conan* into the theaters by a few weeks.

Conan also begat *The Beastmaster,* another 1982 entry into the field. The film starred Marc Singer as Dar, a muscleman who could speak to animals. Featuring the ever-popular queen of the "B"s, Tanya Roberts, this enjoyable minor effort was directed by Don Coscarelli.

Director Peter Yates' *Krull* (1983) was a big-budget bomb. Trapped in a strange fusion of S&S with SF-type effects, star Ken Marshall performed his heroics to empty theaters.

Miles O'Keefe and Sean Connery were the stars of 1984's *Sword of the Valiant,* director Stephen Weeks' low-budget retelling of the legend of Sir Gawain and the Green Knight. O'Keefe's performance did nothing to erase the memory of his awful debut as the lord of the jungle in Bo Derek's *Tarzan.*

Conan's 1984 sequel, *Conan the Destroyer,* suffered two insurmountable losses—*Conan* director-writer John Milius, and *Conan* co-star Sandahl Bergman. Arnold's performance is again okay, but even Grace Jones in a Bergmanesque role can't save this good-looking but ultimately pointless effort. Director Richard Fleischer, veteran helmer of much better films—*The Vikings, 20,000 Leagues Under the Sea,* and *Fantastic Voyage*—seems as defeated by the script as everyone else.

Red Sonja was a Dino De Laurentiis attempt to follow up on the success of

Conan. This 1985 movie featured Arnold Schwarzenegger in a Conan-like role, but unfortunately, the task of carrying the film fell to newcomer Brigette Nielsen. Even director Richard Fleischer couldn't coax a performance from the splendid-looking but wooden Nielsen (Tanya Roberts look out!). Sandahl Bergman was the villainess in this mishmash.

Another 1985 S&S entry was director Richard Donner's medieval epic, *Ladyhawke,* starring Rutger Hauer and Michelle Pfeiffer as, respectively, a knight who is a wolf by night and a beauty who is a hawk by day. Saddled with a strange musical score and the miscast Matthew Broderick, the film had only a modest success.

Disney's long-anticipated animated feature *The Black Cauldron* was finally released in the summer of 1985 and didn't live up to expectations.

Director Ridley Scott's expensively mounted late 1985/early 1986 release, *Legend,* was a superlative, if flawed, fantasy. Tim Curry, in a tour de force acting performance, stole the film as the evil, horned Darkness.

Rock video stylist Russell Mulcahy directed 1986's *Highlander,* an epic fantasy about immortal warriors fighting across the ages. Unfortunately, the film was more style than substance and never realized its potential.

Robert E. Howard's Conan. The following Conan stories appeared in *Weird Tales:* "The Phoenix and the Sword" (December 1932); "The Scarlet Citadel" (January 1933); "The Tower of the Elephant" (March 1933); "Black Colossus" (June 1933); "The Slithering Shadow" (September 1933); "The Pool of the Black One" (October 1933); "Rogues in the House" (January 1934); "Queen of the Black Coast" (May 1934); "The Devil in Iron" (August 1934). "The People of the Black Circle" (September, October, November 1934); "A Witch Shall Be Born" (December 1934); "Jewels of Gwahlur" (March 1935) "Beyond the Black River" (May, June 1935); "Shadows in Zanboula" (November 1935); "The Hour of the Dragon" (December 1935–April 1936); and "Red Nails" (July–October 1936). Other Conan stories appeared in such magazines as *Fantastic Universe Science Fiction, Space Science Fiction, The Fantasy Fan,* and *Magazine of Horror.*

In 1946, Arkham House published a collection of 24 of Howard's Conan stories under the title *Skull-Face and Others.*

Beginning in 1950, Gnome Press, a superior small publishing company, began issuing a series of Conan hardcovers. The first was titled *The Hour of the Dragon* and later retitled *Conan the Conqueror.* This first book was followed by *The Sword of Conan, King Conan, The Coming of Conan,* and *Conan the Barbarian.*

L. Sprague de Camp, cover artist Frank Frazetta, and Lancer paperbacks (later Ace/Berkley Books) began publishing a series of paperback collections of Howard's Conan stories, adding new adventures written by de Camp or de Camp and Lin Carter, as well as old Howard originals rewritten by de Camp. These included: *Conan, Conan of Cimmeria, Conan the Freebooter, Conan the Wanderer, Conan the Adventurer, Conan the Buccaneer, Conan the Warrior, Conan the Usurper, Conan the Conqueror, Conan the Avenger, Conan of Aquilonia,* and *Conan of the Isles.*

Illustrated Conan novels include: *Conan and the Sorcerer, Conan: the Flame Knife, Conan the Mercenary,* and *The Treasure of Tranicos.* Other Conan novels include *The Blade of Conan* and *The Spell of Conan.*

Marvel Comics' *Conan the Barbarian,* written by Roy Thomas and drawn by Barry Smith, appeared in 1970, and it was through this popular comic book that most of Conan's modern fans first met their hero.

Dragonslayer

Mythic and Fabulous Beasts. *The Flying Serpent*, starring George Zucco and directed by Sherman Scott, was a silly 1945 release concerning a prehistoric bird guarding Aztec teasures and secrets.

Miranda was a 1948 film directed by Ken Annakin and starring Glynis Johns as a mermaid anxious to see the sights of London. A warm, witty fantasy, this romp was a much-needed hit for Gainsborough Studios.

Mr. Peabody and the Mermaid, starring William Powell and Ann Bythe, was Hollywood and director Irving Pichel's answer to Britain's *Miranda*, released the same year. This slight, but amiable, comedy concerns a fisherman who lands a mermaid and then tries to keep her at his home.

Also from the water was the monster in 1954's 3-D hit, *The Creature from the Black Lagoon*. Directed by cult favorite Jack Arnold and starring Richard Denning and Julie Adams, this story of South America's "Gill-man" had plenty of thrills and chills.

The Snow Creature was a 1954 snow job directed by W. Lee Wilder and featuring Paul Langton. Low-budget and low-quality hokum about the Abominable Snowman.

Revenge of the Creature (1955) was the inevitable sequel to the first Gill-man film. Starring John Agar, it too was directed by Jack Arnold and released in 3-D.

The third in the Black Lagoon series, *The Creature Walks Among Us* (1956), starred Jeff Morrow and Rex Reason. Director Arnold added a sense of pathos and pity for the monster to this story of surgeon Morrow's attempt to make an oxygen breather of the Gill-man.

Man Beast was 1956's Abominable Snowman abomination. It starred the ever-popular Rock Madison and was directed by Jerry Warren.

Yet another such release was 1957's *Abominable Snowman of the Himalayas*, a fair version starring Peter Cushing and Forrest Tucker. Based on a BBC play written by Nigel Kneale, and skillfully directed by Val Guest, this Hammer production is clearly the best of the various Yeti pictures.

Another 1957 film was the interestingly titled *From Hell It Came*. Starring Tod Andrews and an ambulatory tree trunk, this strange little "B" picture was directed by Dan Miller.

No "B" programmer, 1967's grandiose musical *Doctor Doolittle* featured marvelous (or at least unusual) happenings (star Rex Harrison warbling "Talk to the Animals") and strange beasts (the fabulous Pushmi-Pullyu, the world's only dancing two-headed llama). Directed by Richard Fleischer, this entertaining flop cost $18 million and returned just $9 million.

Q (a.k.a. *The Winged Serpent*) was another film about an Aztec deity, this one living atop a Manhattan skyscraper and swooping down to eat city inhabitants. Starring the often-strange, always-watchable Michael Moriarity, this 1982 Larry Cohen film is fun if taken in the right vein.

Director Ron Howard's contribution to the long-dormant mermaid film subgenre was 1984's highly successful *Splash!*, starring a wet and wonderful Daryl Hannah and a funny Tom Hanks. This was a much-needed boost for the sagging fortunes of the Disney organization.

Unicorns are the mythic beasts lusted after by Tim Curry's Darkness in Ridley Scott's underrated 1986 box-office failure, *Legend*. Also starring Tom Cruise, this imaginative fantasy features many fabulous monsters and beautiful settings.

Mythic Beasts in Legend and Folktales. The Basilisk/Cockatrice comes from a "cock's egg" hatched by a snake or a toad. The Basilisk most resembles a reptile, while the Cockatrice most resembles its parent rooster. The mere sight of one of these monstrous beasts was enough to cause death. This winged serpent somewhat resembled George Zucco's *The Flying Serpent.*

The Griffin (or Gryphon) has the wings, claws, and head of an eagle, while his tail and hind paws are those of a lion.

The Hippogriff is the offspring of a mare and a griffin. This beast was said to have the body of a horse and the front parts of a griffin, complete with wings, beak, and claws.

Pegasus, the winged horse of the Greeks, makes a magnificent appearance in Harryhausen and Schneer's *Clash of the Titans. Titans* also had Harryhausen's brilliant interpretation of Medusa, the Gorgon — one of three sisters who had snakes on their heads in place of hair and whose look could turn men to stone.

The Manticora, a lionish four-legged monster with the head of a man and the claws of a griffin, was a vicious maneater.

The Centaur, from Greek mythology, was half-man, half-horse. These outlaw creatures inhabited Thessaly until they were destroyed by Hercules.

The Sphinx, from Egyptian mythology, had a woman's head, the loins of a bull, the wings of an eagle, and the claws of a lion.

Other creatures of myth include the Chimera, the Behemoth, the Kraken, the Siren, and the Phoenix.

Films by the Stars of *Dragonslayer*. Among the films of (Sir) Ralph Richardson (1902–1983): *The Ghoul* (1933), *The Return of Bulldog Drummond* (1934), *Bulldog Jack* (1935), *Things to Come, The Man Who Could Work Miracles* (both 1936), *The Citadel* (1938), *Q Planes* (1939), *The Four Feathers* (1939), *The Citadel* (1938), *Q Planes* (1939), *The Four Feathers* (1939), *The Day Will Dawn* (1942), *Anna Karenina, The Fallen Idol* (both 1948), *The Heiress* (1949), *The Sound Barrier* (1952), *The Holly and the Ivy* (1953), *Richard III* (1956), *Our Man in Havana* (1959), *Oscar Wilde* (1960), *The 300 Spartans, Long Day's Journey into Night* (both 1962), *Doctor Zhivago, The Wrong Box* (both 1966), *Khartoum* (1967), *Oh, What a Lovely War, The Bed Sitting Room, The Looking Glass War, David Copperfield* (all 1969), *Tales from the Crypt* (1971), *Alice's Adventures in Wonderland* (1972), *O Lucky Man* (1973), *Rollerball* (1975), *Watership Down* (1978, voice), *Time Bandits, Dragonslayer* (both 1981), *Wagner (1983), Greystoke* (1984), many others.

Awards, Honors, Best Film Lists, Etc. In 1981, *Dragonslayer* was nominated for two Academy Awards: Best Original Score (Alex North) and for Best Visual Effects (Dennis Muren, Phil Tippett, Ken Ralston, and Brian Johnson). It lost on the latter count to *Raiders of the Lost Ark.*

The 5,000 Fingers of Dr. T

A Child's Fantasy. A silent *Peter Pan* was filmed in 1924 by producer-director Herbert Brenon. Photographed by the great Chinese-American photographer James Wong Howe, this was one of the earliest filmings of James Barrie's children's classic.

Walt Disney's 1953 animated version, directed by Wilfred Jackson, is (like many Disney versions of well-known children's stories) the one most people think of first, unless they're old enough to remember Mary Martin's stage and television productions.

Babes in Toyland was also made several times. The 73-minute 1934 version, directed by Gus Meins, starred Stan Laurel and Oliver Hardy. The wooden soldiers, who repel the Bogeymen, were the inspiration for the film's retitling as *March of the Wooden Soldiers*.

The 1961 filming of *Babes in Toyland*, directed by Jack Donohue and starring Ray Bolger, Tommy Kirk, and Annette Funicello, was a too-cute Disney dud.

Disney created an enduring child's fantasy nanny in 1964's smash hit, *Mary Poppins*. Starring a perfectly cast Julie Andrews as the "practically perfect" nanny who can fly and do other magical things, this Robert Stevenson–directed film is wonderful for kids of all ages, if a bit overlong at 140 minutes.

Based on a book by Ian Fleming of all people (he created James Bond), *Chitty Chitty Bang Bang*, directed by Ken Hughes, was an attempt to duplicate *Mary Poppins'* success. This 1968 film about a flying car seemingly had all the right ingredients—including Dick Van Dyke—but it misfired on all cylinders. Poor special effects.

Released in 1971, *Willy Wonka and the Chocolate Factory*, directed by Mel Stuart and starring Gene Wilder and Jack Albertson, was an enjoyable kids' fantasy. Based on Roald Dahl's book *Charlie and the Chocolate Factory*, the film featured music by Anthony Newley and Leslie Bricusse, including the hit song "Candy Man." The film is meant to teach kids a number of lessons, but, as Leonard Maltin notes, "cruel edge taints film's enjoyment."

Films by the Stars and Crew of *The 5,000 Fingers of Dr. T.* Hans Conried has made a number of genre films besides *Dr. T*, including *The Twonky* (1952), about a television set taken over by an alien intelligence. His other appearances in the fantasy genre are in *Siren of Baghdad* (1952), *The Monster That Challenged the World* (1957), *The Magic Fountain* (1961, voice of the Owl), *The Phantom Tollbooth* (1968, voice), *The Shaggy D.A.* (1976), *The Cat from Outer Space* (1978), *Oh God! Book II* (1980), and more.

Among the other films of Hans Conried: *Dramatic School* (1938), *It's a Wonderful World* (1939), *Dulcy* (1940), *Underground, The Gay Falcon* (both 1941), *Joan of Paris, Saboteur, The Big Street, Nightmare, Once Upon a Honeymoon, Journey into Fear* (all 1942), *Hitler's Children, Hostages, A Lady Takes a Chance, Crazy House* (all 1943), *Passage to Marseille, Mrs. Parkington* (both 1944), *The Senator Was Indiscreet* (1947), *My Friend Irma, On the Town* (both 1949), *Nancy Goes to Rio, Summer Stock* (both 1950), *Three for Bedroom C, The World in His Arms, Big Jim McLain* (all 1952), *Davy Crockett, King of the Wild Frontier* (1955), *Bus Stop* (1956), *Jet Pilot* (1957), *Rock-a-Bye Baby* (1958), *My Six Loves* (1963), *The Patsy* (1964), *The Brothers O'Toole* (1973), others.

Among the films of Roy Rowland (1910–) *A Stranger in Town, Lost Angel* (both 1943), *Our Vines Have Tender Grapes* (1945), *Boys' Ranch* (1946), *The Romance of Rosy Ridge, Killer McCoy* (both 1947), *Tenth Avenue Angel* (1948), *Scene of the Crime* (1949), *The Outriders, Two Weeks with Love* (both 1950), *Excuse My Dust* (1951), *Bugles in the Afternoon* (1952), *The 5,000 Fingers of Dr. T, Affair with a Stranger, The Moonlighter* (all 1953), *Rogue Cop, Witness to Murder* (both 1954), *Many Rivers to Cross, Hit the Deck* (both 1955), *Slander, These Wilder Years, Meet Me in Las Vegas* (all 1956), *Gun Glory* (1957), *The Seven Hills of Rome* (1958), *The Girl Hunters* (1963), *The Gunfighters of Casa Grande* (1964), and others.

Works of Dr. Seuss (Theodor Seuss Geisel). Among this prolific and popular author's works: *And to Think That I Saw It on Mulberry Street* (1937), *The 500 Hats of Bartholomew Cubbins* (1938), *The King's Stilts* (1939), *Horton Hatches the Egg* (1940), *McElligot's Pool* (1947), *Thidwick, The Big-Hearted Moose* (1948), *Bartholomew and the Oobleck* (1949), *If I Ran the Zoo* (1950), *Scrambled Eggs Super!*

(1953), *Horton Hears a Who!* (1954), *One Beyond Zebra* (1955), *If I Ran the Circus* (1956), *The Cat in the Hat, How the Grinch Stole Christmas* (both 1957), *The Cat in the Hat Comes Back!, Yertle the Turtle and Other Stories* (both 1958), *Happy Birthday to You!* (1959), *One Fish, Two Fish, Red Fish, Blue Fish, Green Eggs and Ham* (both 1960), *The Sneetches and Other Stories* (1961), *Dr. Seuss's Sleep Book* (1962), *Hop on Pop, Dr. Seuss's ABC* (both 1963), *Fox in Socks, I Had Trouble in Getting to Solla Sollew* (both 1965), *The Foot Book* (1969), *I Can Lick 30 Tigers Today and Other Stories* (1969), *Mr. Brown Can Moo! Can You?* (1970), *The Lorax* (1971), *Marvin K. Mooney, Will You Please Go Now?* (1972), *Did I Ever Tell You How Lucky You Are?, The Shape of Me and Other Stuff* (both 1973), *There's a Wocket in My Pocket!, Great Day for Up!* (both 1974), *Oh, The Thinks You Can Think* (1975), *Hooper Humperdink. . . ? Not Him!* (1976), *Oh Say Can You Say?* (1979), *Hunches in Bunches* (1982), and others.

Geisel has also published at least ten books of verse as "Theo Le Seig," and written and illustrated numerous other works. Several of his works, including *How the Grinch Stole Christmas* and *The Lorax*, have been adapted for television as half-hour animated specials by Geisel and directed by the great Warner Brothers director, Chuck Jones.

It's a Wonderful Life

Angels and Guardian Angels. *Here Comes Mr. Jordan*, starring Robert Montgomery, Edward Everett Horton, and Claude Rains, this Alexander Hall–directed fantasy has set the standard for the subgenre since its 1941 release. It concerns a prizefighter who is mistakenly called to heaven by angel Horton. When returned to earth, the fighter finds his body's been cremated and another must be found for his forty years of life still owed him.

A bland operetta, 1942's *I Married an Angel*, was the next entry in the heavenly visitors category. Directed by W.S. Van Dyke, this silly film was the final pairing of Jeanette MacDonald and Nelson Eddy. The film also featured *Mr. Jordan's* Edward Everett Horton.

A curious wartime contribution was 1943's *A Guy Named Joe*, starring the always-interesting Spencer Tracy. Directed by Victor Fleming, this not-especially-successful tale has deceased flier Tracy returning to oversee pilot Van Johnson's romance.

The Horn Blows at Midnight concerned angel Jack Benny's attempt to destroy the earth with a blast from Gabriel's horn. Director Raoul Walsh does a fine job of wringing laughs from this 1945 film's unusual and original premise.

Unfortunately for 1946's *Angel on My Shoulder*, it arrived late in the *Mr. Jordan* cycle. This particular version had gangster Paul Muni being returned to earth in the body of a judge. Directed in derivative style by Archie Mayo, this is one Muni film not to set the VCR for.

Robert Cummings played an angel sent to the Old West to help a gambler go straight in *Heaven Only Knows*. Directed by Albert S. Rogell and co-starring Brian Donlevy, this 1947 version offered little new. It was later retitled *Montana Mike*—heaven only knows why.

In 1947's *The Bishop's Wife*, Cary Grant is an angel sent to earth to reorder the priorities of a bishop more concerned with building a cathedral than assisting his flock. It's very old-fashionedness and delightful performances—by Grant, David Niven, and Loretta Young—make it a whimsical delight and a Christmas perennial.

For Heaven's Sake, a 1950 release, concerns the efforts of angels Clifton Webb and Edmund Gwenn to help Broadway producer Robert Cummings save his marriage to Joan Bennett. Directed and written by George Seaton, this bit of fluff has not aged well.

The Pittsburgh Pirates (who at this writing could use some heavenly help) are assisted by an angel in improving their win-loss record in *Angels in the Outfield*. Directed by Clarence Brown and starring Paul Douglas, Janet Leigh, and Keenan Wynn, this 1951 fantasy is as engaging as it is expertly produced.

Diane Cilento was *The Angel Who Pawned Her Harp*, a 1954 British fantasy of an angel out to help needy earthlings. Directed by Alan Bromly, this 76-minute film also featured Felix Aylmer and Alfie Bass.

An odd entry in the genre was the 1956 filming of the Rogers and Hammerstein Broadway musical, *Carousel*. Gordon MacRae plays carnival barker Billy Bigalow, who returns 15 years after his death to help straighten out his family's fortunes. Directed by Henry King, this wide-screen extravaganza also featured Shirley Jones.

The Angel Levine was a 1970 fantasy starring the irrepressible Zero Mostel. Directed by Jan Kadar, the film concerns black angel Harry Belafonte's attempts to help out a pathetic Jewish tailor. Well-told tale.

Disney's 1973 *Charley and the Angel* concerns storekeeper Fred MacMurray's attempts, with help from angel Harry Morgan, to set his life in order before being called to heaven. A moderately successful entry, directed by Vincent McEveety.

The Heavenly Kid was released in 1985 and starred Lewis Smith as a greasy '50s teen who died in his hot rod only to pop up in the '80s to help a young nerd become "cool." Directed by Cary Medoway, this feeble attempt at comedy is as forgettable as they come.

Heaven Can Wait was director-star Warren Beatty's 1978 remake of *Mr. Jordan*. Also starring Julie Christie and James Mason, this hugely successful fantasy showed there was still life left in the old subgenre.

Films by the Stars of *It's a Wonderful Life.* Among the films of James Stewart: *Murder Man* (1935), *Rose Marie, Next Time We Love, Wife Versus Secretary, Small Town Girl, Speed, The Gorgeous Hussy, Born to Dance, After the Thin Man* (all 1936), *Seventh Heaven, The Last Gangster, Navy Blue and Gold* (all 1937), *Of Human Hearts, Vivacious Lady, Shopworn Angel, You Can't Take It with You, Made for Each Other* (all 1938), *Ice Follies of 1939, It's a Wonderful World, Mr. Smith Goes to Washington, Destry Rides Again* (all 1939), *The Shop Around the Corner, The Mortal Storm, No Time for Comedy, The Philadelphia Story* (Academy Award), *Come Live with Me* (all 1940), *Pot O' Gold, Ziegfeld Girl* (both 1941), *Magic Town* (1946), *Call Northside 777* (1947), *On Our Merry Way, Rope, You Gotta Stay Happy* (all 1948), *The Stratton Story* (1949), *Malaya* (1949), *Winchester 73, Broken Arrow, The Jackpot, Harvey* (all 1950), *No Highway, The Greatest Show on Earth* (both 1951), *Bend of the River, Carbine Williams* (1952), *The Naked Spur, Thunder Bay, The Glenn Miller Story* (all 1953), *Rear Window, The Far Country* (both 1954), *Strategic Air Command, The Man from Laramie* (both 1955), *The Man Who Knew Too Much* (1956), *The Spirit of St. Louis, Night Passage* (both 1957), *Vertigo, Bell, Book and Candle* (both 1958), *Anatomy of a Murder, The FBI Story* (both 1959), *The Mountain Road* (1960), *Two Rode Together* (1961), *The Man Who Shot Liberty Valance, Mr. Hobbs Takes a Vacation, How the West Was Won* (all 1962), *Take Her She's Mine* (1963), *Cheyenne Autumn* (1964), *Dear Brigitte, Shenandoah, The Flight of the Phoenix* (all 1965), *The Rare Breed* (1966), *Firecreek* (1967), *Bandolero* (1968), *The Cheyenne Social Club* (1970), *Fool's Parade* (1971), *That's Entertainment* (1974), *The Shootist* (1976), *Airport 77* (1977), *The Big Sleep* (1978), *The Magic of Lassie* (1978).

Among the films of Donna Reed: *The Getaway* (1941), *Shadow of the Thin Man*, *The Courtship of Andy Hardy*, *Calling Dr. Gillespie* (all 1942), *The Human Comedy*, *Dr. Gillespie's Criminal Case*, *Thousands Cheer* (all 1943), *See Here, Private Hargrove*, *The Picture of Dorian Gray* (both 1944), *They Were Expendable* (1945), *Faithful in My Fashion* (1946), *Green Dolphin Street* (1947), *Chicago Deadline* (1949), *Saturday's Hero* (1951), *Scandal Sheet*, *Hangman's Knot* (both 1952), *From Here to Eternity* (AA, 1953), *The Caddy*, *Gun Fury* (both 1953), *The Last Time I Saw Paris*, *The Far Horizons* (both 1955), *Ransom*, *Backlash*, *The Benny Goodman Story* (all 1956), *Beyond Mombasa* (1957), *The Yellow-Headed Summer* (unreleased, 1974).

Awards, Honors, Best Film Lists, Etc. In the 1946 Academy Awards race, *Wonderful Life* was nominated for Best Picture, Best Director, Best Actor, Best Editing (William Hornbeck), and Best Sound Recording (Richard Van Hessen and Clem Portman). The National Board of Review Awards of 1947 listed it as one of the year's best films. The Golden Globe Awards for 1946 gave Frank Capra the Best Director award. In *Time* Magazine's annual "Ten Best" list for 1946, the film was again cited as one of the year's ten best. The American Film Institute member survey of the Greatest Fifty American Films (1977) ranks it at number twenty-six. And according to the Annual Top Money-making Films of 1946–47, *It's a Wonderful Life* was the eleventh top-grossing film.

Jason and the Argonauts

Ancient Mythology. One of the earliest, if not *the* earliest such production was French film pioneer Georges Melies' 1905 production of *Ulysses and Giant Polyphemus*.

Kirk Douglas starred in the 1954 Italian production of *Ulysses*, directed by Mario Camerini. This was a robust adventure film with star Douglas at his enthusiastic best.

Directed by Pietro Francisci, the low-budget but well-made 1957 Italian epic *Hercules* was imported by Joseph E. Levine and became, inexplicably, a huge hit. It made a star of lead Steve Reeves. The sequel, *Hercules Unchained*, released two years later, was also successful—thus beginning the Italian "muscles and swords" wave of similar productions.

The Minotaur, a 1960 film starring Olympic gold medal winner Bob Mathias, was directed by Silvio Amadio and was yet another entry in this overcrowded field.

Others include: *Loves of Hercules* (1960, Mickey Hargitay and Jane Mansfield), *Goliath and the Barbarians* (1960, Steve Reeves), *Hercules and the Captive Women* (1961, starring Reg Park), *Hercules in the Haunted World* (1961, Reg Park), *Ulysses Against the Son of Hercules* (1961, Georges Marchal), *Mighty Ursus* (1961, Ed Fury), *Three Stooges Meet Hercules* (1961), *Hercules in the Vale of Woe* (1963, Kirk Morris), *Hercules, Samson and Ulysses* (1963, Kirk Morris, Richard Lloyd, Enzo Cerusico), *Hercules the Invincible* (1963, Don Vadis), *Hercules Against Rome* (1964, Alan Steel), *Hercules Against the Barbarians* (1964, Mark Forest), *Hercules Against the Moon Men* (1964, Alan Steel), *Hercules Against the Sons of the Sun* (1964, Mark Forest), *Hercules and the Tyrants of Babylon* (1964, Rock Stevens), *Hercules of the Desert* (1964, Kirk Morris), *Hercules, Prisoner of Evil* (1964, Reg Park), *Hercules vs. the Giant Warriors* (1964, Don Vadis), *Hercules and the Princess of Troy* (made for TV, 1965, Gordon Scott), *Hercules in New York* (1970, Arnold Schwarzenegger).

Films by the Stars and Crew of *Jason and the Argonauts*. Among the films of

Don Chaffey (1917–): *The Mysterious Poacher* (1950), *The Case of the Missing Scene* (1951), *Skid Kids* (1953), *The Secret Tent* (1956), *The Flesh Is Weak* (1957), *The Man Upstairs* (1958), *Danger Within, Breakout* (both 1959), *Nearly a Nasty Accident, Greyfriars Bobby* (both 1961), *The Prince and the Pauper* (1962), *The Horse Without a Head, Jason and the Argonauts, The Three Lives of Thomasina* (all 1963), *They All Died Laughing* (1964), *One Million Years B.C.* (1966, Harryhausen and Schneer), *The Viking Queen* (1967), *Creatures the World Forgot* (1971), *Charley One-Eye* (1973), *Ride a Wild Pony* (1976), *Pete's Dragon* (1977), *The Magic of Lassie* (1978), *C.H.O.M.P.S.* (1979), *Lassie: the New Beginning* (TV, 1979), others.

Chaffey also directed a number of *The Prisoner* episodes, and several of *The Avengers* episodes.

Among the films of Todd Armstrong (1939–): *Walk on the Wild Side* (1962), *Jason and the Argonauts* (1963), *King Rat* (1965), *The Silencers* (1966), *A Time for Killing* (1968).

Among the films of Nancy Kovack (1935–): *Strangers When We Meet* (1960), *Diary of a Madman* (1962), *Jason and the Argonauts* (1963), *The Outlaws Is Coming* (1965), *Frankie and Johnny, Tarzan and the Valley of Gold* (both 1966), *The Silencers* (1966, also featuring her *Jason* co-star, Todd Armstrong), *Marooned* (1969).

Many Americans, if they know Laurence Naismith (Lawrence Johnson, 1908–) at all, know him from a short-lived television series which aired from 1971 to 1972, *The Persuaders*, starring Roger Moore and Tony Curtis. He also starred in the 1972 children's fantasy, *The Amazing Mr. Blunden.* Among his films: *Trouble in the Air* (1947), *A Piece of Cake* (1948), *The Beggar's Opera* (1952), *Mogambo* (1953), *The Black Knight* (1954), *Lust for Life, Richard III* (both 1956), *Tempest, A Night to Remember* (both 1958), *Solomon and Sheba* (1959), *Sink the Bismarck!* (1960), *The 300 Spartans* (1962), *Cleopatra, Jason and the Argonauts* (both 1963), *The Three Lives of Thomasina* (1963, with *Jason* director Don Chaffey), *The Scorpio Letters, Fitzwilly, Camelot* (all 1967), *The Valley of Gwangi* (1968, Harryhausen and Schneer), *Eye of the Cat* (1969), *Scrooge* (1970), *Diamonds Are Forever* (1971), others.

Like Laurence Naismith, Gary Raymond (1935–) is best known in the United States for his role in a television series, 1965's *The Rat Patrol.* Among the films of Gary Raymond: *The Moonraker* (1958), *Look Back in Anger, Suddenly Last Summer* (both 1959), *The Millionairess, El Cid* (both 1961), *Jason and the Argonauts* (1963), *The Greatest Story Ever Told, Traitors' Gate* (both 1965), *The Playboy of the Western World* (1966), others.

Irish-born Niall MacGinnis (1913–) is probably being seen in the title role of 1953's *Martin Luther* somewhere in the world in a Lutheran church basement or assembly room at this moment. One of his best roles was as Dr. Julian Karswell in 1956's superb horror/fantasy film, *Night of the Demon (Curse of the Demon* in the United States). Among his other films: *Turn of the Tide* (1935), *49th Parallel* (1941), *Henry V* (1944), *Knights of the Round Table* (1953), *Tarzan's Greatest Adventure* (1959), *Pursuit of the Graf Spee* (1957), *The Nun's Story* (1958), *Billy Budd* (1962), *Jason and the Argonauts* (1963), *Becket* (1964), *The War Lord* (1965), *Island of Terror* (1966), *Torture Garden* (1967), *Shoes of the Fisherman* (1968), *Sinful Davey* (1969), and more.

Although more recently famous in the United States for having been TV's second Dr. Who, Patrick Troughton (1920–1988) is probably remembered by more adults for having played the ill-fated priest in 1976's successful horror film, *The Omen.* Among the other films of Patrick Troughton: *Escape, Hamlet* (both 1948), *Treasure Island* (1950), *The Black Knight* (1952), *Richard III* (1956), *The Curse of Frankenstein* (1957), *Phantom of the Opera* (1962), *The Gorgon* (1964), *Scars of Dra-*

cula (1970), *Frankenstein and the Monster from Hell* (1974), *Sinbad and the Eye of the Tiger* (1977, Harryhausen and Schneer), others.

Among the films of Nigel Green (1924–1972): *Reach for the Sky* (1956), *The Criminal* (1960), *Mysterious Island* (1960, Harryhausen and Schneer), *Jason and the Argonauts* (1963), *Zulu*, *The Masque of the Red Death* (both 1964), *The Ipcress File*, *The Face of Fu Manchu* (both 1965), *Let's Kill Uncle*, *Deadlier Than the Male* (both 1966), *Tobruk* (1967), *Play Dirty* (1968), *The Wrecking Crew*, *The Kremlin Letter* (both 1969), *The Ruling Class* (1971), *Gawain and the Green Knight* (1972), etc.

The Sodium Light Process. The "sodium light process," or the "yellow-backing system" is similar to the blue-screen traveling matte process except that it is less complicated and less likely to prove detectable. (See notes on *King Kong*, below, for more on matte photography.) Harryhausen discovered other limitations in the blue-screen process as well. Any foreground element which contained blue could not be used—costumes, water, actors' eyes in closeup, etc. The sodium process eliminated or at least minimized these problems and allowed for greater choices in foreground composition and color.

The sodium light process makes use of a beam-splitting camera which utilizes a prism to split the light entering its lens and send the identical image to two different strips of film. A yellow screen is then lighted from the front by monochromatic yellow light from sodium vapor lamps. The actors, in front of this yellow-lit screen, are lit with ordinary lamps coated with didymium, a chemical which prevents any yellow light from passing through. Yellow is the lowest band in the color spectrum and comes out black since it does not photograph at such low light levels (if you've ever tried to make a photocopy of printed matter covered by yellow "highlighting," only to discover that the highlighted area comes out opaque, you now know why).

The beam splitter ensures that one of the two strips of film records only the actors' actions while the other strip of film is exposed only to the yellow light bouncing off the screen. It is this second strip of film, called the "traveling matte," that is blank where the actors' bodies were exposed but opaque where the background was exposed. An optical printer is then used to composite the two images.

Because the sodium light process could not initially be used with anamorphic (wide-screen) lenses, Harryhausen's reliance on it prevented him from working with anamorphic lenses until he successfully adapted the process for *The First Men in the Moon* (1964).

Today, the sodium light process is used almost exclusively by the Disney Studios.

King Kong

Matte Photography. A matte was originally just a cut-out or mask that prevented some of the film in the camera from being exposed. Later, with the originally photographed area now masked, the earlier portion which had been masked could now be exposed in the camera. Matte shots resulted in the joining in one image or frame elements not really shot at the same time. This process allowed studios to make it appear that a glamorous female star was really in the same shot as a fierce tiger.

"Glass shot" is just another term for a matte painting. The matte artist paints fake elements (a colossal castle or a futuristic city in the clouds) on sheets of glass. In the silent era, the camera actually shot through this glass painting, making it appear that the actors are in the midst of this painted scene. Today, instead of the matte painting and live elements being combined in the camera, they're combined in the optical printer—which blends two or more images on a single frame or piece of film.

Traveling mattes are used to show a moving object against a moving background. This is most often accomplished by filming the actors (or, for example, a model spacecraft) against a blue backing. In this "blue-screen system," the blue background does not register on the film. Later this shot will be combined in the optical printer with another background. Some shots are so complex that many elements may be individually processed and combined for the final effect on screen.

Merian C. Cooper. Cooper became one of the founders of David O. Selznick's new company, and he convinced Selznick to use Technicolor in *Gone With the Wind* (1939). Other Cooper/Ford productions were *The Long Voyage Home* (1940), *Three Godfathers*, *Fort Apache* (both 1948), and *Wagonmaster* (1950).

Cooper, at the age of 78, died at his Coronado, California, home on April 21, 1973.

The Films of Willis O'Brien. Willis O'Brien's film work includes *This Is Cinerama* (1952), *The Animal World* (1956), *The Black Scorpion* (1957), *The Giant Behemoth* (1959), and *It's a Mad, Mad, Mad, Mad World* (1963). O'Brien's Edison films include *R.F.D. 10,000 B.C.*, *Prehistoric Poultry* (two versions), *In the Villain's Power*, *Curious Pets of Our Ancestors*, *Mickey and His Goat*, *Sam Loyd's Famous Puzzles—The Puzzling Billboard*, and *Nippy's Nightmare*.

O'Brien's life was tragic in many ways. He was rarely able to put his talents fully to work and his personal life was full of pain and sorrow. In October 1933, three years after OBie and his wife Hazel separated, she shot both of their sons to death with a .38-caliber pistol and tried to kill herself. Charged with murder, Hazel O'Brien died of natural causes in November 1934. OBie immediately married Darlyne Prenett on November 17, 1934.

Willis O'Brien died at his home after a heart attack on November 8, 1962. He was 76 years old.

Films by the Stars of King Kong. Among the other actors in *King Kong* was Noble Johnson, a light-skinned mulatto who made a career out of playing Indians and a variety of ethnic types. He was a Cossack in Cooper and Schoedsack's *The Most Dangerous Game*, a Chinese man in *The Mysterious Dr. Fu Manchu*, a Polynesian in *Moby Dick* (1930), and a Nubian in *The Mummy* (1932). His other films included *Robinson Crusoe* (as Friday, 1922), *The Ten Commandments* (1923), *The Navigator* (1924), *Hands Up* (1926), *Vanity* (1927), *Redskin* (1928), *The Four Feathers* (1929), *She* (1935), *Conquest* (1937), *The Ghost Breakers* (1940), *Jungle Book* (1942), *She Wore a Yellow Ribbon* (1949), and many others.

Fay Wray's other films include: *Street of Sin* (1928), *The Four Feathers* (1929), *The Texan*, *Dirigible* (both 1930), *The Bowery* (1933), *Madame Spy* (1934), *They Met in a Taxi* (1936), *Murder in Greenwich Village* (1937), *The Jury's Secret* (1938), *Adam Had Four Sons* (1941), *Small Town Girl* (1953), *Queen Bee* (1955), *Crime of Passion* (1956), and *Tammy and the Bachelor* (1957). Her one television series, *Pride of the Family*, aired in 1953.

Bruce Cabot's other films include: *Murder on the Blackboard* (1934), *Let 'Em Have It*, *Show Them No Mercy* (both 1935), *Fury* (1936), *Legion of Terror*, *Love Takes Flight* (both 1937), *Homicide Bureau*, *Dodge City* (both 1939), *Wild Bill Hickok Rides* (1942), *The Desert Song* (1943), *Angel and the Badman* (1947), *Fancy Pants* (1950), *Best of the Badmen* (1951), *The Quiet American* (1958), *The Comancheros* (1961),

Hatari (1962), *Cat Ballou* (1965), *The War Wagon* (1967), *The Green Berets* (1968), *Big Jake* and *Diamonds Are Forever* (both 1971).

Bruce Cabot died of cancer in May 1972, at the age of 68.

The Work of Max Steiner. Max Steiner wrote the following pieces of music for *King Kong:* "King Kong," "Jungle Dance," "The Forgotten Island," "A Boat in the Fog," "The Railing," "Aboriginal Sacrifice Dance," "Meeting with Black Men," "Sea at Night," "Stolen Love," "The Sailors," "The Bronte," "Cryptic Shadows," "The Cave," "The Snake," "Humorous Ape," "The Peri," "Furioso," "The Swimmers," "The Escape," "Return of Kong," "King Kong March," "Fanfare No. 1," "Fanfare No. 2," "Fanfare No. 3," "Agitato," "Elevated Sequence," "The Train," "The Aeroplane," and "Dance of Kong."

A *few* of the many RKO pictures that Steiner scored: *Rio Rita* (1929), *Cimarron* (1930), *The Public Defender* (1931), *The Lost Squadron, The Most Dangerous Game* (both 1932), *Little Women, Son of Kong* (both 1933), *Of Human Bondage, The Gay Divorcee* (both 1934), *The Informer, Top Hat* (both 1935), and *Follow the Fleet* (1936).

Max Steiner died in 1971.

Until John Williams did the same for *Star Wars,* few films were as helped by their music as *King Kong.* Almost every critic attributes much of the movie's success to its powerful and evocative score.

Sets and Props from *King Kong* Used in Other Movies. One of the test reel's spiders made an appearance in OBie's *The Black Scorpion* in 1957, and *She* (1935) made use of the massive gate. The wall itself was destroyed by fire for the famous burning of Atlanta sequence in Selznick's *Gone With the Wind* in 1938. Pathé's "Skull Island" sets appeared in a Bela Lugosi serial, *The Return of Chandu,* filmed in 1934.

In the mid–70s, David Allen filmed a Volkswagon television ad which lovingly parodied *King Kong.* Allen used the original armature from one of the Kong models for his own model Kong.

Giant Monster Films. Besides O'Brien's other such pictures (*The Lost World, Son of Kong, Mighty Joe Young,* and *The Black Scorpion*), the genre has included everything from ants to rabbits, and seen a seemingly endless flood of (often) radioactivity-produced monsters from Japan, the only country to have been attacked by an atomic bomb.

OBie's one-time protege and ultimate successor, Ray Harryhausen, created 1953's *Beast from Twenty Thousand Fathoms.*

James Whitmore and James Arness starred in the superior giant ants picture, 1954's *Them!,* directed by Gordon Douglas. Walt Disney's *20,000 Leagues Under the Sea* featured a fight between Captain Nemo's crew and a giant squid.

Japan's 1954 film *Godzilla* (released in the United States in 1956 with added footage featuring Raymond Burr) begat a whole slew of slumbering monsters unleashed upon Tokyo and the world by radiation, pollution, and other man-made elements.

Tarantula, which crawled out onto movie screens in 1955, featured Leo G. Carroll and an enormous spider. *The Deadly Mantis* was another entry into the subgenre and was released in 1957.

Jeff Morrow would later regret starring in 1957's laughable *The Giant Claw.* This camp classic features a giant roc unlikely to scare a two-year-old child, the result of cheap Mexican special effects work.

After *The Spider* invaded theaters in 1958, the British-made *Gorgo* briefly revived giant reptiles with one of the screen's surprise hits of 1959.

The Giant Behemoth, also made in 1959, followed, giving Gene Evans a rare starring role, and the Danish-made *Reptilicus* (1961) was a worthy successor to *The Giant Claw*.

Harryhausen's 1968 *Valley of Gwangi* is not a great film, but its effects work is fine and it was unfairly overlooked or dismissed critically when it came out. Harryhausen pitted cowboys on horseback against dinosaurs, a theme dear to the heart of his old mentor, Willis O'Brien.

Night of the Lepus, a 1972 film, took giant monsters about as far as the subgenre could go — its monsters were giant bunnies! It's amusing to see the bemused and timid monster bunnies push railroad cars and other miniature props around.

The giant monsters keep coming, although their heyday was the fifties. Even Dino De Laurentiis returned to the subgenre in 1986 with another *King Kong* sequel. This one, called *King Kong Lives!*, saw the comatose giant ape (after his fall from the World Trade Center towers) getting an artificial heart and fathering a little Kong. It was critically lambasted and did minuscule business, quickly disappearing from the few theaters that booked it.

Lost Horizon

The Hidden Paradise, or Lost Worlds. An early entry in this category was *The Lost World* (1925). Also a "Giant Monster" film, this silent production starred Wallace Beery as Professor Challenger.

Mysterious Island (1929), was an early Technicolor version of the Jules Verne story, directed by Lucian Hubbard and starring Lionel Barrymore. It was remade in 1969 under the title *Captain Nemo and the Underwater City*, starring Robert Ryan in the title role.

She (1935), a "lost" film, starred Helen Gahagan (later Helen Gahagan Brown, who opposed Richard Nixon for the United States Senate) in the title role and featured Randolph Scott. The directors of this tale of an immortal queen (who can be made mortal by love) were Irving Pichel and Lansing G. Holden.

Two Lost Worlds (1950) starred a pre–*Gunsmoke* James Arness in a story of shipwrecked survivors on an uncharted island. Uses stock footage from *One Million Years B.C.* Plodding.

The Lost Continent (1951) was a routine thriller starring Cesar Romero and John Hoyt on an expedition to a prehistoric mountaintop in search of a missing rocket.

Brigadoon (1954) was director Vincente Minnelli's attempt to film the successful stage musical. Starring Gene Kelly, Van Johnson, and Cyd Charisse, the movie concerns two Americans in Scotland who discover a village which appears only once in every 100 years.

The Mole People (1956), a "Lost Horizon-ish" horror film, starred John Agar and takes place in an underground Sumarian civilization which has been hidden from the upper world since 3000 B.C.

The Land Unknown (1957) starred one-time screen Tarzan Jock Mahoney in another "uncharted prehistoric monster" refuge film.

Journey to the Center of the Earth (1959) was directed by Henry Levin and featured James Mason, Pat Boone, and Arlene Dahl in a colorful version of the Jules Verne tale.

The Lost World was remade in 1960, starring Claude Rains and Michael Rennie. Okay, if not up to the silent original.

Mysterious Island (1961) was directed by Cy Enfield and starred Gary Merrill,

Joan Greenwood, and Michael Craig. This version featured Herbert Lom as Captain Nemo and giant animals animated by stop-motion whiz Ray Harryhausen.

Atlantis, the Lost Continent (1961), directed by George Pal, has fine special effects and is a great deal of fun, if a bit corny. The film starred Anthony Hall and Joyce Taylor.

Ursula Andress starred in a remake of *She* in 1965. This Hammer production was directed by Robert Day and featured horror/fantasy stalwarts Peter Cushing and Christopher Lee.

In 1973, director Charles Jarrott unleashed a musical remake of *Lost Horizon*. This soulless production starred Peter Finch, Liv Ullman, Michael York, Sir John Gielgud, and, as the High Lama, Charles Boyer. Simply awful.

Walt Disney's *Island at the Top of the World* (1974) was an uninspired version of the Jules Verne story starring David Hartman and Donald Sinden. Directed by Robert Stevenson, this was no *20,000 Leagues Under the Sea*.

The Films of Frank Capra: *Fultah Fisher's Boarding House* (1922), *The Strong Man* (1926), *Long Pants, For the Love of Mike* (both 1927), *That Certain Thing, So This Is Love, The Matinee Idol, The Way of the Strong, Say It With Sables, Submarine, The Power of the Press* (all 1928), *The Younger Generation, The Donovan Affair, Flight* (all 1929), *Ladies of Leisure, Rain or Shine* (both 1930), *Dirigible, The Miracle Woman, Platinum Blonde* (all 1931), *Forbidden, American Madness* (both 1932) *The Bitter Tea of General Yen, Lady for a Day* (both 1933), *It Happened One Night* (Academy Award), *Broadway Bill* (both 1934), *Mr. Deeds Goes to Town* (1936), *Lost Horizon* (1937), *You Can't Take It With You* (1938), *Mr. Smith Goes to Washington* (1939), *Meet John Doe* (1941), *Arsenic and Old Lace* (1942, released 1944), *It's a Wonderful Life* (1946), *State of the Union* (1948), *Riding High* (1950), *Here Comes the Groom* (1951), *A Hole in the Head* (1959), *Pocketful of Miracles* (1961). Also, *Why We Fight Series* during WWII, and *Bell System Science Series* (TV).

Films by the Stars of *Lost Horizon*. Among the films of Ronald Colman (1891–1958): *The Toilers* (1919), *The Black Spider* (1920), *Handcuffs or Kisses* (1921), *The White Sister* (1923), *Tarnish* (1924), *The Sporting Venus, The Dark Angel, Stella Dallas* (all 1925), *Kiki, Beau Geste* (both 1926), *The Magic Flame* (1927), *The Lovers* (1928), *Bulldog Drummond* (1929), *Raffles* (1930), *The Unholy Garden, Arrowsmith* (both 1931) *Bulldog Drummond Strikes Back* (1934), *Clive of India, A Tale of Two Cities* (both 1935), *Under Two Flags* (1936), *Lost Horizon, The Prisoner of Zenda* (both 1937), *If I Were King* (1938), *The Talk of the Town, Random Harvest* (both 1942). *The Late George Apley* (1947), *A Double Life* (Academy Award, 1948), *Champagne for Caesar* (1950), *Around the World in Eighty Days* (1956), and *The Story of Mankind* (1957).

Among the films of Sam Jaffe (1893–1984): *We Live Again, The Scarlett Empress* (both 1934), *Lost Horizon* (1937), *Gunga Din* (1939), *13 Rue Madeleine* (1946), *Gentleman's Agreement* (1947), *The Asphalt Jungle* (1950), *The Day the Earth Stood Still* (1951), *Ben Hur* (1959), *A Guide for the Married Man* (1967), *Guns for San Sebastian* (1968), *The Great Bank Robbery* (1969), *The Kremlin Letter, The Dunwich Horror* (both 1970), *Bedknobs and Broomsticks* (1971), and *Battle Beyond the Stars* (1980).

Among the films of Thomas Mitchell (1892–1962): *Six Cylinder Love* (1923), *Theodora Goes Wild* (1936), *Lost Horizon, The Hurricane* (both 1937), *Only Angels Have Wings* (1938), *Stagecoach* (Academy Award), *Mr. Smith Goes to Washington, The Hunchback of Notre Dame, Gone With the Wind* (all 1939), *Our Town* (1940), *Out of the Fog* (1941), *The Black Swan* (1942), *Bataan, Flesh and Fantasy* (both 1943), *The Sullivans, Wilson* (both 1944), *Adventure* (1945), *It's a Wonderful Life* (1946), *High*

Barbaree (1947), *Alias Nick Beal* (1949), *High Noon* (1952), *Destry* (1954), *Handle With Care* (1958), and *Pocketful of Miracles* (1961).

Among the films of Edward Everett Horton (1886–1970): *Too Much Business* (1922), *Ruggles of Red Gap* (1923), *The Nutcracker* (1926), *The Terror* (1928), *The Sap* (1929), *Holiday* (1930), *The Front Page* (1931), *Trouble in Paradise* (1932), *Soldiers of the King, Alice in Wonderland* (as Mad Hatter) (both 1933), *The Gay Divorcee, Top Hat* (both 1935), *The Man in the Mirror* (1936), *Lost Horizon* (1937), *Bluebeard's Eighth Wife* (1938), *Ziegfeld Girl, Here Comes Mr. Jordan* (both 1941), *The Magnificent Dope* (1942), *Thank Your Lucky Stars* (1943), *Summer Storm, San Diego I Love You* (both 1944), *Arsenic and Old Lace* (1942, released 1944), *Down to Earth* (1947), *The Story of Mankind* (1957), *Pocketful of Miracles* (1961), *The Perils of Pauline* (1967), *Cold Turkey* (1970), and others.

Among the films of Jane Wyatt (1912–): *One More River* (1934), *The Luckiest Girl in the World* (1936), *Lost Horizon* (1937), *Kisses for Breakfast* (1941), *The Kansan* (1942), *The Iron Road* (1943), *None But the Lonely Heart* (1944), *Boomerang, Gentlemen's Agreement* (both 1947), *Pitfall* (1948), *Bad Boy, Task Force* (both 1949), *Our Very Own* (1950), *The Man Who Cheated Himself* (1951), *Never Too Late* (1965), *Tom Sawyer* (TV, 1973), *Treasure of Matecumbe* (1976), others.

Among the films of John Howard (1913–): *Annapolis Farewell* (1935), *Lost Horizon, Bulldog Drummond Comes Back* (both 1937, and other B.D. films in series), *Disputed Passage* (1939), *The Philadelphia Story, The Invisible Woman* (1940), *The Mad Doctor* (1941), *The Undying Monster* (1942), *Isle of Missing Men* (1943), *The Fighting Kentuckian* (1949), *The High and the Mighty* (1954), *The Unknown Terror* (1958), *Destination Inner Space* (1966), *The Destructors* (1967), many others.

Among the films of Margo (1918–1985): *Crime Without Passion* (1933), *Winterset* (1936), *Lost Horizon* (1937), *The Leopard Man* (1943), *Gangway for Tomorrow* (1944), *Viva Zapata* (1952), *Who's Got the Action?* (1963), others.

James Hilton (1900–1954) and the Movies. Not only were many of Hilton's books turned into successful films, but he also wrote several of them and several other screenplays as well, including 1942's popular wartime drama, *Mrs. Miniver.*

Among the films of James Hilton: *Knight Without Armour, Lost Horizon* (both 1937), *Goodbye Mr. Chips, We Are Not Alone* (both 1939), *Random Harvest* (1942), *The Story of Dr. Wassell* (1943), *So Well Remembered* (1947), and more.

Cutting and Trimming in Film and Literature. There is much precedent for Frank Capra's elimination of the first two reels—about 20 minutes—of *Lost Horizon.* As far back as Mary Shelley's *Frankenstein*, creators of fiction struggled with the perfect length. In Shelley's case, she originally wanted to begin the book with Victor Frankenstein's creation of the monster, but her husband, the poet Percy Bysshe Shelley, convinced her (wrongly) to lead up to that momentous event.

Parts of *King Kong* (the spider sequence, see that chapter) were cut because they disrupted the flow of the film, and scenes showing a still-alive Dallas (the doomed Captain) woven into a cocoon of sorts to provide food for the creature in *Alien* (1979), were cut to speed up the film's pace. As with *King Kong*, the scene (Ripley obliterates him with the flame-thrower) was horrific and brought the film to a standstill.

When some film fanatics object to cuts, they fail to realize a basic truth of filmmaking (and novel writing): The audience won't miss what they don't know they're missing. And many cuts and trims drastically improve a film. The exciting, fast-paced action-adventure film *Gunga Din*, which I remember with fondness from my boyhood, has been restored— to its detriment. The restored scenes slow the film down and pad out its length unnecessarily.

Awards, Honors, Best Film Lists, Etc. In 1937, *Lost Horizon* was nominated for the following Academy Awards: Best Interior Decoration (Stephen Goosson); Best Film Editing (Gene Havlick, Gene Milford); and Best Supporting Actor (H.B. Warner). It won the first two. It also appeared on the *New York Times* Ten Best list for 1937, and is listed among the Fifty Most Significant American Films (Performing Arts Council of USC, 1972).

Popeye

The Comic Strip Hero. In 1936, *Flash Gordon*, artist Alex Raymond's popular comic strip hero, came to the screen in a 13-part serial directed by Frederick Stephani, and starring Buster Crabbe, Jean Rogers, Charles Middleton, Frank Shannon, and Priscilla Lawson. Cheaply done, the "chapter play" was a hit at the time and became an all-time camp classic. The two sequels were *Flash Gordon's Trip to Mars* (1938), and *Flash Gordon Conquers the Universe* (1940).

Dick Tracy, a 1937 Republic serial in 15 episodes, brought Chester Gould's famous police detective to cinema life. Directed by Ray Taylor and Alan James, and starring Ralph Byrd (as Tracy), Kay Hughes, Smiley Burnette, Lee Van Atta, and John Piccori, this cliffhanger saw Tracy bring an end to the terrorist activities of the notorious "Spider Gang." Tracy and company reappeared in a 1938 sequel, *Dick Tracy Returns*.

Chic Young's perennially popular comic strip *Blondie* arrived in movie theaters in 1938. Starring Arthur Lake as Dagwood, Penny Singleton as Blondie, Larry Simms as Baby Dumpling (later Alexander), Majorie Kent as Cookie, Jonathan Hale as Mr. Dithers, and Daisy as Daisy, and directed by Frank Strayer, this first filming spawned two dozen sequels before the line ran out in 1951.

Warren Hull was the eponymous *Mandrake the Magician* and Al Kikume was his sidekick Lothar in Columbia's 1939 serial. This 12-parter was directed by Sam Nelson and Norman Deming. There were many nefarious goings-on by a gang headed by "The Wasp," a master criminal seeking control of a radium-energy machine. Fortunately, his plans are foiled by the world-famous magician Mandrake.

That same year, 1939, also saw the release of two other serials starring comic strip heroes. The first to hit the theaters was Universal's 12-part chapter play, *Buck Rogers*, starring Larry "Buster" Crabbe, Constance Moore, Jackie Moran, Anthony Warde, and Henry Brandon. Buck and Buddy, our two heroes, crash in the Arctic and are kept alive for 500 years by "Nirvano" gas. They awaken to a world run by arch-gangster Killer Kane. Their efforts to overthrow Kane find Buddy and Buck visiting Saturn for help from the Saturians. After many advances and setbacks, Buck, Buddy, and Dr. Heuer (C. Montague Shaw) defeat Kane and his forces.

Later in 1939, *The Lone Ranger Rides Again*, a 15-parter from Republic, was released. Directed by old pros William Witney and John English, it starred Robert Livingston in the dual role of Bill Andrews/The Lone Ranger. Tonto was played by Chief Thunder Cloud, and J. Farrell MacDonald was baddie Craig Dolan.

The comic strip heroes kept coming to the silver screen. In 1940, it was *Terry and the Pirates*'s turn. Directed by James W. Horne, this 15-part Columbia effort starred William Tracy as Terry Lee, Granville Owen as Pat Ryan, and Joyce Bryant as Normandie Drake. Others in the cast included Allen Jung, Victor De Camp, Sheila Darcy, Dick Curtis, and J. Paul Jones. This action-packed cliffhanger had it all: lost civilizations, hidden jungle temples, a dragon lady, a pet gorilla, "Tiger Men," and a villain named Fang.

Republic's directing team of William Witney and John English were the men behind the camera for 1940's *Adventures of Red Ryder*, a western starring Don "Red" Barry, Noah Beery, and Tommy Cook (as Little Beaver). There was gunplay, doublecrossing, stagecoach races, land grabbing, and lots of riding around the studio's back lots.

One of the few comic strips to come to the screen in feature form during this time was 1940's *L'il Abner*, based on Al Capp's hugely successful characters. This Albert S. Rogell–directed short feature (78 minutes) included a great many silent film stars, among them Buster Keaton, Edgar Kennedy, Chester Conklin, Billy Bevan, and Al St. John. Despite the presence of these comedy greats, the laughs were few and far between.

A much more successful *L'il Abner* was the 1959 production. This Gene DePaul–Johnny Mercer musical, directed by Melvin Frank, was based on a long-running broadway hit and starred Peter Palmer as L'il Abner, the dim-witted but good-hearted Dogpatch hunk. Leslie Parrish was a luscious Daisy Mae, and others in the cast included Julie Newmar, Stella Stevens, Robert Strauss, Stubby Kaye as Marryin' Sam, and Billie Hayes as Mammy Yokum.

Back to the serials. Both *The Adventures of Smilin' Jack*, starring Tom Brown and Marjorie Lord, a 12-part Universal release, and *The Phantom*, a Columbia 15-parter starring Tom Tyler and Kenneth MacDonald, were released in 1943.

Brenda Starr, Reporter was a serial starring a heroine for a change. Directed by Wallace W. Fox for Columbia, this 15-parter starred Joan Woodbury as ace reporter Starr. Also featuring Kane Richmond and Syd Saylor, the story concerned a satchel of stolen money and a ruthless gang of criminals in pursuit of it.

Prince Valiant came to the screen in 1954 as a feature starring Robert Wagner. Henry Hathaway directed from a script by Dudley Nichols. This colorful adventure also featured James Mason, Janet Leigh, Debra Paget, Sterling Hayden, Victor McLaglen, Donald Crisp, and Brian Aherne.

A bomb called *Dondi* detonated on the nation's screens in 1961. Starring David Kory as the presumably cute war orphan, this Albert Zugsmith–directed film did nothing for star David Jannsen's career.

An overblown, over-budgeted, over-produced adaptation of a successful Broadway musical, 1982's *Annie* was a curiously lifeless version of *Little Orphan Annie*. Directed by John Huston and starring Albert Finney, Carol Burnett, Aileen Quinn (as Annie), Bernadette Peters, Tim Curry, Ann Reinking, and Geoffrey Holder, it's unlikely this film pleased anyone over the age of eight.

Films by the Stars and Crew of *Popeye*. Among the films of Robin Williams (1952–): *Popeye* (1980), *The World According to Garp* (1982), *The Survivors* (1983), *Moscow on the Hudson* (1984), *The Best of Times, Club Paradise* (both 1986), *Good Morning Vietnam* (1987).

Among the films of Robert Altman (1925–): *The Delinquents* (1955), *The James Dean Story* (1957), *Nightmare in Chicago* (1964), *Countdown, That Cold Day in the Park* (both 1968), *M*A*S*H, Brewster McCloud* (both 1970), *McCabe and Mrs. Miller* (1971), *Images, The Long Goodbye* (both 1972), *Thieves Like Us, California Split* (both 1974), *Nashville* (1975), *Buffalo Bill and the Indians* (1976), *The Late Show* (as producer), *Three Women* (both 1977), *Welcome to L.A.* (as producer), Remember My Name (as producer), *A Wedding, Quintet* (all 1978), *A Perfect Couple, Rich Kids* (as producer), and *Health* (all 1979), *Popeye* (1980), *Come Back to the Five and Dime, Jimmy Dean, Jimmy Dean* (1982), *Streamers* (1983), *Secret Honor* (1984), *Fool for Love* (1986), *Beyond Therapy* (1987).

Among the films of Shelley Duvall (1950–): *Brewster McCloud, McCabe and*

Mrs. Miller (1971), *Thieves Like Us* (1974), *Nashville* (1975), *Buffalo Bill and the Indians* (1976), *Annie Hall, Three Women* (both 1977), *The Shining, Popeye* (both 1980), *Time Bandits* (1981), *Roxanne* (1987).

Superman

Superheroes. *The Adventures of Captain Marvel* was a Republic Pictures 12-part serial released in 1941. Directed by William Witney and John English, it depicted the adventures of a caped superhero who was transformed from a young boy named Billy Batson into Captain Marvel by the magic word "Shazam!" (S is for Solomon's wisdom, H is for Hercules' strength, A is for Atlas' stamina, Z is for Zeus' power, A is for Achilles' heel, and M is for the speed of Mercury.)

Captain Marvel was played by the popular Tom Tyler, Frank Coghlan was the puny Billy Batson, and Nigel de Brulier was Shazam, the old mystic whose very name invokes the mighty Captain Marvel.

Tom Tyler returned as a mysterious masked hero in Columbia Pictures' 1943 serial *The Phantom.* Tyler was both the Phantom and Godfrey Prescott in this 15-parter directed by B. Reeves Eason.

The Batman, directed by Lambert Hillyer, was a 1943 serial in 15 parts. It starred Lewis Wilson as Bruce Wayne/Batman, Douglas Croft as Dick Grayson/Robin, J. Carrol Naish as Dr. Daka, and William Austin as Alfred the butler.

In 1944, a 15-part serial called *Captain America* (AKA *Return of Captain America*) was released. Dick Purcell played the dual role of Grant Gardner/Captain America, Lorna Gray was spunky Gail Richards, and Lionel Atwill was Dr. Maldor/Scarab. John English and Elmer Clifton directed.

Another Batman cliffhanger, *Batman and Robin* (AKA *The New Adventures of Batman and Robin*) was released by Columbia Pictures in 1949. Robert Lowery played Bruce Wayne/Batman, John Duncan was Dick Grayson/Robin, and B-movie great Lyle Talbot was Commissioner Gordon. The 15-parter was directed by Spencer Gordon Bennet.

Batman became a twice-weekly television show in 1966. This high camp series, which did much to sully the once-popular caped crusader, was played for the broadest laughs possible, and the first episode of each two-parter ended with a cliffhanger, *à la* old serials. The first double episode, "Hey Diddle Riddle/Smack in the Middle," featured Frank Gorshin as the Riddler and Jill St. John as Molly.

Adam West played Bruce Wayne/Batman, Burt Ward was Dick Grayson/Robin, Alan Napier was Alfred, Neil Hamilton was Commissioner Gordon, Madge Blake was Aunt Harriet Cooper, and Stanford Repp was Chief O'Hara. Yvonne Craig played Barbara Gordon/Batgirl from 1967 to 1968. Both West and Ward were so identified with their roles that their careers stalled out for many years after the series left the air.

Batman premiered in January 1966 and became an overnight sensation. Veteran movie and television stars competed for the honor of playing a guest villain or making a cameo appearance. However, *Batman* somehow lost some of its appeal over the first summer hiatus, and the ratings continued to decline precipitously until the series finally was cancelled in March of 1968.

A feature film *Batman,* starring West and Ward as well as Cesar Romero, Burgess Meredith, Frank Gorshin, and Lee Meriwether, was released in 1966 to indifferent response.

A made-for-TV movie, *Wonder Woman,* starring Cathy Lee Crosby as Wonder Woman, was aired in 1974. Directed by Vincent McEveety, this modernized version was not especially successful. Though a trained athlete, blonde Cathy Lee Crosby was not right for the part.

More successful was the television series *Wonder Woman,* which ran from 1976 until 1979. A "period piece," the series pitted raven-haired Lynda Carter, as Wonder Woman/Diana Prince, against various Nazi agents threatening the United States and the world during World War II. Not an athlete, Lynda Carter looked the part — which Cathy Lee did not. The series also starred Lyle Waggoner (late of the *Carol Burnett Show*) as Steve Trevor, and Richard Eastham as General Blankenship.

Captain America and *Captain America II,* television movies starring Reb Brown as Steve Rogers/Captain America, were aired in 1979. Rod Holcomb directed the first film. The second film, directed by Ivan Nagy, boasted suave Christopher Lee as Miguel.

Supergirl, a 1984 Salkind production, starred Helen Slater as the "Girl of Steel" and featured an all-star cast: Faye Dunaway, Peter O'Toole, Peter Cook, Brenda Vaccaro, Mia Farrow, Simon Ward, and Marc McClure. Still, the script and the direction, by Jeannot Szwarc, were found lacking by audiences and the film was a super bust in the United States, earning only $6 million domestically against an estimated negative cost of $30 million.

Awards, Honors, Best Film Lists, Etc. *Superman* was awarded the 1978 Academy Special Achievement Award (to Les Bowie, Colin Chilvers, Denys Coops, Roy Field, Derek Meddings, and Zoran Perisic for Special Visual Effects). The National Board of Review Awards for 1978 voted it "among the Best English-Language Films." In the British Academy Awards for 1978, it won Most Promising Newcomer (for Christopher Reeve) and the Michael Balcon Award (Outstanding British Contribution to Cinema) for Les Bowie, Colin Chilvers, Denys Coop, Roy Field, Derek Meddings, and Zoran Perisic for their special effects.

The Thief of Bagdad

Arabian Nights. *Aladdin and the Wonderful Lamp* (1917) was a silent version of the famous tale. Directed by S.A. Franklin and C.H. Franklin, it starred Elmo Lincoln (the first screen Tarzan), Buddy Messinger, and Gertrude Messinger.

Ali Baba Goes to Town (1937), a musical comedy, sent Eddie Cantor backwards in time and also starred Gypsy Rose Lee (under her real name Louise Hovick). Directed by David Butler, the film also featured Tony Martin, Roland Young (of *Topper*), and John Carradine.

Arabian Nights (1942) was directed by John Rawlins and starred John Hall, Sabu, Maria Montez, Turhan Bey, and Shemp Howard (of The Three Stooges) as Sinbad. Slight but corny fun.

Ali Baba and the Forty Thieves (1944), directed by Arthur Lubin, was a Technicolor romp starring the ubiquitous Jon Hall and Maria Montez, and featuring Turhan Bey and Andy Devine. A prince, Ali Baba (Hall), pretends to be a thief to regain his crown.

A Thousand and One Nights (1945) starred Cornel Wilde as Aladdin and featured Evelyn Keyes as a female genie. Directed by Alfred E. Green, and more than slightly tongue-in-cheek, it also starred Phil Silvers, horn-rimmed glasses and all, as Wilde's sidekick. Rex Ingram played a role similar to his part in *Thief.*

Sinbad the Sailor (1947) starred Douglas Fairbanks, Jr., who was attempting to duplicate his famous father's success in adventure and fantasy films. This stage-bound, often turgid, Technicolor production was directed by Richard Wallace and featured Maureen O'Hara, Anthony Quinn, and Walter Slezak. Sinbad searches for the treasure of Alexander.

Aladdin and His Lamp (1951) featured John Sands as Aladdin and starred Patricia Medina and Noreen Nash. Boring version of the classic tale.

Lucille Ball starred in *The Magic Carpet* (1951) in her pre–*I Love Lucy* days. Directed by Lew Landers, this routine effort concerned the Caliph's son's return as the Scarlet Falcon. Also in the cast were John Agar and Raymond Burr.

Son of Ali Baba, starring that son of Arabia, Tony Curtis (as Kashma Baba), and directed by Kurt Neumann was released in 1952. Piper Laurie was also in this lighthearted romp.

France's *Ali Baba and the Forty Thieves* was a 1954 version of the classic tale directed by Jacques Becker and starring the great French comic Fernandel.

Another son showed up in 1955's 3-D release of *Son of Sinbad*. This time it was Dale Robertson in the title role, fighting to save Sally Forrest from evil Vincent Price.

Sabu and the Magic Ring (1957) saw the return of Sabu to the genre that made him a star. This version starred the fine black actor William Marshall as the genie who appeared when Sabu rubbed the ring. Directed by George Blair, the story and the acting were tired and listless.

The Seventh Voyage of Sinbad (1958) is one of the best and most exciting films in the subgenre. Directed by Nathan Juran, it starred Kerwin Matthews as a resourceful and brave Sinbad, Kathryn Grant (before she became Mrs. Bing Crosby), Torin Thatcher as the evil magician Sokurah, and Richard Eyer as the youthful genie. Ray Harryhausen's superior stop-motion model animation gives Sinbad some marvelously realistic monsters, like cyclops and dragons, to battle. The film features the justly famous "living skeleton" sword fight and a great musical score by Bernard Herrmann.

Alas, *The Wizard of Baghdad* (1960) is no *Seventh Voyage*. Starring Dick Shawn as the genie, and Diane Baker as the beautiful princess, this George Sherman–directed feature means to be a satire of the subgenre, but is, instead, a yawner.

The Wonder of Aladdin (1961), starring Donald O'Connor as Aladdin and Vittorio De Sica as the genie, aren't all that wonderful. But the picture, directed by Henry Levin, is funny enough for young kids.

Guy Williams, who found fame among the kiddie set as the star of Walt Disney's television series *Zorro*, played the title role in *Captain Sinbad* (1963), a well-made United States/West German production directed by SF and adventure great Byron Haskin. Swashbuckling and exciting, it's a good rainy afternoon movie.

Sword of Ali Baba (1965) was a remake of 1944's *Ali Baba and the Forty Thieves* directed by Virgil Vogel and starring Peter Mann in the title role. Gavin MacLeod, who played Hulagu Khan, was a pudgy character actor stuck in villainous roles before hitting television stardom in *The Mary Tyler Moore Show* and playing the romantic lead in the long-running series *The Love Boat*.

A Spanish version of *A Thousand and One Nights* was released in 1968. Directed by Joe Lacy (Jose Paria Elorrita), it starred Jeff Cooper, Raf Vallone, and Luciana Paluzzi, and featured all the standard ingredients—a handsome hero, a flying carpet, and an evil vizier (boo!).

Ray Harryhausen returned to Sinbad with 1974's *Golden Voyage of Sinbad*, starring John Philip Law as the peripatetic sailor, cult favorite Caroline Munro as his main squeeze, Margiane, and TV's fourth Doctor Who, Tom Baker, as the evil magician Koura. Harryhausen's effects, including a sword battle with a six-armed living statue, are marvelous, and the direction, by Gordon Hessler, is fine.

In *Sinbad and the Eye of the Tiger* (1977), however, Ray Harryhausen has trotted out his all-purpose hero once too often. Starring a too-pretty Patrick Wayne as Sinbad—and featuring *another* Dr. Who, Patrick Troughton—this Sam Wanamaker-directed picture is notable for its effectively animated baboon and for Peter Mahew (Chewbacca the Wookie in *Star Wars*) in a small part as a mechanical minotaur.

Directed by Kevin Conner, 1979's *Arabian Adventure* is yet another version of the Arabian Nights tale, featuring Christopher Lee, Milo O'Shea, Peter Cushing, and Mickey Rooney in a fun-filled picture pleasing to both adults and kids.

Films by the Stars and Crew of *The Thief of Bagdad.* Among the films of Sir Alexander Korda: *The Duped Journalist* (1914), *Tales of the Typewriter* (1916), *Magic* (1917), *Yamata* (1919), *A Vanished World* (1922), *The Stolen Bride* (1927), *Her Private Life* (1929), *The Princess and the Plumber* (1931), *Marius* (1931), *Wedding Rehearsal* (1932), *Men of Tomorrow* (1933), *The Rise of Catherine the Great* (1934), *The Private Life of Don Juan* (1934), *The Scarlet Pimpernel* (1934), *Sanders of the River, The Ghost Goes West* (both 1935), *Things to Come, Men Are Not Gods, Rembrandt* (all 1936), *The Man Who Could Work Miracles* (1937), *The Divorce of Lady X* (1938), *Q Planes, The Four Feathers, The Spy in Black* (all 1939), *Conquest of the Air* (1940), *That Hamilton Woman* (1941), *To Be or Not to Be, Jungle Book* (both 1942), *Perfect Strangers* (1945), *Anna Karenina, The Winslow Boy, The Fallen Idol* (all 1948), *The Third Man* (1949), *Seven Days to Noon* (1950), *Tales of Hoffman, The Wonder Kid* (both 1951), *The Sound Barrier* (1952), *The Captain's Paradise* (1953), *Hobson's Choice, The Belles of St. Trinian's* (both 1954), *The Man Who Loved Redheads* (with John Justin, 1955), *Richard III* (1956), and many others. After 1940, Korda served mainly as executive producer for London Films.

William Cameron Menzies (1896–1957) will always be remembered for his superior art direction, notably for the original *Thief of Bagdad*, and especially for *Gone With the Wind*. As a director, Menzies fared less well, with only two of his efforts rising above the disappointing: *Things to Come* and *Invaders From Mars*. Two of his films are camp classics—*The Whip Hand* and *The Maze*.

As art director he also made: *Robin Hood* (1922), *The Thief of Bagdad* (1924), *Tempest* (1927), *The Dove* (Academy Award, 1928), *Bulldog Drummond* (1929), *Alice in Wonderland* (1933), *Things to Come* (and dir., 1936), *The Adventures of Tom Sawyer* (1938), *Gone With the Wind* (1939), *Our Town, Foreign Correspondent* (both 1940), *King's Row* (1941), *For Whom the Bell Tolls* (1943), *Ivy* (1947), *Arch of Triumph* (1948), *Around the World in Eighty Days* (1956), and others.

As director Menzies made *Always Goodbye, The Spiders* (both 1931), *Almost Married, Chandu the Magician* (both 1932), *Wharf Angel* (1934), *Things to Come* (1936), *The Green Cockatoo* (1940), *Address Unknown* (1944), *Drums in the Deep South, The Whip Hand* (both 1951), *The Maze* (1953), and *Invaders from Mars* (1954).

Sabu (Dastagir, 1924–1963) was soon reduced to playing roles in various grade-B films as his career languished after *Jungle Book*. Several films, like 1942's *Arabian Nights*, tried with minor success to cash in on *Thief*. Appealing as a teenager, Sabu, like many other child stars, did not age well. He died of a heart attack at age 59.

Among the films of Sabu: *The Drum* (1938), *The Thief of Bagdad* (1940), *The Jungle Book, Arabian Nights* (both 1942), *White Savage* (1943), *Cobra Woman*

(1944), *Tangier, Black Narcissus* (both 1946), *The End of the River* (1947), *Maneater of Kumaon* (1948), *Song of India* (1949), *Hello, Elephant* (1952), *Jaguar, Jungle Hell* (both 1956), *The Mystery of Three Continents* (1959), *Herrin der Welt* (West German, 1960), *Rampage* and *A Tiger Walks* (both 1963).

Among the films of Conrad Veidt (1893–1943): *Five Sinister Stories, The Cabinet of Dr. Caligari* (both 1919), *The Hunchback and the Dancer, The Indian Tomb, Der Januskopf* (all 1920), *Waxworks* (1924), *Lucrezia Borgia, The Hands of Orlac* (both 1925), *The Student of Prague* (1926), *The Beloved Rogue, The Man Who Laughs, The Last Performance* (all 1927), *Rasputin* (1930), *Congress Dances* (1931), *Rome Express* (1932), *The Wandering Jew, F.P. 1 Does Not Respond* (both 1933), *Jew Suss, Bella Donna* (both 1934), *The Passing of the Third Floor Back* (1935), *Under the Red Robe* (1936), *Dark Journey, The Chess Player* (both 1937), *The Spy in Black* (1939), *Contraband, The Thief of Bagdad, Escape* (all 1940), *A Woman's Face, Whistling in the Dark, All Through the Night* (all 1941), *The Men in Her Life, Nazi Agent, Casablanca* (all 1942), and *Above Suspicion* (1943).

June Duprez should have become a star after *Thief*, but Merle Oberon, Korda's wife, disliked her and Hollywood sycophants apparently put Duprez on an informal blacklist. Still beautiful decades after *Thief*'s release, Duprez lives in London. Among her films: *The Crimson Circle* (1936), *The Spy in Black, The Four Feathers* (both 1939), *The Thief of Bagdad* (1940), *None But the Lonely Heart* (1944), *And Then There Were None* (1945), *Calcutta* (1946), *That Brennan Girl* (1947), and *The Kinsey Report* (1963).

Rex Ingram (1895–1969), like Sabu, found he was repeating himself in films like 1945's *A Thousand and One Nights*. Among the films of Rex Ingram: *Hearts in Dixie* (1929), *The Sign of the Cross* (1932), *King Kong, The Emperor Jones* (both 1933), *Captain Blood* (1935), *The Green Pastures* (1936), *Huckleberry Finn* (1939), *The Thief of Bagdad* (1940), *The Talk of the Town* (1942), *Sahara, Cabin in the Sky* (both 1943), *Dark Waters* (1944), *King Solomon's Mines* (1950), *Tarzan's Hidden Jungle* (1955), *The Ten Commandments, Congo Crossing* (both 1956), *God's Little Acre* (1958), *Watusi* (1959), *Desire in the Dust, Elmer Gantry* (both 1960), *Hurry Sundown, Journey to Shiloh,* (both 1967), and others.

Among the films of John Justin: *The Thief of Bagdad* (1940), *The Gentle Sex* (1943), *Journey Together* (1945), *Call of the Blood* (1947), *The Sound Barrier* (1951), *Melba* (1953), *The Man Who Loved Redheads* (1955), *Safari, Island in the Sun* (both 1956), *The Spider's Web* (1961), *Savage Messiah* (1972), *Valentino* (1977), *The Big Sleep* (1978), *Trenchcoat* (1983), and others.

Co-director Michael Powell, born in Canterbury in 1905, has divided his career between the films of realism like *One of Our Aircraft Is Missing* (1943) and films of fantasy like *A Matter of Life and Death* (1946), *The Red Shoes* (1948), and *The Tales of Hoffmann* (1955). Powell is recognized as one of the masters of the color film, though his most personal—and artistically and morally troubling—film was 1960's black-and-white film, *Peeping Tom*. *Peeping Tom*, about a photographer who films the death throes of his female victims as he impales them on the sharpened tip of his camera tripod, was condemned at the time of its release, but today it is considered a disturbing look at voyeurism and the art of filmmaking—itself a sanctioned form of voyeurism. Among Michael Powell's other films: *The Edge of the World* (1937), *49th Parallel* (1941), *The Life and Death of Colonel Blimp* (1943), *Black Narcissus* (1946), *Honeymoon* (1961), *Age of Consent* (1969), and many others.

Miklos Rozsa (1907–) has scored many great films, and he won Academy Awards for his music for *Spellbound* (1945), *A Double Life* (1947), and *Ben Hur* (1959).

Awards, Honors, Best Film Lists, Etc. *The Thief of Bagdad* won three Academy Awards in 1941: Best Cinematography (Color), Georges Perinal; Best Interior Decoration (Color), Vincent Korda; and Best Special Effects, Lawrence Butler and Jack Whitney. It was also nominated for Best Original Score (Miklos Rozsa).

Time Bandits

Child as Hero. *Time Bandits* shares with *The 5,000 Fingers of Dr. T.* a number of the films on its list of "A Child's Fantasy."

Other films that might fall into this subgenre include the enormously successful *E.T. — The Extraterrestrial*, Steven Spielberg's 1982 science-fiction fantasy of a young boy who befriends a little lost alien. Starring Henry Thomas as the youthful hero, ably abetted and assisted by his brother and sister (Robert MacNaughton and Drew Barrymore), this wondrous work showed the universal appeal of love and friendship.

Joe Dante's underrated space fantasy *Explorers* was one of 1985's less successful films. However, its story of three young boys who make their own spacecraft from junk and venture forth to meet aliens is a sweet and clever enterprise.

Also a box-office underachiever, Walt Disney's 1986 fantasy *The Flight of the Navigator* offered kid-sized adventure galore — and the voice of Pee Wee Herman as well. Director Randal Kleiser's tale of a twelve-year-old boy who disappears in 1978 only to turn up the same age eight years later starred young Joey Cramer. His parents were played by Cliff De Young and Veronica Cartwright, and Howard Hesseman was on hand as a NASA scientist.

Two other unsuccessful 1986 films presented kids and teens as heroic: *Space Camp*, with Kate Capshaw; and *Solarbabies*.

Films by the Stars of *Time Bandits*. Among the films of Sean Connery: *No Road Back* (1956), *Hell Drivers, Time Lock, Action of the Tiger* (all 1957), *Another Time Another Place* (1958), *Darby O'Gill and the Little People, Tarzan's Greatest Adventure* (both 1959), *The Frightened City, Operation Snafu* (both 1961), *The Longest Day, Dr. No* (both 1962), *From Russia With Love* (1963), *Marnie, Woman of Straw, Goldfinger* (all 1964), *The Hill, Thunderball* (both 1965), *A Fine Madness* (1966), *You Only Live Twice* (1967), *Shalako* (1968), *The Molly Maguires* (1970), *The Red Tent, The Anderson Tapes, Diamonds Are Forever* (all 1971), *The Offense* (1973), *Zardoz, Murder on the Orient Express* (both 1974), *The Terrorists, The Wind and the Lion, The Man Who Would Be King* (all 1975), *Robin and Marian, The Next Man* (both 1976), *A Bridge Too Far* (1977), *Meteor* (1978), *The Great Train Robbery, Cuba* (both 1979), *Outland* (1981), *Five Weeks One Summer, Wrong Is Right* (both 1982), *Never Say Never Again* (as James Bond once again, 1983), *Sword of the Valiant* (1984), *The Name of the Rose* (1986), *The Untouchables* (1987), and others.

Topper

The Ghost in Films. Naturally, this subgenre boasts a very full roster. A number of entries follow:

Ghost Train (1931, with Jack Hulbert). Train passengers stranded in a haunted train station. Remade in 1941.

The Ghost Walks (1934, with John Miljan). Phony party ghost's place taken by a real one.

The Return of Peter Grimm (1935, with Lionel Barrymore). A man returns as a ghost to check on how his family is coping without him. An earlier version was released in 1925.

The Scoundrel (1935 with Noel Coward; Academy Award for original story). A cynical writer's ghost returns to find the true meaning of life.

Earthbound (1940, with Warner Baxter). The ghost of a murder victim aids his widow in bringing the killer to justice.

The Ghost Breakers (1940, with Bob Hope and Paulette Goddard; remade in 1953 as *Scared Stiff* starring Martin and Lewis). Chills and laughs in an eerie Cuban mansion.

The Remarkable Andrew (1942, with William Holden). The ghosts of Andrew Jackson and others come to the aid of a framed city bookkeeper.

A Guy Named Joe (1944, with Spencer Tracy). Ghostly flyer returns to aid pilot Van Johnson during World War II.

The Uninvited (1944, with Ray Milland and Gail Russell). Returning to her mother's house, a girl is haunted by an apparently evil spirit.

Ghost Catchers (1944, with Olsen and Johnson). Wacky duo assists Southern colonel and family in a haunted mansion.

Halfway House (1944, with Sally Ann Howes). Interesting fantasy concerns group of people brought together in an inn which was destroyed by bombs a year before.

A Place of One's Own (1944, with James Mason). Elderly couple's companion is possessed by the ghost of a long-dead girl.

Ziegfeld Follies (1944—released 1946, with Fred Astaire and William Powell). All-star musical is introduced by Ziegfeld's ghost in heaven. Uneven, but Fred Astaire dances.

Wonder Man (1945, with Danny Kaye). Two twins—one serious, one a nightclub performer. When the entertainer is killed, his brother must take his place and is helped by his sibling's ghost.

The Unseen (1945, with Joel McCrea). Governess is haunted by strange mystery.

Dead of Night (1945, with Michael Redgrave). A gathering of people under mysterious circumstances, with several strange tales told. Brilliant performance by Michael Redgrave as a ventriloquist harrassed by his murderous dummy.

The Time of Their Lives (1946, with Abbott and Costello). Revolutionary ghosts haunt country estate.

Curse of the Cat People (1946, with Kent Smith). Atmospheric sequel to the classic *Cat People*.

Ghosts of Berkeley Square (1947, with Robert Morley). Two ghosts are doomed to haunt a house until it is visited by royalty.

Portrait of Jennie (1949, with Jennifer Jones and Joseph Cotton). A penniless artist is inspired by a mysterious girl he meets under strange circumstances.

You Never Can Tell (1951, with Dick Powell). A murdered dog returns in the form of a human private detective to expose his killer.

Ghost Chasers (1951, with Leo Gorcey and Huntz Hall). Programmer with those popular nitwits, the Bowery Boys, up against the supernatural.

Pandora and the Flying Dutchman (1951, with James Mason). Ava Gardner falls in love with ghostly sea captain Mason and dies so she can be with him.

Ghost Ship (1952, with Hazel Court). Yacht haunted by a murdered woman.

Francis in the Haunted House (1956, with Mickey Rooney). The talking mule, minus usual partner Donald O'Connor, takes on ghosts.

The Headless Ghost (1958, with Clive Revill). Students in haunted house.

The Invisible Creature (1959, with Sandra Dorne). Ghost complicates murder plot.

House on Haunted Hill (1959, with Vincent Price). Guests must spend the night in spooky mansion to win $50,000 each.

The Ghost of Dragstrip Hollow (1959, with Jody Fair). Hotrod gang and haunted house.

Thirteen Ghosts (1960, with Charles Herbert). Family inherits haunted house replete with a spooky housekeeper—Margaret Hamilton, *Oz*'s wicked witch.

Tormented (1960, with Richard Carlson). Low-budget effort from director Bert I. Gordon.

The Innocents (1961, with Deborah Kerr). Version of Henry James' novel *The Turn of the Screw*, with children being possessed by dead servants.

The Ghost and Mr. Chicken (1965, with Don Knotts). Unassuming comedy with a small-town reporter finding scares in an eerie mansion.

The Ghost in the Invisible Bikini (1966, with Tommy Kirk and Boris Karloff). A-I nonsense about a motorcycle gang and a corpse.

Blackbeard's Ghost (1968, with Peter Ustinov). The pirate's ghost helps protect his descendants' home from takeover by gangsters in this Disney romp.

Scrooge (1971, with Albert Finney and Alec Guinness). Dickens' classic tale as a so-so musical.

The Legend of Hell House (1973, with Roddy McDowall). Researchers study occult phenomena in haunted house.

The Ghost of Flight 401 (TVM, 1978, with Gary Lockwood). Ghostly pilot Ernest Borgnine turns up in the cockpit.

Ghost Story (1981, with Fred Astaire). Flabby rendition of Peter Straub's horrific novel.

Ghostbusters (1984, with Bill Murray). Ghosts and spirits of the undead in modern Manhattan against a trio of ghostbusters. Great special effects helped this comedy to reap millions.

Films by the Stars and Crew of *Topper*. Among the films of Norman Z. McLeod: *Monkey Business* (1931), *Horse Feathers* (1932), *If I Had a Million* (episode), *Alice in Wonderland* (both 1933), *It's a Gift* (1934), *Pennies from Heaven* (1936), *Merrily We Live* (1938), *Panama Hattie* (1941), *The Kid from Brooklyn* (1946), *The Secret Life of Walter Mitty, The Paleface* (both 1947), *My Favorite Spy* (1951), *Never Wave at a WAC* (1953), *Cassanova's Big Night* (1954), *Alias Jesse James* (1959), and others.

The films of Cary Grant: *This Is the Night, Sinners in the Sun, Merrily We Go to Hell, Devil and the Deep, Blonde Venus, Hot Saturday, Madame Butterfly* (all 1932), *She Done Him Wrong, Woman Accused, The Eagle and the Hawk, Gambling Ship, I'm No Angel, Alice in Wonderland, Thirty-Day Princess* (all 1933), *Born to Be Bad, Kiss and Make Up, Ladies Should Listen, Enter Madame* (all 1934), *Wings in the Dark, Last Outpost, Sylvia Scarlett* (all 1935), *Big Brown Eyes, Suzy, Wedding Present, Romance and Riches* (all 1936), *When You're in Love, Toast of New York, Topper, The Awful Truth* (all 1937), *Bringing Up Baby, Holiday* (both 1938), *Gunga Din, Only Angels Have Wings, In Name Only* (all 1939), *His Girl Friday, My Favorite Wife, The Howards of Virginia, The Philadelphia Story* (all 1940), *Penny Serenade, Suspicion* (both 1941), *Talk of the Town, Once Upon a Honeymoon* (both 1942), *Mr. Lucky, Destination Tokyo* (both 1943), *Once Upon a Time, Arsenic and Old Lace, None But the Lonely Heart* (all 1944), *Night and Day* (1945), *Notorious* (1946), *The Bachelor and the Bobby Soxer, The Bishop's Wife* (both 1947), *Mr. Blandings Builds His Dream House, Every Girl Should Be Married* (both 1948), *I Was a Male War Bride* (1949),

Crisis (1950), *People Will Talk* (1951), *Room for One More*, *Monkey Business* (both 1952), *Dream Wife* (1953), *To Catch a Thief* (1955), *The Pride and the Passion*, *An Affair to Remember*, *Kiss Them for Me* (all 1957), *Indiscreet*, *Houseboat* (both 1958), *North By Northwest*, *Operation Petticoat* (both 1959), *The Grass Is Greener* (1960), *That Touch of Mink* (1962), *Charade* (1963), *Father Goose* (1964), and *Walk, Don't Run* (1966).

Among the films of Roland Young: *Sherlock Holmes, Moriarity* (both 1922), *The Unholy Night* (1929), *Madame Satan, New Moon* (both 1930), *One Hour With You, Wedding Rehearsal, The Guardsman, David Copperfield* (all 1932), *His Double Life* (1933), *Ruggles of Red Gap* (1934), *One Rainy Afternoon, The Man Who Could Work Miracles* (both 1936), *Call It a Day, King Solomon's Mines, Topper* (all 1937), *Ali Baba Goes to Town, Sailing Along* (both 1938), *The Young in Heart, Topper Takes a Trip* (both 1939), *No No Nanette, The Philadelphia Story* (both 1940), *Flame of New Orleans, Topper Returns* (both 1941), *The Lady Has Plans, They All Kissed the Bride, Tales of Manhattan* (all 1942), *Forever and a Day* (1943), *Standing Room Only* (1944), *And Then There Were None* (1945), *Bond Street* (1947), *The Great Lover* (1949), *Let's Dance* (1950), *St. Benny the Dip* (1951), *That Man from Tangier* (1953), and others.

Other Actors in *Topper.* Billie Burke (1885–1970) was born Mary William Ethelbert Appleton Burke. A stage star who married Florenz Ziegfeld, Miss Burke made her screen debut in 1916 in *Gloria's Romance.* From the 1930s on, she played mainly society matrons, but she is best remembered for her role of Glinda, the good witch, in *The Wizard of Oz* (1939).

Arthur Lake, born Arthur Silverlake in 1905, played the harassed elevator boy/bellboy the Kerbys delight in mystifying. His *Blondie* film series (28 features over 12 years) in which he played Dagwood Bumstead, started in 1938, the year after *Topper* came out.

Hedda Hopper (1890–1966), who played Mrs. Styvesant, was born Elda Furry. She began her acting career in the silent era with *Virtuous Wives* (1919), but gained fame and notoriety as one of Hollywood's most powerful gossip columnists.

Ward Bond (1903–1960) appeared in many John Ford and John Wayne movies as either a villain or a two-fisted, hard-drinking Irishman. He was a dependable character actor in films (like *The Searchers*, 1956), but he did not achieve stardom until he starred on television in *Wagon Train* in the late 1950s. Bond had the smallest of bit parts in *Topper*—he was one of the cabbies who gets into a fight with Cosmo and the Kerbys.

Topper on Television. *Topper*, which first aired on CBS October 9, 1953, ran for two seasons on that network, then one on ABC, and as a summer replacement on NBC in 1956. Ann Jeffreys was Marion, Robert Sterling was George, and Leo G. Carroll was Cosmo Topper. The Kerbys also had a ghostly St. Bernard named Neil.

The Wizard of Oz

Films by the Stars of *The Wizard of Oz.* Judy Garland (1922–1969) was born Frances Gumm to vaudeville-performing parents. She became a phenomenal success, with a devoted cult following, but could not cope with the stresses of her private life. The films of Judy Garland: *Every Sunday* (live short), *Pigskin Parade* (both 1936), *Broadway Melody of 1938* (1937), *Thoroughbreds Don't Cry, Everybody Sing, Listen Darling, Love Finds Andy Hardy* (all 1938), *The Wizard of Oz, Babes in Arms, Andy Hardy Meets a Debutante* (all 1939), *Strike Up the Band, Little Nellie Kelly* (both 1940), *Ziegfeld Girl, Life Begins for Andy Hardy, Babes on Broadway* (all

1941), *For Me and My Gal, Presenting Lily Mars, Girl Crazy* (all 1942), *Thousands Cheer* (1943), *Meet Me in St. Louis* (1944), *Ziegfeld Follies, The Clock* (both 1945), *The Harvey Girls, Till the Clouds Roll By* (both 1946), *The Pirate* (1947), *Easter Parade, Words and Music* (both 1948), *In the Good Old Summertime* (1949), *Summer Stock* (1950), *A Star Is Born* (1954), *Judgment at Nuremberg* (1960), *A Child Is Waiting* (1962), and *I Could Go on Singing* (British, 1963).

Ray Bolger (1904–1987) is best known as the Scarecrow in *Oz*, but he also scored many Broadway successes, including *Where's Charley*. His film appearances were uniformly excellent, but the movies didn't know what to make of him—a problem shared by Bert Lahr. The last living principal actor in *Oz*, Ray Bolger died in January 1987.

The films of Ray Bolger: *The Great Ziegfeld* (1936), *Rosalie* (1937), *Sweethearts* (1938), *The Wizard of Oz* (1939), *Sunny* (1941), *Stage Door Canteen* (1943), *Four Jacks and a Jill* (1944), *The Harvey Girls* (1946), *Look for the Silver Lining* (1949), *Where's Charley, April in Paris* (both 1952), *Babes in Toyland* (1960), *The Daydreamer* (1966), *The Entertainer* (TV, 1975), *The Captains and the Kings* (TV, 1976), *Heaven Only Knows* (TV), *The Runner Stumbles, Just You and Me Kid* (all 1979), and *That's Dancing* (1984).

Among the films of Jack Haley (1899–1979): *Follow Thru* (1930), *Sitting Pretty* (1933), *Poor Little Rich Girl* (1936), *Rebecca of Sunnybrook Farm, Alexander's Ragtime Band* (both 1938), *The Wizard of Oz* (1939), *Moon Over Miami* (1941), *Higher and Higher* (1943), *Scared Stiff* (1944), *People Are Funny* (1945), *Vacation in Reno* (1947), and *Norwood* (1969).

Among the films of Margaret Hamilton (1902–1985): *Another Language* (1933), *These Three* (1936), *The Wizard of Oz* (1939), *Invisible Woman* (1941), *State of the Union* (1948), *Thirteen Ghosts* (1960), *Rosie* (1967), *The Anderson Tapes*, and *Brewster McCloud* (both 1971).

Among the films of Bert Lahr (Irving Lahrheim, 1895–1967): *Faint Heart, Flying High* (both 1931), *Zaza, The Wizard of Oz* (both 1939), *Ship Ahoy* (1942), *Always Leave Them Laughing* (1949), *Mr. Universe* (1951), *Rose Marie* (1954), *The Second Greatest Sex* (1956), and *The Night They Raided Minsky's* (1968).

Awards, Honors, Best Film Lists, Etc. In the Academy Awards for 1939, *The Wizard of Oz* took Best Song (Harold Arlen and E.Y. Harburg, "Over the Rainbow"), Best Original Score (Herbert Stothart), and a Special Oscar for Judy Garland, "for her outstanding performance as a screen juvenile during the past year." It was nominated for Best Picture but lost to *Gone With the Wind*.

According to the American Film Institute Survey (1977), *Oz* is among the Top Ten Greatest American Films. On the list of the Fifty Most Significant American Films (Performing Arts Council of the University of Southern California panel of film producers and critics), *Oz* is number 27.

Bibliography

Books

Armes, Roy. *A Critical History of British Cinema*. New York: Oxford University Press, 1978.
Bettelheim, Bruno. *The Uses of Enchantment*. New York: Alfred A. Knopf, 1976.
Brooks, Tim, and Marsh, Earle. *The Complete Directory to Prime Time Network TV Shows, 1946 to Present*. New York: Ballantine, 1979.
Brosnan, John. *Movie Magic*. New York: Plume, 1976.
Campbell, J.F. *The Celtic Dragon Myth*. Edinburgh: John Grant, 1911.
Capra, Frank. *The Name Above the Title*. New York: Macmillan, 1971.
Cline, William C. *In the Nick of Time*. Jefferson, N.C.: McFarland, 1984.
Cocteau, Jean. (Edited and annotated by Robert M. Hammond.) *Beauty and the Beast: Scenario and Dialogs*. New York: New York University Press, 1970.
Culhane, John. *Special Effects in the Movies*. New York: Ballantine, 1981.
Doyle, Brian. *Who's Who of Children's Literature*. New York: Schocken, 1968.
Dunn, Linwood G., and Turner, George E. *The ASC Treasury of Visual Effects*. Hollywood: ASC, 1983.
Editors of Time-Life Books. *The Enchanted World*. Alexandria, VA: Time-Life, 1984.
Eyles, Allen. *The World of Oz*. Tucson, Ariz.: HPBooks, 1985.
Feiffer, Jules. *The Great Comic Book Heroes*. New York: Bonanza, 1965.
Finch, Christopher. *The Making of* The Dark Crystal, *Creating a Unique Film*. New York: Holt, Rinehart, and Winston, 1983.
Fuller, Muriel. *More Junior Authors*. New York: H.W. Wilson, 1963.
Glatzer, Richard, and Raeburn, John, eds. *Frank Capra—The Man and His Films*. University of Michigan Press, 1975.
Goldner, Orville, and Turner, George E. *The Making of King Kong*. New York: Barnes, 1975.
Gottesman, Ronald, and Geduld, Harry, eds. *The Girl in the Hairy Paw*. New York: Avon, 1976.
Halliwell, Leslie. *Halliwell's Film and Video Guide*. 5th edition. New York: Scribner's, 1986.
_____. *Halliwell's Filmgoer's and Video Viewer's Companion*. 8th edition. New York: Scribner's, 1984.
Harmetz, Aljean. *The Making of the Wizard of Oz*. New York: Alfred A. Knopf, 1977.
Harryhausen, Ray. *Film Fantasy Scrapbook*. Cranbury, N.J.: Barnes, 1972.
Hayes, R.M. *Trick Cinematography*. Jefferson, N.C.: McFarland, 1986.
Hilton, James. *Lost Horizon*. 49th printing. New York: Pocket Books, 1961.
Hogarth, Peter, and Clery, Val. *Dragons*. New York: Viking, 1979.
Holiday, Frederick William. *The Dragon and the Disc*. New York: W.W. Norton, 1973.

Howard, Robert E., and de Camp, L. Sprague. *Conan.* New York: Ace Fantasy, 1984.
_____. *Conan the Freebooter.* New York: Ace Fantasy, 1984.
_____. *Conan the Wanderer.* New York: Ace Fantasy, 1984.
Kael, Pauline. *Kiss Kiss Bang Bang.* Boston: Atlantic Monthly/Little, Brown, 1968.
Katz, Ephraim. *The Film Encyclopedia.* New York: Perigee, 1982.
Keylin, Arleen, and Bent, Christine, eds. *The New York Times at the Movies.* New York: Arno, 1979.
Kirkpatrick, D.L. *Twentieth-Century Authors.* New York: St. Martin's, 1983.
Knight, Damon. *In Search of Wonder.* Chicago: Advent, 1967.
Korda, Michael. *Charmed Lives.* New York: Random House, 1979.
Lahr, John. *Notes on a Cowardly Lion.* New York: Limelight, 1984.
Langman, Larry. *A Guide to American Screenwriters: The Sound Era, 1929–1982.* Vol. 1. New York: Garland, 1984.
Leese, Elizabeth. *Costume Design in the Movies.* New York: Frederick Ungar, 1977.
Lehner, Ernst and Johanna. *A Fantastic Bestiary.* New York: Tudor, 1969.
Lentz, Harris M., III. *Science Fiction, Horror and Fantasy Film and Television Credits.* 2 Vols. Jefferson, N.C.: McFarland, 1983.
Lovelace, Delos W. *King Kong.* New York: Ace, 1976.
Lum, Peter. *Fabulous Beasts.* New York: Pantheon, 1951.
Maland, Charles J. *Frank Capra.* Boston: Twayne, 1980.
Maltin, Leonard, ed. *TV Movies and Video Guide.* New York: Signet/N.A.L., 1986.
Medved, Harry and Michael. *The Hollywood Hall of Shame.* New York: Perigee, 1984.
Nash, Jay Robert, and Ross, Stanley Ralph. *The Motion Picture Guide A-B, 1927–1984.* Chicago: Cinebooks, 1985.
Nicholls, Peter, ed. *The Science Fiction Encyclopedia.* Garden City, N.Y.: Dolphin, 1979.
Parish, James Robert, and Pitts, Michael R. *The Great Science Fiction Pictures.* Metuchen, N.J.: Scarecrow, 1977.
_____, and Mank, Gregory. *The Best of M-G-M: The Golden Years: 1928–1959.* Westport, N.Y.: Arlington, 1981.
Peary, Danny. *Cult Movies.* New York: Delta, 1981.
Perry, George. *The Life of Python.* Boston: Little, Brown, 1983.
Pollock, Dale. *Skywalking: The Life and Films of George Lucas.* New York: Harmony, 1983.
Propp, Vladimir. *Morphology of the Folktale.* Austin: University of Texas Press, 1968.
Rose, Brian Geoffrey. *An Examination of Narrative Structure in Four Films of Frank Capra.* Ann Arbor, Mich.: University Microfilms International, 1982.
Roud, Richard, ed. *Cinema: A Critical Dictionary.* New York: Viking, 1980.
Rovin, Jeff. *The Fabulous Fantasy Films.* New York: Barnes, 1977.
Sarris, Andrew. *The American Cinema.* New York: E.P. Dutton, 1968.
Schechter, Harold, and Everitt, David. *Film Tricks.* New York: Quist, 1980.
Scherle, Victor, and Levy, William Turner. *The Films of Frank Capra.* Secaucus, N.J.: Citadel, 1977.
Schickel, Richard. *The Men Who Made the Movies.* New York: Atheneum, 1975.
Slusser, George, and Rabkin, Eric S., eds. *Shadows of the Magic Lamp.* Carbondale: Southern Illinois University Press, 1985.
Smith, Thorne. *Topper, A Ribald Adventure.* New York: Grosset & Dunlap, 1926.
Steegmuller, Francis. *Cocteau.* Boston: Atlantic Monthly/Little, Brown, 1970.
Steinberg, Cobbett. *Reel Facts.* New York: Vintage, 1982.

Steinbrunner, Chris, and Goldblatt, Burt. *Cinema of the Fantastic.* New York: Galahad, 1972.
Taylor, Al, and Roy, Sue. *Making a Monster.* New York: Crown, 1980.
Teichmann, Howard. *Fonda, My Life As Told to Howard Teichmann.* New York: N.A.L., 1981.
Terry, Bridget. *The Popeye Story.* New York: Dell, 1980.
Thomas, Tony. *Music for the Movies.* Cranbury, N.J.: Barnes, 1973.
Tvrdikova, Michael. (translated by Vera Gissing.) *Folktales and Legends.* London: Octopus, 1981.
Vermilye, Jerry. *The Great British Films.* Secaucus, N.J.: Citadel, 1978.
Von Gunden, Kenneth, and Stock, Stuart H. *Twenty All-Time Great Science Fiction Films.* New York: Arlington, 1982.
Walker, Joseph and Juanita. *The Light on Her Face.* Hollywood: ASC, 1984.
Wansell, Geoffrey. *Haunted Idol: The Story of the Real Cary Grant.* New York: Ballantine, 1985.
Warren, Bill. *Keep Watching the Skies!* Vol. 1. Jefferson, N.C.: McFarland, 1982.
Weiss, Ken, and Goodgold, Ed. *To Be Continued. . .* New York: Crown, 1972.
Willis, John. *Screen World Annual.* New York: Crown, yearly.
Wilson, Robert. *The Film Criticism of Otis Ferguson.* Philadelphia: Temple University Press, 1971.

Periodicals and Journals

Beauty and the Beast
Films and Filming, June 1964, pp. 27–28.
_____, February 1978, pp. 28–33.
Monthly Film Bulletin, November 1947, p. 161.
National Board of Review Magazine, Feb.–Mar. 1948, pp. 8–9.
New York Times, December 24, 1947, p. 12.
Sequence, Spring 1948, pp. 28–30.
Theatre Arts, January 1948, pp. 20–26.
Variety, December 24, 1947, p. 13.
Yale French Studies, Vol. 17, No. 4 (Summer 1956), pp. 14–20.

Conan the Barbarian
American Fantasy, Vol. 1, No. 2 (May 1982), pp. 4–15.
American Film, May 1982, pp. 32–37.
Christian Science Monitor, June 10, 1982, p. 18.
Cinefantastique, Vol. 11, No. 3 (September 1981), pp. 16–37.
_____, Vol. 12, Nos. 2/3 (April 1982), pp. 22–71.
Fantasy Newsletter, Vol. 5, No. 8 (September 1982), pp. 10–11.
Film Comment, May–June 1982, pp. 26–28.
Los Angeles Times, May 14, 1982, Calendar, p. 1.
Moviegoer, Vol. 1, No. 5 (May 1982), pp. 14–19.
New Leader, June 14, 1982, p. 19.
New Statesman, August 27, 1982, p. 24.
New York, May 24, 1982, p. 68.
New York Post, May 14, 1982, p. 49.
Newsday, May 14, 1982, Part II, p. 11.
Newsweek, May 17, 1982, p. 100.

Time, May 24, 1982, p. 76.
Variety, March 17, 1982, p. 24.

The Dark Crystal

American Cinematographer, December 1982, pp. 1282–91, 1312–16, 1318, 1320–1324.
Christian Science Monitor, January 6, 1983.
Cinefanatastique, Vol. 13, No. 4 (April–May 1983), pp. 24–55.
Los Angeles Times, December 17, 1982.
Monthly Film Bulletin, February 1983, p. 39.
New Statesman, February 18, 1983.
New York Post, December 17, 1982.
Newsday, December 17, 1982.
Newsweek, December 27, 1982, p. 61.

Dragonslayer

Christian Science Monitor, July 2, 1981.
Cinefantastique, Vol. 11, No. 3, (September 1981), p. 46.
Cinefex, No. 6, October 1981, pp. 30–61.
Films in Review, October 1981, p. 497
Jump Cut, No. 26 (1981).
Los Angeles Times, June 29, 1981, p. 2.
Monthly Film Bulletin, February 1982, p. 26.
New Statesman, February 12, 1982, p. 28.
New York, July 20, 1981, p. 60.
New York Post, June 26, 1981, p. 39.
Newsday, June 26, 1981, p. 10.
Newsweek, July 13, 1981, p. 81.
Time, July 6, 1981, p. 69.
Variety, June 19, 1981, p. 2.

The 5,000 Fingers of Dr. T

America, June 27, 1953, pp. 345–346.
American Cinematographer, January 1953, pp. 16–17, 42.
American Film, October 1978, p. 69.
Commonweal, July 3, 1953.
Films in Review, 1953, pp. 151, 154.
New York Times, June 20, 1953, p. 20.
New Yorker, June 27, 1953, pp. 58–59.
Newsweek, June 15, 1953, pp. 100–102.
Theatre Arts, May 1953.
Time, June 22, 1953.
Variety, June 17, 1953, p. 6.

It's a Wonderful Life

American Film, April 1979, p. 25.
_____, May 1980, p. 43.
_____, March 1980, p. 41.
Films in Review, Vol. 2, No. 4 (April 1951), pp. 32–38.
The Nation, December 28, 1946.
National Board of Review Magazine, Feb.–March 1947, pp. 5–8.
New York Times, December 25, 1946, p. 19.

Newsweek, December 30, 1946, pp. 72–73.
Video, July 1986.
Variety, December 25, 1946, p. 12.

Jason and the Argonauts
America, August 10, 1963.
American Film, June 1981, pp. 47–52.
Cinefantastique, Vol. 11, No. 4, (December 1981), pp. 24–45.
New Yorker, August 24, 1963.
New York Times, August 8, 1963, p. 19.
Newsweek, July 8, 1963.
Time, July 19, 1963, p. 78.
Variety, June 5, 1963, p. 6.

King Kong
American Film, Dec.–Jan. 1977, pp. 14–23.
Cinefex, No. 7, January 1982, pp. 4–72.
The Nation, 136, No. 3533 (1933), p. 326.
New York Times, March 2, 1933.

Lost Horizon
America, March 20, 1937, p. 576.
New York Herald Tribune, March 4, 1937, p. 16.
New York Times, March 4, 1937, p. 27.
New Yorker, March 6, 1937, p. 78.
Time, March 8, 1937, p. 78.
_____, June 8, 1986, p. 82.
Variety, March 10, 1937, p. 14.

Popeye
American Film, December 1980, pp. 30–36, 73–74.
Christian Science Monitor, December 18, 1980, p. 19.
Film Quarterly, Spring 1981, p. 42.
Films in Review, February 1981, p. 122.
Monthly Film Bulletin, March 1981, p. 54.
New Leader, January 12, 1981, p. 20.
New Statesman, April 10, 1981, p. 28.
New York, Dec. 29, 1980–Jan. 5, 1981, p. 47.
New York Post, December 12, 1980, p. 39.
Newsweek, December 22, 1980, p. 72.
Playboy, October 1982 (Playboy Interview).
Saturday Review, February 1981, p. 80.
Time, December 22, 1980, p. 72.
Variety, December 10, 1980, p. 30.
Village Voice, December 17–23, 1980, p. 70.

Superman
American Film, May 1979, pp. 33–44.
_____, May 1981, pp. 57–63.
Cinefantastique, Vol. 8, No. 4, (1979), pp. 12–18.
_____, Vol. 11, No. 2, (Fall 1981), pp. 4–7.

Films in Review, January 1979.
Journal of Popular Film and TV, Vol. 9, No. 2, (Summer 1981), pp. 78–82.
New Republic, January 13, 1979, p. 27.
New York Times, December 15, 1978.
Newsweek, January 1, 1979, pp. 46–51.
Time, November 27, 1978, pp. 59–61.
Variety, December 13, 1978.

The Thief of Bagdad
Films in Review, March 1958, pp. 150–151.
New York Times, December 6, 1940, p. 28.
Variety, October 16, 1940, p. 16.

Time Bandits
Christian Science Monitor, January 17, 1982, p. 19.
Cinefantastique, Vol. 12, No. 1, (February 1982), p. 50.
Film Comment, Nov.–Dec. 1981, pp. 49–54.
Film Quarterly, Vol. 36, No. 1 (Fall 1982), pp. 41–46.
Los Angeles Times, November 16, 1981, Calendar/p. 1.
Monthly Film Bulletin, August 1981, p. 163.
New York, November 16, 1981, p. 116.
New York Post, November 6, 1981, p. 39.
Newsday, November 6, 1981, Part II/p. 7.
Newsweek, November 9, 1981, p. 92.
Time, November 9, 1981, p. 81.
Variety, July 22, 1981, p. 3.
Village Voice, Oct. 28–Nov. 3, 1981, p. 52.

The Wizard of Oz
New York Times, August 18, 1939.
Variety, August 16, 1939, p. 14.

Index

Boldface numbers indicate a photograph on that page. A **boldface** title indicates one of the fifteen films covered individually.

281

B

Back to the Future 53
Badham, John 53
Badlands 20
Baker, Kenny 188, 196
"The Ballad of Fultah Fisher's Boarding
　House" 127
Barboo, Luis 16
Barnett, Robby 37, 39
Le Baron Fantome 9
Barry, David 165
Barry, John 161, 163
Barrymore, Ethel 80
Barrymore, John 80
Barrymore, Lionel 72, 80, 81
Barrymore, Maurice 80
Barwood, Hal 48, 53, 54, 56
Batman 161
Baum, Frank J. 214, 215
Baum, L. Frank 214–215, 220, 229
Baum, Maud Gage 214, 215
Baxter, John 151
The Beast From 20,000 Fathoms 93, 98
Beatty, Ned 155, 162–163, 167
Beauty and the Beast viii, 1–13, 47
Beaver, Jim 154
Becket 161
Beery, Wallace 217, 218
Belcher, Stephen 2
Bel Geddes, Barbara 80
La Belle et la Bête: see **Beauty and the
　Beast**
La Belle et la Bête: Journal d' un Film 2
Bells of St. Mary's 81
Ben Casey 137
Benaderet, Bea 65
Bennett, Barbara 207
Bennett, Constance 200, **202, 205,** 207,
　208, 209
Bennett, Joan 207
Bennett, Richard 207
Benson, Sheila 186
Benton, Robert 161
Berard, Christian 2, 10
"Berg." 16, 46
Berger, Ludwig 179, 181
Bergman, Ingrid 81
Bergman, Sandahl 17, 24, **25,** 26
Berkeley, Busby 139
Berle, Milton 226
"Bert." 71
The Best of M-G-M: The Golden Years:
　1928–1959 217
The Best Place To Be 80

The Best Years of Our Lives 84
Bettelheim, Bruno 7
Between Time and Timbuktu 37
Big Trouble in Little China 53
Big Wednesday 21
Billingsley, Sherman 65
The Bingo Long Travelling All-Stars and
　Motor Kings 53
Biro, Lajos 178
The Birth of a Nation 134
Bishop, Joey 65
Black, Art 77, 132
"Black Colossus" 20, 22
Blackman, Honor 90
Blake, Yvonne 168
Blandick, Clara 212, **216,** 219
Blithe Spirit 210
Bloom, Claire 98
Bludorn, Charles 146
The Blue Lagoon 53
Bob Eddy Comedies 127
Bodimeade, John 169
Bolger, Ray 212, **216,** 217, 220, 221, **226,**
　227, 228
Bolt, Robert 96
Bond, Ward 74, 81
Bonnie and Clyde 167
Boorman, John 44
Booth, Connie 196
Bosch, Hieronymous 197
The Boston Herald 107
Boston Transcript 212
The Bostonians 167
Bought 207
Bowie, Les 165
Bowker, Judi 98
Bradbury, Ray 92, 93, 215
Brando, Marlon 154, 161, 162, 166–167,
　168, 169
Bray, Peter 142
Bray, Robert 65
Bray Studios 163
Brazil 137, 196
Breaking Away 147
Brewster McCloud 146
Bride of the Monster 150
Bringing Up Baby 200, 209
"Bron." 2
Brooks, Tim 64, 66
Brosnan, John 185
Brownlow, Kevin 206
Buffalo Bill and the Indians 145
The Bulleteers 159
Bullfinch's Mythology 94
The Bullwinkle Show 66
Bumping into Broadway 206
Bunnell, David 54

H

I

J

K

Index